NORTHMAN: JOHN HEWITT (1

John Hewitt in the Linen Hall Library, Belfast.

Northman: John Hewitt (1907–87)

An Irish Writer, His World, and His Times

W. J. Mc CORMACK

OXFORD
UNIVERSITY PRESS

OXFORD
UNIVERSITY PRESS

Great Clarendon Street, Oxford, OX2 6DP,
United Kingdom

Oxford University Press is a department of the University of Oxford.
It furthers the University's objective of excellence in research, scholarship,
and education by publishing worldwide. Oxford is a registered trade mark of
Oxford University Press in the UK and in certain other countries

First Edition published in 2015

Impression: 1

Published in the United States of America by Oxford University Press
198 Madison Avenue, New York, NY 10016, United States of America

British Library Cataloguing in Publication Data
Data available

Library of Congress Control Number: 2015934239

ISBN 978–0–19–873982–1

Printed and bound by
CPI Group (UK) Ltd, Croydon, CR0 4YY

For Keith Millar
and for John Montague:
Keepers of the flame

Acknowledgements

I am grateful to the committee of the John Hewitt Society for their original invitation to write a life of the poet, and especially to Tony Kennedy for his patience in dealing with an author sometimes more reflective than active. I am also happy to acknowledge funding provided by the Arts Council of Northern Ireland to launch the project.

John Hewitt's nephew and literary co-executor, Keith Millar, has been exceedingly helpful in sorting out obscure family relationships, lending me some material not yet in the public domain, and on every occasion evincing that confident scepticism which is part of his and Hewitt's inheritance from dissent. His permission to quote from Hewitt's published and unpublished writings, also Roberta Hewitt's journal, diaries, and letters, without which *Northman* would have been impossible, is gratefully acknowledged.

Evelyn Barrett, Helen Beaney, Paul Bew, Ciaran Brady, Rae-Ann Byatt, Helen Carr, Richard Davies, Mary Denver, Denis Donoghue, Jeffrey Dudgeon, Philip Flanagan, Brendan Flynn, Peter Forsaith, Frank Gallagher, Katrina Goldstone, John and Mary Gray, Myrtle Hill, Sidney Jackson, Keith Jeffery, Greta Jones, S. B. (Brian) Kennedy, Martin Kettle, the late Siobhán Kilfeather, Carla King, Linda Linney, Paul MacAveny, Fearghal McGarry, Philip Magennis, Janet Maybin, Neil Maybin, John Montague, Róise ní Bhaoil, Proinsias O Drisceoil, Eunan O'Halpin, Connal Parr, Eve Patten, Jean-Paul Pittion, Paul Rassam, the Revd Robin Roddie, Briad and Peter Rowan, Alastair Smyth, Damian Smyth, Brenda Stewart, Ferenc Takács, Zoe Watson, Veronica Watts, Danielle Westerhof, Lawrence Whyte, Nicholas Whyte, and John Wilson have all assisted with advice, information, or support.

Quotations from the published and unpublished writings of John Hewitt, likewise from Roberta Hewitt's journal, appear by kind permission of the John Hewitt Trust.

Mrs Marie Heaney generously authorized publication of an excerpt from her late husband's letter to John Hewitt, written on the occasion of Roberta's death.

At Oxford University Press, Jacqueline Baker, and my copy editor Phil Dines diplomatically handled the occasional squall of contradiction and exasperation which buffets an author from time to time. For their support and direction, I remain grateful. Lydia Shinoj oversaw production skilfully.

In Cushendall, I found the same kindness, wit, and hospitality that the Hewitts encountered more than sixty years ago. For local wisdom and good company I especially thank Alex McKillop, Joe Blaney, Maria McAllister, Charlie and Bernadette McDonnell. Part of Chapter 1 was presented at the John Hewitt Summer School in 2008, in Garron Tower on the Antrim coast.

Library staff at Belfast Central Library, the Methodist Historical Society of Ireland, the Queen's University Belfast (including Geraldine O'Beirn and Paula

McComish at the Agri-Food and Biosciences Institute), the Linen Hall Library (most notably John Killen), and the University of Ulster at Coleraine (Frank Reynolds, Jayne Dunlop, and Cheree McGill); archivists at the Public Record Office of Northern Ireland, the National Library of Ireland (notably the ever-helpful Tom Desmond), the Royal Irish Academy, the Arts Council of Ireland, the University of Leeds (Brotherton Collection), the University of Reading, and the Herbert Gallery (Coventry) have provided me with a variety of materials, some of them not yet catalogued and others scarcely recognizable from the descriptions I submitted.

To each and all my heartfelt gratitude.

Contents

List of Plates

All photographs courtesy of Keith Millar, except where otherwise indicated.

List of Abbreviations

Ancestral	*Ancestral Voices; the Selected Prose of John Hewitt*, ed. Tom Clyde (Belfast: Blackstaff, 1987)
Brotherton	Brotherton Collection, University of Leeds Library
CEMA	Council for the Encouragement of Music and the Arts (Northern Ireland)
COV	Coventry Historical Centre, holding archives of the Herbert Art Gallery, and related material
COVC	Coventry Cathedral Archives
JH	John Harold Hewitt
Journal	The manuscript journal kept by Roberta Hewitt (née Black) from 1947 onwards, preserved in PRONI at D 3838/4/6 and 7
Journal TS	The journal in its two-volume typescript form in the possession of Roberta Hewitt's nephew, Keith Millar (JH's literary co-executor). The typescript differs from the manuscript in a number of helpful ways, by the inclusion of some pre-1947 material and later photographs
Linen	The Linen Hall Library, Belfast
Longley/Ormsby	John Hewitt, *Selected Poems*, ed. Michael Longley and Frank Ormsby (Belfast: Blackstaff, 2007)
NLI	National Library of Ireland, Dublin
North	John Hewitt, *A North Light; Twenty-Five Years in a Municipal Art Gallery*, ed. Frank Ferguson and Kathryn White (Dublin: Four Courts, 2013)
Ormsby	*Collected Poems of John Hewitt*, ed. Frank Ormsby (Belfast: Blackstaff, 1991). Includes several chronologies and a lengthy introduction amounting to a mini-biography
PEN	International PEN (founded in 1921 as Poets, Essayists, Novelists)
PRONI	Public Record Office of Northern Ireland
QUB	Queen's University Belfast
RTH	Robert Telford Hewitt, the poet's father
TCD	Trinity College Dublin (library)
UU	University of Ulster (Coleraine)

Yea, for sooth, once again I saw as of old, the great treading down the little, and the strong beating down the weak, and cruel men fearing not, and kind men daring not; and the saints in heaven forbearing and yet bidding me not to forbear.

William Morris

So deeply are ideologies and economic factors intermeshed, so clearly is the individual dyed in the colours of his period, and driven by the currents of his time. So, too, when I make what I think is a free act of choice, I still wonder what distant bugle's echo is beckoning or in what mass movement I shall shortly find myself. I have only to examine the history of my personal opinions to have revealed to me the fluctuating climate of general ideas over the same period.

John Hewitt

The true work of art continues to unfold and create within the personality of the spectator. It is a continuous coming into being.

Mervyn Levy

Prologue

Generous, courageous, of independent mind, the poet John Hewitt (1907–87) occupies an anomalous place in the literary world. His life's work is celebrated at *two* annual gatherings—a week-long summer festival in the city of Armagh, and a shorter event in the Glens of Antrim. These are organized by the highly experienced John Hewitt Society.

Nor is it difficult to find the literary work. Two *Collected Poems* have appeared, the first in 1968 under the imprint of an enterprising London publisher, McGibbon and Kee. The firm's acceptance of Hewitt was encouraged by the quiet diplomacy of John Montague, a fellow Ulster poet. The second *Collected Poems*, from Blackstaff Press of Belfast in 1991, was edited by Frank Ormsby, another Ulster poet.

Hewitt's career was deeply frustrated. The first slim hardback volume came just in time for his 41st birthday in 1948. Rejected by the Belfast Museum and Gallery for the post of director in 1952, he had to wait five years before escaping—to exile. More intimate disappointments also took their toll. He and his wife Roberta were devoted to each other, but they were unable to have children. This is a book about both of them.

Like oxygen, politics was in the air he breathed every minute. Sometimes it burned him up, mostly it kept him lively. He distrusted almost every form it took, yet remained endlessly engaged. As a gallery director in Coventry, he did business with 'Eastern Europe', and evidently found more than borrowable paintings there. Nothing bores or embarrasses the post-New Left of today more than Old Left *earnestness*, a term now used to discredit sincerity. In response to Hewitt's engagement in and disengagement from Ulster politics after 1972, it is tempting to apply a modified version of George Orwell's brutally frank dictum about Jonathan Swift—'one of those people... driven into a sort of perverse Toryism by the follies of the progressive party of the moment'. But no.

Hewitt was sincere; more to the point, he was constantly thoughtful. The poems do not seduce, either by rapid attraction or the lure of an undisclosed treasure. Easy readers will happily settle for either of the above, but cannot muster enough mental energy for the discipline of reflective reading. And Frank Ormsby's wonderfully helpful second version of Hewitt's *Collected Poems* unwittingly played into these lazy hands—it provided far too much.

In British terms, he might be read as a late disciple of William Morris (d.1896), but in some respects only; or a successor to the Anglo-Welsh poet Edward Thomas, killed in the Great War. Among Irish writers, his closest associates were Austin Clarke (1896–1974) and Roy McFadden (1921–99). In place of poets, two contrasting Ulster painters—John Luke (1906–75) and Colin Middleton (1910–83)—provide more immediate guidelines for an understanding of their friend and mentor. Though Hewitt was always the poet, he spent many arduous years working as an art curator.

And this double career generates an imbalance for the biographer. The poet was a private man whose surviving papers, though numerous, revolve within relatively small circles. A collection of compositional notebooks preserves some material for a variorum edition of the poems but, frankly, that's not what Hewitt needs. His *Selected Poems* (Blackstaff, 2001, judiciously edited by Ormsby and Michael Longley) make his best case because—yes—he was prolix.

Despite a wealth of material, we know comparatively little about Hewitt's compositional methods, for the notebooks are filled with transcriptions, and rarely admit evidence of the choppings and changings, the crossings out and incompletions which—for example—make Yeats's manuscript remains so exciting. In Joycean terms, there is no 'scribbledehobble'. An admission is frankly made in 'On the Preservation of Work Sheets', which acknowledges the replacement of 'showy' words in favour of 'word proposing word'. Yeats, in 'The Municipal Gallery Revisited' (a poem Hewitt mirrored), wrote that 'No fox can foul the lair the badger swept'. The younger poet's badger hygiene in the archives department has stylistic implications beyond the phase of composition. For the transcriptions effectively obscure the evidences of composition, so that—to borrow momentarily from the French—*écriture* is accompanied by erasure. By this term, introduced in *Writing Degree Zero* (1953; in English 1967), Roland Barthes sought to differentiate the act of writing from *both* the writer and the substance of what's written.

Two further sources, still an imbalance, remain for comment. Archives preserved in Coventry provide a marvellously detailed narrative of Hewitt's involvement in the post-war British scene, his contribution to, and (lesser) conflict with, institutional art collecting. If we leave aside the Old Masters which passed through his hands on loan, even a shortlist of contemporary names is breathtaking: David Bomberg, Elisabeth Frink, Barbara Hepworth, L. S. Lowry, F. E. McWilliam, Henry Moore, Ben Nicholson, John Piper, Victor Pasmore, William Scott, Stanley Spencer, Graham Sutherland et al. And there were various other kinds of association with Jacob Epstein, E. M. Forster, Philip Larkin, Wyndham Lewis, Dylan Thomas, Rebecca West.... Inevitably, these archives figure prominently in the pages which follow, not just because they are available in good order, but because Hewitt was a very good curator of twentieth-century British art, proud of a regionalist base in the English Midlands.

The final source to be acknowledged is Roberta Hewitt's journal. Begun in 1947, and written up regularly, this chronicle of domestic and professional life provides wonderful detail of Hewitt's activities, while at the same time indicating the extent to which—within the conventions of those days—the husband's career lay outside the wife's sphere. It is of course *her* journal, but the element of frustration at being tied to voluntary work (no career, no salary) is only one indicator of the Hewitts' shared difficulties. Again and again, it is the landscape of 'North Antrim Revisited' which excites and unites them.

The journal raises an issue about its author's husband—his reticence in discussing emotional intimacy. If the matter is passed over without serious comment, I am liable to be accused of complicity. On the other hand, I have no reason to indulge theories of interiorized Calvinist Puritanism, latent homosexuality, and any other one-size-fits-all speculation. Roberta records incidents of emotional and sexual difficulty. There is no equivalent record on her husband's side. But Hewitt preserved the journal after her death, and arranged for it to enter the public domain with these passages intact. It may be wiser to interpret his seeming reticence as *reserve*, that is, as a postponing of direct expression for better use in time to come.

In so proposing, I have in mind Wordsworth's famous Preface to the *Lyrical Ballads* in which he declared that:

> poetry is the spontaneous overflow of powerful feelings: it takes its origin from emotion recollected in tranquillity: the emotion is contemplated till, by a species of reaction, the tranquility gradually disappears, and an emotion, kindred to that which was before the subject of contemplation, is gradually produced, and does itself actually exist in the mind. In this mood successful composition generally begins, and in a mood similar to this it is carried on...

This is not an easy philosophy of art to implement, and the implication of vocational inwardness carries with it negative charges, which Keats summarized as the 'egotistical sublime'. We will return to Keats in trying to characterize Hewitt the poet's experience of, or representation of, Time.

Historians and literary scholars (editors, critics, etc.) differ in method according to the material under examination. They generally vary also in procedure and objective. The historian absorbs source material and, in discussing it, aims for a synthesis of knowledge and understanding. Detailed footnotes will allow the reader to check sources, but quotation is sparing. The literary critic, by contrast, is more generous with quotation on the page, because s/he knows the average reader has immediate access to editions of Shakespeare's drama, the poems of Tennyson, or Joyce's *Ulysses* where more is available for critical comparison. S/he aims for something more open (incomplete?) than synthesis. Understanding and interpretation grow through research and reflection, but, in a sense not to be cavalierly dismissed, the original work remains—however detail, structure, and source may have been clarified.

The literary biographer has a footstool of penitence in each camp. S/he is a historian, particularly but not exclusively, of an individual person. S/he is also concerned with a period, not coterminous with the person's life but not hugely exceeding it. There are influences and determinations to be investigated, some historical, none prophetic. But, in the other camp, the plays, poems, or novels exist according to literary conventions, some of which are complex and intelligent in themselves, while others derive from generic practices dating back several centuries. Thus Hewitt's literary biographer is at times torn between socialism and the sonnet, family affection and syllabics.

Northman traces a poet's career in ten chapters and three 'appends'. At four points in the narrative, a 'Break for Text' is introduced to allow for a close examination of Hewitt's writing: in the early 1930s, the post-war years, the early Troubles (1971), and the final years of his life. As indicated in 'The Poet Breaks Through' (my *in medias res* first chapter) Hewitt's work is integral to the biography.

In speaking of the Ulster writer, I do not suggest that Hewitt's world should be identified with his native province or native island. While his range of non-Anglophone literary reference was not wide, an understanding of the poetry would be enhanced by some attention to contemporary thought in Europe—even to such arcane thinkers as Walter Benjamin in the 1920s and 1930s or Albert Camus in the post-war decades. This is not an argument to expose debts and influence but rather to suggest affinities, and to place Hewitt in a broader discussion than has been the case so far. Biography can prepare the ground for such enquiries, but should not host them.

Like all of us, he had his contradictions—indebted to the Romantics, yet stolidly pragmatic; ardently progressive in his politics, yet deeply attached to traditional crafts and country speech. He was not cuddly nor did he suffer fools in the manner noted by St Paul: singing in his cups was never a contribution. But he was not just sociable; a kindly host, he had an active social conscience. And that, in his own view, doomed him an outsider in his home town.

The poem 'Interim' (written in May 1940), promptly refers to its author's 'slow skill'. On a larger scale, slow time—with Keatsian echoes neither amplified nor ignored—may constitute an underpinning concern. While there will be abundant evidence of Hewitt's involvement in politics, an appreciation of his achievement in its totality will depend on recognition of some less transient unifying theme. Stated bluntly, the poetry with the visual arts, the arts with the politics, the pacifism and anger, can resemble a patchwork quilt, not a Grecian Urn. Certainly, political interpretations of his career should be wary of insisting on contemporary 'relevance', whether in the 1930s or the twenty-first century. Hewitt's politics always had a historical dimension which itself was cut across by an inner reflective stillness. Instead of the patchwork quilt, I prefer the image of a biographic kaleidoscope (or Joycean 'collideorscape'), observing patterns rather than narrating a mechanical progress towards vindication.

This biography attempts to represent the poet (and his life, and his wife) primarily through the testimony they left behind, the imprint they made on the minds and emotions of responsive friends, colleagues, neighbours, readers, fellow artists, fellow activists in this cause or that. The great philosopher Blaise Pascal once observed that he had written a long letter because he had not the time required for a short one. Respecting slow time, I would say that getting the right measure of my subject matter was a constant preoccupation, neither inflating the man into a hero nor reducing the achievement to the scale of mere typicality.

Bill Mc Cormack

PART I

FROM BELFAST, SENT TO COVENTRY

1

The Poet Breaks Through: *No Rebel Word*, London, 1948

THE FIRST BOOK

Like many others in the 1930s, the young man wrote poems, submitted them to the criticism of friends, and to the more practical judgement of magazine editors. Belfast was not a literary centre comparable to London, Edinburgh, or Dublin. A native of the town, he aspired to be the director of its art gallery. And, again like many in the 1930s and 1940s, he engaged with politics, of the left-wing kind. Various futures potentially lay ahead, various distractions, disappointments, and delays. Perseverance was no guarantee of recognition, least of all in Belfast, where being taken down a peg or two was a ritual of initiation, a rite of passage.

John Hewitt's literary biography began with the publication of *No Rebel Word*. The proofs, when they finally arrived on 8 November 1947, were long overdue. Belfast worked Saturdays, so the poet took the original typescript and one of two sets of proofs to his office in the civic museum, leaving his wife Roberta at home with the other set. She had typed the work for submission to a London publisher. Almost a year would pass before the book finally appeared. Thus, Hewitt was over forty years old when his first collection appeared in early winter 1948. Well-educated, married more than a dozen years, established in a profession he enjoyed, he had (however briskly) entered middle age.

Less personal markers say more. There is something mordantly apt in his attending the belated Irish funeral of W. B. Yeats (1865–1939) in the same year which saw the publication of *No Rebel Word*, a delayed beginning, a belated conclusion. The great man had died nine years earlier in January 1939. Hewitt's tribute in the heavy-bannered *City of Belfast Museum and Art Gallery Quarterly Notes* was diplomatically built around a description of an 1889 portrait of the poet. Between Yeats's death in the south of France and his re-interment in Sligo, the largest undiplomatic slaughter in the history of mankind had occurred.[1] The war directly impinged on Hewitt's world, as citizen of Belfast with its shipyards and strategic location, as a left-winger of universalist affinities, as poet. But the simple chronology of his literary debut is almost equally important. He was a delayed man, in some respects out of sequence, or dislocated, just as Yeats's proper funeral was belated.

[1] For JH on the Second World War, see his contribution to *The Honest Ulsterman* no. 64 (1979/80), pp. 24–7.

In 1937, he had made attempts to interest notable London publishing houses, including Jonathan Cape, in his work. Nothing came of these initiatives. The gradual intensification of political concern on the Left, and then the onset of war, reduced the opportunity to join the ranks of writers with a metropolitan profile. Unquestionably, part of Hewitt resisted this otherwise desirable progression. His regionalism of theme and tone did not sit easily with the pursuit of a London imprint. After the war had well and truly begun, he arranged for the private circulation of *Conacre*, a long poem printed in Belfast in spring 1943. Appropriately, the opening line speaks of the 'itch of contradiction' as a motivating, if negative, power.[2]

The earliest trace of *No Rebel Word* appears in 'fragments', prefacing a journal kept by the poet's wife from 1948 until her death. Referring to what may have been a broadsheet or a pamphlet, the document records a price of 1/6d, under the date of January 1945. Exactly what this now-missing item contained is impossible to know—perhaps a single poem entitled 'No Rebel Word'. For it will be a curious feature of the full collection eventually published in November 1948 that the phrase nowhere appears.[3] Two months after the apparent offering for sale of the spectral item, forty poems were despatched to Cape, and quickly rejected. For 16 May, the fragments record Hewitt or his wife posting a collection, specifically named *No Rebel Word*, to Macmillan (who published Yeats), only to have it returned with a 'nice letter'.[4] In the early summer of 1945, Oliver Edwards, a university teacher with a special interest in Yeats's poetry, invited the Hewitts to call on the great man's widow in Dublin.

Hewitt's persistence after the act of deliberate self-publication can be traced in some detail. The one traceable side of the correspondence with the London-based publishers, Frederick Muller, opens in March 1946. However, there is every indication that contact had been established earlier and that a typescript prepared by Roberta Hewitt had probably reached Muller several months previously. As the book did not appear until (in good Irish rural idiom) 'the mouth of Christmas' 1948, the experience was deeply frustrating.

Muller's was a firm in a middle way of business, issuing books on sport and topography, occasional political topics, and a small quantity of literary material. Count Carlo Szorza's *Contemporary Italy: Its Intellectual and Moral Origins* (published in 1946) was a hangover from wartime concerns. *The Fair Rivers of Southern England* (1947) was more typical. Like most small houses, Muller's had a reliable 'core' author, important for the scale of return rather than the merit of the work. In this case, the author was a poet or poetess, the perennial Patience Strong whose moralisms decorated calendars and greeting cards. In 1947, the Irish southerner, Ewart Milne (1903–87), published *Boding Day Poems* with Muller, but little extensive interest in Irish matters, literary or otherwise, attached.

[2] For the text of 'Conacre', see Ormsby, pp. 3–12.

[3] *Journal TS*, vol. I, p. 3. This skeletal entry follows a longer note about *Conacre* (also 1/6d), which elicited appreciative letters from Ethel Mannin and Herbert Read. Davy McLean took sixty-two copies of *Conacre*.

[4] Letters of rejection are gathered in PRONI, D/3838/7/10.

On 19 March 1946, the managing director wrote of *No Rebel Word*:

> We would like to do this, but cannot at the moment, give you any sort of idea of the date of publication, because our publication side is hopelessly confused.... I feel that the poem called IRELAND should be omitted and I should be glad, if possible, to get Mr Geoffrey Taylor to write an introduction.[5]

By the 'publication side' he may have meant production because, even after war-time restrictions had ended, problems of supply in the paper industry affected book printing. The idea of an introduction by Taylor, lately poetry editor of the Dublin-based *The Bell*, gives some indication of Muller's lack of full confidence in the book's capacity to sell on its own merits.[6] But the discussion of an individual poem opens up more significant areas of editorial assessment.

Whatever minor differences of opinion may have endured, a contract dated 15 April 1946 was drawn up and accepted. Towards the end of the month, Muller's secretary, Nora Landsbury, took up the one discordant theme, evident in response to Hewitt's own comment: 'With regard to the poem IRELAND, I will ask our reader about it and let you know further. I think you are probably right about not "plugging the Irish aspect".'[7] This had been the poet's own interpretation of the advice, in which he appears to concur in deleting a poem written as far back as February 1932.[8] No allegation of delaying things can be made against Miss Landsbury for, before the day was out, she had spoken to Muller's anonymous reader by telephone, and could report in a postscriptum to her letter, 'you are quite right. The "Irish aspect" was what he had in mind.' At that point, the poem 'Ireland' was dropped from the typescript. Thirty-six remained.

Then, for ten months, nothing further happened. Of course, the many other sides of Hewitt's life were not inactive. While awaiting word from the English capital about his future on the British scene, he was establishing contacts in very different circles. In September 1946, the redoubtable nationalist critic Daniel Corkery (1878–1964) graciously acknowledged Hewitt's awareness of his work, all the more remarkable in someone of 'planter stock'—Hewitt's own mode of introducing himself. The author of *The Hidden Ireland* conceded a very limited familiarity with Ulster: 'I am sorry to say I do not know your end of our country at all—I spent one day—and only one day—in Belfast—and naturally only saw one side of its life.'[9]

Then, in February 1947, Muller reported a New York firm's interest in an American edition.[10] The arrangement had many attractions. Good quality paper and binding was available in the United States. From an American typesetting, a British edition could be derived with minimal alterations to the title page and preliminaries. Unit costs were thus reduced and, finally, Hewitt's copyright would be protected in the

[5] For the text of 'Ireland', see Ormsby, p. 58.
[6] On Taylor (1900–56), see Terence Brown, *Ireland's Literature* (Dublin: Lilliput, 1988), pp. 141–51.
[7] PRONI, D/3838/3/14, Muller to JH 19/3/1946.
[8] For a chronology of individual poems, see Appendix II (pp. 543–68) in Ormsby.
[9] PRONI, D/3838/5/1, Daniel Corkery to JH, September 1946.
[10] PRONI, D/3838/3/14, Muller to JH, February 1947.

United States. In March, Hewitt despatched a new manuscript (or, more likely, typescript) for transmission to New York, as requested. In some minor way, it differed from the original accepted in London. However, despite these encouraging overtures, in June the American company (Devin-Adair) decided against *No Rebel Word*, much to the irritation of everyone east of the Atlantic. In fairness to Muller, inactivity during the first half of 1947 may be explained by his reliance on the American deal, but the impact on Hewitt can be imagined.

A further four months elapsed. On the last day of October 1947, the publisher despatched two sets of proofs with Roberta's original typescript back to the patient author. But, at the earliest moment of their response to Muller, John and Roberta were at odds about whom *No Rebel Word* should be dedicated to. This was a domestic issue for a couple who lived closely together. He wished to acknowledge his wife's role in his life and in the evolution of the book. She, on the other hand, urged the case for honouring his widowed mother.

Correction of proofs now threw Hewitt back into an exacting scrutiny of work he had completed years earlier. After the agreed elimination of 'Ireland', no substantial changes appear to have been proposed in the correcting process. There may have been, however, a highly localized issue of orthography or, more simply, spelling. Two younger poets, Robert Greacen (1920–2008) and Valentin Iremonger (1918–91), were putting together an anthology of *Contemporary Irish Poetry*, to be published by Faber and Faber. They had chosen three of Hewitt's poems, including 'Little Loch' (a significant text) or so John Bunting of Muller's office informed him. The immediate problem involves the manner in which permission for this secondary publication should be granted and by whom. A smaller, but perhaps more significant, point concerns the spelling of the word 'loch/lough'.

Hewitt had, by 1947, embarked on an investigation of regionalism as a social philosophy better equipped to deal with modern living and the enjoyment of culture than the centralizing doctrines of capitalism or Soviet-style Marxism to which he had been attracted. His world, as reflected virtually on every page of *No Rebel Word*, was conceived of glen and stream, mountain side and birdsong. It was not just a generalized landscape, incidentally enlivened with fine natural description. Place was repeatedly named—Antrim, Glenariffe, Kilmore, Parkmore, Waterfoot. Elements of these names involved an unofficial language, or the merger of two languages, to give embodiment to their history and their several dimensions. Should one spell the word in question L-O-C-H or L-O-U-G-H? In a sense, the answer involved the specification of a readership, regional or metropolitan.

For *No Rebel Word*, its publisher and author agreed on the longer spelling, more or less standard English instead of vestigial Gaelic. But the question of Hewitt's work appearing in Faber's anthology also raised questions of control. The inclusion of 'The Glens', 'Townland of Peace', and 'The Little Lough' brought welcome acknowledgement of his standing among contemporary Irish writers, many of them his juniors. No unpleasantness broke out between poet and publisher, but Muller was careful to point out that profit was hardly to be expected from a first volume. In return, the control of reprint permissions was his business.

In May 1947, the *Irish Times* hosted a symposium on literary publishing in which this back-room turmoil was reflected. M. J. MacManus, a learned bibliophile, had discussed on radio the apparent failure of poets under the age of thirty to publish in book form. Replying, the poet/diplomat Iremonger declared that 'the books he is looking for rest snugly on the shelves of British publishing houses'. If, in this remark, Iremonger means submitted typescripts, then his analysis would fit Hewitt's case. But Iremonger proceeded to eliminate that interpretation: 'today the works of Roibeárd Ó Faracáin, Austin Clarke, Patrick Kavanagh, Maurice Craig, Robert Greacen, John Hewitt [*sic*], Freda Laughton, Donagh MacDonagh, Roy McFadden, Ewart Milne, W. R. Rodgers etc. all bear British publishers' imprints, and consequently, in the circumstances of today, their books are very much delayed'.[11] Hewitt had not yet acquired a British imprint.

On 11 November 1947, Muller acknowledged receipt of the corrected proofs. There was, he regretted, no chance of the book being ready when Hewitt would address Scottish PEN in the New Year. The issue of permissions was resolved by the end of the month. Any sting of rebuke Hewitt may have felt was mollified once proofs were in the hands of Patric Dickinson at the BBC. By mid-December, Bunting—by now the editor handling Hewitt's correspondence—proposed a formula to cover acknowledgements whenever poems were pre-published; it referred to 'Mr John Hewitt's volume of collected poems, *No Rebel Word*, which will be published shortly.' The wording is not quite what one might expect in reference to a first collection, suggesting as it does that the general corpus of Hewitt's earlier work has been gathered into collective form. For whatever reason, we should note that Hewitt had excluded 'Conacre' from the volume to be published by Muller, another instance to prove how uncollected *No Rebel Word* was (and is).

The December correspondence suggested publication in March 1948. On New Year's Day, Hewitt's great friend, Colin Middleton, wrote from rural Norfolk, 'Do your damdest [*sic*] for the next month or two. I'm painting hard again.'[12] On 21 February, Hewitt duly addressed the PEN Club in Glasgow, having brought along advertising material for a new magazine, *Irish Writing*, edited by David Marcus (1924–2009). On the second-last day of March, Bunting dolefully reported Hewitt's book still at the binder's. Indeed, on 4 July, he was reporting that *No Rebel Word* was still at the binder's. Two months later again, a glimmer of hope was emitted from London: the announcement that it was due from the binder's within three weeks, for publication in October 1948. And so it nearly was.

Hewitt's prolonged anticipation of a first appearance between his own hard covers witnessed more than one change of fortune and tentatively uncovered others. In the political realm, to which he paid close attention, the big development had been Labour's success in the post-war general election of July 1945, followed rapidly by the death of his beloved father. The Education Act (Northern Ireland) of 1947 became operative on 1 April 1948 with the effect, amongst others, of releasing teachers from the requirement to give religious instruction. Reform in education,

[11] *Irish Times*, 8 May 1947, p. 6.

[12] PRONI, D/3838/7/24. JH acted as an unofficial selling agent for Middleton.

together with the radical new National Health Service, gave promise of genuine social amelioration; all good news to a staunch man of the Left. Such hopes, of course, depended on the strength of central government in overcoming the still conservative majority in Stormont. The summer 1947 issue of *The Northman* had published Hewitt's clarion call for 'Regionalism; the Last Chance'. The reasoning behind the article, and other statements on the same theme, infuses the poetry of *No Rebel Word* without concealing the 'itch of contradiction'.

The provoking delays—caused in part, I suspect, by Muller's difficulty in paying his binder—encouraged other kinds of literary activity or cultural engagement. In April 1948, Hewitt published 'The Laying on of Hands' in *The Bell,* a short story with consequence. May Morton (1876–1957), fellow poet and an avid reader of his work, wrote to congratulate him and to encourage other successes in the same genre. Secretary of the Belfast centre of International PEN, and for years vice-principal of the Girls Model School, May provided a compromising kind of encouragement, well intentioned but unambitious. Soon the English poet and editor, Geoffrey Grigson (1905–85), would also counsel a balancing of verse with prose of related theme. He also proposed an alternative publisher, Routledge & Kegan Paul.

A good deal of Hewitt's energy also went into managing the affairs of Middleton and other artists. This was not part of his formal obligations at the Belfast Museum, but voluntary assistance given to aspiring writers—some of them beyond hope—and to established painters. Central to both needful constituencies was what one might term free cultural public space, a thing at a premium in hard-pressed, hard-bitten 1940s Belfast. David McLean ran a bookshop with useful display facilities in its window. For aesthetic effect, Middleton had supplied a 'posh slice of hessian' for a suitable backdrop. At the beginning of 1948, however, McLean was refusing to show a new picture, when a prompt sale was just what the painter ordered. Isolated in Norfolk from his former associates in Ulster, Middleton was, in compensation, within reach of London and the resumption of public gallery activity after the wartime closures. He was particularly taken by a new exhibition of classic Indian art and also by renewing intimate relations with old favourites by Van Gogh and (especially) Cézanne. Unexpectedly to come face to face with the latter's 'Card Players' was, Middleton insisted, like 'a whiskey on top of a belly full of Guinness'. In the winter of early 1948, Middleton's energetic, thoughtful letters, as much as the chore of negotiating local deals, made cheerful inroads on Hewitt's frozen condition as nearly fully published poet.

March brought further support. Marcus, the Cork-born Jewish editor of *Irish Writing*, accepted 'Overture for Ulster Regionalism' and 'Swan'. Two days later, the Dublin art critic James White (1913–2003) wrote to declare, 'your work continues to delight me'. This was to mitigate an *Irish Times* oracle who had found Hewitt too level-headed, even prosaic. And opportunities to write and publish prose, lucrative opportunities at that, continued to arise. The invitation to write an 'Ulster' volume under Festival of Britain's auspices was baited with a fee of £100, plus £25 travel expenses. Prose was an attractive option for a poet long frustrated by the vicissitudes of contractual procrastination with Muller. His poetic themes were amenable to prosaic treatment, while his sturdily maintained commitment to regionalism required that medium. Whether as poet or prose writer, a greater range of outlets became available if one were to ply both trades. *The Ulster Young Farmer* sent proofs of an article by Hewitt—by no means the last—in mid-May, while *No Rebel Word* remained mured in some bookbinder's store in London.[13] On 25 August 1948, Muller's informed Hewitt of two guineas due for poems included in *A Thousand Years of Irish Verse*, but never mentioned the volume they were supposedly publishing. In her journal, Roberta wrote, 'we were both mad—they collect their share but won't bring out [the] book, that is several royalties they have now which had nothing to do with them'.[14]

Some consolation accrued south of the border. Hewitt's 'Overture [or Ode?] for Ulster Regionalism' was broadcast on the Athlone wavelength of Radio Eireann at the beginning of the month, though muffled reception in Belfast made Austin Clarke's murmured commentary almost inaudible. From England, news of Gordon Bottomley's death depressed John and Roberta all the more for the publisher's failure to get *No Rebel Word* into his hands. At the end of August, proofs arrived from Devin-Adair of an anthology for which ten poems had been originally selected. Only eight of these were now included, with texts modified here and there. Generally despondent about her husband's literary career, Roberta thought the New Yorkers no better than Frederick Muller and his binders—'unsatisfactory people'. She was concerned at the prolonged strain of waiting, anxiously hoping that the book would at least be available for her husband's forty-first birthday.

And—by a whisker—it was. The parcel of advance copies was mistakenly delivered to Hewitt's mother's home, and she complacently neglected to inform him, until eventually phoning her son at work on 25 October. After a hasty lunch, Roberta dashed to her mother-in-law's home to rescue the book. 'Johnny had said I could open it... It isn't a bad looking wee book for now, red linen back not too bad paper for now, and a nice plain blue wrapper.'[15] The two women to whom it was dedicated sat together enjoying their much-delayed acknowledgement. Further to emphasize continuing post-war austerities, Roberta's journal records the essential business of collecting her rations en route to the Belfast Museum with the author's copies. That evening over tea, man and wife continued to discuss *No Rebel Word*, finally issued if not yet in the shops. 'How precious it is to us—it is nice for me for I know when and where the poems occurred and I am the other one that makes the WE, mostly.'[16]

Wasting no time, Hewitt sent complimentary copies where a favourable response might win further recognition. John Masefield (1878–1967), who had become poet laureate in 1930, sent a formal acknowledgement. Far more satisfying was the letter of Myfanwy Thomas, daughter of the Anglo-Welsh poet, Edward

[13] Eagle-eyed bibliographers will have noticed that, on the spine of *No Rebel Word*, the lettering does not run from top to bottom (as in British, Irish, and general American practice) but follows the Continental pattern by which the lettering is read from the bottom upwards: this may indicate that Muller had sent Hewitt's book to a foreign binder, with consequent delays.

[14] *Journal*, PRONI, D/3838/4/6. [15] *Journal*, PRONI, D/3838/4/6.

[16] *Journal*, PRONI, D/3838/4/6.

Thomas (1878–1917), who had been killed in France before the publication of his first (and only) full collection. On 10 November 1948, she wrote to Hewitt, commenting on the strategies adopted by some readers in placing *No Rebel Word* in a literary context. 'I am sure my father would have been proud to think that someone felt your work was in his tradition.' In Belfast, warm endorsements were close at hand. Milly Morton, sister of May, confided that, in the poems of *No Rebel Word*, she found herself 'nearer to my friend John Hewitt in that they manifest a quality in him in which I can share—the feeling and awareness of the spirit in nature'. She went on, 'I find it difficult to explain just what I mean but you have so exactly expressed my own reactions to scenes I have loved. Particularly this is so in "Glenariffe and Parkmore".'[17] These tributes did not, and today still do not, fully lift John Hewitt's reputation clear of a line of minor English writers—Gordon Bottomley and others. Milly Morton half-consciously read *No Rebel Word* through the prism of Wordsworth as taught at school. Masefield's influence might be traced also, or that of his Georgian generation.

The response of individuals mattered to Hewitt, who preserved notes and cuttings. Reuben Jackson (born 1884), an Englishman of working-class origins but settled in Antrim since 1924, wrote on 9 March 1949, enclosing a pamphlet of his own.[18] Jackson praised *No Rebel Word*, adding that he sought no advertisement of his poetry, knowing the futility of all such efforts.[19] Sales of Hewitt's book were indeed poor. In July 1950, more than 500 copies remained in the publisher's stock room. On 26 September, Muller wrote to Hewitt regretting 'that NO REBEL WORD has not succeeded better'.[20] Yet the poet had made his mark, if not in commercial terms. With D. H. Lawrence, he could say 'Look, we have come through.' He did not publish a book again in London for twenty years until, in 1968, the new and enterprising firm of MacGibbon & Kee issued the first *Collected Poems*. The years 1945–48 eventually bore fruit.

CHALLENGING IDENTITY

There is little or nothing Coleridgean about John Hewitt, no opium, no albatross. Nor—frankly—is Hewitt comparable aesthetically to the co-author of *Lyrical Ballads* (1798), or to the solitary critic in *Biographia Literaria* (1817). Nevertheless, when in 1948 the Belfastman began to choose a few poems by Ulster writers of the past for republication, he did so using a famous phrase from 'Kubla Khan': 'ancestral voices'.

[17] PRONI, D/3838/7/24, Milly Morton to JH, 10 November 1948.

[18] This was probably *The Rhyme of a Whirling Sphere*, printed by J. Sherratt in Altrincham earlier in 1948.

[19] See Catalogue 75 (March 2009) from the Belfast booksellers, P & B Rowan, item 231.

[20] PRONI, D/3838/3/14, Muller to JH, 26/9/1949. Hewitt bought eighteen copies at 5/- each. It is striking how few copies are recorded in COPAC. Apart from the copyright libraries, only the Universities of Exeter and York are credited, and the former acquired *No Rebel Word* as part of a John Betjeman collection. NLI, QUB, and the Linen Hall Library (Belfast) also possess copies, though these are not listed in COPAC. Allowing for some holdings which elude the modern electronic system, one still finds only a small 'take-up' of the book in 1948.

The very resonance of the two words might be an adequate explanation, though—on sharper enquiry—what Hewitt printed in successive issues of *Rann* was scarcely remote in time or literary pedigree. This little 'quarterly of Ulster poetry' had various editors but, through twenty issues Hewitt acted as an internal editor-archivist under the heading 'Ancestral Voices'.[21] Most of the poems he excavated were nineteenth- or late eighteenth-century in origin. Coleridge's fuller phrase, 'ancestral voices prophesying war', might have been closer to the mark, for the year of *Lyrical Ballads* in England was that of bloody rebellion in Ireland and its more bloody suppression. The United Irishmen, who planned the 1798 Rebellion, surface in Hewitt's prose and provide the theme for a play which he never published.[22] There was no shortage of historical material, but drama was not his regular stock-in-trade. Evictions, executions, famine, insurrections, trials all recurred, in action and in recollections. Those events, social or mental, reverberated in the country of Hewitt's growing up, in the Easter Rising of 1916 (when he was eight), in the Irish War of Independence between 1919 and 1921, and in the more claustrophobic sectarian incidents of 1920 in Derry, Banbridge, and Belfast.

The years between these incidents and *No Rebel Word* were dominated by the Second World War and, as its prelude, a hectic decade in which John Hewitt played a vocal part. At the moment of his breakthrough, the poet occupied a curious position. Contrary to much popular opinion, there was a substantial literary movement in Ulster, at least by Irish standards. Secondly, Protestant Northern Ireland, which Hewitt frequently slated for its philistinism, contributed in due measure, perhaps more so. But, under closer scrutiny, the happy illusion breaks down. MacNeice tended to be regarded as Anglo-Irish rather than Irish; this in keeping with his origins in the Anglican Church of Ireland—his father was an ordained minister. Patrick Kavanagh (1904–67), a Catholic, hailed from Monaghan, an Ulster county which lay south of the border established in 1920/21: an Ulster poet in his parochial concerns, but in no sense attached to Northern Ireland. W. R. Rodgers (1910–69), a Presbyterian minister who fled the manse for London and California, was brilliant, inconsistent, and frugal in poetic output. Roy MacFadden (1921–99), baptized in Belfast's Anglican Cathedral, pursued a joint career of solicitor and poet. The philistinism was less scattered, more concentrated in power—the sectarian divisions more thoroughly regimented than any artistic movement or dispute.

Paradoxically, Hewitt's friends in wartime and austerity Belfast were well able to criticize. Personal judgement flourished, partly as a consequence of the nonconformist tradition preferring conscience over authority, and partly as a result of the Catholic minority's being pitted against an entrenched establishment. Equally positive, though Hewitt might have disagreed, was the absence of any extensive state patronage of the arts. Even if the divided character of northern society inhibited a shared culture, to be acknowledged by all, its mutually suspicious constituencies

[21] See Tom Clyde, *Irish Literary Magazines: An Outline History and Descriptive Bibliography* (Dublin: Irish Academic Press, 2003), pp. 216–18.

[22] See the first item in JH, *Two Plays: The McCrackens [and] The Angry Dove*, edited by Damian Smyth (Belfast: Blackstaff Press, 1999).

practised the verbal arts to a high degree. This was the era of debating societies and book clubs or, to be more exact, the 1930s had been that era. By the time Hewitt's first book appeared, post-war changes were bringing different tensions to the surface.

No Rebel Word's dust jacket declared 'John Hewitt is one of the leading poets of Ireland.' Within a few lines, the blurb writer has shifted ground. The work 'is firmly in the English tradition, the tradition of Wordsworth, Clare and Edward Thomas, but he is as indigenous to Ulster as Robert Frost is to New England'. Publishers like to pitch widely on behalf of little-known authors, but the launching of these poems required careful square-dancing between categories and rival classifications. Leaving aside the detail that Edward Thomas was almost Welsh by birth, though (by implication) not *indigenous* in some way evident in the cases of Hewitt and Frost, one finds the issue of land and landscape decisive in shaping Hewitt's public image. Wordsworth, John Clare, and Thomas unquestionably wrote about nature, and did so by reference to specific places, all of which could be subsumed under the banner of England or the English tradition. Oddly enough, the blurb found no room for Thomas Hardy, dead just twenty years. Nevertheless, Hewitt is placed in powerful supportive company.

The implied Irish context is wholly unspecified. Who were the leading poets of Ireland in 1948? In London's eyes, the most notable was MacNeice; his *Collected Poems 1925–48* would appear the year after *No Rebel Word*. He had been born in the same year as Hewitt, but had 'arrived' to a degree his contemporary could never rival. In a different perspective, a loud claimant for attention was Patrick Kavanagh, whose important third volume, *A Soul For Sale*, had appeared in 1947. If MacNeice had been assisted by a public school and Oxford education, the self-educated Kavanagh had risen above what he called the peasantry. Others were less well known. Rodgers had broken on to the scene mid-war with *Awake! And Other Poems* (Secker & Warburg, 1941), and McFadden also reached a London readership with *The Heart's Townland* (Routledge, 1947).[23] Hewitt was trailing in several wakes, in danger of being knocked off course or even sunk without trace. All four poets were, in some sense or other, indigenous to the province of Ulster, not just to Ireland. The only major Irish poet born outside Ulster, and active in 1948, was the Dubliner Austin Clarke, much of whose work in this period was fugitively published.[24]

A 'tree of identities' has been proposed to solve the riddle of Ulster Protestantism, and adopted to salve the pain of those bound to 'settler ideologies'.[25] Metaphors

[23] For useful introductions, see Michael Longley's essay, in W. R. Rodgers, *Poems* (Loughcrew: Gallery, 1993), pp. 11–22, and Philip Hobsbaum's, in Roy McFadden, *Collected Poems 1943–1995* (Belfast: Lagan, 1996), pp. xix–xxiii.

[24] Padraic Colum (1881–1972) emigrated to the United States and, while still read in Ireland, had ceased to be a contemporary poet. Like James Stephens (1882–1950), he also wrote extensively in prose. Among the lesser poets F. R. Higgins had died in 1941, G. W. Russell in 1935, Francis Ledwidge in 1917, and several emergent talents (notably Thomas MacDonagh) in 1916. Seamus O'Sullivan (1879–1958) continued to publish verse but was of more consequence as editor of *The Dublin Magazine*.

[25] See Pamela Clayton, *Enemies and Passing Friends: Settler Ideologies in Twentieth Century Ulster* (London: Pluto Press, 1985), pp. 86, 102–3 (citing JH).

proliferate. R. G. Marsh has drawn attention to Hewitt's frequent announcement of a 'pedigree' invoking Ulster, Ireland, the British Isles, etc. in various ways. This flexible identity by declared affiliation was expressed with some vigour, most notably by the formulation: 'My hierarchy is this: Ulster, Ireland, British Isles, Europe. And any man who omits one step is guilty of treason to his people and to humanity.' Of course, 'his people' begs the central question, and the charge of treason to humanity smacks of overacting based—could it be?—on a half-repressed unease.[26]

Five years after *No Rebel Word*, and the *Rann* articles reprinting nineteenth-century Ulster verse, Hewitt embarked on a more personal enquiry. Writing as John Howard in the Dublin-based magazine *The Bell*, he published a three-part essay in autobiography. Much of the thrust in 'Planters' Gothic' searches for what he called *synthesis*, commencing with family history in County Armagh. Oddly enough, no *ur*-Hewitt of the seventeenth century, landing from Somerset or Warwickshire, is traced. There are other, less accidental gaps. Hewitt has nothing to say about events in Kilmore, County Armagh, during the 1790s. No rebel word inflects the brief autobiography, and only a most passing reference to the counter-revolutionary Orange Order is conceded. Yet the parish just north of Armagh city had been central to conflicts leading to the formation of the Order in 1795. Though neighbouring Loughgall more often features in accounts of these sectarian but large-scale battles, a recent historian has indicated how closely Kilmore was involved. Clashes between Protestant and Catholic weavers had played their part in the growth of larger-scale violence. The arrest of two United Irishman delegates in 1798 on their way to France led to the hanging of Father James Quigley, a Kilmore man.[27]

Hewitt will write a good deal in prose about eighteenth- and nineteenth-century weavers, their radical politics, their poems and songs. In 1953, he remained silent on the involvement of his craft-heroes on both sides of the communal strife which fed into the 1798 Rebellion, even though he was meditating upon 'ancestral' themes in the parish his grandparents came from. There is nothing peculiarly culpable in this silence, for Hewitt's forebears did not hang pedigrees above the chimney-breast or brag of martial valour. His enquiry into origins, and into wider themes of justice and beauty, ethics and history, repeatedly brought him face to face with uncomfortable facts which he did not evade.

On one point of nomenclature, Hewitt took steps to distance himself from general practice. Writing about his grandmother, he declared 'I still resent the imprecise publicists who chatter glibly of "The Ulster Scots", or, in the deplorable American phrase, "The Scotch-Irish", as if every Ulster Protestant must necessarily be of Scottish descent.'[28] Despite this anti-partisan inclination, Hewitt found himself

[26] R. G. Marsh, 'John Hewitt and Theories of Irish Culture: Cultural Nationalism, Cultural Regionalism and Identity in Northern Ireland', PhD thesis, QUB, 1996, p. 201.

[27] Patricia Reilly, *A Journey Through Time: A History of Kilmore Parish, County Armagh* (Armagh: Trimprint, 2009), pp. 110–11, 113–14. The parishes of Kilmore and Loughgall were among those in the county proclaimed in the autumn of 1796 under the Insurrection Act.

[28] 'Planters' Gothic'; see *Ancestral*, p. 8.

on several occasions looking to an inherited tradition for guidance or just an explanation of how he found himself to be where he was.

In the years since Hewitt died in 1987, the violent contestation of identities has abated, but, on the other hand, the dissemination of literary careers, residencies, reputations, and glittering prizes has grown exponentially.[29] This is not a bonanza of two benefits for the price of one. Literary reputation cannot, unaided, result in, or substitute for, critical judgement; indeed there is depressingly abundant evidence that reputation is now preferred to careful, discriminating judgement.

His was a life's work, the life half over when he broke through.

[29] Cf. Peter McDonald, 'The Fate of "Identity": John Hewitt, W. R. Rodgers, and Louis MacNeice', *Irish Review* no. 12 (Spring–Summer 1992), pp. 67–74.

2

Belfast Beginnings, 1907–29

The city emerged out of a lively but modest eighteenth-century town in which Enlightenment ideas spread among some of the dissenting citizenry. It grew in size after the Famine of 1845–47, as distressed country folk (most of them Catholic) moved eastward in search of work and survival. Belfast by mid-century flourished at the head of an extensive linen industry, becoming the manufacturing centre for an area stretching well beyond the Lagan valley.[1] By the 1880s, when the notion of Home Rule for Ireland gained ground, Belfast was a model base for opposition and inter-communal strife. Home Rule bills were defeated in 1886 and 1893 by parliamentary opposition, but populist loyalism remained a potent force in Irish politics, buttressed by the city's prosperity not only through linen but also shipbuilding and allied trades.

When John Harold Hewitt was born on 28 October 1907, the city perhaps had passed its zenith, but the natal place—Cliftonpark Avenue—and its attachment to a predominantly Protestant district, indicated the fractured condition of civil society. On Agnes Street, of which the Avenue was a direct continuation, stood a Methodist church which the Hewitts attended. Despite both parents' piety, the boy was not christened, a decision based on his father's supposedly recent disagreement with the minister. Here too was another fracture; inside the generally tight compact of opinion and belief within a reformed Church in Ireland, occasional demonstrations of the old Protestant value of conscience could occur. In this case, it exemplified the principle that an ordained clergy did not simply dictate to a compliant laity; and the protesting layman or -woman relied confidently on an informed independence.

The disagreement between minister and school principal is sketched in an autobiographical essay Hewitt published in 1953, eight years after his father's death. The facts appear plainly simple, though family names were changed—not beyond recognition—and a silhouette of literary fiction is visible here or there. His mother's family had occupied the principal's residence since 1894; when Elinor Robinson's husband (Robert Telford Hewitt, hereinafter RTH) succeeded to the post, the Hewitts came too. Eileen, the first and only daughter, was born on 20 February 1902; John Harold, the first and only son, on 28 October 1907. Neither child was

[1] The classic account is E. R. R. Green, *The Lagan Valley 1800–50: A Local History of the Industrial Revolution* (London: Faber, 1949), which JH reviewed. For a more recent survey, with useful statistics, see Philip Ollerenshaw, 'Industy', in *An Economic History of Ulster 1820–1939*, edited by Liam Kennedy and Philip Ollerenshaw (Manchester: Manchester University Press, 1985), pp. 62–108, esp. 86.

baptized, indicating a five-year or longer disagreement with the minister.[2] A synopsis of this appears in the first instalment of the poet's lightly disguised memoir, 'Planters' Gothic':

> For some time before I was born my father had difficulties with his school-manager, a red-faced white-haired man who, without his [clerical] collar, might have looked happier polishing glasses. My father was so convinced of this man's duplicity he decided that such a person was not fit to baptise me. He could not easily call on the services of any other cleric and, anyhow, rated the convention so unimportant that I was never baptised. This has given me a sense of liberation.[3]

The allegation, if it had ever been uttered, that a Methodist minister resembled a barman or publican was grave indeed, especially if sustained over a half a decade. The son's light-hearted and middle-aged treatment of the matter admits a few wobbles from straight narrative—was it firm belief that the incumbent secretly drank or limited belief in the necessity of baptism which motivated RTH?[4]

The elder Hewitt's withholding his children from baptism prompts a second glance at arrangements for his wedding in 1900. He and his bride, and their families, attended the Agnes Street Methodist church in Belfast, yet the marriage was conducted at Greenhill Cottage, near Bangor, and registered in Newtownards, a market town ten miles from Belfast on 12 July, of all days, by special licence.[5] Behind the minor obscurities and uncertainties, RTH is clearly established as one who did not slavishly follow convention on the issue of marriage venues or the baptism of children. In 1910, Edward VII died. Later in the year, the major Protestant churches in Ireland combined their evangelical strength along lines first worked out in an agreement between the (Calvinist) Presbyterians and the (generally Arminian) Methodists. The broad division in Irish society was further entrenched, and room for dissent squeezed. Local economic conditions reflected sharply this semblance of an anti-Catholic defence league, principally through employment and housing. The Great War brought a short-term buttressing of Ulster's prosperity, but also copper-fastened fervent loyalty to the Empire by all except an increasingly restive nationalist minority, and the socialist few. These talismans of cohesion, neatly compacted in the

[2] The possibility that she was baptized in a neighbouring church has been examined; records for Agnes Street, Carlisle Memorial, Duncairn, and Shankill reveal no evidence of this.

[3] JH, 'Planter's Gothic', *Ancestral*, p. 28. See also 'Outside the Creeds', Ormsby, p. 276.

[4] In the ten years 1903–14, no fewer than seven ministers served at Agnes Street, despite the standard period being three years (and no more). In different reference sources, E. B. Cullen and J. R. Clinton are listed for 1907, the latter staying just one year. In 1914, the incumbent was Robert James Black (born near Beltonanean Mountain (near Cookstown, County Tyrone), who also served only one year. Roberta Hewitt's paternal (Black) ancestors came from the same district.

[5] According to the certificate preserved in the Registry Office, Werburgh Street, Dublin, the marriage was conducted 'according to the usages of the Methodist Church and under the authority of a special licence', the latter granted by the secretary of the Methodist Conference. The officiating minister was the Revd E. B. Cullen. The Secretary of Conference from the Conference of June 1898 until June 1901 was the Revd John Oliver Park, who hailed from County Monaghan. I am grateful to Paddy Gillan and Robin Roddie for their separate pursuits of the Hewitt/Robinson wedding. In *Kites in Spring* (1980), Hewitt devoted a number of sonnets to family events in Bangor, see Ormsby, pp. 258, 262, 264, etc. See also Ormsby, p. 262, for 'My Parents' Courtship'.

slogan 'Home Rule is Rome Rule', were urgent in their contemporary vehemence. Nationalism, from Parnellite Home Rulers to the conspirators of the Irish Republican Brotherhood, preferred an older rhetoric in which ancestry and literature were venerated.[6]

Largely thanks to Yeats, who drew inspiration from Gaelic tradition, the idea of cultural genealogy was widely respected in mid-twentieth-century Ireland. In Ulster, with its rival tribes or traditions, the practice was all the more seemingly urgent. In the essays called 'Planters' Gothic' (1953), John Hewitt explored his ancestry in County Armagh, the parish of Kilmore. It is a curious piece, valuable for its level-headed account of what is now usually called 'identity', but also evasive (or creative). The name 'Howard' is substituted for 'Hewitt', and 'Robertson' for 'Robinson' (the poet's mother's maiden name). He speaks of 'strange oscillations of identity' rather than any solid unitary item.[7] Earlier, in September 1941, he began a sonnet with the line 'Among the many selves that throng my flesh...' which places the child-self pre-eminent in the final lines.[8] A later unpublished poem begins, 'Sentences that begin with "I" imply / an absence...'[9] In keeping with this fugitive strategy, Hewitt used a surprising range of pseudonyms during his career, including Causerie, J. Horne, Jack Horne, John Horne, John Howard, John H. Hurst, Cormac Mac Airt, MacArt, McHugh, Harold Shepherd, Richard Telford, John Thorne, and (I contend) a set of expanded initials J. H. H. K. Others probably await detection in, for example, the *Forum* supplement to *Irish Jewry* (1937). Frank Ormsby points out that John Hill, guilty protagonist of 'The Bloody Brae', bears its author's initials—and more—as if a *nom de plume* had been secreted inside a text.[10]

In Ireland, notoriously or gloriously, the past is regarded as a womb of identity, with a biological-generational model of identity everywhere assumed. The past in Hewitt's work is an unsettled relationship between history and personal growth, investigated repeatedly. Quite a late poem, 'The Long Bridge', narrates a story from Victorian Belfast about a man carrying his aged father to the workhouse; then the centre shifts when the poet-as-scholar takes over, drawing attention to a Balkan folk tale on the same theme.[11] Pick-or-twist is a characteristic mode of discovery in Hewitt's sceptical interrogations of the past.

[6] For an account of this retrospective revivalism which gives prominence to Belfast, see Richard Kirkland, *Cathal O'Byrne and the Northern Revival in Ireland 1890–1960* (Liverpool: Liverpool University Press, 2006).

[7] JH, 'Planters' Gothic', *Ancestral*, p. 6.

[8] Ormsby, p. 431, where the sonnet features among previously unpublished poems.

[9] See UU, Hewitt, Box 1, Folder S.

[10] Ormsby, p. xlviii.

[11] The poem is dedicated to Keith Millar, nephew of Roberta Hewitt (née Black), son of her sister Peggy Black who married Andrew Millar. Hewitt indicates in a note to the poem that the 'grandson of the old man' was Samuel Somerset Keith (1858–1955). Ormsby (p. 600) uncharacteristically nods when he identifies the dedicatee with the 'grandson of the old man', whereas there is no blood relationship between Keith Millar and S. S. Keith, the latter being the second husband of Keith Millar's Black grandmother. The point is important only in that Hewitt's concern is with a less stream-linear kind of history. S. S. Keith died in a geriatric ward at a very advanced age, and the poem acknowledges the constitutive potential of imagined things: 'Clearly, it was part of his reality; / he believed every word of it'.

'Planter's Gothic', used for the old church at Kilmore which enclosed the remains of a round tower from the period of Celtic Christianity, was coined by the architectural historian, Denis O'Dea Hanna. In his summary, the settlers arrived in Ulster when (elsewhere) the Gothic style was yielding to the Renaissance. 'In the preoccupation of founding a settlement, the arts in the province did not keep pace with the times.' Consequently, 'a strange and unique architecture was born'.[12] Though Hewitt frequently used the term 'planter' to characterize his background, his ancestors were *planted* rather than *planting* folk; tenants, not possessors. Indeed the point is more or less conceded in the essay:

> These Howards [*sic*] came over most likely as camp followers of some of the Devon or Somerset planters whose traditions still blossom every May in the broad orchards of Armagh and the Loughshore. So far as I know, they were Episcopalians, with an odd secession, now and then, to the Society of Friends or the Methodists.[13]

Others who arrived in County Armagh in the seventeenth century included Gaelic-speaking Scots, an awkward detail for those who find the division of Planter and Gael captivating.[14] In a letter to Mary O'Malley, Hewitt could with equanimity assign both the firebrand nationalist John Mitchel and the gentle mystic George W. Russell to the camp of 'good northern planters', when his intention was to demonstrate the variety of seedlings.[15] He rarely looked back earlier in Irish history than the Reformation, though he noted mythological figures such as Ossian, and Lir's lonely daughters; the fifth- and-sixth century saints Patrick and Columcille also feature, but not much.[16] St Columcille serves in the cause of the Belfast Peace League and a play originating in wartime, 'The Angry Dove'. In most cases, Hewitt's recourse to ancient mythology is fired by short-term need.

Not only the Hewitts, but the Redpaths also—the poet's paternal grandmother's family—came from the parish of Kilmore. Jane Redpath was born there in 1839; her future husband, John Hewitt, in 1841. In an earlier generation, the wife of Mark Hewitt died of famine fever in 1847, contracted 'from a poor starveling who came to her half-door begging for a bite to eat'.[17] Mark Hewitt had been a huxter and a 'quack' doctor, terms which carried less opprobrium then than now; he travelled from fair to fair, selling what he could, including drenches and doses and 'cures'. He had no formal education. Writing in the mid-twentieth century about this dim layer of family legend, Hewitt acknowledged the fatal importance of the Famine in east Ulster though, until recently, orthodox history tended to imply a curious Protestant immunity from the consequences of potato blight. It is not

[12] Denis O'D. Hanna, *The Face of Ulster* (London: Batsford, 1952), p. 33. See Geoffrey Taylor's review in the *Irish Times*, 7 June 1952, p. 6. It is some indication of the small circle of Irish literary activists in which Hewitt moved that Taylor was both poetry editor for *The Bell* (which published 'Planters' Gothic') and author of the Introduction to Hewitt's *No Rebel Word*.

[13] JH, 'Planters' Gothic', *Ancestral*, p. 6.

[14] See Maolcholaim Scott, 'When the Planter was the Gael', *Fortnight* 316 (April 1993), pp. 24–7.

[15] Mary O'Malley, *Never Shake Hands with the Devil* (Dublin: Elo Press, 1990), p. 121.

[16] For a recurrent early concern with Patric (JH's spelling), see Break for Text I, esp. pp. 33–40.

[17] JH, 'Planter's Gothic', *Ancestral*, p. 7.

surprising that his grandparents left Kilmore and County Armagh. Having married in 1858, when the groom was just seventeen, they fled from Belfast on Christmas Day and settled in Glasgow.

This young John Hewitt became a member of the Orange Order, either—his grandson speculated—because it was an institution familiar since his childhood in 'the cock-pit' of Armagh, or because it offered protection in a strange, challenging urban society where he might otherwise go under. He worked for a seed merchant, preserving into his old age an ability to recognize plants and seed merely by passing them through his fingers. In a poem of 1976, the poet John Hewitt envies this skill, but then notes his own ability to recognize by touch the covers of different weaver poetry volumes on a shelf, the last harvest of 'that rich word-hoard vivid long ago, / when seasons marked the time and it ran slow'.[18] The earlier John Hewitt and Jane had eleven children, three of whom appear to have died in infancy. Mark Hewitt visited with country provisions to ease the household economy. Jane Redpath's brother also turned up, despite a lifetime's habit of bigamy, trans-Atlantic land deals on a small scale, and an air of charming incompetence.

Despite all this, the poet's beginnings were urban. His Belfast-born mother, Elinor Robinson, lived from 1877 until 1958. Roy McFadden recorded a widespread opinion that, in manner or personality, John Hewitt was 'considered to be a Robinson' though the available evidence is slight.[19] In the year of their marriage, RTH qualified as a primary teacher, and went to work first in Sandy Row, a staunchly Orange district in south Belfast. All who knew father and son agreed that the poet venerated, admired, and imitated RTH, having been taught by him at the Methodist-managed primary school in Agnes Street. Little oedipal conflict there. Elinor Hewitt had also trained as a primary teacher, though their son tells us little of her career, which ended on marriage. Both parents dabbled in amateur painting, with watercolours for the most part. RTH played the cello.

Despite the membership of the first John Hewitt, little or no trace of Orangeism can be found in the network of inter-family alliances—with Robinsons, Blacks (perhaps a lapse among them), Urquharts, Todhunters, and Millars—surrounding the second. The denominational attachment of these households ranged across the Protestant spectrum. The Hewitts' Methodism appears at first glance to place them among the Protestant majority in Northern Ireland. However, the census of 1911 indicates clearly the smallness of that specific community: in the city of Belfast, the proportions were as follows: Presbyterian (33.7 per cent), Church of Ireland (30.5 per cent), Catholic (24.1 per cent), Methodist (6.5 per cent), and others (*c.*5.5 per cent).[20] While 'the whole Protestant community' was invoked in politico-sectarian

18 See Ormsby, p. 239, 'The Seedsman (J. H., 1841–1922)', first published in *The Irish Press*.

19 See 'My Grandmother Robinson', '96 Clifton Park Avenue and the Robinsons', and 'Grandfather Robinson Dies in 1898' in the collection *Kites in Spring* (1980), Ormsby, pp. 260–1. In the first of these, Hewitt writes 'Church-going, comely, critical, sedate, / deep down my terror of her still endures.' These poems were written in 1978, and the notebook original of the first bears an annotation '1915', suggesting the period at which the boy Hewitt thus regarded his grandmother.

20 For discussion of these proportions in relation to a major political issue, see David Fitzpatrick, 'Methodism and the Orange Order in Ireland', *Bulletin of the Methodist Historical Society of Ireland* 17 (2012), pp. 5–38, esp. p. 16.

debates, the constituent churches related to class, property, and authority in distinctive ways.[21] In their decidedly minority condition Methodists maintained significant differences; they retained their original eighteenth-century notion of the itinerant preacher by limiting ministers to short periods (often just three years) on any one 'circuit'. And whereas both the Anglicans and Presbyterians could relate to state-establishment (in England and Scotland respectively), Methodists valued their independence everywhere. If their reputation has been shaped around fervent opposition to gambling and alcohol, the basis for these prohibitions lay in extensive contact with the working poor where 'vice' too often destroyed lives.

The inheritance of social conscience was not imposed, nor resisted. *Kites in Spring* (1980) includes a sonnet recording RTH's trip to Liverpool with Uncle Joe Love for a Keir Hardie rally, and their subsequent conversion to the Labour cause.[22] Nor did it originate solely with the poet's father. Uncle Sandy, a brother of RTH who worked in the print trade, emigrated to the United States in search of a fortune, but refused to work as a blackleg (strike breaker). However, he joined up for the Great War—see 'The Volunteer'—and was killed in 1917.[23] Trouble was brewing in Ireland and, in a divided city like Belfast, the parties to imminent conflict often had little familiarity with each other, at least in personal and positive terms. In 1919, when what most southerners came to call the War of Independence began, a Catholic family moved in next door to the Hewitts, and John became friendly with their son, Willie Morrissey. The experience is recalled in one of the four-square sonnets of recollection which Hewitt put together in 1980:

> With these folk gone, next door was tenanted
> by a mild man, an Army Officer,
> two girls, a boy, left in his quiet care,
> his wife, their mother, being some years dead.
> We shortly found that they were Catholics,
> the very first I ever came to know.
> To other friends they might be Teagues or Micks;
> the lad I quickly found no sort of foe.
>
> Just my own age. His Christian Brothers' School
> to me seemed cruel. As an altar boy
> he served with dread. His magazines were full
> of faces, places, named, unknown to me.
> Benburb, Wolfe Tone, Cuchulain, Fontenoy.
> I still am grateful, Willie Morrissey.[24]

[21] For a historical background, see David Hempton and Myrtle Hill, *Evangelical Protestantism in Ulster Society 1740–1890* (London: Routledge, 1992), esp. pp. 145–87: 'From Religious Revival to Protestant Identity'. See also Terence Brown, *The Whole Protestant Community; the Making of a Historical Myth* (Derry: Field Day, 1985).

[22] Ormsby, p. 269.

[23] *North*, pp. 4–5; Ormsby, pp. 119–20.

[24] The names in line 13 relate to high points in Irish Catholic or national history. The Battle of Benburb took place in 1646, in County Tyrone. Theobald Wolfe Tone (1763–98) was leader of the United Irishmen. Cuchulain was the defender of Ulster in proto-historic epic literature. In 1745, Fontenoy (in modern Belgium) was the site of a major battle in the War of the Austrian Succession;

Safe from the reputed violence of the Christian Brothers, Hewitt enrolled first at Inst. (the Belfast Royal Academical Institution), but transferred after a year to Methodist College (1921–24) to complete his secondary education. There are some minor obscurities in this routine progress. Why the change of secondary school? Methody no longer has any records to enlighten the enquirer, but financial considerations may have been at work. Some time after the Second World War, Hewitt began a sketch-memoir of his schooldays. Apart from one John Falconer, who instilled a love of Wordsworth, most of the teachers mentioned were women, including one the teenager 'admired beyond the limits of calf love'. Another, impressed by his wide range of reference, enquired what he had been reading. She proudly took the list (Emerson, Shaw, Tolstoy, Wells, and several political authors) to the headmaster, who wrote in panic to the boy's father about dabbling in socialism. RTH chuckled. Bible study 'was among the more intelligent activities', encouraging an interest in recent scholarship and a liberal attitude towards dogma. But the memoir contradicts itself on a crucial point. At the outset, Hewitt recalls a perpetual 'absence of corporateness, identity' whereas, towards the close, he explains the negligible occurrence of bullying to 'our feeling of corporate antagonism' towards offenders. On leaving in 1927 (according to the memoir), he had an unresolved notion of collective life.[25] Ulster in the 1920s had little patience with unresolved folk.

A somewhat younger pupil at Inst. was the playwright and novelist John Boyd (1912–2002) with whom Hewitt would collaborate in editing *Threshold* (1957–90). Hewitt's schooling took place within an encircling repression. *A North Light*, a dossier of autobiographical chapters, has almost nothing to say about the schools, nothing but eventual graduation to recall of the university; far more about cricket. This silence may echo in succeeding pages. One measure of the tensions generated, and the courage displayed in Northern Ireland's formative months and years, can be found in the poet's father and his continued membership of a Dublin-based trade union. Despite the turmoil of inexact partition, acts of isolated viciousness, and intimidation, RTH remained active.

The Morrisseys were, by now, under threat from larger forces than the Christian Brothers, and their reinforced minority status branded as inferiority. Though Belfast had the most formidable concentration of nationalist residents, both Tyrone and Fermanagh had a nationalist-controlled county council in 1920—though not for much longer. Retaliation cropped up anywhere. In May 1922, the Annesleys of Castle Wellan, County Down, experienced their 'first battle' on a dark but fine night.[26] In July, three young men were shot dead in the tiny isolated village of Cushendall by Crown forces. Political repression began early, with the abolition

the Irish Brigade of exiles distinguished themselves in routing a British force. For the poem 'The Irish Dimension', see Ormsby, p. 303; for a prose account of this childhood relationship, see 'The Family Next Door', *Threshold* no. 23 (Summer 1970), pp. 14–19.

25 'The Old School Tie', preserved in UU, Hewitt, Box 9. The five-leaf manuscript is unfinished, partly corrected, at times illegible, and undated.

26 Mabel Annesley, *As the Sight is Bent* (London: Museum Press, 1964), p. 29.

of the proportional system which allowed Catholic majorities to elect nationalist-controlled local councils (1922). There followed extensive gerrymandering of electoral boundaries. A paramilitary police, modelled on the pre-war Ulster Volunteer Force, but also resembling in motivation some of the *Freikorps* units of post-war Germany, came into existence in 1920 and under ministerial control two years later. By the end of 1922, the apparatus of sectarian control—electoral, legal, and extra-legal—was firmly entrenched. It was against this monopolist practice of formal democracy that John Hewitt and his wife would protest all their lives. Against it and within it.

Constitutional rearrangements in 1920/22 had an immediate impact on RTH, an active member of the Dublin-based Irish National Teachers' Organisation (INTO). Founded in 1868, INTO could boast of being the oldest white-collar trade union on the island, representing the vast majority of lay teachers at the primary level. Its ethos was decidedly secular. When T. J. O'Connell was elected general secretary in 1916, it steadily moved to affiliate with what passed for the southern Left. O'Connell not only became a Labour Party deputy in Dáil Eireann, he succeeded the English-born Thomas Johnson as party leader from 1927 to 1932. The poet's father, regularly attending union conferences in Dublin, elevated the politics or economics of class and employment above state boundaries, oaths to monarchs, or the palaver of nationality.

After Methodist College, John crossed the road to redbrick Queen's University, where he read English, French, and History, the first in his family to acquire third-level education. It was not an uninterrupted process, taking six years (1924–30) in all. Failure in one or another of his subjects led to the retaking of exams, and more than one 'year out'. The problem was compounded by a period of double registration, at Queens and at the local teacher-training college.[27] 'At Queen's [library] free access to the books was denied ordinary students.'[28] Instead he was more seriously involved with *The Northman*, a literary journal with which he maintained contact even after graduation. Its early pages maintained an admirable ecumenism of the spirit; books reviewed were heavily Protestant-pious, local advertisers included whiskey distilleries. Some of Hewitt's prose contributions have yet to be listed, including an experimental piece, 'Kelly', blending a feverish narrative of the Great War with spasmodic recollections of Ulster places and Ulster lassies:

> It had been a stiff run that time after he had left the billet madame had been bloody decent so had yvonne hed seen that bloody fool start courting her on the landing belgian stairs are all to too steep not deep enough like the ones in Mrs. Maclegans war is hell Mrs. Mac had aspidistra in her parlor window mustn't think of maggie now or yvonne get out of this first.

[27] For the damning but inconsequential failings, see Sarah Ferris, 'An Exemplary Protestant: A Study of the Myth of John Hewitt and its Place within Contemporary Literary Debate in Northern Ireland', PhD thesis, Newcastle University, 1998, p. 11. For Hewitt's post-war retrospect on his university, see JH,'The Bitter Gourd', in *Ancestral*, pp. 117–19.

[28] John Boyd, *Out of My Class* (Belfast: Blackstaff, 1985), p. 113.

In another, 'Fragment from the Gospel According to St Thomas', a very different prose style is rehearsed:

> And the master said: I hate no one. And ye are mine. Then spake the eldest again: Master, I dreamed that the land should be free, even from Jordan to the great water. Wherefore I followed after Judas of Galilee, and when he went down I followed after thee. . . .[29]

These items represent no unsung youthful genius, but they do indicate the extent to which he committed himself to prose fiction as well as poetry. They also display a range of external influences—George Moore (1852–1933) in 'Fragment from the Gospel', and T. S. Eliot (1888–1965) in '*Via* Great Victoria Street' (a poem signed J. H. H. K.)—which in turn illuminate his unease on the topic of Christianity in modern culture. The story 'Tundra', until now assigned to 1946, takes an earlier place in his chronology. The geographical term also recurs in a late poem, 'The Search', 'where you reside now was once tundra'. Thus Hewitt provides a discreet hint that the pursuit of history, in Ireland so doggedly maintained in the cause of identity, brings us to the pre-human, a desolate non-landscape devoid even of vegetable life, remote, vast, and featureless.[30] In sardonic contrast, 'Tundra' of *The Northman* is a brief sketch about a teacher in the classroom, its obscure title reflecting the pervasive gloom and cultural pessimism of the 1920s inaugurated for young poets by *The Waste Land* (1922). Its content may throw light on Hewitt's search for a job that offered greater challenges to the mind and the imagination.

Beyond school and student circles, Hewitt's interests are difficult to trace. He may have taken an interest in soccer; if he did, it was not maintained into adult life. He may have visited the home of Francis Joseph Bigger (1893–1926), a noted Belfast antiquary, nationalist, and friend of Roger Casement. In 'The Red Hand', he wrote:

> I can remember moving here and there
> about the dream packt [*sic*] rooms of your old home
> stopping a moment to return the stare
> of some green coated volunteer
> who gazed with pity from his tarnish [sic] frame[31]

[29] For (1) 'Kelly', see *The Northman* 1, no. 6 (December 1928), pp. 40–1. The following are also unquestionably Hewitt's work, signed in various ways: (2) J. H. Hewitt, 'The Legend Concerning the Beggar and the Brothers', *The Northman* 2, no. 3 (June 1929), p. 14; (3) J. H. Hewitt, 'The Singer of the Caravan', *The Northman* 2, no. 4 (December 1929), p. 20; (4) 'The Lantern in the Dark; a Parable', *The Northman* 3, no. 2 (March 1931), p. 18; (5) John Hewitt, 'Fragment from the Gospel According to St. Thomas' *The Northman* 3, no. 4 (Winter 1931), pp. 37–8; (6) J. H. H., untitled review of five books, *The Northman* 3, no. 4 (Winter 1931), pp. 21–4; (7) an anonymous story, 'Tundra', appeared in *The Northman* 3, no. 5 (Spring 1932), pp. 20–1, and was later published by Hewitt in the *Ulster Teachers' Union Bulletin* 2, no. 6 (March 1946), pp. 14–15.

[30] See John Wilson Foster, 'The Landscape of Planter and Gael in the Poetry of John Hewitt and John Montague', *Canadian Journal of Irish Studies* 1, no. 2 (November 1975), p. 27.

[31] UU, Hewitt, Notebook 10 (# XLIX). For a more detailed account of 'The Red Hand', see Break for Text I, pp. 33–40. For an account of Bigger's intellectual milieu, see Richard Kirkland, *Cathal O'Byrne and the Northern Revival in Ireland 1890–1960* (Liverpool: Liverpool University Press, 2003), pp. 87–122: 'F.J. Bigger and the Ardrigh Coterie'.

A familiarity with the contents of Ardrigh, Bigger's house on the Antrim Road, would certainly have opened young Hewitt's eyes to political and social notions beyond those inculcated or tolerated in Methody or Queen's. In turn, confirmation of the familiarity suggested in the lines just quoted would sharpen any examination of Hewitt's attitudes towards the mythic-cum-cultural nationalism of the Bigger circle. But the source for these lines included pseudo-autobiographical passages in which the 'I' is incompatible with the John Hewitt of historical and contemporary report: indeed some of these passages are incompatible one with another (see Break for Text I, pp. 33–40).

Through Queens, he met Patrick Maybin (1916–76), a medical student, who remained a close friend and a (very self-effacing) fellow writer. Maybin's father, Hugh (d.1936), was founder-headmaster of the Wallace High School in Lisburn, and the family also had an interest in farming.[32] Patrick had seven siblings, amongst whom new ideas and the latest novels freely circulated. Medicine and radical politics featured prominently in the younger Maybins' plans: the eldest, Kathleen (b.1903) became secretary to R. Palme Dutt, a leading theoretician in the Communist Party of Great Britain; Nora (b.1905) became a doctor, married a fellow doctor and settled in Sligo; Dorothy (b.1909) became a hospital social worker; Hester (b.1911) visited the Soviet Union in 1961, before emigrating to New Zealand. Kathleen Maybin's illegitimate son, Richard Maybin (d.2010), remained loyal to the Communist Party, even in its decline. Looking back over their friendship in the 1960s, Hewitt would declare, 'I have gained much from Patrick's talk; but the silences between us have been more nourishing than any other human silences I have experienced.'[33]

Several of his future long-term associates were active in university clubs—Ray Rosenfield was Assistant Secretary to the Literary and Scientific Society, and H. O. Meredith (who taught economics) was President of the Drama Society. More remotely, Maribel Huxley ran the Hispanic Society. Two years younger than Hewitt, the future pioneer of Atlantic history, David Beers Quinn (1909–2002), was an undergraduate, contributing poems to *The Northman*.[34] Quinn, like Hewitt, was of a left-wing disposition which curtailed his early research in official archives. One feature recurring in *The Northman* was the termly report of the Officers'

[32] The school had been established in the nineteenth century by Sir Richard Wallace's bequest, but was left to its own devices. On its reconstitution in 1901, Maybin became headmaster, but still was obliged essentially to rent the school from trustees—hence his interest in farming.

[33] *North*, p. 141. Maybin's published poems include 'The Astronomer', *The Bell* 4, no. 6 (September 1942), p. 389; 'Colleen', *Lagan* 1 (1943), p. 67; 'Conscripts', *Lagan* 2 (1944), p. 52; 'A Larch Tree in Spring', *Poetry Ireland* 8 (January 1950), p. 14; 'The Monks at Ards', *Lagan* 1 (1943), p. 67; 'Two poems' [i.e. 'Thought from Abroad' and 'A Lark in February'] *Lagan* 3 (1945), p. 87. See also 'North African Retrospect' [prose], *Lagan* 2 (1944), pp. 87–90. UU, Hewitt, Box 19, contains mss of poems by Maybin ('Conscripts', 'Epitaph for my Father', 'Italian Moonlight', and 'Rain'); also a folder containing two bodies of work (1) two short stories, and (2) 'The Poems of Patrick Maybin', twenty items typed up after his death by Neil Maybin.

[34] 'No messenger has come', *The Northman* (Winter 1931), p. 61; 'Tree magic', 'Trees', and 'Antagonists', *The Northman* (Spring 1932), pp. 23, 26, and 33; 'Three poems', *The Northman* (Summer 1932), pp. 20–1. During Quinn's presidency of the Historical Society at Queens, complaints were made about the low wages paid to waitresses in the Students' Union (see *The Northman* 2, no. 6 (June 1930), p. 38). Quinn's major work was *England and the Discovery of America, 1481–1620* (1974).

Training Corps with which neither Quinn nor Hewitt had any contact. Another future historian of distinction, Theodore Moody (1907–84) of TCD and the Radio Téilifís Eireann (RTE) authority, was then a member of the Belfast Peace League.

'The Champion of the Jews' (1926), a cumbersome and abandoned poem in what the teenager regarded as the Spenserian mode, promises very little in its opening lines:

> O see yon castle with its turrets gilded
> In the last splendours of the dying sun.
> So many years have gone since it was builded
> That time and its grey mossy stones are one.[35]

The promise is faithfully kept at some length, yet the narrative of a mediaeval hero rescuing wrongly imprisoned Jews is a very early indication of commitments he will make, locally and in the British media, in the 1930s. Perhaps the conceit in the last line quoted above, where time is merged or identified with 'grey mossy stones', is an early indication of his concern with gradations or (in grossly mechanical terms) the *gears* of time, its multiple velocities or anti-velocities.

The time taken out (1927–29) to follow a teacher-training course at Stranmillis College might be seen as an unremarkable insurance against hard times—a personal tundra—to come. This digression repeated a manoeuvre authorized by Methody in his final year in the school; with the matriculation requirements behind him, Hewitt had been allowed to attend art classes at the Belfast College of Technology. Art, English, French, History, teacher-training: these swerves amounted to conscientious indecision about a future vocation with, perhaps, a crisis of self-confidence, faith, or another of the crooked paths to maturity. Of his time at Stran we know little, though in 1965 he recalled a debate in which he participated as an advocate of socialism 'over 30 years ago'.[36] Having reverted to Queens, he was awarded a BA General Degree (Pass) in July 1930. More consistently, he had started to write poems, preserved in fair-copy notebooks which later became a trademark in his reputation.[37] There is one further, possible, digression to be considered both here and in Append B.

In 1926, the Holborn Publishing Company issued a pamphlet of twenty pages, *Africa Calling: a Missionary Play*, by John Hewitt. As the poet was, at the same time, publishing occasional poems under pseudonyms and in decidedly left-wing periodicals, it must seem unlikely that the playwright was the same man. The dialogue is wooden, the plot elementary. The action, stretched over more than four years, involves three students who become Methodist missionaries in Africa. Only a very few details would encourage further enquiry about the play's authorship in the present context. Two of the students are named Oliver and Roland (after the famous paladins of Charlemagne's reign), and their surnames (Dees and Dales) are almost as indistinguishable as the great mediaeval champions themselves. Second,

[35] UU, Hewitt, Box 15. [36] Linen, JH to John Boyd, 8 May 1965.

[37] Quite a number of early notebooks are described as 'The Better Poems of John Hewitt' on a preliminary leaf. Composition may have occurred some time before the date assigned to a fair copy, but the difference is unlikely to affect interpretation.

a hymn tune, 'Bertha', is mentioned in stage-directions; this is an actual composition (published by W. Heslop) but Bertha also was the name of several women in Charlemagne's family (including his mother, a sister, and a daughter). This undercurrent of echoes might be thought the work of a clever if wayward undergraduate with literary interests. The issue of authorship is discussed in Append B (pp. 263–7). The surface topic of the play should be recalled when Hewitt's occasional religious engagements both in Belfast and Coventry are considered.

For an all-too-brief record of the Belfast Left of the mid-1920s, one could hardly do better than consult *Labour Opposition*, a monthly paper which ran from March 1925 to June 1926. Published by the Independent Labour Party (ILP) (North Branch), it attracted notable speakers to Belfast, among them G. D. H. Cole and James Maxton. Its association with the broader ILP brought lustre and uncertainty: from May 1925, the masthead clarified the paper's constitutional outline with the additional words 'of Northern Ireland'. Contributors included many known to the Hewitt family, or later to John Hewitt himself—A. L. Agnew (1896–1977), Thomas Carnduff, Margaret M'Coubrey, and David McLean. An official Labour candidate in the municipal elections of January 1926, Mrs M'Coubrey was a leading member of the cooperative movement who may have helped Hewitt's first published poem gain admission to *The Irish Statesman*. The ILP (North Branch) played a left-opposition role in Belfast, opposed both to the Unionist Party and to ideological nationalism. Its narrow ground narrowed with every passing decade, until the ILP disintegrated, and, as the Northern Ireland Labour Party, it continued without strings attached.

On several occasions Hewitt recalled an event of 1926 which bore in on him for decades, though he appears only to have written of it after the Second World War. He heard the Revd Dr Alexander Irvine (1863–1941) address a public meeting in Belfast and, to his surprise, was mightily impressed by the oratory. Irvine was renowned for *My Lady of the Chimney Corner* (1913), a moving tribute to his mother who raised a family in circumstances of dire poverty. There are, however, discrepancies in the available evidence. Hewitt claimed to have been 'asked by [his] father to accompany him to the Doctor's first lecture of the 1926 visit'. According to Irvine, he was a last-minute stand-in for a London speaker who had failed to show up; he was not delivering a series of lectures, but visiting his sister in Antrim town. He was, it appears, persuaded to step off a bus and address *c.*3,000 workers at a temperance meeting in an unnamed hall. RTH could not have known in advance of Irvine's presence at the event; his son was silent on the topic, location, and time of Irvine's performance.[38]

The discrepancies are insignificant as far as 1926 is concerned, though they draw attention to Hewitt's life-long avoidance of diary-keeping. The same year saw his

[38] Cf. JH, 'Alec of the Chimney Corner', *Ancestral*, pp. 38–47 (p. 39), and Alexander Irvine, *A Fighting Parson* (London: Williams & Norgate, 1930), p. 240. On the approximate date of this public meeting, the *Irish Times* report (30 July 1926) of Irvine's participation in a League of Nations event in Geneva is helpful. In *A Fighting Parson*, Irvine places his visit to Ireland after his stay of several weeks in Geneva ('the poorest of poor intellectual playgrounds'). See also a memo in UU, Hewitt, Box 14, 'Heard lecture by Irvine in CIYMS', that is, in the Church of Ireland Young Men's Society.

first use of a notebook (or least the first of those preserved). It contains not verse, but prose. Much of it owes a debt to Oscar Wilde's parables; the final item, 'The Parcel of Thorns' strikes a decidedly religious (if also sardonic) note:

> I saw a man with a parcel of thorns: and so I thought of Jesus: a clergyman with his dull dark clothes—a parcel of thorns under his arm—running for a bright red tram.
>
> He was thinking of his garden, and how well it was going to look in the summertime [*sic*], tho' wintry autumn's subtle smell of rotten leaves and rain hung round and over his desolate dank grasst [*sic*] lawn, unbright save for soot drencht [*sic*] chrysanthemums.
>
> I heard him tell a friend in the tram that the thorns were for his garden so he wasn't thinking of Jesus.[39]

In a larger notebook, 'Poems 1924–27', he transcribed numerous pieces taking up the decade's great social concern—unemployment—for example, 'The Agitator in the Dock', 'Protest and a Plan', 'Unemployed Again' (in sixteen numbered stanzas), and 'On the Conservative Anti-Union Bill' (in May 1927). The focal event of these years was the General Strike of May 1926.[40] When the latest of these prose poems or verse was written, Hewitt had not reached the age of twenty, and no definitive statement of his beliefs and commitments can be advanced. The mix of Christianity and socialism was long familiar, with F. D. Maurice's *The Kingdom of Christ* (1838) regarded as a starting point for the modern dialogue. Hewitt's 'The Bloody Brae: a Dramatic Poem' (written 1936, broadcast 1954) and 'The Angry Dove' (*c.*1952) deal with Irish Christianity in contrasting historical contexts, the first exploring themes of guilt and repentance, retribution, and redemption arising from a (legendary) massacre of Catholics in 1642, the other set in Celtic Ireland before the Church became subject to full Roman authority. These longer and more polished works should be borne in mind when skimming through Hewitt's juvenilia with their chess board of religious and political concerns. The later 'Salute to the Red Army, from a Script for Celebration' (February 1943) belongs to an adjacent class.

When he graduated from Queen's in 1930, he had already published verse in a Dublin-based paper, edited by the celebrated poet-painter AE (George William Russell, 1867–1935), a County Armagh man like the Hewitts of old. His first published poem appeared in the 21 December 1929 issue of *The Irish Statesman* and was reprinted several times. First titled 'Christmas (in style of Lindsay)', it made only discreet attempts to veer away from orthodoxy.[41]

[39] UU, Hewitt notebook, 'Prose Sketches and Pieces', p. 39. Later, he studied Lord Alfred Douglas's sonnets (see UU, Hewitt, Notebook 30, p. 26).

[40] UU, Hewitt, Notebook 2, pp. 161–241 *passim*. It has been claimed that JH and his fellow-poet, Thomas Carnduff, 'exchanged caustic correspondence' about the Belfast Poetry Circle in the *Belfast Telegraph* of 30 July 1926. I have not located any such item, and it is difficult to imagine how letters could be exchanged within one issue of a newspaper which published very few letters from readers.

[41] Vachel Lindsay (1879–1931) was an American who practised 'singing poetry'. See Ormsby, pp. 664–6, for an extensive account of variants and reprints. 'A friend of Robert and Elinor Hewitt sat with Russell on a committee in Dublin and his name was familiar in the Hewitt household as a pioneer as a pioneer of the co-operative movement', Ormsby, p. xliv. The friend may have been Margaret M'Coubrey, who was active in various radical bodies.

After graduation, he was still in touch with *The Northman*, which transcended the usual faults of student publications; during the 1930s, its occasional contributors included Frank McDermot (an elected but independent-minded politician in the south), Major-General Hugh Montgomery, and the historian/novelist Hugh Shearman.[42]

Independence of mind came early to Hewitt. In *A North Light* (an autobiography unpublished in his lifetime), he recalled an episode from the 1920s in which he was called on to officiate at a secular funeral. 'I have never been able exactly to define my fluctuating and wavering religious beliefs; and, at that time, as I was closer to atheism than I usually have been, I agreed…' The circumstances are perhaps more remarkable than the performance (in the main, delegated to someone else). Hewitt had been approached by David McLean, who would long maintain a progressive bookshop in Belfast, following the death of an old woman in the Castlereagh Hills. Her son and husband were staunchly non-believing, an attitude Hewitt attributed to the lingering influence of the United Irishmen and also that of his rhyming weavers. Hewitt's soft agnosticism was no match for the 'granitic *non credo*' of the widower, and a series of oppositions and gaps develops in his late account of the incident. He and McLean are essentially young urbanites, in contrast to the deceased and the chief mourner who were farmers of advanced years. Their philosophical outlook is not attributed to modern philosophy but to a thoroughly eclipsed eighteenth-century radical enlightenment. In his account of two such funerals, what Hewitt rescues are traditional phrases and conventions of rural life. 'The old man was borne on the shoulders of his kin to the marches of his land'; usually, coffins were rested on four chairs which were then turned over, a ritual 'called "whummelin" the chairs, making the chairs safe again for living folk to use'.[43] Both burials took place in Belfast City Cemetery. Hewitt at this time attended a 'men's fellowship' group at York Street Non-Subscribing Presbyterian Church, where all and sundry were welcome.

Northern Ireland at this date was not a decade in existence. The 'troubles' of 1919–22 were very recent; the Great War in many painful lingering ways would remain even closer. The unionist defiance of parliament in September 1912—through the Solemn League and Covenant—had led to the arming of a sectional population. Hewitt's invocation of the United Irishmen has about it an air of nostalgia rather than practical belief. And with these epochal changes had come the consolidation of Belfast as an industrial capital, an urban powerhouse marked off from the surrounding hills, glens, river-courses, loughs, and inlets, while drawing on them for materials and manpower. In retrospect, we can see that industrial decline had set in even before Belfast achieved status as a capital, creating an imbalance of confidence and anxiety. The city as such was always to be Hewitt's home—Belfast,

[42] For a broad view of north–south relations during JH's lifetime, see Dennis Kennedy, *The Widening Gulf: Northern Attitudes to the Independent Irish State 1919–49* (Belfast: Blackstaff, 1988).

[43] UU, Hewitt, Box 5. In a letter to Alan Warner, 15 September 1973 (Private collection), JH described this document or documents as 'finished years ago, maybe 10 or 12, and use[d] now as a "quarry" for odd chapters & as a source of reference'.

followed by Coventry—and the spiritual or literary benefactions he drew from nature required effort and vindicated it.

In September 1927, Eileen Hewitt married Norman Cecil George Todhunter, a bank official, in the Agnes Street church.[44] In doing so, she left the family home at No. 96 Cliftonpark Avenue when her brother was not quite twenty. Her husband's occupation promised well for the future, even for the Crash of 1929 and the Depression which followed. The Blacks had more in common with the Hewitts, but there were differences also. When Roberta was born on Portland Road, Larne, on 30 October 1904, her father (Robert Shepherd Black) was conducting a watchmaker's business on the same premises. Her mother was Robina (1882–1955; née Urquhart, a Presbyterian family). Jim Urquhart (born in Scotland), Robina's brother, had run a similar business in York Street, Belfast, where the young dwarfish woman met her future husband. She became pregnant at the age of sixteen, and the Urquharts insisted on marriage, though Robert Black was fifteen years older than his bride.

The pregnant bride was taken in by her widowed mother-in-law (Black), though little comfort resulted. The child (variously called Elizabeth, Lissie, and, finally, Lilian) was born with curvature of the spine in July 1899. A second daughter (Margaret, or Peggy) arrived eleven months later, and was briefly farmed out to another Black relative, named Campbell. Abject poverty threatened insecure families in the pre-welfare industrial jungle of Belfast: one eloquent testimony by a survivor, whose influence on Hewitt came early, recalled children 'scratching the offal in the gutter ways for scraps of meat, vegetables, and refuse'.[45]

The Blacks never reached the foul bottom, but were healthily aware of it. Things improved when Robert Shepherd Black got out of Belfast, and found a job in Larne, where Roberta was born into relatively settled circumstances. However, the family was soon on the move yet again. When she was about three, they moved back to Belfast, settling in Agnes Street near the primary school in which RTH taught.

The 1890s had thrown many small traders and shopkeepers into financial difficulty, and downward mobility was not an exceptional condition. Nor was alcoholism, to which Robert Shepherd Black succumbed at some point. He ran a small shop at No. 13 Agnes Street, and mainly carried out watch repairs. When John Harold Hewitt was born in October 1907, the local teacher mentioned the proud fact to his shopkeeper neighbour, and so the two families came to know each other. But the Black family defied easy knowing. It is found readily enough in the 1911 Census at the Agnes Street address, with daughters Elizabeth (aged ten), Margret [*sic*] (nine), and Roberta (six) duly listed. However, in the same census, the residents of No. 29 Annalee Street include Elizabeth (nine), Margaret (four), and Robina (aged one), the children of Samuel Black (bread-server) and his wife Maggie. Also present in the household is Ellen Campbell. All these and other

[44] Todhunter was born *c.*1904 in England; his mother was a native of Belfast; in 1911, the family lived in Cork. Late in his successful career, Norman Todhunter's signature appeared on currency notes issued by a Belfast bank.

[45] Alexander Irvine, *From the Bottom Up; a Life Story* (London: Eveleigh Nash, 1914), p. 13.

residents are Presbyterians. As some Christian names of these Black children appear in both households, and the name Campbell occurs in relation to each, it is reasonable to assume a degree of relationship. Under 'occupation', Ellen M. Campbell, sister-in-law of Samuel Black, is listed as 'farmer's daughter', by which we *might* deduce that the Blacks—Robert Shepherd and Samuel—were a farmer's sons, drawn into Belfast in the latter third of the nineteenth century. Certainly, Roberta's family produces no modest genealogy to rival that of the Hewitts. It was only in 1944 that Robina Black (née Urquart) disclosed that Roberta's great-great-grandfather on the Black side had come from France, settling in Clogher (County Tyrone) changing the family name from Swartz or Schwartz, and making his livelihood as a small-time seed merchant, a trade closely allied to farming. Even her grandfather used French as his preferred or first language while travelling to sell seed; having married a woman named Shepherd from near Dungannon, he died when their son Robert was only three months old.[46] These uncomfortable details were not widely known even in the family when Roberta and her sisters were growing up.

It would appear that Robert Shepherd Black signed the Ulster Covenant in September 1912, as did four members of the Redpath family also residing on Agnes Street.[47] In 1952, his daughter recalled a childhood incident when, on a warm summer day, the family had visited a cousin of her father's at Lissan, near Cookstown (County Tyrone). Up in the moss, cutting turf, she heard the two men talking about 'the territorials' with smiles and gestures meant to bamboozle the child; 'I knew something daring was happening and the Papishes were "in for it"'.[48] Tyrone was a mixed county, Lissan a strongly Protestant district; the county regiment of Ulster Volunteers has been estimated at more than 7000 men.[49]

When Black died in July 1915, aged about fifty (Roberta was ten), the family were obliged to give up the premises. His widow, though no business woman, opened a boot shop around the corner on the Crumlin Road, not far from Belfast's jail. The youngest daughter went to work in the Flax Control Board at the age of fourteen as the Great War ended, and remembered the turmoil of her late-teen years:

> the Sinn Fein prisoners in the Crumlin Road [Jail] banging every night[.] It would start punctually at 11pm and they would wail and bang for well over an hour but we were very sorry for them very secretly in our house. Peggy and I were shot at in Cooper Street one day—just going to work, just because we were Protestants—they knew us because we went across every day.[50]

She more than once characterized her family background as Christian Socialist, evidently from the Urquhart side.

[46] Roberta Hewitt, Diary 1944 (April).

[47] R. S. Black of Agnes Street signed in Belfast City Hall; see digitized records available on the PRONI website.

[48] *Journal*, PRONI, D/3838/4/7, 20 July 1952. The 'territorials' (a new term) drew on the illegally armed units which had backed up the Ulster Covenant agitation.

[49] A. T. Q. Stewart, *The Ulster Crisis* (London: Faber, 1967).

[50] *Journal*, PRONI, D/3838/4/7, 21 June 1952.

By 1921, the two younger Black girls were employed in the Blackstaff Spinning Company in clerical jobs. The oldest, Lilian, opened a shop in Bangor, County Down, but took ill. Roberta was obliged to stand in, but (by her own too frank admission) was a complete failure, perhaps because facing the public alone was not her strongest suit. Jobs in Arnott's Department Store (7/6 a week) and the Saxone Boot Shop followed, but evidently did not satisfy her. Ulster Protestant emigrants preferred Canada or Australia over the United States. On 21 June 1929, Roberta registered at the Immigration Office, Quebec, having crossed the Atlantic on the Duchess of York. She proceeded next day to Hamilton, a large steel town in Ontario, arriving with £7 in reserve.[51] Though she had years of experience of office work in Belfast, and some of the retail trade, at least part of her employment in Canada was as a domestic housekeeper.[52] Just over a year later, she entered the United States in September 1930, registering at Buffalo, New York, with the Department of Labor.[53] The immigration officer may have been Irish; his name was Michael Costello. By March 1931, Roberta was living in Rockville Centre, a small prosperous town in Nassau County, Long Island. Around the same time, her mother remarried to a retired post-office supervisor. Samuel Somerset Keith (1858–1955), a somewhat deaf six-foot Methodist widower with stony good looks, brought no money but gave the girls' mother 'companionship and affection until he died'.[54] He had a son and three daughters by his first marriage.

All three of Robina Black's daughters married: Lilian to Norman Kirkham (a clergyman); Peggy to Andrew Millar. At the time of Peggy's marriage, she was head bookkeeper at the Blackstaff Spinning Company. Andy served on local committees, and sponsored improvement schemes, including one to develop small businesses; it did not work when Lilian set up shop beside her mother. Roberta's family had little or no secondary education, and their social position wobbled between the respectable working class and the *petit bourgeoisie* (if French is allowed here). Physical handicap afflicted Mrs Black and her eldest daughter; innate intelligence blossomed in Peggy and Roberta.

Peggy nursed an occasional grudge against Hewitt and sometimes queried his local fame as a writer. Mrs Keith, on the other hand, usually marked John's birthday with a book token. Lilian, the eldest and most disadvantaged in life and often in need of a domestic bailout, was helpful in dealing with her nephew and niece. Peggy and Andy's two children were academically talented. Anne took a degree at Trinity in Dublin, and married into the south; Keith, who spent a good deal of time with John and Roberta, followed the scientific route to become a radiologist. By comparison, the Hewitts were a small band, with education central to their lives. After the passing of Robert Black in 1915, everyone—Hewitt and Black alike—manifested a capacity for long and active lives. In 1951, Roberta was still visiting her mother's sisters, Nessie and Ella Urquhart (born *c.*1888). The following

[51] Roberta Hewitt, Diary 1944 (June) recalling her emigration fifteen years earlier.
[52] *Journal*, PRONI, D/3838/4/6, p. 34, Good Friday, 1948.
[53] PRONI, D/3838/1/1/6–7. [54] *Journal TS*, vol. I, prelims.

summer, Mrs Keith (née Urquhart) advertised for an assistant in the shop she would not abandon. On the other side, at Christmas 1949, Roberta remembered her long-dead father's trick of producing cough sweets from a door lock in Agnes Street.

It is possible that she was more experienced sexually than Hewitt, having lived abroad and away from her family for several years. (John never crossed the Atlantic.) She had been briefly engaged to a young man named Weldon. John too had been previously *affianced*; around 1930 he became engaged to Dorothy Edna Roberts (1909–84), the fourth child of a chemist by trade. The Hewitts and Roberts attended the same Methodist church, and the intended marriage can be fitted into an equally abandoned notion that he might become a missionary overseas. The Methodists liked their missionaries to be married. When Dorothy died in 1984, she earned a very late sonnet, 'Hesitant Memorial'.[55]

Though Roberta was occasionally inclined to think him under the thumb of a mother and elder sister—and many people remarked on his likeness to his mother—the painter Markey Robinson (no expert in these matters) regarded Roberta as the dominant one in her relationship with Hewitt. This is a view we shall have reason to examine in some painful detail, especially for a period *c.*1953–56. All the evidence indicates that he existed in a decidedly self-contained world, from which he could issue confident judgements about art, literature, and politics.

According to tradition, her return from the United States was intended as a brief holiday. She had evidently acquired quite a mature interest in the arts for, after arrival back in Belfast, her first encounter with John Hewitt occurred at a Rodin exhibition in the Belfast Gallery. They had of course been casually aware of each other as neighbours; in 'My Future Wife' (a uxorious sonnet originally called 'Summer 1921', written in February 1979) Hewitt dwells on 'her student friend all company supplied / and in their walks no third had any share'.[56] The moment of their resolved contact is worth noting, after this shy observation. Some time in 1933, less than three years into his first job, he had apparently agreed to attend a Friday night concert in the local jail, hardly the lot of an ideal civil servant with no responsibility for music. He established that the performance, starting at 7.00 p.m., would be over by 8.45 at the latest. On the Thursday he wrote to Roberta (calling her Ruby) enjoining her to telephone before 12.30 p.m. 'to decide on plan of Campaign'. He signed off 'yours with-a-hug-and-a-kiss not to mention a bruise or two'.[57]

[55] Ormsby, pp. lxxi, 394. Dorothy Roberts's date of birth, 5 April 1909 (not 1911 as given elsewhere) establishes that she would have reached her majority by 1930. She may have become a typist in the Post Office in February 1925; see *London Gazette*, 6 March 1925, p. 1617.

[56] Ormsby, p. 302.

[57] See *Journal TS*, vol. I, prelims, where Keith Millar inserts a photocopy of the original letter.

Break for Text I

'The Red Hand', a Young Man's Poemosaic

John Hewitt's legendary notebooks, dating from 1924 and sustained through most of his long career, constitute a rich source for textual scholars while posing some difficulties for the biographer. Indeed his procedures reveal a lot less about the art of composition than the bulk of the manuscript would suggest. However, Notebook 10 is an important exception. Whereas most items in the series assemble individual poems in fair copy, Notebook 10 is largely given over to a numbered sequence of poems gathered under the title, 'The Red Hand', this being the heraldic emblem of Ulster. A number of poems bear light correction, and there is evidence of late additions near the close of the notebook. Certain details indicate late 1934 as a date of composition for several poems, but the project clearly began earlier and had for a provisional title 'Uladh', the Gaelic name for Ulster. No single period of composition can be exactly established.

Notebook 10 has a simple title page on which 'The Red Hand' is designated 'a poemosaic', evidently a coinage of Hewitt's. The notebook is neither paginated nor foliated, but the untitled and numbered parts of 'The Red Hand' (eighty-seven of them) take up pp. 3–75, with a further twenty-two pages occupied by untitled and unnumbered poems. It is not entirely clear that these latter are wholly distinct from the sequence of numbered items. Already, we have a problematic manuscript, the bulk of which shows evidence of careful ordering by Hewitt, and the rest leaving open the question of order. A poemosaic indeed, with the relation of parts and fragments to a larger composition left finally indeterminate.

An initial perusal shows that 'The Red Hand' is repeatedly concerned with two kinds of proper noun—names of places, names of persons. To instance the first of each kind mentioned—Ulster and Hugh McDiarmid (1892–1978)—is to highlight both tension and association. The third poem (#III) addresses the Scottish poet to approve the demand that his people go back 'beyond the tarnisht thought / and old familiar lilt of Burns', yet proceeds to deplore Ulster's lack of a William Dunbar (*c.*1460–*c.*1520). Ulster had strong links to Scotland, not all comfortable: prominent among these was the settlement of Protestant Scots in what had been an archaic Gaelic Irish pre-Reformation Ulster.

The ensuing litany of place names—including Antrim, Broughshane, Clady, Dunluce...the Quoyle, Ram's Island, Saintfield, Trooper's Lane...—is overwhelmingly Ulster-focused, with a strong bias towards the eastern counties of Antrim and Down. Two cases deserve closer comment here. In the line 'Clonroot is the townland where I belong' (#X) Hewitt refers to a place in the parish of Kilroot, County

Armagh, where a few elderly Hewitts still lived in 1911; his grandfather had left the county in the late 1850s. The line is neither true nor untrue; it exemplifies a recurrent theme in which fact and invention, autobiography and the dramatic monologue of a non-Hewitt take turn-about.[1]

The first stanza of #X incorporates place names into something other than a litany:

> The names I mean are Browndod, Malone
> Dunluce, Dunseverick, bone of my bone.

This is followed immediately with 'The words of a song are the soul of a race'. Hewitt's interest in ethnicity finds another outlet in #VII where 'the shouting Briton ... the sallow Roman ... the Saxon ... the dark Keltic Christian with his cross ... the red Scot ... the ... English trooper ... the gaunt Scot' all march through a sonnet which offers two hardly compatible conclusions. First, of the 'races' named 'what I am is only what they were'; second, 'time & this island tied a crazy knot'. Where Kelt or Keltic recurs in 'The Red Hand' Hewitt generally disapproves.

The second place name deserving particular comment is one which recurs frequently in the pages which follow: Cushendall. In the final stanzas of #X, Hewitt proposes two substitutions, one national, the other biblical:

> Let the lakeland poets of England fade
> before the glory that quivers & comes
> out of the sunset over Knocklayde
> to the clear hard throb of protestant drums
> arise with the memory of martyrdoms[.]
>
> On every name will a new fame fall
> of gentleness working its wonder on wrath;
> instead of Nazareth Cushendall;
> yet if a voice shoud [*sic*] on Calvary call
> Christ will have taken the Gray Man's Path.

If the fading of Coleridge and Wordsworth seems an ambitious hope, and Protestant drums sound like a poor harbinger of gentleness, a certain logic informs the second stanza. The Gray Man's Path was noted in Brewer's *Dictionary of Phrase and Fable* (1898) as 'a singular fissure in the greenstone precipice near Ballycastle, in Ireland'. Knocklayde is a mountain in the same vicinity—the logic of associating this landscape with Christ rests on the association of Patrick, the Romano-British-born patron saint of Ireland, with another Antrim mountain, Slemish, where he was held a slave in his youth. Cushendall lies further south on the Antrim coast, a small village which the Hewitts regularly visited from the 1940s to 1965. 'Instead of Nazareth Cushendall' suggests a kind of nativized Christianity, a religion rooted in local landscapes and landmarks; similar ideas

[1] 'Scottish Interlude', one of the 107 sonnets making up *Kites in Spring* (1980) refers to 'certain kitchen-friction in Clonroot' involving a young stepmother introduced to the Hewitt household by the poet's great-grandfather Mark Hewitt (b.1816); see Ormsby, p. 273.

had occurred to G. W. Russell (AE) in the mid-1890s. In the late 1940s, Hewitt's most closely attested religious anxieties and longings will arise in the Catholic chapel at Cushendall (see Chapter 5).

'The Red Hand' is almost equally profuse with the names of diverse individuals historical and contemporary, including F. J. Bigger (antiquarian); Samuel Burdy (agriculturist); Sir Edward Carson (lawyer and politician); Sir Arthur Chichester (soldier); St Columba (missionary); Cuchulain (saga hero); Samuel Ferguson (poet); Frederick McNeice (unnamed but recognizably the bishop father of Louis MacNeice); John Milton (poet); [Rory] McQuillan (patron of Franciscans); Sergeant Robert Quigg (winner of the VC); Hans Sloane (physician); Ted Vizard (footballer). Famous, infamous, or nearly unknown, most of these are Ulster heroes to Hewitt, a few are villains (notably Carson). Two sonnets (#XLVII–XLVIII) praise the Revd Alexander Irvine (1863–1941), a radical preacher whom Hewitt had first heard in 1926, and met in 1934. Some truly dreadful lines (#LII) condemn opponents of Charles Stewart Parnell:

> May terror blight whoever shook
> John Redmond's hand or Healy's hand
> and let hell's fury scorch the book
> that drivels love of native land [.]
>
> But I reserve my deepest curse
> for Gaelic speakers[,] folkdance folk[,]
> for them I keep a savage verse
> the thing has gone beyond a joke.[2]

Nothing else so baldly discloses the incomplete control Hewitt exercised in 'The Red Hand'. The sequence is less a finished composition than a series of highly revealing excursions into disturbed districts of his imagination, for which the ritual of onomastics offers some redress, and the citation of heroes and villains leads to triumphalism, complacency, or crude prejudice. What, then, can the biographer learn from it?

First, the subtitle—'a poemosaic'—challenges the notion of composed unity by introducing the art made of broken marble as a metaphor for literary work. Sceptics may feel that the choice revealed more desperation than inspiration on Hewitt's part. Unpublished and excluded from accounts of his emergence as a poet, 'The Red Hand' is not to be mistaken as a transitional work. It is more a breaking yard in which intimidating psychic blocks are reduced to manageable size. Conventional discussions of poetry refer (in English) to 'the work' in a manner which is glossed (in Latin) as the *corpus*, the product, the 'body', where English 'work' also denotes the *process* of working (in this case, writing, composing, or shaping), *labor* in Latin. Hewitt's long career as a poet might be considered as an unresolved, brave plumbing of the fissure between *corpus* and *labor*.

[2] There is strong evidence that this poem could not have been written earlier than 1937 when Clark Gable starred in *Parnell*, generally regarded as his worst film; see first stanza of #LII, line 4: 'sunk to Hollywood from hell'.

Much of the sequence employs rhyme and stanza. An exception occurs in #LIV where the style of 'A Game of Chess' in T. S. Eliot's *Waste Land* (1922) impinges:

Where shall we go on Saturday
Where do we ever go
A pint at Rooneys going to the match
a half'un coming home
the tea at half past six
shopping with the missus
down the Shankill
down North Street...

With further reference to 'the kids', this clearly is *not* autobiography; its questions suggest a quandary, not a search for illumination. Later in the poem, billboard Christianity is echoed. #LV follows with a sketch of pigeon keeping in the backyard, and #LVI a scene of urban drabness in which revivalists 'lift their red faces to heaven / as they stood [*sic*] in a fairy ring'. Nativized Christianity, in this tiny fragment, remains self-debased despite the influence of faery.[3]

Soccer had not been part of Hewitt's formal schooling, though the game was popular in Protestant Belfast. It is mentioned just twice in *Kites in Spring, a Belfast Childhood* (1980), a sequence of 107 sonnets: first to record an amateur player who married the poet's aunt Edith, and second to describe waste-ground matches (but also to discuss cricket).[4] One of the longer pieces in 'The Red Hand', #LVIII is replete with professional footballers' names—Bill McCracken, Elisha Scott, and a dozen others. 'Naming these I bring / before my eyes the crowded shouting stands...' Rollo, that is David Rollo (1891–1963), played for a series of Belfast teams, for Blackburn Rovers and Port Vale; he also played for Ireland. Hewitt's account of Rollo ('count the memory sweet') rates his ability 'above dim Red Branch deeds in worth' instancing 'the great Ted Vizard humbled to the earth'—Vizard (a Welsh international) last played against Rollo in January 1914, when Hewitt was six years old. The mixing of memory and desire may contribute to an attempted democratizing of Eliot's use of Greek myth to show up shoddy contemporaneity, but the relationship of the poet's life to the poetry shimmers with unlikelihood. Hewitt's politics may register:

O it will be a poor and niggard age
can spare no column on its figurd [*sic*] page
between reports of commissar or king
or small dictators hoarsely blustering
can spare no column written crisp and terse
in praise of centerhalves [*sic*] and goalkeepers.

[3] The passage raises the question of JH's church attendance, especially any familiarity with revivalist rhetoric. While some childhood experience may be gathered from *Kites in Spring; a Belfast Childhood* (1980), one sonnet 'Year of Grace and My Greatgrandfather' deals with conversion and resistance to conversion among a farming family in 1859 (Ormsby, p. 259).

[4] Ormsby, pp. 263, 307.

Bathos, evident here and in other last lines, is the strategy of a peculiar literary self. #LVIII, for all its particular detail and the tribute to memory, opens with an admission that 'I never knew the greatest cracks of all / safe in the goal or deadly with the ball...'[5] The I-narrator is spectator only, perhaps spectator through record books. A string of players' names culminates in a tribute to

Gallagher
that intricate and deft artificer
who wove his patterns thro' the Scots' defence
then out and back with poet's insolence[.]

Other players named in these lines include Bill Scott, and Tom Scott who, together with 'the Scots' defence' provide an emphatic, perhaps stammering, repetition. David Rollo, the footballer of line 3, echoes for the attentive reader with Rollo Gillespie (1766–1814) of #XLV, the latter a dashing imperial soldier, though nothing but a nominalist link (and birth in Ulster) is shared. Hewitt goes out of his way to establish that Tom Scott was 'not kin by blood' to the other two of the same surname.

Various authors contribute a rhythm, a tone, or a characteristic turn of phrase to Hewitt's eclectic, evolving style including Vachel Lindsay, Patrick McGill, Walt Whitman, and, inevitably, W. B. Yeats. From the last resource, 'The Man Who Dreamed of Faeryland' (1891) became an influential text, its four verse paragraphs opening—'He stood... He wandered... He mused... He slept...' until the final line insists 'The man has found no comfort in the grave.'[6] Hewitt's variations (cf. #XXI, 'I stood upon the crest above the sea'; #XXXIV, 'I stood upon a little hill in Down'; #LXVI, 'I left this dreamy townland'; #LXXIX, 'I walkt with ghosts on Donegore';) paradoxically consolidate a fixed, perhaps anxiously clinging and non-exchangeable identity.

Yet, in the middle of #XXXIV, 'I lost my ache of self my heart gone out / into the shapes among the dykes of stone...' Thanks to the poet's fondness for names, this dark epiphany can be located quite exactly not only in a place but a time of year. The place is close to Lough Altnadue (or Altnadua) in mid Down, and to a quarry ('the gash of quarry with its clayred wound') now used by apprentice rock climbers. The month is August when corn in 'new stacks thatcht' is 'hardly weathered yet,' though the closely observed bird life (gulls settling 'on the low marish places') offers little sense of natural harmony. The dialect word *marish* (cf. French *marais*) contributes to this disturbance for the reading intruder, by resembling but refusing quite to be *marshy*. So too with the speaker's account of his condition:

I was in all and yet included all
that are and [illegible word] of earth was but projected
from the stord [*sic*] images within my mind
like God or chaos dreaming forth a world[.]

[5] *Crack* is an Ulster dialect word for play, good fun, humour, banter; latter-day *craic* is pseudo-Gaelic.

[6] W. B. Yeats, *The Poems*, edited by Daniel Albright (London: Everyman's Library, 1992), pp. 64–6.

It had not been before me and woud [*sic*] end
when my will wisht. I coud [*sic*] control its end[.]
Then as I stood a cry from one behind
emerging from the souterrain's cool gloom
[illegible word] sudden frenzy to my lulling sense[.]

Here to this hill well walld [*sic*] from ranging beast
one hurried gasping with the terrible word
of Patric landed with his murderd [*sic*] god
to north there by the green mouth o' the Quoyle[.]
Why must another god break into my dream?

At some level, this narrative chimes with accounts of journeys in time explored through exactly contemporary historical novels by Joseph O'Neill, notably *Wind from the North* (1934) and *Land Under England* (1935). It also treats of psychological disturbance, whether in the poet or in a narrating persona. Finally, it provides a framework in which the arrival in Ulster of the first Christian missionary with his murdered god can be denounced as intrusion into an older idealism or dream. The writing does not live up to this lofty theme: the evasive or awkward use of the abstract pronoun 'one' for the person emerging from a souterrain who, a few lines later, brings news of Patric's landing may mask a withheld personal datum or reveal a deficiency in nimble rhetoric. The souterrain disrupts the binary inner schedule of then-time (Patric) and now-time: souterrains were shallow underground stone passages designed for storage or concealment, they remain difficult to date, and some are of relatively modern construction.

One minute further textual parallel, to an author far better known than O'Neill, deserves consideration. Yeats's *Last Poems* (1939) included 'Man and the Echo', opening with the lines 'In a cleft that's christened Alt / Under broken stone I halt'. The poem is remembered for lines 11–12—'Did that play of mine send out / Certain men the English shot?' Its celebrity was guaranteed by this question, if not perhaps by its deeper thematic. The 'cleft christened Alt' is tautological, a vacant phrase or undeclared translation for, in Gaelic, the word Allt or Aillt means a cleft, a narrow glen, or the side of a glen: what is remarkable in Yeats is the verb chosen to effect the vacancy—to christen. Less obscurely, anglicized Alt is a common place-name element in Northern Ireland, the best-known instance being Altnagelvin near Derry, where a modern hospital stands. The place (name) to which Hewitt refers, Altnadua, literally might mean the Glen of the Tribes, the Glen of the Axes, or the Glen of the Sandbank.[7] A question for the reader might be: did the place in County Down strike the poet as symbolically apt because he had read 'Man and the Echo' and found themes there which concerned (even perturbed) him? If a comparison of the two poems, unequal in poetic quality, were to establish common thematic ground, then 'The Red Hand' dates from the very late 1930s, in part at least. That, in turn, would indicate the extent to which Hewitt persisted in writing and copying lengthy semi-coherent, semi-experimental work while at the same

[7] The place name does not appear in the nineteenth-century Ordnance Survey materials. For the alternative reconstructions given above, I am grateful to Proinsias O Drisceoil and Róise ní Bhaoil.

finishing a body of competent formal poems. On the level of geographic setting, #XXXIV bears comparison with a sonnet Hewitt copied into Notebook 15 on 11 April 1933, and also—more tellingly with 'The Little Lough', a later and tougher poem included in *No Rebel Word* (1948).[8] An enigma gradually emerges, in which the very size of Hewitt's notebook archive acts as a veil through which only occasional and discontinuous evidences of composition are discernible. Not just the acts of writing, but their order in time, remain to be established—and this despite Frank Ormsby's pioneering edition of so many poems. The much commented-upon reticence of his personality, domestic and public, is also a foundation stone of his prolific art.

Patrick is sustained through much of the later 'Red Hand' sequence. The final poem, #LXXXVII, offers juxtapositions, laments, and even ambitions. The speaker, on St Patrick's Eve, is reading about Henry Joy McCracken (1767–98) and his 'ardor violent'; he deplores the absence of latter-day supporters for 'ardor violent', and implicitly compares McCracken to the late Edward Carson (1854–1935). From this detail, #LXXXVII can be dated no earlier than 22 October 1935. Further comparison places Carson against Jemmy Hope (1764–1846), like McCracken a United Irishman rebel. The sonnet's sestet addresses Ireland, and proposes a future in which high treason (i.e. Carson's Volunteer activities in 1912–14) 'shall not buy prosperity / for ever'.

Notebook 10 then leads smoothly enough into the unnumbered poems, for the first of these opens with a wearied dismissal of Deirdre, Gráinne, Cuchulain, Fionn, and other Celtic Revival types, not all of them children of the 1890s' Twilight. Austin Clarke's *The Vengeance of Fionn* was published as late as 1917, with dust jacket commendation by G. W. Russell (AE), and both James Stephens and Yeats continued to use the heroic names.[9] Hewitt, however, insists that 'what this island needs / is not a new myth or a more remarkable legend / but a new shape of being'. The argument is taken no further in Notebook 10, though shape will be a recurrent concern in the mature poems. Instead, the litany of names resumes: 'Sarsfield, Tone, McCracken, Connolly, and Casement' are briefly invoked, men of action all, in specific Irish historical situations and conditions. But, 'They went forth to battle / and now we have the worst slums in Britain [*sic*], puerpal [*sic*] sepsis. Censorship / the Sweep Stakes and compulsory Irish.'[10] The tone of the poems is now sharply critical of modern society, with occasional and unexplained lunges at the Church of Ireland and the Church of Rome. A long poem ('The hall is packt...' describes

[8] See Ormsby, pp. 420, 648. UU, Hewitt, Notebook 25, gives 2 October 1941 as the date of fair copy, under the title 'The Little Lough That Has No Name'. But Notebook 46 (labelled 'The Better Poems of John Hewitt') contains a revision, 'Memory of Donegal (Burtonport)'.

[9] Clarke's *Vengeance* appears to have a renewed circulation in 1935, the year in which Russell died.

[10] 'They went forth to battle, but they always fell' is the opening of a poem by Sheamus O Sheel, a shadowy figure associated with Joyce Kilmer. The instances of social malfunction listed here relate more obviously to the Irish Free State (slums, censorship, compulsory Gaelic) than to Northern Ireland, though working-class Belfast housing was deplorable. Puerperal fever, a dangerous condition in women after childbirth or abortion, was recognized as in part the result of poverty, insanitary living conditions, and inadequate medical services. In May 1937, the *Irish Times* carried several articles and reports about the Dublin Fever Hospital in which cases of puerperal sepsis and fever were noted.

an evangelical mission rich with sacrificial *verismo*—'The red fac't countrygirls stand up and shout . . .'. In this and succeeding poems, Hewitt builds a nervous, sardonic, and yet captivated image of Ulster Christianity as refracted through an outraged self. Much of this is too bad to be true ('O Christ you are either a pig with a spurting throat . . .'). Beneath the poem just quoted, he wrote at some considerably later date a poem of nine lines clearly about his father: the tone is wholly positive, the detail affecting. It ends:

He gives a breath of cleanness to a room
but never tells a soul what he believes[.]

The haunted Christology is then taken up again in a poem incorporating some Scots dialect and a tincture of the nativized religion associated with young G. W. Russell—'Christ . . . smoking & colloguing with tinkers in Tyrone / or giving sweets to children in Sandy Row.' The remaining leaves of Notebook 10 are devoted to first-person testimonies by several heroes, including the deist John Toland (1670–1722), the founder of Irish Quakerism William Edmondson (1627–1712), and the United-man James Hope. Between Edmondson and Hope, an unnamed person recounts his privileged upbringing, titled relatives, literary efforts ('printed songs to fill the mouth of famine when people I lovd [*sic*] were dying by the road'), imprisonment, and death from tuberculosis at Naples, aged twenty-six. Hewitt did not name this paragon, clearly identifiable as Frederick Richard Chichester (1827–53), styled Earl of Belfast. Perhaps he felt, even in the inner sanctum of Notebook 10, that an Eton-educated scion of the conquering Chichesters should not be admitted, despite his lectures in working men's clubs, his *Masters and Workmen; a Tale Illustrative of the Social and Moral Condition of the People* (1851), and other good works. Francis Joseph Bigger published a short account of Chichester in *The Belfast Municipal Art Gallery and Museum Quarterly* of December 1908. A second by John J. Marshall followed in December 1937, by which time Hewitt had joined the Belfast Gallery and Museum staff, and had begun work on 'The Red Hand'.

Notebook 10 is a carefully inscribed and undated copy of poems written in the 1930s, most of them (perhaps all) arranged as a sequence. Though some lines and themes are traceable in published work, it is an essentially private record of a private mind. Hewitt's outer life for the same period may be helpfully illuminated by textual archaeology, allowing him to step out from the souterrain of composition. 'Let the forgotten speak from the broken binding.'

3

Ulster Art and a Wider Politics, 1930–39

Belfast underwent the traumas of an armed independence campaign, despite (or because of) the establishment of a regional parliament in 1920.[1] In 1922, contemplating post-war Britain and Ireland, Winston Churchill remarked on 'the dreary steeples of Fermanagh and Tyrone emerging once again. The integrity of their quarrel is one of the few institutions that [remains] unaltered.' The notion of an endemic sectarian division, elevated to the status of a permanent institution in its own right, owed much to Churchill's father, Randolph, who had played the Orange card in 1886 to defeat Irish Home Rule. Despite the manifest survival of the quarrel after partition in 1920 (or 1922), Northern Ireland did take a few halting steps towards modernity.

In the late 1920s, just before Hewitt joined its staff, Belfast Museum and Art Gallery sold off conventional works received through a bequest—'a thoroughly discreditable jumble of Victorian trash', in his later and unpublished opinion—to purchase contemporary art.[2] Since 1928, Davy McLean's tiny Progressive Bookshop in Howard Street championed causes unwelcome at the elephantine City Hall (1906) nearby. Unmoved by these marginal developments, the steeples remained numerous as ever. A native younger than Hewitt has left a useful schema of Belfast's spiritual geography:

> In the small area between my own home and my primary school, there was one Methodist [church], two Presbyterian, one Congregationalist, one Anglican, one Elim tabernacle, one Gospel Hall belonging to the Plymouth Brethren, one Unitarian and one Christian Scientist church. Only the Roman Catholic areas in the west, therefore, belong to a single united church which can claim to speak for the whole community.[3]

As the shift from perfect tense to the tense imperfection of the 1980s' present indicates, this is at once a generous and a nervous cartography. In many respects, the

[1] For a solid account of the transitional processes, originating as a QUB thesis, see Bryan A. Follis, *A State under Siege: The Establishment of Northern Ireland 1920–25* (Oxford: Clarendon Press, 1995).

[2] *North*, p. 12. The bequest had been Sir Robert Lloyd Patterson's, and the disposal of it recommended by Frank Rutter. In *Art in Ulster 1: 1557–1957* (Belfast: Blackstaff, 1977), Hewitt added another sharp comment: 'the executors, making a fair assessment of the good taste of the city's aldermen and councillors, stipulated that the substituted paintings should be acquired for the gallery, by the Contemporary Art Society in London, and not by the Libraries, Museum and Gallery Committee of the [Belfast] Corporation' (p. 78).

[3] Geraldine Watts, 'John Hewitt: the Non Conformist Conscience of Northern Ireland', MLitt thesis, TCD, 1987, p. 16.

town persisted in its supposedly ancient ways. Catholic and Protestant working-class populations lived apart to a considerable extent, and were employed apart also. The press was divided along similar lines, education even more thoroughly regimented by both sides. Yet there is a case for seeing Belfast, at the time of Hewitt's coming of age, not as some kind of local anachronism but as an unusual instance of near-universal urban anomie, a mix of Dante and William Burroughs. The mugwumps could fend for themselves in their camps; cultural opportunities were to be excavated from their own resources, perhaps their own entrails. The reptiles chose to live discreetly apart—Roman alligators over there, Protestant crocodiles right here. Insularity was near universal, even if the important island for many in the unionist community was the other island, the one 'across the water'. Without any land-link bringing in new ideas, and with little passing traffic from overseas, Belfast was Small Town writ large. The film *Ascendancy* (1982, directed by Edward Bennett; premiered in Berlin, 1983) catches the polished philistinism of middle-class Belfast in 1920 to a T. The film's title, of course, lends plausibility to an age-old diagnosis, whereas—to choose an American parallel—Dashiell Hammett's novel *Red Harvest* (1929) invites a contemporary and comparative perspective.

Inside this civil battleground, a very small cultured minority did as best it could. In the mid-1920s, the city hosted an exhibition of work by Nathaniel Hone (1831–1917), 'that greatly neglected landscape master' as Hewitt later called him; Frank Rutter and Thomas Bodkin gave public lectures. As Hewitt's father was a competent watercolourist, these events came to his attention.[4] The transitional years were marked by a significant bonding between father and son. The parental family, always closely knit, was undergoing change: Eileen, his only sister, had married in 1927. Coming of age often introduces a diminished relationship as the young man slips anchor and heads into uncharted water. In 1927, when John was approaching twenty, his father took him to Belgium. Art featured on their itinerary, the young man being particularly impressed by Jan van Eyck's 'Adoration of the Lamb' in Ghent Cathedral. They also spent time in Bruges.[5] Two years later, they visited Paris when John (in retrospect at least) felt 'the usual disappointment at the Mona Lisa'. Among the innumerable works he saw, and admired, Puvis de Chavannes' 'Saint Genevieve Looking Across Paris' in the Pantheon especially appealed.[6] In the summers of 1930 and 1931, he returned to Paris on his own. The pupil-son mutated into a fellow-adult with shared passions for things of the mind and things of beauty.

John Hewitt's versified socialism of these years has been traced directly to RTH's trade-union and labour activities, to his dedicated committee-work and the public meetings which father and son attended together. Ormsby lists a number of visiting speakers from the Left who impressed, including James Maxton (1885–1946) of the Independent Labour Party (ILP), Shapurji Saklatvala (1874–1936, Communist MP for Battersea), and John Wheatley (d.1930), Minister for Health in Ramsay MacDonald's 1924 government.[7] Whether Hewitt's inclination to name heroes deserves analysis in itself, or in relation to Thomas Carlyle's lectures

[4] *North*, p. 12. [5] *North*, p. 19. [6] *North*, p. 20. [7] Ormsby, p. xliii.

On Heroes and Hero Worship (1841), or might less comfortably be referred to the reputations of Edward Carson, Lloyd George, Benito Mussolini, and Adolf Hitler, remains for consideration elsewhere.[8]

Finished at university by the summer of 1930, Hewitt took stock of himself with pedantic accuracy—he was five feet and nine inches 'standing up'. One day, waiting in the barber's shop, he spotted a newspaper advertisement: the Belfast city museum needed an art assistant. In pursuit of support like all the other candidates, he approached a councillor-cum-trade-unionist; 'although he was far to the Right I admitted my leftist views which he told me to keep to myself till the appointment was made'.[9] Much has been written and said about Hewitt's left-wing position then and later. A perspective on the 1930s is offered in an obituary for his friend, the novelist Sam Hanna Bell: Belfast was 'rife with sectarianism as always but there was also poverty and such poverty that any man of sensitivity sought the only possible means of amelioration—left-wing politics'. The reflection elegantly mixes the aesthetic and political, sensitivity and socialism. The hopes of young Hewitt and young Bell were to be disappointed many times over, but more recent reliance on cultural tradition(s) as a hopeful amelioration of (or consolation for) left-wing radicalism may prove no more fruitful.[10]

Life in the museum was routine. As the newest member of staff, he was given very humble accommodation, which had the advantage of being virtually out of sight. J. A. S. Stendall (1887–1973), whom John Hewitt would later hope to succeed, was a naturalist from Chester interested in owls and spiders. In addition to the professionals, the museum employed menial staff. In 1930, their selection called for vigilance. However, a Catholic city councillor who had long served on the committee held the right by custom to appoint one charwoman (usually a widow) when her co-religionist predecessor died or retired. All the other non-professional staff who served during Hewitt's twenty-six years were Protestant—except one, a transferee from the Parks Department.

The first exhibition in which he was practically engaged showcased Yugoslav painting and sculpture, a detail which suggests that the gallery was not quite so provincial as received opinion insists. In his accompanying notes for the public, Hewitt flamboyantly threw over the discretion recommended by the trade-unionist councillor; Krsto Hegedušić (1901–75), he declared, 'paints like a Dutch communist of the sixteenth century', adding bathetically, 'in other words like Breughel'.[11] As it happens, Hegedušić was a Marxist dedicated to peasant culture. To his surprise, Hewitt learned that the actual arranging of pictures would be decided by the curator's wife, a woman of such remarkable shortness that viewers had to stoop before the exhibits.[12]

[8] *The Labour Opposition*, a Belfast monthly publication of the ILP (North Branch), published one article under the pseudonym Student, which made effective use of Carlyle's heroism. Its opening paragraph ('You readers of this newspaper...') resembles in hortatory style JH's first contribution to *The Irish Democrat* of 1937.

[9] *North*, p. 22.

[10] Sean MacMahon, 'Obituary: Sam Hanna Bell', *Linen Hall Review* 7, nos. 1–2 (1990), p. 7.

[11] *North*, p. 42. [12] *North*, p. 43.

Though such an exhibition was exotic, and the traffic in new ideas no more than a trickle, Belfast acquired some permanent residents from beyond its tribal dichotomy. The Ukrainian-born painter Paul Nietsche (1885–1950) began to visit *c.*1926, and soon settled down as a notable figure on the local artistic scene. A decade later, Zoltan Frankl (1894–1961), a Hungarian-born Jewish *emigré* industrialist, arrived with his wife Anny Lewinter to establish textiles factories and, during his long sojourn, became a major collector of twentieth-century Irish painting.[13] The visual arts proved more responsive to international stimuli than the literary ones, largely because the 'language barrier' does not exist in sculpture or watercolour or oils. It would be a constant complaint of John Hewitt's that literature in Northern Ireland was a poor relation within a family of cultural practices not well endowed in any discipline.

Frank Ormsby's capacious edition of Hewitt's *Collected Poems* takes as its starting date 1929, the year before his appointment as junior art assistant in November 1930. The 'unpublished' and 'uncollected' sections—blessedly incomplete—preserve many items which indicate the poet's ambition and energy more than his talent, an imbalance hardly unexpected in a young man still at university until July 1930. Even the political interests have an unexpected inclusiveness. Two poems of this transitional period catch the satirical edge of the 'low dishonest decade' just dawning—'Bradford Millionaire' (written July 1931) borrows its title from *The Waste Land* (1922) to mock the suburban businessman, while the (surely?) ironic 'Chant for the Five-Year Plan' (November 1930) reveals more disenchantment with Soviet culture than Hewitt will admit ten or twenty years later. While he is commemorated primarily as a poet, it could not have been clear at the outset that such would prove to be the case. There are weak and noisy poems, written while other engagements attracted his closer attention. The publication of 'Ireland' in the BBC's flagship journal *The Listener* (18 May 1932), boded well, yet the poem failed to get into *No Rebel Word* in 1948.

Jack Carney (1887–1956), a close associate of Sean O'Casey and a stalwart communist, wrote in *The Irish Worker* of February 1932 that, 'the influence of Soviet Russia has reached out to the Queen's University. There is a fine poem on the 5-Year Plan [in *The Northman*], written to the swinging style of the late Vachel Lindsay. It comes from the pen of John Hewitt. Hewitt is a newcomer in the field of Irish poetry. He will be heard of again.'

Hewitt was never an impressive swinger, and more than one reader has wondered if a dimension of parody or mockery informs the 'Chant for the Five-Year Plan'. Whatever the motive or the reservation implicit in its five loud stanzas, praise in the Irish mouthpiece of Comintern was unlikely to go unnoticed by Stormont's special branch officers.[14]

[13] For a brief but moving tribute to the Frankls, see the opening paragraphs of Terence Fulton, 'Through the Artist's Eyes; Presidential Address to the Ulster Medical Society in the Session 1981–82', *The Ulster Medical Journal* 51, no. 1 (1982), pp. 1–22. A plaque in their honour was unveiled in 2013 on the Malone Road house where they lived.

[14] R. G. Marsh, 'John Hewitt and Theories of Irish Culture; Cultural Nationalism, Cultural Regionalism and Identity in Northern Ireland', PhD thesis, QUB, 1996, pp. 204–5.

At the museum, one of his duties was to conduct parties of visitors through the material on public view. In the autumn of 1932, sculpture by Auguste Rodin (1840–1917) attracted great attention. John spotted 'the youngest of the three daughters of a genial little widow who had been very friendly with my parents'. Having emigrated to Canada some years earlier, Roberta Black was home again, evidently in pursuit of culture. Hewitt's memoir coolly records *two* Americans, the second 'a pleasant looking fellow, by the cut of his clothes' whom 'she had met on board ship'. Though they had docked in Queenstown, Southampton, or London, he was still at her side in Stranmillis, a tenacity which carries the suggestion of her greater sexual maturity—she was three years older—than Hewitt's. He also recalled her use of the American past participle 'gotten'.[15]

In a town as small as Belfast, and inside one of its populations, a prior contact between the two families was hardly surprising, even with the difference of class and education between their parents. Despite her American experience, Agnes Street had provided common ground at least for a few years. Further shared concerns would include the Peace League, for which Roberta acted as local secretary, the Left Book Club (where they met John Kilfeather, publican, bibliophile, and a Catholic), and the British National Council for Civil Liberties.[16] Roberta's fellow travelling American disappeared from view.

In 1933, John and Roberta travelled to Welwyn Garden City, Hertfordshire, for the ILP's Summer School. Founded in 1920, the city itself constituted 'progressive' politics, designed to overcome the sharp opposition of rural and urban experiences and to introduce modern design to families of limited income. Among left-wingers, George Orwell included, there was some hankering for rural virtues.[17] By 1933, the Left in Britain was undergoing serious crises of priority, purity, and conscience.[18] Nevertheless, Jimmy Maxton MP enthralled the two Irish listeners, mainly due to his rhetoric, but partly for the red bandana which he wore 'like a pirate chief'.[19] Fred Jowett (1864–1944), an ILP veteran whose mother had been a Chartist, also impressed the Hewitts: his work was represented in John's library in 1987. Two young Germans earnestly warned of Hitler's potential for catastrophe but few appreciated the urgency of their message; 'only Jennie Lee, a girl in a white frock . . . spoke with any answering seriousness'.[20] Roberta would look back to the Summer School thirty or so years later, deploring the compromises accepted by Lee. Others whom they encountered in 1933 were the Labour pacifist Fenner Brockway and a Chinese poet whom they befriended at the end of the decade.

[15] *North*, p. 48.

[16] See Hewitt, 'The Peace League', *Northman* 2, no. 3 (Autumn 1934), and *Northman* 3, no. 4 (Winter 1935/36). Hewitt's role appears to have been that of a moderator, for which he might not seem best suited. The article in *Northman* (Winter 1935/36) diplomatically refers to opinions 'broadly if not widely held'. Unfortunately, *Ancestral* includes none of his political writing from the 1930s and 1940s, whether in *The Museums Journal*, *The Northman*, *The Northern Star*, or more ephemeral proletarian magazines.

[17] See Valentine Cunningham, *British Writers of the Thirties* (Oxford: Oxford University Press, 1989), p. 238.

[18] For an account of the tensions between various groups inside and outside the Labour Party in this context, see Gordon Brown, *Maxton* (Edinburgh: Collins/Fontana, 1986), pp. 256–69.

[19] *North*, p. 60. [20] *North*, p. 61.

On 7 May 1934, John Hewitt and Roberta Black were married in a civil ceremony at Belfast's registry office, his address No. 7 Fortwilliam Park, hers No. 180 Crumlin Road; witnesses were Robert Telford Hewitt and Samuel Somerset Keith (the bride's stepfather). R. T. Hewitt's participation in a non-church wedding was further evidence of his warm-hearted tolerance. The couple later honeymooned in Paris, having taken possession of a small flat at No. 45 Malone Road. It was probably on this trip that Hewitt smuggled *Ulysses* with its blue paper covers into the United Kingdom by means Joyce would have approved—'tied to my braces and hanging in the seat of my plus fours'.[21] The smuggling into Ulster, through England, of a 'Free State' author's work in a French edition chimes well with an ambitious project of summer 1934, 'Uladh' or—later—'The Red Hand: A Poemosaic'.[22] The sequence of poems took its first name from Hewitt's native province, through the Gaelic name for Ulster, transmuting itself in turn through the province's heraldic sign, the Red Hand (in Gaelic, *Lámh Dearg*). This device, loosely associated with the O'Neill clan, acquired a powerful ambiguity in the twentieth century when it conjured, for some, the identification of Catholic nationalism with 'red' socialism, a spectre which haunted and eluded Hewitt in the mid-1930s. 'Poemosaic' likewise conjured a unity of the verbal icon with the fragments (tesserae), distinguishable from and yet collectively being the poem.[23] Two late collections, *Tesserae* (1967) and *Mosaic* (1981) derive their titles from the experiment of 1934, the significance and value of which are discussed in Chapter 8 ('Defending Barbara Hepworth before the Ratepayers').

Back home by the end of September, John threw himself into one of his most daring engagements outside formal employment. Founded the previous year as the Northern Irish Guild of Artists, the Ulster Unit was a collective for whom he hung their one and only exhibition in December. The Guild renamed itself in tribute to the English-based Unit One where Paul Nash was a dominant spirit. Though Nash was moving steadily towards Surrealism, others associated with Unit One included Edward Burra (1905–76), Barbara Hepworth (1903–75), Henry Moore (1898–1986), Ben Nicholson (1894–1982), and Victor Pasmore (1908–98), with the poet and critic Herbert Read (1893–1969) acting as intellectual promoter and curator. A forcing house for the British avant-garde in the 1930s, Unit One remained unique. While the Belfast offspring was less venturesome, and lasted less than a year, many of Unit One's leading painters and sculptors would reappear in Hewitt's life after he had migrated to Coventry's Herbert Gallery. 'This kind of Puritanism in art was sympathetic to my nature', Hewitt recalled of Unit One when working on a book of memoirs.[24]

The Ulster Unit issued its own manifesto:

> In oil painting, watercolour, sculpture, modelling, etching, and pottery, it is unanimously agreed that the artist must be consistent, simple, sincere, must not seduce the

[21] *North*, p. 75. At his death, Hewitt still had a copy of the 1932/23 Olympia Press edition of *Ulysses*, without any dust jacket.

[22] UU, Hewitt, Notebook 17; Ormsby, p. 597. For a brief discussion of this work, see 'Break for Text I'.

[23] See Ormsby, p. 597; UU, Hewitt, Notebook 17.

[24] *North*, p. 77.

material from its natural integrity, but must seek the realisation of his consciousness of order within the physical limits imposed by wood, stone, clay, glass, or paint.

Little of Nash's Surrealism had crossed the North Channel, and the opportunities for an unfettered avant-garde art practice might seem discouraged by a 'downright' attitude (requiring unanimity) among Ulster practitioners. But the December exhibition in Locksley Hall (attached to a café) was a sizeable occasion, with eighty-two works on show, twenty-one of them pieces of sculpture or pottery. Hewitt physically arranged the exhibition and wrote an introduction for the little catalogue. He also bought three paintings, and a Stone Mask by George McCann (1909–67). The show was nicely timed, with the catalogue offering distinctive and unique Christmas presents.

Not all of the artists involved have gone down in the history books, though Colin Middleton and John Luke were part of the wider group.[25] Exhibited painters included Lady Mabel Annesley (1881–1959), Kathleen Bridle (1897–1989), Elizabeth Clements, W. R. Gordon (1872–1955), and Margaret Yeames—a remarkably 'Protestant' list of names.[26] Jean McGregor, who seems to have provided twelve of the pottery or sculpture items, was essentially a local practitioner of a craft, who did not exhibit much elsewhere. Always on the fringes, William McClughin (1900–71) became bogged down in concerns about technique—'tenacious as an octopus when he had hugged an argument to his mind', according to Hewitt, a close and enduring friend.[27]

McCann certainly deserves attention in the context of Hewitt's evolving interests. Born in Belfast the son of a monumental sculptor (that is, tombstone-maker), George studied at the Royal Academy of Art in London where he met Moore, Epstein, and Eric Gill. In 1934, he was teaching at the Royal School in Armagh, yet acted as the bridgehead between the (far from unanimous) influences he had taken up in London and the local Ulster scene. A second piece by McCann exhibited by the Ulster Unit was 'Abstraction'. In 1939, he joined the Inniskilling Fusiliers, survived the war, and returned to Northern Ireland in 1946. Under the pseudonym George Galway he published a collection of short stories in 1942.[28] His wife, Mercy (née Hunter, 1910–89), a widely travelled art mistress at Banbridge Academy, was half-Russian on her mother's side.

Hewitt's purchase of the McCann Mask, together with three paintings, indicates a financial commitment which, as a junior civil servant with no private income, was bordering on the foolhardy. Throughout his working career, and more so after retirement, he and his wife were never comfortably off, and the accommodation

[25] For an early exercise in support for the artist, see JH's 'Colin Middleton, a Biographical Sketch', *The Bell* 4, no. 5 (August 1942), pp. 338–9. Hewitt met Middleton through the Unit, and the latter contributed a black-and-white image for the catalogue's cover.

[26] See Hewitt's later note, 'The Lady Mabel Annesley's Collection of Contemporary Wood Carvings', *Belfast Municipal Art Gallery and Museum Quarterly Notes*, 61 (June 1939). For his later account of the Ulster Unit, see Hewitt, *Art in Ulster I: 1557–1957: With Biographies of the Artists by Theo Snoddy* (Belfast: Blackstaff, 1977), pp. 100–3.

[27] See Theo Snoddy, *Dictionary of Irish Artists: 20th Century*, 2nd edn (Dublin: Merlin, 2002), p. 369.

[28] George Galway, *Sparrows Round my Brow* (Newcastle, Co. Down: Mourne Press, 1942).

they bought involved mortgages which pinched. His collecting, though it has left a splendid monument at the University of Ulster and the Ulster Museum, was exacted at a price. In poetry, he tried to stretch his wings, writing in November 1934 to Macmillan & Co., seeking encouragement to submit for their Contemporary Poets anthology. Success on this level was accompanied by an invitation to submit a full collection. Hewitt's choice of advocacy took the shape of favourable opinions from Lascelles Abercrombie, Gordon Bottomley, and, more positively, Janet Adam Smith (assistant editor of *The Listener*). However 'circumstances' prevented Hewitt from doing the bigger thing until the spring of 1937, when thirty-eight poems were despatched to London. And returned.[29]

The mid-1930s saw Hewitt develop his professional and political life in Belfast, while also exploring an isolated portion of his native province. In autumn 1934, he finally met the ageing Revd Alexander Irvine (1863–1941) at a Labour meeting in York Street; this was to be a year of few poems—just two in Ormsby's listing. Irvine, a charismatic orator and radical in his social teaching, had impressed Hewitt in 1926. He stayed with Eileen and Norman Todhunter in 1938 when John Luke painted his portrait.[30] The old veteran died three years later, but re-emerges in Hewitt's psychic life some years later. The relationship between the two men, though slight in terms of personal contact, involves issues of vocation, the son–father bond, and the fictions generated by the act of writing. Irvine, on his side, appears to have corresponded more with Eileen Todhunter than with her brother.

As an early marker, we found that Hewitt responded to a public address in Belfast by the American-based but Antrim-born preacher. Bred in poverty, a casual labourer turned miner turned soldier, Irvine exemplified the capacity of man to overcome dire circumstances and retain his humanity. Hewitt heard but did not meet the charismatic and doughty social reformer in the year of *Africa Calling*. According to Irvine, the subject of his impromptu address in 1926 was Temperance, rather than politics or religion (see Chapter 2, 'Belfast Beginnings', p. 26). The teenager much later recorded that he had gone, albeit reluctantly, with his father. Certainly there had been no shortage of public meetings to attend in the Belfast of those days. Apart from the mainstream churches, the variety stretched from the near-deism of Non-Subscribing Presbyterians to the effusive Christodelphians, with Jock Troup (1896–1954) of the Cripples Institute somewhere in-between. The Irish Alliance of Christian Workers' Unions was mainly concerned with organizing missions, but had links with the Christian Socialist Revd Bruce Wallace (d.1939), founder of *The Belfast Weekly Star* in 1880 whom Hewitt celebrated in verse.[31] Given his interest in John Ball (1338–81) and other early rebels, one hopes

[29] University of Reading, Macmillan & Co. Records, letters of JH dated 26 November 1934 and 21 April 1937.

[30] Watts, 'John Hewitt: the Non Conformist Conscience of Northern Ireland', p. 57; JH, 'Alex of the Chimney Corner', in *Ancestral*, p. 44. On the issue of JH and Irvine in 1926, see Append C, 'Alex Irvine, Luther, and Rebellion'.

[31] Ormsby, pp. 155, 598. However JH's little poem is simply titled, 'B. O. W.', while the Christian Socialist's full name was John Bruce Wallace.

he did not miss N. Bonaparte Wyse's talk on 'Early Communism: Jack Cade as Bolshevist'.[32] All of these entertainments were on offer in January 1926. Hewitt's first sighting and hearing Irvine cannot have occurred any earlier than August of that year.

When he and his wife heard Irvine again in 1934, the latter preached in a Belfast suburban church on 'sin in its Greek connotation meaning missing the mark, the target'—a decidedly non-Calvinist view. The poet was so impressed that he wrote two sonnets and sent them to Irvine: these have not been published. Shortly afterwards, a more openly political meeting was arranged in the Labour Hall, York Street, where the two men met, the elder being seventy-one, the younger twenty-six or -seven.[33] An apparent contrast of venues—Presbyterian church and Labour or trade union hall—essentially defines what Hewitt found intriguing about Irvine.

The same year saw Hewitt embark on his poemosaic (see Break for Text I). To judge by 'Providence 2' (first published 1974), ethics, agency, determinism are all at play:

> The beetle near my foot
> tempts providence in me;
> my inadvertent boot
> is God's own mystery.[34]

Noting it as 'the diffuse and sprawling Part XXV of the unpublished poemosaic', Steven Matthews quoted from 'The Return' (September 1935) lines which acknowledge the contrast of rural calm and urban riot, yet propose 'it is not wars we remember / but the chiselled face... the temple, the sonnet: these are Man'.[35]

A year later poet and preacher met again, by accident, in a Belfast café, and the next morning for breakfast in Irvine's hotel, the Kensington in College Square. Hewitt is prolific with some details, parsimonious with others, and his essay 'Alec of the Chimney Corner' is the cumulative yet gappy account we have of his relations with Irvine.[36] This visit to Belfast had not been advertised in the newspapers,

[32] Jack Cade (d.1450) led a Kentish rebellion against Henry VI, and came to feature in Shakespeare's *Henry VI Part 2*. Apart from seeking a reduction of taxes and the eradication of corruption at court, the rebels had a political demand with some local appeal in Belfast—the recall from Ireland of Richard Plantagenet, Duke of York.

[33] These dates—1926, then 1934—of Irvine's visits to Ireland are already established in Hewitt's first account of him; see JH, 'Portrait of Dr. Alexander Irvine: the Man', *Belfast Municipal Museum and Art Gallery Quarterly Notes* 63 (December 1939), pp. 1–5. The portrait, by John Luke, was painted in August 1938, when Irvine stayed with Eileen (née Hewitt) and Norman Todhunter.

[34] Ormsby, p. 149.

[35] Steven Matthews, *Irish Poetry: Politics, History, Negotiation: the Evolving Debate 1969 to the Present* (Basingstoke: Macmillan, 1997), p. 52. Thematically, #XXV of 'The Red Hand' deals with the visit to Rathlin and the depressing return to Belfast ('the city of our dreadful night'); textually it stands almost independent of 'The Return' as dated 1935 in JH, *Compass: Two Poems* (Belfast: privately printed, 1944). Some lines from #XXV are incorporated in the later text, but examination of the ms also reveals that #XXV is an incomplete poem, with gaps between groups of lines and sometimes gaps within a line.

[36] See *Ancestral*, pp. 38–47. Hewitt mentions an interview he gave to the BBC in 1961, describing the Labour Hall meeting with Irvine, but complaining that the gist of his account was omitted from the broadcast.

as on earlier occasions, and it emerged that Irvine's Labour Hall oration had offended the city fathers, the Unionist Party, the YMCA, the Rotarians—and, naturally, the newspapers. Irvine had, in Hewitt's words, 'consorted with atheists and communists', an allegation close to that later whispered about Hewitt himself in 1952. Time does not fly.

Rejected and liberated, 'the old actor' announced that there were unpopular things to be said in Ulster, values to be maintained. Growing old and based in America, he needed someone locally to lead youngsters in the right direction. Would Hewitt take on this duty, this mission?[37] Of the consequences, Hewitt merely tells us that he was to expect contact from the youngsters in question. The preacher-reformer's objective is never disclosed, except by blurred implication:

> I invited three young men to the flat one evening. But here the ambiguity which cut through Irvine like a geological fault was painfully laid bare. For the Irvine they respected and the jargon they used for their regard was cast in the evangelical mould. To them he was the revivalist *par excellence*, not different in kind but in degree from the roaring fundamentalists and niggling literalists who played so great a part in the lives of the Ulster working-class non-conformists of that period.... Irvine's books, other than *The Carpenter and His Kingdom* which contained among other things the sermon on sin...did not interest them. His politics they never guessed. His professional skill they had no awareness of. So, rather on a note of bewildered cordiality, we parted. A letter or two passed between us. We never met again.[38]

The Belfast sermon on sin was preached in 1934, whereas *The Carpenter and His Kingdom* had appeared in 1922. Its fourteenth chapter, however, is 'Missing the Mark'. Like many preachers, Irvine had innocently recycled old reliables, confident, surely, that the congregation would not recognize the source. He gave Hewitt a copy of the book, laying bare his economy of divine truth. On the other side of these imprecisions, Hewitt insinuates that the three evangelically attuned students took to *The Carpenter and his Kingdom* as distinct from Irvine's more socialistic writings. Here he distorts the book's contents. Paragraphs are headed 'The democracy of the new religion...Why working men were chosen...Denunciation of the rich...The mind of a Capitalist...Social democracy in the Kingdom...'[39] It would be nigh impossible to read *The Carpenter* without realizing the author's left-wing political views.

The events of 1935 are occasionally traceable in 'The Red Hand', where ##XLVII–XLVIII are the sonnets presented to Irvine in 1934, but #XXV recounts the trip to Rathlin the following year. Apart from unsettling a conclusion that the poemosaic is at some level a chronological narrative, the order of poems complicates any settled view of Hewitt's attitude towards Edward Carson. Poem #XLIII recalls the occasion when, as a boy of four, he was taken to hear Carson

[37] 'Alec of the Chimney Corner' was written in Coventry in the early 1960s, and first published in *The Honest Ulsterman* 4 (August 1968), pp. 5–12; see *Ancestral*, p. 43.

[38] *Ancestral*, pp. 40–3. Irvine visited Belfast for the last time in 1938.

[39] Alexander Irvine, *The Carpenter and His Kingdom* (New York: Scribners, 1922). For the passage on sin, quoted accurately enough by JH, see p. 206. No copy of the book is preserved in Hewitt's library at UU.

speak at Six Roads End, in County Down. It is plausible to conclude that this piece was prompted by Carson's death in October 1935, for #L describes the funeral, the silent crowds lining the street, the cultured bishop (Frederick McNeice) presiding,

> and on no distant day
> the angry men will see by easy sign
> that North and South each worker is a friend...

In conclusion, Carson's political career is bluntly called treason. Yet John and Roberta Hewitt stood in St Anne's Cathedral; saw the coffin; heard the bishop. Was Carson's funeral the occasion of Irvine's return to Ulster in 1935 though, like Hewitt, the old actor could denounce the chicanery, 'the crooked lawyer and the party hack' with a wealth of detail?

Irvine's importance in Hewitt's life involves two texts, one of 1926, the other of 1948. It will be obvious that the purpose of introducing Irvine into a consideration of *Africa Calling* and its authorship (see Append B, '*Africa Calling* [1926], Unwanted Words') relies on two data. First, that Irvine was a famous missionary and howling pulpit success, though more active on the home or city missions (including New York) than in 'the dark continent', and that he apparently wanted the poet John Hewitt to undertake some duty or vocation of a related kind. Second, that Hewitt's account of his initial efforts in this connection centres on a group of three students, just as the 'missionary play by John Hewitt' compares the careers of three students-become-missionaries.

But a mean-spirited chronology inhibits any causal linking of the two: the play was in print by 1926, the short-lived duty or mission undertaken by the poet in 1934. Indeed, the account we have of his meeting with three students dates from no earlier than 1961, when Hewitt was comfortably settled in Coventry. This problem of timetabling may take us beyond its immediate content or, rather, discloses the inevitable compaction and overlap of psychically charged material. Between 1934 and 1961, a fictional reworking of Hewitt's engagement with the Revd Alex Irvine appeared under the priestly title 'The Laying on of Hands'. Published in *The Bell* in April 1948, when Peadar O'Donnell (1893–1986) occupied the editorial chair, the short story echoed the incident of 1934. Given the hostile perspective employed by Sarah Ferris in summarizing this material, it is as well to examine it in some detail.[40]

In Hewitt's story, a variety of narrative filters and disguise names are used to rearrange the still recognisable terms of the pact between Irvine and Hewitt which concludes 'Alec of the Chimney Corner'. The fictitious person entrusted with the

[40] Dr Ferris, in the preliminary material of her dissertation, summarizes matters thus: 'Chapter Six develops the theme that Hewitt's essays on Irvine are artfully tailored to the demands of his career at significant moments and that his contradictory estimates of Irvine's integrity amount to a cynical manipulation of his "hero's" legendary status in Northern Ireland. It is suggested that this aspect of Hewitt was a crucial factor in his rise to prominence which followed shortly after he published "Alec of the Chimney Corner" in 1968.' See Sarah Ferris, 'An Exemplary Protestant: A Study of the Myth of John Hewitt and its Place within Contemporary Literary Debate in Northern Ireland', PhD thesis, Newcastle University, 1998, p. 6.

mission is Dick Griffin, referring to the character in F. L. Green's *Odd Man Out*, but also echoing the Richard Telford pseudonym used by Hewitt *The Irish Democrat* in which O'Donnell was also involved. The nameless narrator describes an encounter while travelling to Dungannon with Tom, 'a famous explorer author', whose books were inferior to his public lectures—'that is, all except, his very first, on the Congo Rubber Scandal'.[41] The last detail, conjuring up Roger Casement's career, adds to the story's fictionality. The crucial passage, couched in a suave rhetoric only fiction can manage, had Tom (otherwise nameless) reported as declaring:

> So this is my last testament. I should have stayed here always. I shouldn't have cast my pattern of action over so wide an area. I should have stayed and done my work here. The life of a man of good-will is always a crusade. I only made forays and brief raids. I didn't occupy and consolidate. Now it's got to be done. Things have dropped behind here. There must be someone to supply the drive, so that we may catch up. There must be one voice for justice. One voice for progress and tolerance. Someone to light the little fires that are languishing and guttering out all over the province. Someone not bound to a political party, nor tied to a particular creed. You've got to be that voice, be that torchbearer. I've made it my business to meet most of the likely young fellow here, and you are the likeliest. Don't ask me how I know. I just know. It will be a big job. I could have done it, but things panned out differently. I don't suppose you believe in the laying on of hands—Well, anyway, Dick, you're nominated.[42]

If writing had to contend with other obligations in the mid-1930s, the religio-social mission did not feature. In 1935, Hewitt attended a Museums Association conference in Bristol, boosting his professional claims. For their summer holidays that year, he and Roberta spent a week on Rathlin Island off the Antrim coast, a location memorably served by Michael McLaverty, short story writer and novelist, in *Call My Brother Back* (1939). A feature which struck them was the burial side-by-side of Catholic and Protestant in the local graveyard. This observation is a fair indication of how little they had ventured into rural Ireland by 1935, for such a practice is common in pre-Victorian churchyards; Kilmore in Armagh, where John's ancestors came from, is a good example. But exploring and embracing the countryside became a vocation. Whereas most Irish urbanites favoured a country retreat in the far west (Connemara for Dubliners; Dingle for the Cork people; Donegal for the Belfast liberal professions), the Hewitts chose the Antrim Glens. The highland area was desolate but hauntingly beautiful. Close enough to Belfast, there are points in some of the upper glens offering large views of Scotland with no intervening sea visible. Hewitt's growing interest in regionalism was fed by these unexpected proportions of the near and the far.

'The Return' sought to gather his experiences of 1934/35 into a satisfactory whole. Rathlin provided a rugged and rural starting point, with the return to Belfast in riot providing a contrast. The trip to Bristol offered a chance to explore the local

[41] JH, 'The Laying on of Hands', *The Bell* 16, no. 1 (1948), p. 31. Ferris implies that Irvine is named, indeed is a central character in the story, which he certainly is not.

[42] JH, 'The Laying on of Hands', p. 35.

countryside; at Meare Lake in Somerset, excavations of an Iron Age village led to 'some sort of mystical conversion, a true turning towards, and away from, not to be expressed in orthodox religious terms, but rather, an upspringing of self realisation'.[43] The poem offers two contrasting perspectives: first 'cold and lonely intervals of self' (l. 39) which presumably related to his experience before the rich encounters with Roberta and now a revelatory remote past; then, 'the clogging grease of self' (l. 223) which threatened to impede a convergence of thought and physical being.[44] Often taken for a no-nonsense individualist, Hewitt, in these years, more than once interrogates the sticky mirages of self.

The following year, the couple travelled to Colchester in Essex for a summer school at the Adelphi Centre. This utopian project had been established on a farm at Langham bought by the critic John Middleton Murry (1889–1957). Together with the poet Max Plowman (1883–1941), he proposed a pacifist community to study 'the new socialism'. Compared with occasional gatherings in Davy McLean's bookshop, this was an elite corps of bohemian geniuses and eccentrics. The Hewitts met George Orwell (1903–50), Rayner Heppenstall (1911–81), and other stars, some dim, some distant. Everyone had a daily manual chore, performed for the collective good. In the kitchen, Orwell and Hewitt shared potato-peeling duties. The art critic and anarchist Herbert Read lectured, but Hewitt could not remember him sweeping the floor. If some individuals were stimulating, the Adelphi Centre (in retrospect) was a 'steaming fish tank of supercharged egos'. Later, Murry degenerated into 'a Red-baiting fascist Messiah'.[45] At the time, Belfast drew strength from the Peace Pledge Union and, when the Adelphi Centre took in sixty Basque children (refugees from the Spanish Civil War), Roberta, as secretary of the Belfast Peace League, assisted in fund- and morale-raising. Two young Basque visitors stayed with the Hewitts in their new accommodation at No. 15 Westland Drive, one of them (Laura Martinez) returning in 1939 for almost six months.

The Adelphi Centre excursion was followed rapidly by Hewitt's commencing work on one of his longest verse undertakings, a dramatic poem, 'The Bloody Brae', the early portion of which is recorded in a notebook dated to August 1936.[46] Years later, it was broadcast on radio (though not written for the medium), performed in the Lyric Theatre, published in *Threshold* (autumn 1957), and collected in *Freehold and Other Poems* (1986). On one level, the Adelphi gathering and the play share an important theme—the gross folly of war. But 'The Bloody Brae', set in an isolated part of east Antrim in the early seventeenth century, encapsulates and re-enacts the theme through the intensifying lens of guilt. John Hill, a trooper who killed (amongst others) Bridget Magee and her suckling child, cannot know rest or hope of salvation until he somehow earns forgiveness. Hill, it goes without saying, was a Protestant; Bridget a Catholic.

Despite these neat arrangements, Hewitt drastically modifies the historical context. Though he publicly stated that the play was based on a 'legendary and largely fictitious event...which is supposed to have taken place in Islandmagee, Co.

[43] *North*, p. 115. [44] Ormsby, pp. 14, 19.
[45] *North*, pp. 59–61. [46] UU, Hewitt, Notebook 21.

Antrim, in January 1642', the preliminaries to the text specify 'Early XVIII [*sic*, *recte* XVII] century'.[47] By declining to specify a year, he removes the action from 1641–42, a period dominated in Ulster history by the uprising of Catholics and the sudden massacres which Hewitt alludes to later in 'The Colony'. By extension John Hill's overwhelming realization of guilt is not mitigated by any implied half-justification in 'enemy action'. One might conclude that Hewitt dramatizes a spiritual condition in which Protestant guilt is objective. Within the text, a speaker identifies Hill—'He wears the habit of a Cromwell trooper, / a trooper at the head of a penny ballad'—in a manner to date the original action even later than 1642. Apparently at odds with this, Hill urgently speaks of 'this night, this place, and seventy years ago', further dissolving any historical given, while intensifying immediacy. Of course, 'The Bloody Brae' attends to mental action (and reflection), not the cut and thrust of warfare, and the identification is phrased in terms of popular commemorative iconography. It bears comparison with Yeats's 'The Dreaming of the Bones' (1919), without the Noh palaver.

During the last years of peace, Hewitt appeared diligently in the museum/gallery's *Quarterly Notes*. For the most part his topics were strictly professional, for example, recent donations made by the Contemporary Art Society (December 1938). However, he occasionally allowed an overlap between the professional and the domestic, as when he wrote up a portrait of Alexander Irvine, a picture painted in the Hewitts' home while the subject was staying with the Todhunters.[48]

While in London visiting exhibitions, he and Roberta responded to anxieties about a proposed carve-up of Abyssinia (the Hoare–Laval Pact, 1935), and heard George Padmore (1902–59), a stocky West Indian, address a meeting in the Livingstone Hall. Hewitt spoke and, 'overcome by emotion', contributed £1. Padmore was a prolific anti-fascist and anti-racist writer at the time, fond of quoting Marx. 'Never let it be forgotten that "Labour with a white skin cannot emancipate itself where labour with a black skin is branded."'[49] Admirable, if heady, stuff. On the street afterwards, police dispersed the crowd before it could march on Westminster.

> When Roberta and I, our excitement not all dissipated, found our way to Charing Cross, I bought a copy of *The Daily Worker* dated for the next day, and read in it an inexact account of the meeting we had just attended and the demonstration which had fizzled out. This was one of those little things which, all through the agitations of the Thirties, kept us out of the Communist Party.... [O]nly that which is achieved by honesty is worth attempting...defeat is never so overwhelming when your hands are clean.[50]

[47] John Hewitt, *Freehold and Other Poems* (Belfast: Blackstaff Press, 1986), p. 47. JH refers in a note to D. H. Akenson, *Between Two Revolutions* (Port Credit, Ontario: Meany, 1979) 'for an informed reference' to the largely fictitious event. Akenson does not provide, but to some degree confirms, JH's original source in 1936.

[48] 'Portrait of Dr Alexander Irvine (by John Luke)', *Belfast Municipal Art Gallery and Museum Quarterly Notes* 63 (December 1939), pp. 1–5.

[49] Karl Marx, *Capital, a Critique of Political Economy*, vol. 1, trans. Ben Fowkes (Harmondsworth: Penguin, 1976), p. 414.

[50] *North*, p. 100.

A counsel of bourgeois perfection Padmore would hardly have commended.

Prejudice lay even closer to home. The London-based National Council for Civil Liberties took a cool look at the altering nature of law enforcement in Northern Ireland. A small local committee was established in Belfast, which included Professors Robert Mitchell Henry (Classics) and Alexander MacBeath (Adult Education)—with the precocious Hewitt—to examine the Special Powers Act (April 1922). In addition to her secretarial role, Roberta occasionally lured the inevitable plain-clothes man on a wild goose chase. Henry (1873–1950) interviewed a number of 'witnesses', mainly victims of the Act Hewitt described as 'a useful manual for counterrevolution'.[51] In 1936, the Council concluded that the Royal Ulster Constabulary lacked autonomy from a politicized administration, going on to accuse the Unionist Party of creating 'under the shadow of the British Constitution a permanent machine of dictatorship'.[52] Praised in *The Irish Worker* two years earlier, Hewitt's left-wing radicalism had now implicated him in formal denunciation of the state for which he worked.

These were factors not forgotten when the post of director at the Belfast Museum fell vacant in the Cold War early 1950s. In a published essay of 1972, he proudly named Henry and MacBeath—both were safely dead and beyond official sanction—as fellow contributors to the enquiry, adding that this had been 'his first acquaintance with the nature of state authority and its techniques of the opened letter and the tapped telephone'.[53] Of Henry, he observed 'There can be few at his old university who can recall that honourable career of independent thought and action in a context of compromise, expediency, and obscurantism.'[54] He added, for good measure, that Henry had written a book called *The Evolution of Sinn Fein,* published in Dublin in 1920. MacBeath delivered a lecture to the British Association visiting Belfast in 1952, entitled 'A Plea for Heretics'.

The Council was deliberately infiltrated by at least one Irish lobby in Britain, later to become the Connolly Association: the latter's serpentine development and switches of name made a contribution to uncertainty about Hewitt's political journalism. While few could deny the accuracy of the Council's analysis with regard to the RUC and the Unionist Party, his position vis-à-vis employers was further compromised when he took a hand in establishing an avowedly political newspaper, *The Irish Democrat.*[55]

Sometime early in 1937, he was invited to meet a group of three at the Brown Horse, a city centre public house in Library Street. A decision had already been

[51] *North*, p. 73. Earlier R. M. Henry had resigned as chairman of the Trade Board in Belfast in protest at efforts to cut workers' wages. See Paddy Devlin, *Yes We Have No Bananas* (Belfast: Blackstaff, 1981), p. 54.

[52] *Irish Times*, 25 May 1936, quoting *Report of a Commission of Inquiry Appointed to Examine the Purpose and Effect of the Civil Authorities (Special Powers) Acts (Northern Ireland) 1922 and 1933* (London: Council or Civil Liberties, 1936).

[53] 'No Rootless Colonist', first published in *Aquarius* 1972; reprinted *Ancestral*, pp. 146–57 (p. 151).

[54] *North*, p. 73. Henry and MacBeath were well known in 1936 as activists; Hewitt's naming them in 1972 was intended to *recall* their contribution to a liberal politics.

[55] For a contrasting view of *The Irish Democrat*, in its several incarnations, see Simon Prince, *Northern Ireland's '68: Civil Rights, Global Revolt and the Origins of the Troubles* (Dublin: Irish Academic Press, 2007), pp. 92–7.

taken to launch the paper, and the business of the moment was to appoint Hewitt literary editor. This he agreed to do, contributing under the *nom de plume* Richard Telford, which can hardly have fooled anyone, given his father's renown in Belfast. The project was backed by socialistic republicans who, in 1934, had broken with the IRA to form a short-lived Republican Congress. The leading figures were Peadar O'Donnell, Frank Ryan (1902–44), and the brothers Gilmore (George and Charlie).[56] O'Donnell, a novelist and playwright, unquestionably had literary interests; the Gilmores were distinguished in such company by coming from a Protestant family, sometime resident in Belfast. Ryan edited *The Irish Democrat* after his temporary return from Spain (March 1937) to recover from battle wounds. Back with the republican forces, he was taken prisoner (March 1938), and later 'liberated' by Franco into German hands.

Unfortunately, Hewitt left no details of who was present in the Brown Horse, though he suspected them of being 'fellow-travellers' if not card-carrying members of the Communist Party. Frank Ormsby gives the names Edward Boyle, George Hill, and Joe Sherlock, adding that Hewitt at this time or shortly afterwards was also literary editor of *Forum*, a supplement issued with the short-lived journal *Irish Jewry*.[57] Of the three names on offer, Sherlock remains the most opaque; as a minor poet Edward Boyle recurs under several variants of his name; the third is probably the journalist George Herbert Hill (1898–1969) who published an anti-war memoir-novel, *Retreat from Death*, in 1936. This last identification fits into Hewitt's distinctly vague memory of the Left Book Club's Belfast adherents—'somehow a symbolical figure, George Hill the quiet newspaper man, with the authority of Ulster's only war-novel behind him'.[58]

It seems likely that either O'Donnell or Ryan would have vetted the candidate literary editor. The former had been active in Belfast during railways strikes, coordinating the activities of the IRA and a Revolutionary Workers' Group in sabotage, and so was vividly familiar to the Special Branch. An active supporter, Malachy Gray, a shop steward with bookish interests and a sometime communist, has left reminiscences of Belfast in those days without making reference to an *Irish Democrat*, to which he regularly contributed.[59] Hewitt's account of the episode deserves extended quotation:

> As, unfortunately, we could not carry on our editorial work in the snug of *The Brown Horse*, a little office was found up a stairway near the Great Northern Railway, and to this address I was committed to having my monthly budget delivered on time. I wrote my inaugural manifesto, bidding the proletarian writers of Ireland to unite and deluge

[56] See George Gilmore, *The 1934 Republican Congress*, 2nd edn (Inistioge: George Brown Memorial Committee, 2011). The congress identified the Belfast leadership as 'among the most reactionary factors in the I.R.A.' (p. 36).

[57] Ormsby, p. xxxiii. For some details of JH's contributions to *Forum*, see Tom Clyde's useful (but incomplete) lists in 'The Prose Writings of John Hewitt; a Bibliography', MA thesis, QUB, 1985.

[58] *North*, p. 66. The passage continues, 'still distinct, but without that authority, his henchman the sporting journalist, and their friend the red-nosed linotype operator who tapped out surrealist poems on long galley strips'. None of these latter convinces as a Brown Horse conspirator.

[59] Malachy Gray, 'A Shop Stewart Remembers', *Saothar: Journal of the Irish Labour History Society* 11 (1986), pp. 109–15.

us with the stories, the verses...born out of their immediate class and national struggle. I also reviewed George Orwell's *The Road to Wigan Pier*. When I had these typed, I decided against posting in the normal way, for it was accepted that the mails in Northern Ireland were under continual surveillance...So, rather than inform the authorities, if they did not already know, that Richard Telford was in fact John Hewitt, I took my envelope down town to *The Democrat* office. I knocked on the door, but got no reply; so I dropped my stuff through the letterbox. Something prompted me to try the door handle. It opened straight away. I went in and saw my envelope lying at an angle in the wire-mesh catcher. This seemed a most insecure way of doing business, so I took out my envelope, stuck it in my pocket and went home, delivering it later by another method.[60]

The museum man, custodian of treasures if not secrets, unimpressed by the lack of security, kept plugging away, until (in his account) two of the *Democrat*'s local sponsors left to work in England. Then it was thought more efficient to shift the editorial office. Though Hewitt draws no such implication, it is likely that the change reflected a tightening of political security among editors. 'In these circumstances I wrote less and less for it, my final contribution being an appreciation of Jack B. Yeats, based on a review of Tom McGreevey's little book.'[61] Hewitt was no unqualified admirer of Jack Yeats.

The account of his engagement with *The Irish Democrat* raises a few problems. MacGreevy's book was not published until 1945. By then, the paper briefly edited by Frank Ryan had long ceased publication (December 1937). However, a London-based successor, *Irish Freedom* (first issued 1939) changed its name to *The Irish Democrat* in 1942 and it was these later papers which were affiliated to the Connolly Association. Malachy Gray edited *Irish Freedom* for the latter half of 1939. What is obvious from Hewitt's autobiographical notes is the fact that he had not kept cuttings from the pre-war *Democrat*. Tom Clyde indicates that the review of MacGreevy appeared in *The Irish Democrat* of October 1945 under the title 'Most Interesting Irish Painter of His Generation'.

The problems do not disappear with the cuttings. Hewitt's account of his involvement with *The Irish Democrat* appears in *A North Light*, a typescript, the covers of which carry his Coventry address of March 1960 onwards. Of course, the contents may have been written much earlier, different chapters composed perhaps at quite different times. Yet, if his claims about *The Democrat* (his own usual way of referring to it, even in the paper itself) do not stand up, then the North Light project (never completed) is to some degree compromised. For the moment, staying with the 1930s, we have to report that Hewitt's (or Richard Telford's) Manifesto certainly appeared in issue no. 2, and that 'A WORKER'S BOOK PAGE, edited by Richard Telford' commenced with the issue of 3 April.[62]

[60] *North*, pp. 68–9.

[61] *North*, p. 69. Hewitt's memory may have overlooked the gap between the paper he contributed to and its eventual namesake successor.

[62] *The Irish Democrat* of 1937 was one of many short-lived radical-left papers of the 1930s; some of its regular contributors reappear in *The Irish Worker* of May 1938 onwards; *Irish Freedom* (1939 onwards, a London-based paper edited by Michael McInerney and others), at least once reprinted material from *The Irish Democrat* of 1937 (see issue 20 of August 1940, p. 2). In December 1941, *Irish*

A review of *The Road to Wigan Pier* (published March 1937) appeared, with the Manifesto framed within it. Hewitt enthused about Orwell, 'author of three good novels and a grand work of reminiscences [who] is now out fighting in Spain'. He described the new book as 'really two books in one', the first of which is treated in considerable detail, a report on living conditions among the English working class. The second, however, required more than praise: 'in this part so many controversial issues are raised that it is better to postpone consideration and discussion of that section till our next issue, when I hope to treat at length of the points that require comment, criticism or approval'.

As luck would have it, *The Daily Worker* of 17 March 1937 carried a review by Harry Pollitt (1890–1960). The general secretary of the Communist Party (GB) could not endorse Orwell's perspective on English working-class life nor his implied political remedies. In 1939, Pollitt would (privately) deviate from the Moscow line in order to recommend prompt support for the war against Hitler and, as a result, he was obliged to stand down briefly. His replacement was R. Palme Dutt, for whom Kathleen Maybin worked. But in 1937, Pollitt was the voice of orthodoxy, from which Hewitt dissented either out of naivety, mischief, or loyalty to an author he admired beyond partisan considerations.

Towards the end of his highly positive review, Hewitt returned to the theme previously deferred till the next issue of *The Irish Democrat*: 'Orwell concludes this section of his challenging summary by remarking that "it is quite likely that fish and chips, art silk stockings, the movies, the radio, strong tea and Football Pools have between them averted the revolution".' In Hewitt's eyes, this is magnificent stuff, only to be improved on by an extension of the analysis to other parts of the British Isles, including Ireland. 'What about it, you intellectuals, you workers? Derry and Dublin are clamouring for your exposures. Read Orwell and you will have no trouble about style or approach.' The second instalment of his response to *Wigan Pier*, dealing with the controversial aspects, never appeared in *The Irish Democrat*. Seizing on the Left Book Club's March 1937 Choice, he had kicked off in a crypto-communist paper—with the wrong foot. The fact that Hewitt had met and liked Orwell (at the Adelphi Centre), and may have disclosed this detail to the paper's controllers, probably explains the non-appearance of an argumentative sequel to the review.[63] But Orwell's own prejudicial observations—ranging from 'a dark, small-boned, sour, Irish-looking man, and astonishingly dirty' to 'Comrade

Freedom cites *The Irish Front* as its predecessor, and a second *Irish Democrat* commences publication in 1945. If Hewitt became confused about which ephemeral paper he reviewed Orwell for, the makings of confusion existed independent of his memory. In a more specifically literary context, *The Bell* has been treated by Larry White as developing themes explored by *The Irish Democrat* of 1937.

[63] *The Road to Wigan Pier* was commercially published in March 1937. By that time the author was in Republican Spain, where he quickly discovered tensions smouldering between orthodox communists and various other left-wing groups, notably anarchists. Ironically, in his initial attempt to reach Spain, he had consulted John Strachey, but in the end he made his way there through ILP contacts. By the time Strachey in *The Irish Democrat* was denouncing Trotskyite betrayal in Catalonia, Orwell had already experienced the 'May Days' in which the two factions had come to blows in Barcelona. Consequently, no further review of *Wigan Pier* could be tolerated in *The Irish Democrat*, for its author was already known to have rejected the orthodox interpretation; see Orwell's *Homage to Catalonia* (1938) and other writings in *Orwell in Spain*, edited by Peter Davison (London: Penguin, 2001).

X, author of *Marxism for Infants*'—doubtless alienated the *Democrat*'s joint sponsors. Even in Orwell's own view, *The Road to Wigan Pier* was 'not very left-wing'.[64]

'Richard Telford' made his debut in late March 1937, and is not traceable after 1 May; in other words, he lasted little over a month. The Manifesto as published certainly matches the summary Hewitt typed up perhaps thirty years later; but it also deviated from the stern tenor of the paper as a whole. Despite the cautious use of a pseudonym, Hewitt began, 'This is mine, my own manifesto, for I shall be responsible of this page of The Democrat. The Literary Page. Whoopee. We're going places.' Having called for Workers' Short Stories, he went on to hope for 'a new and wise social order of friendship and joy'. Frank Ryan was made of sterner stuff.

Hewitt's problems were two-fold. He was not a nationalist and he was not a communist. His identifiable reviews are both non-Irish in subject matter, dealing with (a) the Paris Commune, and (b) the Spanish Civil War.[65] There is an anonymous review of Leslie Daiken's *Goodbye Twilight* (1936), an anthology of committed Irish verse, which might also stem from Hewitt's hand, for it complains about the reduction of 'the Irish Struggle' to a Free State versus Republic confrontation, and likewise about the contributors' ignorance of contemporary poetry. But on the final appearance of A WORKER'S BOOK PAGE, the anonymous and favourable review of W. J. Maloney's *The Forged Casement Diaries* (published a year earlier) does not read like his work, even in disguise. The feature on Francis Sheehy Skeffington, emphasizing the pacifism of that less celebrated casualty of 1916, is more likely to have been at least sponsored by Hewitt.

Having thus stripped back Hewitt's involvement with *The Irish Democrat* to a few weeks and a very few articles, we should nonetheless record the paper's general character. First, though Frank Ryan was its editor, the initiative had been taken by Peadar O'Donnell, who became a long-term friend of Hewitt's. Second, it was printed for the Progressive Publications Society (of No. 64 Great Victoria Street, Belfast) by the Ralahine Press (of St Anthony's Place, Temple Street, Dublin): thus, it was a cross-border production. Owen Sheehy Skeffington (1909–70), son of the murdered pacifist, presided at the Dublin launch of the paper; he and his mother (Hanna) and—I believe—his French wife Andrée (under the initials ADS) were contributors.[66]

64 George Orwell, *The Road to Wigan Pier* (London: Gollancz, 1937), pp. 8, 35. For Orwell's self-assessment, see Bernard Crick, *George Orwell: A Life* (London: Secker, 1980), p. 181. 'Part Two', which discussed class in highly non-Marxist terms, occupied pp. 151–264, omitted from the Left Book Club edition.

65 *The Paris Commune of 1871*, by Frank Jellinck, was reviewed by R. T. on 10 April 1937; *Estampas de la Revolucion Espanois* (based on artwork by Sini) was reviewed anonymously on 3 April; *Intellectuals and the Spanish Military Republic* (published by the Spanish Embassy) was reviewed by R. T. on 17 April; a review of *The Defence of Madrid* by Geoffrey Cox appeared on 24 April over the initials R. F. (or perhaps R. P., the printing is smudged) but not R. T.: this could be a typo-error. In the next issue, 1 May 1937, the Workers' Book Page is still edited by Richard Telford, but nothing is either signed or initialled to indicate Hewitt's authorship.

66 In her biography of Skeffington, the widow unhelpfully refers to the paper as *The Irish Weekly Democrat*, but generally confirms his role up to 5 June 1937 when his last contribution was deeply critical of the IRA's narrowness of political vision; see Andrée Sheehy Skeffington, *Skeff: a Life of Owen Sheehy Skeffington, 1907–70* (Dublin: Lilliput, 1991), p. 85. Her husband's column was called 'And Yet It Moves' (taken from Galileo's *sotto voce* remark at the time of his recantation). She makes no reference to Hewitt.

Ernie O'Malley's valuable support was reported in the first issue.[67] One can detect lines of demarcation, perhaps even 'fault lines'. The younger Sheehy Skeffingtons, man and wife, were members of the French Communist Party. In some contrast, Frank Ryan and O'Malley (1898–1957) were Irish republicans first and foremost, but also determined anti-fascists. These were far from identical positions.

Hewitt was not the only contributor who slipped through the categories—Kerry-born Thomas MacGreevy (1893–1967) was a poet, a devout Catholic, and an art curator; the Scot, T. B. Rudmose-Brown, taught modern languages in Trinity College, Dublin, and authored the dirtiest Irish dirty joke never committed to paper; the American Nancy Cunard was a patron of Samuel Beckett, but also a vastly rich communist.[68] Mary Manning, a dramatist later involved in the heroic effort to film Joyce's *Finnegans Wake*, contributed an Open Letter. They represent one loosely associated tendency in *The Irish Democrat*, linked (I believe) through Owen Sheehy Skeffington. Indeed, on 17 April, the paper carried an account of his severance from a Dublin-based periodical for which he had been writing a Foreign Affairs column; *Ireland Today*'s editor, Jim O'Donovan, later engineered the IRA bombing of Coventry in early 1939. Skeffington went on to contribute a similar column to the *Democrat*.

The other noteworthy tendency became increasingly evident after 'Richard Telford' dropped out of sight. In May, the anarchists of Barcelona were condemned with astonishing promptness for being 'in effect' a fascist force in the rear of the Anti-Franco coalition.[69] This Stalinist perspective was hammered home on 8 August with John Strachey's unqualified defence of Stalin's purges in the Red Army officer-corps.[70] By these same tokens, nothing more about George Orwell could ever appear under the *Democrat*'s banner, even if Hewitt had delivered a full review of *Wigan Pier* to the Belfast office—by whatever method.

As far as book reviewing was concerned, Hewitt's departure made room for Malachy Gray, whose first signed contribution appeared on 19 June—a review of *Hitler's Conspiracy Against Peace*.[71] From June onwards, *The Irish Democrat* gave increasing prominence to statements and positions emanating from the Communist Party of Ireland (1933–41). By August Desmond Ryan (1893–1964), biographer of Patrick Pearse and designer of a socialist-nationalist synthetic history of Irish radicalism, was asserting himself.[72] There are also grounds for seeing the latter half

[67] No reference to *The Irish Democrat* (or indeed to Frank Ryan) can be found in O'Malley's correspondence as now available in *Broken Landscapes: Selected Letters of Ernie O'Malley 1924–57*, edited by Cormac O'Malley and Nicholas Allen (Dublin: Lilliput, 2011).

[68] By 1917 or earlier, Rudmose-Brown had published essays on French literature in *The Irish Review* and *Sinn Féin*; see his *French Literary Studies* (Dublin: Talbot Press, 1917). In 1934, Cunard had financed publication of the vast *Negro Anthology*, to which Beckett contributed a large number of translations.

[69] See 'Trotskyite Sabotage in Barcelona', *The Irish Democrat*, 8 May 1937, p. 8.

[70] Evelyn John St Loe Strachey (1901–63) was at this moment a fervent member of the Communist Party (GB) having previously followed Oswald Mosley; later he was prominent in the Labour Party.

[71] Originally written in German under the pseudonym, S. Erckner, *Hitler's Conspiracy* was published by Victor Gollancz in 1937, in Emile Burns' translation.

[72] See *The Irish Democrat*, 21 August, 28 August, 25 September, and 18 December 1937.

of 1937 (after Hewitt's departure) as marking a shift in *The Irish Democrat's* treatment of France (vital because of its Popular Front government, 1936–38) away from the Skeffingtons' endorsement towards partisan or narrower (Stalinist) perspectives; for example, Paul Nizan's novel, *The Trojan Horse*, was reviewed by Gray on 10 July; Desmond Ryan's first contribution (21 August) dealt with the great Paris Exhibition. Other explanations may offer themselves, but the emergence of the 'Irish national question' as the defining socialist issue becomes all the more apparent as one reads into the *Democrat's* successors. In less insular terms, one might also note that Nizan (1905–40) resigned from the French Communist Party in 1939 as a protest against the Stalin–Hitler Pact.[73] Here was a problem for all on the left in Europe, even if *The Irish Democrat* had ceased to exist. The Communist Party of Ireland quickly dissolved itself when the Soviet Union entered the war; otherwise its members would have been allied with perfidious Albion.

Of the successor papers, by far the most enduring has been the second *Irish Democrat*, under the editorship of C. Desmond Greaves (1913–88) from January 1948 to August 1988, and by others before and after. Greaves's post-mortem John the Baptist, Anthony Coughlan, has written perceptively of one for whom a Marxist attention to economics might have been thought central if not primary; instead, 'he was interested above all in the national question and issues of colonialism and imperialism'.[74] The steady displacement of international and socialist issues by the question-begging Irish question certainly played a part in Hewitt's retreat from, or rejection by, *The Irish Democrat* in 1937. But the paper with the sentimental Irish songs, which he would later occasionally buy in Coventry, was Greaves' *Irish Democrat*, not Ryan/O'Donnell's.[75] One cannot exaggerate the importance of the small political news-or-opinion sheet of that time: the Progressive Bookshop advertised in papers like the liberal, if occasionally Bible-quoting, *Voice of Ulster*.[76]

The Irish Democrat (New Series) appeared in January 1945, with an editorial address at Southampton Row, London. Its early contributors included R. M. Fox, Malachy Gray, Vivian Mercier, Ewart Milne, Sean O'Casey, Paul Potts—and John Hewitt. O'Casey at this date was scathing about the poor quality of Northern Irish writing.[77] Hewitt's two traced reviews appeared in a column not unlike the one he edited for *The Irish Democrat* (1937)—this one was 'Pamphlet, Book, and Verse', edited by E. M. Boyle until January 1946, when Boyle's name disappears. The

[73] See Michael Scriven, *Paul Nizan, Communist Novelist* (Basingstoke: Macmillan, 1988).

[74] Anthony Coughlan, 'An Obituary Essay', *The Irish Democrat*, revised and updated 2004, <http://www.irishdemocrat.co.uk/greaves/obituary-essay/>. First published in 1990 by the Irish Labour History Society, Dublin.

[75] Simon Prince quotes JH on 'rage at the betrayal of our dream' when he encountered Greaves' paper, and interprets him in a way consistent with the Two Nations Theory popular among some radical Unionists, see Prince, *Northern Ireland's '68*, p. 99. For the poet's more whimsical reaction, see 'On the Grand Dublin Canal: Musing on the "Two Nations" Theory', in Ormsby, p. 182.

[76] See, for example, *Voice of Ulster* 1, no. 5 (June 1938), p. 7.

[77] 'To *Time and Tide*, Eire's Neutrality', 20 May 1944, in *The Letters of Sean O'Casey, Vol. 2: 1942–54*, edited by David Krause (New York: Macmillan, 1980), pp. 172–5. O'Casey's ire was directed mainly at St John Irvine (1883–1971), a Belfast-born dramatist, regarded by many as having abandoned youthful enlightenment for conformity.

opening issues include one or two articles strangely indulgent, or at least neglectful, of Nazi Germany; in this category one might put 'Most Savage Censorship in Europe' (February 1945, p. 5), dealing with southern Ireland. Appearing in October 1945 (p. 7), Hewitt's notice of MacGreevy's book, while respectful, was unzealous: 'I personally believe him in a number of his assertions and in his general estimate to be mistaken' and, directed perhaps at the paper itself, 'We must look upon the present tide of public approval of [Yeats's] work largely as a fact of high sociological interest.' This, however, was not Hewitt's final appearance in the paper. In December he reviewed *Grey Walls, Stories*, an anthology from which he singled out three contributors for criticism: 'Greacen's last man's meander, Jennet's essay in furtive homosexuality, Gillespie's badly written novelette are thoroughly disappointing.'[78] Thus was an unforgiving review and perhaps self-damaging for its author.

Parallel with (or more precisely, in advance of) *The Irish Democrat* (1937), the even more elusive *Irish Jewry* recruited Hewitt's talents. According to a note he made in May 1943, this Belfast monthly paper was founded by Louis Barnett early in 1937 and, after very few issues, folded under pressure from the local rabbi, Jacob Shachter. Hewitt's role was to edit a literary supplement (*The Forum*) which, by the time of the paper's demise, had Jim MacKinlay for editor. A friend of the Hewitts, Jim will show up occasionally in the pages which follow, but more characteristically he was an absentee from his own family, not a model of dedication.

If Hewitt's recollections of *The Irish Democrat* are patchy, *Irish Jewry* has utterly disappeared from view. From a scrapbook of Hewitt's, we know that the literary editor contributed two poems ('Frost' and 'Swan's Nest'), his wife 'A Surrealist Poem', and his friend MacKinlay a further two poems. James D. Gildea, S. P. McCreery, and Edward Boyle were also represented, not necessarily with their prior knowledge or consent. 'Sawmills 1931', a watercolour sketch by Billy McClughin, appears to have been the one visual feature, at least during Hewitt's editorship. A rare appearance as poet was Roberta's, signing as Ruby Black. Her brief 'Surrealist Poem' encapsulates themes less cogently raised by her husband:

Light up. The end is near.
Slow motion pauses on a speck of time.
The beer gardens in February are green;
With withered Laws
We have no time for succulence.

Hurry!
The barbed wire must be fastened.
We are too old for scarlet reins;

[78] See Charles Wrey Gardiner, ed., *Grey Walls, Stories* (London: Grey Walls Press, [1945]). Robert Greacen contributed 'The Valley of Laughing Skulls'; Leslie Gillespie, 'Auf wiedersehen'; Sean Jennett, 'The Man and the Boy'. More notable contributors were Olivia Manning, Henry Miller, and Stephen Spender. Note also Ian Serrallier (1912–94) who shared *Three New Poets* (1942) with Alex Comfort and Roy MacFadden. Though an amateur in publishing, Gardiner (1901–81) was an influential editor, a supporter of Alex Comfort and the American poet, Kenneth Pachen.

Put on the kettle now the hob is cold,
And prove that Helen was indeed a myth.[79]

The *Irish Jewry* enterprise defies explanation. It evidently lasted for just three issues. Of what little we know the most intriguing detail is Edward Boyle's presence, for he was one of the trio who supposedly drew Hewitt into *The Irish Democrat*. In the scrapbook the name is cumbersomely given as Edward (Malachy) (O') Boyle, and it is noted that (a) he contributed to *Northern Harvest* in 1944 and, less confidently, (b) that he also contributed to *The Irish Democrat*.[80] Unfortunately, though Hewitt claims to have contributed 'reviews, art and film criticism, short stories under pseudonyms' to *Irish Jewry* or its supplement, none of this prose was pasted into the scrapbook. In his bibliography, Tom Clyde lists the following: two editorials (January and February 1937); 'Art Matters' (January); a review of *Goodbye Twilight*, an anthology edited by Leslie Daiken (January); 'Hey Rup! Experimental Films in Belfast' (March); 'The Landscape of John Luke' (March). This still leaves the short stories unaccounted for, with no traced set of *Irish Jewry* to consult. It is very likely that the review of Daiken's anthology served double duty in *Forum* and in *The Irish Democrat*.

Hewitt generally was a scrupulous maintainer of notebooks, a poet with strong political interests. None of these characteristics emerges from the brief engagement with *Irish Jewry*, which never rivalled *The Irish Democrat* in contributors (Mary Manning, Rudmose-Brown, Hannah Sheehy Skeffington). The prose does not seem to have carried any political charge, except perhaps the review of Daiken's explicitly anti-fascist anthology. Of the two poems contributed, just one made it into *No Rebel Word*. By his own admission, the literary supplement was packed with the work of friends. Yet, on the positive side, the theme of the abandoned juvenile poem, 'The Champion of the Jews', is nominally sustained by the very fact of Hewitt's involvement at a crucial moment in European Jewish history.

The Frankls arrived in Belfast in April 1938. Having fled Vienna, they had planned to settle in Australia. But while spending time en route in London, they were approached by Northern Ireland officials who invited them to inspect the possibilities of setting up a business. Under her own name, Mrs Frankl was a well-known designer, and the result of these conversations was Annie Lewinter Ltd, a knitwear business established in Newtownards, in north County Down. This canny manoeuvre by some civil servant rehearsing 'industrialisation by invitation' led the Frankls to make their home on Belfast's Malone Road an open house for artists. If prejudice and persecution in Continental Europe sent a number of refugees to Belfast, it remained more isolated than other cities of its size in the United Kingdom. A few brave socialists invoked the Soviet Union, knowing too little about it, and others longed for the normality of Tunbridge Wells or the rival barricades of Glasgow. *Plus ca révolution*... Political debate was heated, but not widespread. The arrival, in January 1938, of Li-hsi Wang (1901–39)

[79] Preserved in UU, Hewitt, Box 8.

[80] *Northern Harvest*, edited by Robert Greacen, did include a story, 'Wanderer West', by Malachy Boyle (on pp. 55–61). *The Irish Democrat* (1937) published two poems signed E. O'Boyle, and also featured some work by one of Hewitt's circle, the actor Jack McQuoid (1910–77).

a poet of decidedly Marxist allegiances, sprang from the invitation of Belfast's China Campaign Committee. This was the acquaintance John and Roberta had met in Welwyn Garden City.

He stayed for ten days with the Hewitts at No. 15 Westland Drive, Cliftonville. Wang, known in English as Shelley Wang, was en route for Dublin, where the soil was scarcely more fertile. Hewitt clearly recognized the propagandist objectives of Wang's visit, justifiable in the aftermath of Japan's invasion in the summer of 1937. Wang, however, was no Chinese nationalist. What we have of his poems includes a dedication to G. D. H. Cole (voluminous historian of the English Labour Party), invocations of Marx, and resonant phrases such as 'the language of peace is resistance'. Hewitt, in his unfinished memoirs, recalls that Wang's death was reported in *The Daily Worker*, a note of more significance for disclosing the Ulsterman's continuing attention to that paper than for the facts.[81] In 1944, he took part in a Chinese cultural event at Richmond Lodge, where his 'englished' version of poetry by Wang featured, and some children acted a play in 'the authentic Chinese manner'. His niece Deirdre Todhunter 'gonged' in the band and played a double whistle.[82]

For students of the Belfast poet, the significance of the Chinese poet's arrival in Northern Ireland may be localized in a few poems from *The Chinese Fluteplayer* (1974), published thirty-five years after the visitor's death in military action against the invader. Certainly, recollection of Wang as a person and as a writer with strong political commitments stayed within Hewitt, coming back to his mind almost (but not qualitatively) like a Wordsworthian reprise. Hewitt's friend, rival, and occasional legal adviser, the poet Roy McFadden, sharply observed that Hewitt 'endorsed progressive thought and unpopular causes, but he did not offer dedication'.[83] The passage of time between Wang's death 'leading an anti-Japanese squad of writers in occupied territory' and Hewitt's eventual gathering of 'From the Chinese of Wang Li Shi [*sic*]' is only one example of many in which he revealed his dedication to a cause, less in immediate commitment, more in quiet persistence.[84] An account of Wang's death appeared in the BBC's house magazine, *The Listener*, on 6 August 1942, written by Mulk Raj Anand (1905–2004), a Punjabi novelist of humanist rather than communist inclinations.

In Wang's Belfast itinerary, intellectual groups vied with factories. He spoke to the Young Ulster Society and, probably, to another gathering in Queen's University. He gave an interview to the *Irish Times*'s Belfast correspondent, speaking positively about China's attitudes towards the Western powers.[85] On 11 January, Norman Todhunter and Roberta Hewitt drove him to the Mourne Mountains in County Down. In the early evening, at a meal in the Orpheus Café, Belfast, he composed

[81] This account of Wang, and the Hewitts' contact with him, is largely derived from a body of material in QUB Special Collections, catalogued at x PL2822.S45/Exil. See also *North*, p. 78.

[82] Roberta Hewitt's Diary 1944 (February).

[83] Quotation from an untitled typescript preserved in QUB (the McFadden Papers) which was an expanded version for oral delivery of the article, 'No Dusty Pioneer', published in *Threshold* 38 (Winter 1986–87).

[84] The poem was first published in *The Northman* (Autumn 1938), p. 87, where it appears with Wang's name as author.

[85] 'United Front in China', *Irish Times*, 11 January 1938, p. 8.

a poem about his encounter with the rural Irish landscape, writing it directly on to a packet of Kensitas cigarettes. Somebody, almost certainly Hewitt, wrote with the same pen on the other side of the packet, the name of southern Ireland's (then) dominant political movement—Fianna Fáil. And so, Wang was briefed for Dublin. Even later in the day, a competition to translate the poem was organized, with Hewitt constituting one team, his wife and George Musgrove the other. In Wang's opinion, Hewitt won. The Mourne Mountains, as a phrase, had not been employed in the original poem, but were 'mountains shaped like tall loaves of bread'. After he left Ireland, he kept in touch with Hewitt, writing occasional letters from London and then China. Active in the 1920s' peasant movement, he had been briefly head of the Peasant Department of the Kuomintang government in Nanking (1927).

Wang's Dublin hosts included several literary-political figures well known to Hewitt, the most notable being the novelist Peadar O'Donnell. Lecturing on 'Chinese Martyrdom' at the Metropolitan Hall (a Protestant evangelical stronghold) on 14 January, Wang stuck to a broadly nationalist account of his country's woes. An anti-imperialist 'united front' emerged for the occasion, bringing together the left-republican O'Donnell, the Fianna Fáil icon Erskine Childers (junior), Sam Kyle of the Amalgamated Transport and General Workers Union (an English-based dockers' union), and Archie Heron (1894–1971) of the Irish Labour Party. A native of Armagh, and son-in-law of James Connolly, Heron represented the intellectual aristocracy of Irish socialism but, though billed to speak at Wang's meeting, he failed to turn up. Another advertised speaker who did not show up was Dr Hanna, a Presbyterian minister with a strong commitment to international peace movements.[86] O'Donnell held the ring, pointedly arguing that opposition to Japanese militarism must not result in the repetition of John Redmond's mistakes of 1914. 'They realised that the latest British attempts to make peace with this country were not dissociated from the necessity on the part of the General Staff of trying to get a better understanding with America, where Irish influence was important.'[87]

War lay eighteen months ahead or slightly more, as far as Europe was concerned. The discernible lack of unanimity among the politically conscious intellectuals and activists on the Left whom Wang met in Belfast and Dublin accurately reflected divisions in Hewitt's own mind. Though Robert Greacen would recall shortly before his death in 2008 that John Hewitt was the first public speaker he heard advising a Belfast audience that war was inevitable, the pacifist inclinations of the ILP continued to influence his thinking. Writing much later, Roy McFadden contrasted his own 'belligerently anti-militarist' attitudes in the 1930s with Hewitt's, for the older man 'stood back from activism'.[88]

In one specific publication, Hewitt refutes the allegation, though the context is wartime, not the period famous for lowness and dishonesty. At the end of October

[86] R. K. Hanna attended the Paris Peace Conference of November 1931; see *Irish Times*, 12 January 1932, p. 6.

[87] 'Japan Cannot Succeed', *Irish Times*, 15 January 1938, p. 10.

[88] QUB, McFadden Papers, 'No Dusty Pioneer' extended, p. 1.

1941, he wrote to Bertie Rodgers requesting a poem for inclusion in a pamphlet designed to raise funds for the Russian Red Cross. (The *Wehrmacht* at this moment was scarcely fifty miles from Moscow.) 'The verses will not be propagandist or left or Soviet salutes—just typical poems as good as we can get.'[89] Early the following year, *15 Poems* appeared with nine contributors.[90] MacNeice, whom Hewitt was approaching, does not seem to have obliged. Whatever one feels about the contents as propaganda, the pamphlet was officially published by 'The Socialist Party, Belfast' and distributed through McLean's Progressive Bookshop. Of the lesser-known names, William Adair features as a versifier of Marx, against the largely rural background.

Hewitt's own contributions were 'The Little Lough' and 'Sonnet in Autumn', neither remotely political in the common understanding of the term. The sestet of the latter (its concluding six lines) addresses a theme pervasive but not intrusive in Hewitt's work:

> I turn to-day then from the published mask,
> the attitude commended, phrase assayed,
> the imminent insistence of the task,
> because the hard bright berries of the haw
> report an older, an austere law,
> a season older, suddenly afraid.

If the first three of these lines exemplify a 1930s idiom, the point to be noted is the poet's turning away from it. If the final two words disclose the anxiety of late 1941, Frank Ormsby establishes that the poem was written in September 1938, a time of fear, certainly, but not carrying the mood of 1941.

The so-called inconsistencies complained of by McFadden (a non-contributor on this occasion) are not without literary significance. At a technical (some will say finicky) level, Hewitt's rhymes and full echoes deserve close attention. The double role of the word 'older' works to convince the reader of an identification between law and season, the latter also embodied in the 'haw' which is echoed in 'law'. The poems display and investigate dimensions of time in human consciousness, both individual and social. Activism cannot be adequately defined in terms of immediate physical implementation; thought, requiring reflection, takes time; influence, through the written or spoken word, is not inert or passive. The poems written in 1938 were not the most enduring, yet a thematic weight is central to the eight lines of 'Alien Harvest' (written 30 March):

> I cross a laboured plot of ground
> where skilful men with spade and graip
> through weary years of use have found
> the comfort of recurring shape.

[89] PRONI, D2833/C/1/8/1, JH to W. R. Rodgers, 28 October 1941.

[90] These were William Adair, Maurice James Craig (two pieces), Rayner Heppenstall (two), John Hewitt (two), James Mackinlay, R. P. Maybin (two), Colin Middleton (two), Paul Potts (two), and W. R. Rodgers.

I break the sods of my slow mind
with tools that some old craftsman wrought,
yet when the yield is cut, I find
a harvest alien to my thought.[91]

The distinctly different movements of time in the outer landscape and in the poet's reflective mind deserve consideration in a critical rather than biographical framework, though, in the context of his attitudes in late 1939 and the war years, they gain a degree of urgency.

[91] Ormsby, p. 158.

4

The War Years, including Cold War Preliminaries

Pacifists and appeasers, generally opposed in their political affiliation along the left–right spectrum, shared a muddled apprehension of when war might break out. For most acute minds, *Kristallnacht* (9–10 November 1938) made the writing on the wall grimly plain. February 1939's issue of *The Museums Journal* (a British, not Belfast, production) carried a review by Hewitt under the clarion title, 'Curatorship Under the Swastika'. The final sentences read:

> As museum workers it is our duty to read this book... We are an integral part of democratic civilization: the freedom and impartiality we require for the scope and pursuit of our labours are bound up with democratic institutions, and with the collapse of democracy we must inevitably pass into the shadows. Just as these words are being written it is decreed from Berlin that no Jew may enter a museum without a special permit.[1]

The review stood in stark contrast to Hewitt's previous contributions to his professional journal, for example an article (with J. A. S. Stendall) on 'Multiple-Colour Block Case Mounting' (January 1937). Although the *Journal*'s editor takes credit for sending out for review a book of personal testimony and protest, the response constitutes Hewitt urgently bringing together his professional and political concerns in a statement of moral imperatives. It hardly echoes the clumsy narrative of 'The Champion of the Jews' (1926) but certainly follows actively on his editorship of *Irish Jewry*'s literary supplement (1937). The same uneasy linkage of profession and vocation resulted in Hewitt publishing an obituary for W. B. Yeats in the *City of Belfast Museum and Art Gallery Quarterly Notes* (March 1939).

In July, Louis MacNeice and F. R. Higgins engaged in a radio discussion about 'Tendencies in Modern Poetry', broadcast on a variety of BBC regional stations. For listeners in Northern Ireland, the preceding item was 'The Travelling Exhibition of the Ulster Academy of the Arts' by R. T. Hewitt.[2] The younger Hewitt

[1] *Museums Journal* 38, no. 11 (February 1939), pp. 523–5, see p. 525. The book under review was Eva Lips, *What Hitler Did to Us; a Personal Record of the Third Reich*, trans. Caroline Newton (London: Michael Joseph, 1938). Dorothy Thompson, whom the Hewitts would meet in Coventry, contributed an introduction.

[2] See Jonathan Allison, ed., *Letters of Louis MacNeice* (London: Faber, 2010), p. 350. The editor assumes that the talk was given by the poet, not his father, treating the initials as a misprint; but see *Irish Times*, 11 July 1939, p. 4, for a listing of radio programmes giving the poet's father as author of the piece.

was among the audience at home and the next day he wrote to MacNeice congratulating him on his 'advocacy of socialist internationalism' as an invaluable contribution to the 'cultural Sahara' of their native province. This was perhaps further than MacNeice intended to go, but the Ulster poets were at one in rejecting the 'boyo' values of Higgins, a Mayo man by birth and Yeats's trusted assistant at the Abbey Theatre.

The war paradoxically loosened some of the rigid constraints and narrow classifications of Belfast life, allowing a prolific writer to mix in previously irreconcilable quarters. In August 1940, Hewitt (signing as Cormac Mac Airt) published a notice of 'The Poems of Alice Milligan', a doughty nationalist, in *The Irish News*, a paper of all but exclusive Catholic readership. In a notebook of that year, Hewitt, who had never crossed the Atlantic, copied in his 'Letter from America' a jaunty satirical poem best taken as a response to Auden's '1 September 1939', first published in the *New Republic* issue of 18 October 1939 and collected in Auden's *Another Time* (1940). Hewitt's riposte included these lines: 'Back in Europe Oslo fell, / Brussels, Amsterdam as well, / And the French recriminate / their way into a fascist state.'[3]

The following April, in a paper named in honour of its 1790s' radical precursor, he published 'Some Thoughts on Marxism and the War'.[4] Geraldine Watts, a fellow native of Belfast who interviewed him, recorded that 'during the Second World War, he had been interested in the Progressive Workers' Group [with its] strong fellow-traveller leanings'.[5] These associations became possible when the Soviet Union was a valued ally, but that did not commend them in a public servant employed by Unionists in permanent majority. He also expressed a political sentiment dear to the left-republicans, that 'the national struggle was emphatically a class struggle', attributing that view to Jemmy Hope, a United Irishman organizer, a view he would later repudiate.[6]

The war also gave licence for a kind of under-nourished domestic party scene, where visitors could exchange cherished views and dreams. The Hewitts took over a rented flat at No. 18 Mount Charles, in the autumn of 1940, a quiet, broad side-street off University Road. This was to remain home for almost seventeen years, convenient in its closeness to the Belfast Museum and Art Gallery, with neighbours of similar interests living nearby. From the centre of Belfast, Mount Charles was served by two tram routes, one heading ultimately up the affluent and exclusive Malone Road, the other content to terminate in lesser Stranmillis: Hewitt is reputed to have shunned the former, even if it meant waiting in the rain for the latter. Though John Hewitt had a reputation for unsociability, gruffness, or shyness, Roberta's nephew Keith Millar remembers Mount Charles for its many genial parties. (The reputation may have been the work of people Hewitt chose not to encourage.) Roy McFadden recorded the number of non-Irish poets and novelists who found their way there during the war years, including Hamish Henderson, Rayner Heppenstall, Emanuel Litvinoff, John Manifold—but not, lamentably, the ill-fated Sidney

[3] UU, Hewitt, Notebook 46, p. 25.

[4] *The Northern Star* 1, no. 2 (April 1941), pp. 4–6.

[5] Geraldine Watts, 'John Hewitt, the Non-Conformist Conscience of Northern Ireland', MLitt thesis, TCD, 1987, p. 59.

[6] Quoted in Ormsby, p. lii.

Keyes (1922–43), who enlisted in Northern Ireland and was killed in Tunisia at the age of twenty.[7] Visitors from south of the border included Robert Farren who also wrote under the Gaelic version of his name, Roibeárd O Farácháin. Painters also made an appearance, notably Alicia Boyle in red stockings, the ascetic John Luke, Colin Middleton, Paul Nietsche, and the dyslexic Markey Robinson, whose work has become more popular in Dublin through the agency of Hugh Charleton, another Hewitt satellite.

There were discussions of art, politics, and Carl Gustav Jung, poetry readings and, no doubt, arguments. Hewitt's interest in archetype psychology, which infuriated McFadden, was shared by Middleton and by Marie Rodgers, who 'practiced her Jung' in the Hewitts' back attic while they were away. He was not alone in venerating Freud's apostate. Roberta quit her brief reliance on homeopathy and its 'snake's venom' because the practitioner had never heard of Jung and, in any case, was Plymouth Brethren.[8] Individual performances at Mount Charles were satirically noted. Farren always stood up when he was invited to read from a volume plucked by Hewitt out of its place in an absolute shelf order. Howard Sergeant, on the other hand, could only recite while sitting down. This led to debates (not entirely serious) about national characteristics, the differences between English and Irish habits of speech. Once Hewitt declared, 'Spender throws it away.' Those who showed up at Mount Charles may sound in retrospect less important than those (Keyes, Spender, etc.) who did not, yet the traffic of poets 'who make something happen' (to modify Auden) on the stairs to the Hewitts' rooms stands up to historical scrutiny. Henderson (1919–2002) was a bastard by birth, who studied at Cambridge, smuggled Jews out of Nazi Germany, became a major Scottish poet, and formally accepted the surrender of Mussolini's puppet state in 1945.[9] Manifold (1915–85, an Australian) also studied at Cambridge where he joined the Communist Party; in 1938, he aimed, with *Poetry and the People*, to replace the defunct *Left Review*. Both men were committed to the study and proper advance of folk song. Years later, Hewitt remembered another of their wartime visitors, 'the young sailorboy shaken by his Murmansk voyages and the dead bodies on the Archangel quays'.[10]

The war had its refugees in Belfast, the painter Paul Nietsche, and the collector Zoltan Frankl among the Hewitts' friends. The Edinburgh exhibition had prompted Frankl to think of a fully descriptive catalogue of the entire collection, and he asked Hewitt to undertake the project in his spare time. Hewitt had little idea of how to charge for work of this kind—per picture, per hour, per thousand words? He consulted Herbert Read whom he awkwardly flattered; 'you have been pointing the way bravely along the paths of your wisdom'. About Frankl and the

[7] Litvinov, a Jewish poet from London's East End, died in the autumn of 2011. For a further literary perspective on Belfast during the war, see John Boyd, *The Middle of My Journey* (Belfast: Blackstaff, 1990), pp. 13–18.

[8] *Journal*, PRONI, D/3838/4/7, 28 March 1951. For a positive view of Hewitt's interest in Jung see Terence Brown, 'The Poet's Shadow', *Fortnight* (1989), 'Hewitt Supplement', p. vii.

[9] He was on friendly terms with the Dublin-based Marxist critic J. K. Walton, who sent the Scot a lengthy article on the politics of *Gulliver's Travels*.

[10] *North*, p. 132. The young sailor is not identified by name.

collection of pictures he was less flattering. The pictures were 'mostly contemporary British, very mixed...strong in Jack B. Yeats' (an artist Hewitt did not admire). As for Frankl, he was 'large, ornate, rather vulgar, wealthy and pathetically friendly'.[11]

An unpublished poem, 'For the British Troops in Northern Ireland', shows Hewitt attempting even-handed sympathy: an early line places the soldiers 'in a strange country that their fathers wrongd [*sic*]'. A greater clutter of loyalties gathers in 'Sonnet for [a] Class on [the] Philosophy of Marx Held in the Egyptian Room, Old Museum'.[12] The war took its toll on Roberta's health. In August 1942, several friends noted that she had been an invalid for almost three months, or expressed the hope that she might soon be able to return to Belfast from convalescence in the countryside. She was far from idle once she recovered, working as Examiner Grade II in the censorship department of the Post Office from September 1943 to June 1945. These years gave married women an opportunity for full-time employment, while also drawing attention to the unusual circumstances in which the practice was tolerated. Hewitt's political views, as privately expressed, were consistent with his public citations of Marx. Writing to Captain Robin Maybin (RAMC) on New Year's Day 1945, he classified Churchill's attitude towards the Balkans as 'a capitalist ruse to keep Greece safe for the Bank of England'.[13] Whether a serving officer welcomed such frankness may be questioned. Soon, the revelations of genocide in German camps prompted the Hewitts to wonder if people like them—peace leaguers—had been responsible '20 years ago', the exaggerated period distancing their activities back to the 1920s.[14]

A Stormont general election was held on 14 June 1945, thus avoiding any great impact from the Labour triumph of later that year in the UK-wide election. The Hewitts addressed envelopes; Roberta and her sister canvassed, though the former was 'fed up' with the Labour Party—the Northern Ireland Labour Party ran very few candidates. After polling closed, she had what she called 'a romantic adventure' with a wounded RAF lad aged twenty-five who bought her a drink. The extent of this liaison appears to have been a long and depressing street-corner chat till 1 a.m.[15] Other equally minor adventures had or would occur.

One of the few wartime innovations in Belfast's cultural links to the outside world was the establishment of a branch of International PEN. With Hewittt, the original committee members included Thomas Carnduff (1886–1956), McFadden, and Limerick-born Mary Elizabeth (May) Morton (1876?–1956). In December 1942, Belfast delegates attended a PEN dinner in Dublin. Southern Ireland was—comparatively—a land of plenty, with generous rations of butter and tea, not to mention bright nocturnal street lighting. But cross-border relations between the two Irish PEN centres in Belfast and Dublin were not always to remain so cordial as they were during wartime.

11 Brotherton, Read C4363, JH to Herbert Read, 25 January 1945.

12 UU, Hewitt, Notebook 28 (January 1942 into 1943).

13 PRONI, D/3838/3/10–13. R. G. Marsh effectively discusses the correspondence with Maybin in his QUB doctoral dissertation (see Bibliography).

14 *Journal TS*, prelims, 1945 summary.

15 *Journal TS*, 1945 summary.

Meanwhile, opportunities to publish were strictly limited. In the late spring of 1943, Hewitt completed a long-ish poem, 'Conacre', and arranged for its printing and private issue in Belfast as a ten-page pamphlet, stapled together without any protective cover. The title, derived from traditional Irish land-rental custom, was explained in a note taken from the *Oxford English Dictionary*—'the letting by a tenant, for a season, of small portions of land ready ploughed and prepared for a crop'. The word's recognized arrival in the English language can be reliably dated to 1824/25, when the future Liberator of Catholics, Daniel O'Connell, explained its meaning to a House of Commons committee. 'What is the con-acre system?... It is a right to plant a crop, paying sometimes 6, 8 or 10 pounds an acre for that right by the single year, and the crop is detained till that rent is made up.' Between the dictionary definition and the illuminating quotation, the presumption of a legal right is introduced and, in that transaction, one might also detect Hewitt's concern in calling his poem *Conacre*. If the term emerges in pre-Famine rural Ireland, the poet's preoccupations are contemporary, urban, and unstable. He may allude to Goldsmith, Crabbe, Cowper among English-language poets, but the sharper thrust comes earlier from the gallery-man, who notes

> the grave Da Vinci's mural and the plans
> that left hand drew to father bombing planes.

The nervous war years telescope academic knowledge of fifteenth-century speculative drawings backwards and forwards in time to allege complicity in mass murder, the point underscored in Hewitt's visual near-rhyme of the plans and the aeroplanes. Echoing several poems—'On a Political Prisoner', 'Dialogue of Self and Soul', and 'The Old Stone Cross'—he grapples for Yeats and his eugenic dystopia:

> Yet this way madness or a cynic mind
> that in Yeats' [*sic*] ditch hears blind mind thumping blind
> and laughs because the splashing slime is cool
> on the hot brow...

In harness with this traffic across the years of European culture and contemporary destruction, he adds lines referring to his parochial Armagh origins:

> No tweed-bright poet drunk in pastoral
> or morris-dances in the Legion Hall,
> I know my farmer and my farmer's wife,
> the squalid focus of their huxter life,
> the grime-veined fists, the thick rheumatic legs,
> the cracked voice gloating on the price of eggs,
> the miser's Bible, and the tedious aim
> to add another boggy acre to the name.[16]

These lines indicate no capitulation to rural practices or values, even if the tempo of life in the countryside maintained a rhythm gentler than anxious urban bustle,

[16] Ormsby, pp. 9, 11.

the threat of destruction from the skies, and lonely congestion. In March 1944, Hewitt sent *Conacre* to Herbert Read as 'a salute to one of the few civilised Europeans of our time'.[17]

Local recognition came from the English Department of his alma mater. An examination paper tackled by undergraduates on 21 May 1945, the day Heinrich Himmler was captured and the Aussies won a Victory Test Match, presented twenty lines from *Conacre* for critical analysis, which calmly consider a possible ruin/regeneration of the city—'for what was good here can be better still'.[18] This may be regionalism as rural preference, but it also engages with history as human time, though not simply as human time. Geoffrey Taylor, an influential southern editor and critic, moved towards identifying this growing concern of Hewitt's in an article called 'Time and Poetry'.[19] In 1947, *Poetry Ireland* published 'Awareness of Time', unexpectedly playful lines in which William 'Morris at his loom / or prodding his stick in the black letter vat / would call out to Chaucer in the next room / to fetch him Anti-Duhring from the top shelf...'.[20]

The war years brought government into the business of supporting artistic endeavours, partly for the benefit of troops in training, but also to entertain factory workers. A Committee for the Encouragement of Music and the Arts (CEMA) oversaw these provisions, guided in Britain by distinguished leaders such as John Maynard Keynes. At first, CEMA was a purely English affair, but gradually its success led to demands in Scotland for a similar organization. Belfast, proud of its shipyards, and Ulster, conscious of the need to amuse American troops within the confines of the Ten Commandments, would not be excluded. Though CEMA (NI) supported theatre, literature in the form of poetry or fiction did not greatly benefit, despite Hewitt's being a founding member in 1943.[21] Zoltan Frankl was also an enthusiastic committee man and, with Queen's University providing much of the resources from its Adult Education programme, CEMA (NI) was at risk of being a Belfast monopoly. Hewitt lectured in Dungannon, Derry, and other western towns, whereas his pre-war experience had been focused on the province's eastern counties.

At the beginning of 1944, the museum and gallery opened a civil defence exhibition, which Hewitt introduced to wider audiences by giving a broadcast talk, recorded at the Ulster Hall. Laurie Green, the novelist with whom he would shortly quarrel, telephoned his congratulations. Roberta thoroughly approved of her husband's performance, comparing it to the speech of 'Hon. Harry Midgley MP

[17] Brotherton, Read C4362; JH to Herbert Read, 15 March 1944. [18] Ormsby, p. 7.

[19] Geoffrey Taylor, 'Time and Poetry, being a juxtaposition of the old and the new, the old being represented by Thomas Irwin's "Sonnet" and the new by John Hewitt's "The Glens"', *The Bell* 6, no. 3 (June 1943), pp. 210–12.

[20] See Ormsby, p. 493. Published by Friedrich Engels in 1878, 'the Anti-Duhring' was more properly 'Herr Eugen Dühring's Revolution in Science, a Marxist Contribution to German Political-economic Polemics'. William Morris's Kelmscott Press issued a magnificent edition of Geoffrey Chaucer's *Canterbury Tales* in 1896.

[21] He chaired the art committee for six years. His fellow members were L. Beaumont, J. Christie, Denis O'Dea Hanna, Lt-Col J. F. Hunter, J. D. McCord, Nesca Robb, and the Countess of Antrim. See Gillian McIntosh, *The Force of Culture: Unionist Identities in Twentieth-Century Ireland* (Cork: Cork University Press, 1999), p. 137 n. 99.

Traitor', a reference to the latter's defection from the Labour camp to Unionism as Minister for Public Security. Hewitt took pride in his Ulster voice.[22] A few days later, he made a trip to Dublin.

Cross-channel travel was strictly controlled and severely limited during the war years, and southern Ireland (officially Eire, since 1937) offered the only chance of wider horizons. At the beginning of 1944, Hewitt was invited by the organizers of an unusual exhibition in Dublin to deliver a public talk at the Country Shop, a café on Saint Stephens Green (north) frequented by the impoverished intelligentsia. Middleton was also involved. So, on 17 January, Hewitt spoke on 'The Adventure of Subjectivity'. The organizers had arranged for Herbert Read to speak earlier in the month, but he failed to show up. Someone filled the gap by reading aloud a different piece by Read, 'Art and Crisis'.[23] Hewitt had obtained a copy of Read's intended contribution, which eased his allotted task of replying.[24] Behind the venture, a colourful group largely of *emigré* painters known as The White Stag experimented in music, pacifism, psychotherapy, and surrealism. Leading lights were the English-born Basil Rákóczi (1908–79), the even more English Kenneth Hall, and the Irish painters Patrick Scott and Doreen Vanson.[25] A lasting talent among the Stags was the composer Brian Boydell (1917–2000). Wittingly or otherwise, Hewitt had lined up again with the avant-garde. The brief newspaper report may hardly be reliable for the nuances of his argument, but the concluding passage quoted will look odd in retrospect when Hewitt moves to Coventry and declares his aesthetic priorities at greater length. In the Dublin of January 1944, he held that the exploration of greater subjectivity had brought 'an increase of freedom of the artist in the range of his subject matter . . . but no longer can the artist hide behind a façade of technical skill and superficial finish'.[26] When *Conacre* was published, its appearance was not designed to reinforce this argument. Dependence on self-publication did nothing to boost self-confidence. In March, John and Roberta read through 'The Return' in the quiet of Mount Charles; she thought it so good a poem she wanted to have copies printed for personal circulation.[27]

[22] Roberta Hewitt's Diary 1944. Midgley (1892–1957) had served in France during the First World War and, on returning to Belfast, joined the Labour movement. In 1924, he published *Thoughts From Flanders; in Remembrance of All Those Who Fell and Those Who Mourn Their Loss*, a collection of poems, some of which were written at the Front. He was elected to the Stormont Parliament in 1933, supported the Spanish Republic, served in the wartime cabinet, and joined the Unionist Party in 1947. See Graham S. Walker, *The Politics of Frustration: Harry Midgley and the Failure of Labour in Northern Ireland* (Manchester: Manchester University Press, 1985).

[23] S. B. Kennedy, *Irish Art & Modernism* (Belfast: Institute of Irish Studies, 1991), pp. 103–4.

[24] Brotherton, C4362, JH to Herbert Read, 15 March 1944. The copy was supplied by a Mrs Moffett.

[25] The exhibition ran from 4 to 22 January 1944 at 6 Lower Baggot Street, Dublin. See S. B. Kennedy, *The White Stag Group* ([Dublin]: Irish Museum of Modern Art, [n.d.]), p. 158.

[26] *Irish Times*, 18 January 1944, p. 3.

[27] Roberta Hewitt Diary 1944 (March). In 1957, JH wrote appreciatively about the transmission of difficult poetry (Michael Drayton's in 1612) in multiple handwritten copies. 'This privacy of the art had a two-way action. It meant that the potential readership of poetry depended on the extent and nature of the poet's circle of friends and the wider ripples of acquaintance. It also meant that, knowing his audience and its capacities, the poet could be personal, idiosyncratic, and allusive to whatever degree he considered that his audience could take.' *Threshold* 1, no. 4 (Spring 1957), p. 75.

The *Irish Times* provided a surer platform, and Hewitt published numerous poems on its Saturday book-page.[28] Indeed, the south features centrally in the record of his wartime activities as a publishing poet and as a lecturer. The humorist, Lynn Doyle, listed him in an article 'The North Awakes'.[29] *The Bell*, founded by Sean O'Faolain at the prompting of Peadar O'Donnell, was thoroughly committed to literature and criticism. Work collected from its first seven volumes appeared under the title *Irish Poems of To-day* (1944), assembled by Geoffrey Taylor. Austin Clarke was impressed, though he remarked, 'I feel that some of our younger writers are beginning to shake off external influences and search for a closer means of self-expression. Mr John Hewitt, for instance, has not quite escaped from the English pastoral tradition, but the Irish landscape is beginning to appear in his poems.' The review appeared under the caption 'Wanted—a Tradition', which may not have been Clarke's choosing.[30] A far sharper critique of Hewitt appeared in the *Times*' Cruiskeen Lawn column, the satirical work of Flann O'Brien.[31]

Sometime in 1944, Hewitt was invited to inspect the contents of an old house on the outskirts of Belfast, its owner a 'large-knuckled woman in tweeds' descended from a once famous painter (unnamed). His role was probably to value some of the contents for probate or insurance. Reading Hewitt's poems for external, even autobiographical, fact is a risky business, and 'From a Museum Keeper's Album' alludes to several women or to an inheriting woman under several descriptions, one of which casts the person as a Cabinet Minister's aunt. By the end of the poem, he reports that he was allowed to take a keepsake, choosing an album of watercolours depicting 'a series of Chinese tortures of prisoners'.[32] The unexpected chosen material glances back up the poem to the once famous painter and also to the Cabinet Minister, to art and power in orientalist combination. The volume, now rebound and well conserved, is held in the Linen Hall Library.[33] The poem was first published in *The Bell*.

In December 1944, the *Irish Times* issued an anthology of contemporary verse culled from its own pages, edited by Donagh MacDonagh, poet, playwright, district court judge, and son of the executed 1916 leader, Thomas MacDonagh, who had been a poet of great promise in his day. When Desmond MacCarthy came to review the anthology, he picked out several items for individual assessment, including Hewitt's 'The Splendid Dawn', eventually collected in *No Rebel Word*. The poem, MacCarthy suggested, 'is remarkable not only for descriptive power, but for expressing a mood not, as far as I recollect, expressed in verse before. It is not rapture, but a depression.'[34] The reviewer may have forgotten some notable depressives, from Shakespeare to Coleridge or Baudelaire, but he bravely advanced Hewitt's negative sensibility as a poetic merit in itself. (Some allusion to Yeats's

[28] See Ormsby, p. 583, for discussion of several notable examples.

[29] *Irish Times*, 19 August 1944, p. 2.

[30] *Irish Times*, 13 May 1944, p. 2.

[31] *Irish Times*, 16 February 1949, p. 4. Myles na Gopaleen, transcribing a line by JH admired by Austin Clarke, responds, 'I am of all average readers the doyen. My mood induced by the above? Rage.'

[32] Ormsby, pp. 61–3.

[33] I am grateful to John Killen for showing me this curious item.

[34] Advertised in the *Irish Times*, 9 December 1944, p. 2; reviewed in *Irish Times*, 22 December 1944, p. 3.

'The Cold Heaven' might also have been in order.) In 'The Splendid Dawn', an Irish landscape is clearly discernible, though it presents a deserted railway platform on the edge of a 'drab bay' where restless shapes emerge 'upon the hissing slime'.

In a notebook used that year, one page shows commentary and poetic text serving each other oddly. Headed 'Form', it begins 'This verse is slack and yielding but it can hold things that the regular march of syllables could never contain: you must let the cupped hands give with the driven ball.' Apart from a use of cricketing technique—Hewitt kept wicket—as a metaphor for poetry, the introduction appears less to illustrate the succeeding verse and more to comment upon a mental or intellectual dilemma:

My fluctuating thought this year has run
from dry abstraction back to Mary's son,
and round behind him to that shaggy man
in whose slow brain thought's treachery began.[35]

If I am right in dating the page to December 1944, Hewitt provides a challenging Christmas message.

On New Year's Day 1945, Hewitt gave up smoking (not for the last time). January brought the usual blend of domestic, business, and literary activities, and behind them the realization that war might soon end. He reviewed a few books, selected pictures for CEMA, and gave a talk on Robert Frost to the local Poetry Society. His own work still relied for circulation on slim pamphlets printed commercially, stapled pages in a few cases. If it ever achieved material existence, the ghostly first *No Rebel Word* belongs to the same period. *Compass* [working title, *Sea Anchors*], containing just two poems—'The Return' and 'The Ruins Answer'—in a ten-page format, was sold through sympathetic local bookshops, but its real effect was to elicit appreciative letters from literary people in Britain who might help him towards full-scale book publication. Ethel Mannin, Herbert Read, and Richard Church were among the responders.

Compared to the exigencies of pamphlet circulation, radio broadcasting addressed a variety of audiences. Austin Clarke was to the fore in bringing emergent writers to their attention. For example, in February 1945, his Radio Eireann programme 'Living Irish Poets' concentrated on three northerners—W. R. Rodgers, Hewitt, and Maurice Craig (1919–2011). In Belfast, similar kinds of cultural broadcasting flourished under wartime conditions, when people were unable to travel far; after the war, BBC radio increased its output. From a list of about thirty solo broadcasts which Hewitt made between 1946 and 1983, sixteen were made before 1952.[36]

MacNeice, a producer at the BBC in London, invited Hewitt late in May 1945 to propose a synopsis for radio treatment. Within a few days he had nominated Columcille [literally, 'dove of the church'] the early Irish saint (521–597 AD) exiled for provoking a war through unauthorized copying of a psalter. The theme seemed

[35] UU, Hewitt, Notebook 30, p. 12.

[36] See Ormsby, pp. 678–9. All but one of these programmes were broadcast on the Northern Ireland Home Service (BBC).

apt for the times when the war had at last ended, though with revelations suggesting a degree of responsibility at home, even in the Belfast Peace League. Once accepted, the piece itself demanded rapid completion, amid the chores of electioneering and the occasional interruptions of Bertie Rodgers.

The last year of the war found Hewitt trapped in a fictional parody. A Plymouth-born novelist, F. L. Green (1902–53), published *Odd Man Out*, an accomplished exercise in *le roman noir*, later translated to the big screen with James Mason in the title role. Laurie Green had settled in Belfast at the beginning of the thirties, and had absorbed a good deal of the city's capacity for badness (aka 'plain speaking'). He and the Hewitts were on seemingly good terms. According to the poet Robert Greacen, the Englishman was given to chastising his artistic neighbours: 'I'm writing what you and your friends should be writing about, the real dramas going on here. You people ignore what's going on on your own doorstep.'[37] *Odd Man Out* was a thriller about an IRA raid which went wrong. Its central concern, however, was not so much political as psychological or even spiritual. The dying IRA man, seeking a hide-out, becomes an object of greed, an asset to cash in, whose fate tests the integrity of those who encounter him. Among negative observers of the tragedy is one Griffin:

> There was a hardly a platform which he could prevent himself from taking, and from which he theorised in a robust, crisp fashion...And, similarly, when a new artist or novelist, poet, politician, playwright, appeared from amongst the population, Griffin was there to study him from some vantage point and thereafter applaud him or dismiss him.[38]

This was not a unanimous opinion. Robert Greacen knew Hewitt during the 1930s, and recalled with gratitude the older man prophesying war when complacency was generally preferred. Yet the satirical portrait rang true, hit the mark. There were hidden darks, if not hidden depths, in the satirist. Green had been educated by the Salesian Brothers, and *Odd Man Out* is redolent of a period Catholicism in which Evil is a predominant concern. The theme is clumsily outlined by the character Lukey, a painter whose names clumsily link John Luke and Markey Robinson, two Belfast artists with whom Hewitt was on good terms. Moreover, while famously an Englishman in Belfast, Green was partly southern Irish—his father came from Cork. Hewitt makes no reference to these further trenches of difference lying between him and his tormentor. Green's novel attracted greater attention two years later when Carol Reed filmed it in Belfast. The figure of Griffin did not appear in the film, which was well cast with southern Irish actors—Cyril Cusack, Willie Fay, and F. J. McCormick. Conor Cruise O'Brien, writing in *The Bell*, regarded *Odd Man Out* as a more profound enquiry into themes also treated by Liam O'Flaherty in *The Informer* (published 1925; filmed by John Ford, 1935), but that was little consolation to Hewitt, who probably did not notice that 'Griffin' is close to Green in spelling. The novel was republished by Penguin in 1950,

[37] Robert Greacen, *Even without Irene* (Belfast: Lagan, 1995), p. 147.
[38] F. L. Green, *Odd Man Out* (London: Michael Joseph, 1945), pp. 187–8.

keeping Hewitt's discomfort on the boil.[39] The Ukrainian-born, Belfast-resident Paul Nietsche (1885–1950) did a portrait of Green in 1946, but it only reached the Ulster Museum in 1983.

Sarah Ferris has made quite a meal of the poet's response to Green's satire, noting (quite fairly) that Hewitt too promptly reviewed the novel in *Lagan*, a local magazine, and observing (less fairly) how Hewitt tried to absorb the persona of 'Griffin' in his quasi-fictional 'The Laying on of Hands' (1948), a short story published in *The Bell*.[40] The latter has 'Dick Griffin' (cf. 'Richard Telford') as protagonist, potentially the spiritual heir to the Revd Alexander Irvine. Irvine had risen from poverty to international renown, a successful but socially radical preacher, who had once gone incognito to investigate illegal slavery in Tennessee. It is plausible to suggest that Hewitt, a shyer but more sophisticated radical, at some level wished to be Irvine's surrogate or son.

The crucial detail, however, is the death of Hewitt's actual father in July 1945. Apart from the shock of intimate bereavement, the final days and hours had been intensified by unusually warm weather, which the old man found unbearable. Before losing consciousness in the hospital, he had said to his only son, 'no nation can live alone—I have been too much alone'.[41] Quite what John took from this utterance is difficult to fathom. RTH can hardly have been referring to the war just ended in which Northern Ireland had participated (and suffered). The lesser shock of *Odd Man Out* came later in the year. The novel's caricature presents an isolated person who nevertheless has the answer for everybody's mistakes, and pronounces the correct line without reference to inherited authority. 'It is essentially a progressive universe.... And man cannot escape that development.'[42] Hewitt's psychological position between his beloved but ageing father and what might be taken as a fictionalized Irvine was acutely vulnerable to Green's snappy satire.

His fascination with Irvine in the years after the old preacher's death also finds a context in Hewitt's never abandoned position within Ulster Protestantism. Whereas RTH had been brought up a Methodist, and found that attachment compatible with socially progressive ideas and an active role in his trade union, the son veered towards the Non-Subscribing Presbyterians. These congregations rejected the Westminster Confession (1646) and its rigid Calvinism, some of them adopting a veritable Unitarianism and, with that, a more liberal politics. Hewitt's fellow poet, Thomas Carnduff, also found his way into one of Belfast's Non-Subscribing circles though, characteristically, not the same one that Hewitt favoured. In pre-war Belfast, and later in Coventry, the Hewitts occasionally attended a Unitarian church. Liberal politics in Ulster tended to an explicit criticism of violence (as engendered through the major churches and their sectarian confrontations.) Hewitt's (Catholic)

[39] It has been customary to downplay any aggravation felt by JH over this matter, but he deliberately brought it up in 1968 during an interview with the *Coventry Evening Telegraph*.

[40] Sarah Ferris, *Poet John Hewitt (1907–87) and Criticism of Northern Irish Protestant Writing* (Lampeter: Edwin Mellen Press, 2002), pp. 128–31.

[41] *Journal TS*, prelims. [42] Green, *Odd Man Out*, p. 171.

friend John Kilfeather retrospectively suggested that the poet had been an unwitting pacifist in the 1930s because he had not enrolled at the outbreak of the war.[43] In September 1939, he was approaching his thirty-second birthday, a married man, with less than 20/20 vision, not the armed forces' optimum volunteer.

As a 'man of the left', he was unambiguously opposed to the fascist states of Europe, and contributed to the war effort by giving educational talks to recruits. However, his position was open to criticism because of pro-German sympathies among a minority in southern Ireland where he was wont to visit. Neutrality was never an option in Ulster any more than conscription; any distancing from London's position was near-treason. Subtlety could devise few bowers of seclusion. Behind the awkward details of Peace League attitudes and the German connections of his Dublin-based friend Cecil Salkeld, Hewitt the writer was conducting a slow poetic enquiry into the relationship of history and time. A notebook dating from 1945 opens with a quotation from the early sixteenth century:

> Howe shall ye know seasonable tyme? Go upon the lande, that is plowed and if it synge or crye, or make any noyse under thy fete, then it is too wete to sowe; and if it make no noyse and will beare thy horses, thenne sowe it in the name of God.[44]

If this does not illuminate Hewitt's politics or his attitude to the war, it contributes to his practical identification of time with nature and to his concern for the land in his proposals for a regionalist polity.

In December 1945, with the war over, an innovative radio programme brought Hewitt and Colin Middleton together. Art was a topic which challenged broadcasters' evocative skills as when, in autumn 1946, Radio Eireann gathered Hewitt, the southern-born but Ulster-based painter George Campbell, and the critic R. R. Figgis to discuss the question, 'Is There a Renaissance in Irish Painting?' The visual arts remain a constant theme in Hewitt's life not simply because of his nine-to-five job at the museum but because the gathering of poems into a properly circulated volume for critical and appreciative response was remarkably difficult. Wartime in a provincial town bedevilled by sectarian or tribal venom had effectively stalled his reputation at that local, at times venomous, level.

The post-war Labour victory across the United Kingdom had repercussions in Northern Ireland, especially in the sphere of education. A state system threatened both the exclusivism of the Catholic Church and the smugger arrangements available to the Protestant middle classes. Hewitt wrote to London-based Bertie Rodgers in November 1946, sketching the range of obstructive tactics adopted. The Corkonian Daniel Corkery, who had never spent more than a day in Belfast, joined with other 'reactionaries' to stimulate and revive 'the sleeping days of sectarianism' in opposition to an Education Bill. Hewitt can hardly have been convinced that sectarianism had ever gone to sleep for, in the same letter, he described

[43] John Kilfeather, 'Remembering John Hewitt', *Threshold* 38 (Winter 1986/87), pp. 31–6.

[44] UU, Hewitt, Notebook J, front paste-down. I have retained JH's orthography. The passage comes from John Fitzherbert's *Boke of Husbandry* (1523?). JH gives his immediate source as Adrian Bell, *The Open Air; an Anthology of English Country Life* (London: Faber, 1936 [and later editions]).

a stormy Unionist meeting at which the Stormont Minister for Education, Lieutenant-Colonel Samuel Herbert Hall-Thompson, declared 'we have to treat Catholic & Protestant alike' only to be greeted with loud growls of 'Never'.[45] While, at other times, the Colonel had been returned unopposed in his Belfast (Clifton) constituency, in 1945 he had to fight off a vigorous challenge by the Northern Ireland Labour Party.

Mount Charles continued to thrive, though some of the partygoers were old enough to have children in tow. The former Presbyterian minister rubbed shoulders with the former Republican Congress intellectual, which probably took Hall-Thompson's official policy of integration further than he imagined. Rodgers's daughter Harden wrote a poem, 'The Donegal Fairies', based on a story told to her in Mount Charles by Peadar O'Donnell as she was going off to bed. Peace came dropping slow. Christmas 1947 fell into the still-glum economies of post-war shortage. For presents, Roberta left a pullover and a hand-made jar on her husband's sleeping chest. On waking, he rushed downstairs to bring up a red scarf and handkerchiefs (in boxes he had made especially for the occasion). The seasonal fuss about children only served to re-inscribe their own childless condition. John was busy writing a review of *Poor Scholar*, Ben Kiely's study of the novelist William Carleton, for the *Irish News*.

Hewitt's often alleged instinctive revulsion from the religious practices of his nationalist neighbours is not confirmed by his own behaviour in the Glens on Sunday 28 December:

> Johnny and I went to the Chapel. Very dark. Crib, awful plaster figures, very badly cared for and not a candle in the church. There were two people, a man and a woman sitting in the dark and we sat at the back for a while. I could not pray but I tried to concentrate on the spirit of the Church and what it might mean to the coughing woman and the tip-shuffling man.... Johnny was quiet and hoped he would find comfort there.[46]

The incursion into a local Catholic church was more Hewitt's wish than his wife's, though she was deeply attracted to the location of their 'lodge' at the entrance to a convent. *The Bell*, largely run by southerners of formal but irregular Catholic attachment, was in trouble. The new editor, O'Donnell, had appealed to Hewitt for an unpaid contribution to help it survive for three months; Hewitt contributed the aptly named story, 'The Laying on of Hands', and a reef of poems. He also passed on Norman Carruthers' suggestion that the globe in a Mother and Child picture of John Luke's might centre on Ireland. Religion never quite slipped off his internal radar.

On 6 January 1948, Hewitt had a dreamlike experience of writing, which curiously united the sexual and political, at least as recorded in Roberta's journal. The incident had occurred when he was living as a small boy in Cliftonville Avenue; 'he

[45] PRONI, D/2833/C/8/4, JH to W. R. Rodgers, 26 November 1946.

[46] *Journal*, PRONI, D/3838/4/6, 4 January 1948. Until comparatively recent times, the term 'chapel' was generally used in rural Ireland to denote a Catholic church.

was kicking a ball and ran into a man whose coat was open and Jonny saw a rifle. It was during the troubled times here probably about 1922. He often spoke to me about it. Now it is a poem after 25 or 26 years.' First entitled 'Encounter', it appeared in the *Irish Times* of 3 April 1948, when some readers must have seen a connection with Joyce's story of youthful confrontation with pederasty in the *Dubliners*' story 'An Encounter'.[47] In Belfast, some readers may have linked it to Green's sketch of Griffin as a theorist with little experience of society's pains and inflictions.

Hewitt's local preoccupations were woven in and out of his public activities. His appearance in the first (December 1949) issue of *Envoy*, a Dublin literary magazine, threw this arrangement into quizzical relief. The editors of *Envoy* had international tastes and ambitions, signalled promptly by Joseph Hone with an article on the Italian philosopher Benedetto Croce, followed up with a piece by the French critic of politics and culture Julian Benda. Local colour was concentrated in the closing pages of each issue, where Patrick Kavanagh kept his diary open. Hewitt's 'The Farmer's Second Son' now resembles an anticipation of Seamus Heaney's early imagery:

> The farmer's second son has just left school,
> and is a man now, following the plough
> with help at awkward corners, harrowing
> and opening the long potato drills,
> and running after sheep across the mountain,
> the books are shut forever. From now on
> he'll learn in that slow cumulative way,
> by eye and gesture and a well cocked ear
> that listens to the old, the peasant way,
> enough to fill his days with ready labour,
> his nights with quiet dreams to last his life,
> and hand on store of sense and ease of heart
> to a vext age sick for the lack of both.[48]

It is not a particularly successful poem, as poem, even for one sympathetic to its approval of quiet dreams and the old, the peasant way. The rhyming of *way* with *way* must sound lazy or vacuous, unless of course an ironic tonality is detected beneath the plough and the drill. If a boy leaves school at the earliest permitted age, he is a man only in some flattering, deceitful rhetoric. The poem's title, doggedly repeated in the poem's opening words, may suggest an alternative reading, an understated thematic of disinheritance. For the farmer's first son gets the land which the second only labours on. This peculiar tension between a seemingly over-informative title and a smudgy pastoral text is traceable in other forms in Hewitt's other activities—as art connoisseur, international traveller, political 'man of the left', and advocate of regionalism.

[47] While eschewing the Joycean parallel, Ormsby (p. 608) provides a detailed account of textual variants.

[48] *Envoy; a Review of Literature and Art* 1, no. 1 (December 1949), p. [16].

The poem was originally inscribed in a notebook of April 1948 under the title 'For Patrick McDonnell Junior of Cloughglass', its regionalism or parochialism openly declared. It was never collected in Hewitt's lifetime, though the central image informs one critic's influential statement of his prosody, 'Visually his lines are tidy furrows across neat fields or poems; aurally his iambic meters have the regularity of expert but easy ploughing.'[49] The farmer's second son of the poem has yet to become adult or expert, and the fields of Cloughglass are far from neat or easy. In the words of his best editors, 'the disquiet' of Hewitt's poetry, 'is social as well as psychological', though the poem under examination tends to play down, even deny, the latter unease.[50] In August 1951 Roberta recorded his continuing struggle with the piece, trying to make it more objective and to 'eliminate the "I"s'—that is, the first person pronoun.[51] Resting in the Glens, and hard at work with mind and body, Hewitt divided the next day between a sonnet and the task of pulling lint on a nearby farm, owned by a nationalist, but rented out to Murray Emerson. Though the toil exhausted him, and the slyness of farmers taking subsidies outraged him, the Glens and the cottage were home as Belfast could not be. At its best, regionalism was no comfortable retreat to the familiar or ancestral; it was to remain a desire, not an inheritance, a communal desire if only others would join him. Regionalism and the cottage at Tiveragh deserve their own chapter (see Chapter 5).

Hewitt, with the Planter flag provocatively raised, might look like an odd example of disinheritance. But the identity of Planter was assumed for strategic reasons; it is not a literal or historical fact; the Hewitts and Redpaths of Kilmore, County Armagh, would be better understood as settlers, not planters. The original motive for casting himself as Planter may have been a desire to act—in advance of the French term—as a *colon* who refuses. It set off his left-wing affiliations neatly; it drew attention to historical realities without embodying them. In the Northern Ireland emerging after 1920, landlordism still carried a punch, the Church of Ireland in rural parts and the Presbyterian Church in the big towns held the middle and upper classes to their bosoms. The elder Hewitts' Methodism never fitted into the higher compromises of Ulster Protestant society. Inside the household, John was the only, not a second, son; but he was the younger of the two children, dependent in many ways upon his older sister (see 'My Sister', written in November 1978, three years after her death). The close relationship with his father encouraged independent, radical thinking, while it simultaneously offered disarming comfort and agreement; the need to be disinherited was partly to blame for the adoption of a Planter mask.[52]

Ideal disinheritance did not entirely preclude acceptance of an official brief. In March 1949, the British Council offered Hewitt eight guineas for an article

[49] John Wilson Foster, quoted in the introduction to Longley/Ormsby, p. xxiv.

[50] Longley/Orsmby, p. xvii. [51] *Journal*, PRONI, D/3838/4/7, 10 August 1951.

[52] Sarah Ferris discusses Hewitt's deployment of the 'planter' term at considerable length, concluding that it was a myth; her general hostility to the poet, and especially to his reception in Northern Ireland after 1972, diminishes what could have been a shrewd analysis; see her *Poet John Hewitt 1907–1987*, p. 178 etc. For 'My Sister', see Ormsby, p. 284.

on Ulster Poetry, as part of what Roberta dryly termed 'overseas propaganda'. He accepted, though the item has yet to be identified.[53] As the year came to a close, people reflected on a half-century of unprecedented destruction and mass violence. Northern Ireland had suffered a small measure of the bombing (notably in April–May 1941) and the impact of troops on civilian life.[54] To the south, the experience of war had been a lot less direct. Complex feelings of resentment, relief, guilt, and confusion shuttled across the border. On 16 December, the Hewitts took the Dublin train for a dinner organized by the PEN Club. On board the 'Enterprise' they met friends, including the painter Daniel O'Neill; the journey passed quickly. They had booked into Jury's Hotel—'posh' by their standards. On Saturday evening, Hewitt was surprised and pleased by Roger McHugh's knowledge of his work, less impressed by Professor H. O. White's pretences. Kenneth Reddin, a minor literary figure and a judge, brought them to the Hermitage, near Rathfarnham, an eighteenth-century mansion where Patrick Pearse had conducted a school. Roberta was moved by the romantic history of the place—it had been the home of Robert Emmet's beloved; somebody had been hanged there. 'I became a bit of an Irish Republican in the atmosphere.'[55]

The secondary purpose for visiting Dublin was to buy goods still scarce inside the United Kingdom, several pairs of nylon stockings which Roberta smuggled inside her corset. These were to be Christmas presents in Belfast. After the festivities were over, on 27 December they took the bus out of the city up into the Glens. John spent a day reading poetry, work by Edwin Muir, William Soutar, Stephen Spender, and R. S. Thomas. Of these, Soutar (1898–1943) remains the least known, a Scot who became bedridden through infected vertebrae and who wrote in both Scots and English. Antrim was permeated with the influence of Scottish settlers and, reading in their little cottage, the Hewitts felt an affinity with poets from the outer reaches of what John called the archipelago—Muir from Orkney, Thomas in north-west Wales, Soutar from Perth. He suggested to Roberta that perhaps he should give up all committee work, including CEMA, and give more time to writing. Provoked by this, she inwardly recalled that, some time earlier, she had dreamed one night how he had been invited to stand for parliament.

On New Year's Eve 1949, they again attended Mass with neighbours, their individual reactions never unanimous but never consistent. On this occasion, she was moved by the sight of the choirboys; he thought the Catholic faith potentially dangerous, though on other occasions he was the more sympathetic, she the resister. Back in the cottage, he began work on one of his best-known longer poems (see 'Break for Text II'). At a low moment he had started what would become a much cited supposed-political testimony.

There is little evidence that Hewitt had suffered direct bereavement during the Second World War; he had no brothers; other relations were too old or too young;

[53] *Journal*, PRONI, D/3838/4/6, 22 March 1949.

[54] See Brian Barton, *The Blitz: Belfast in the War Years* (Belfast: Blackstaff, 1989).

[55] *Journal*, PRONI, D/3838/4/6, 18 December 1949.

through his civil service job he was exempt from military service.[56] The British government's recognition of 'Red' China in January 1950 suddenly brought back memories of Shelley Wang whom the Hewitts had last seen in 1939. Indeed, John had broken down at the railway station when his Chinese friend said goodbye. For Roberta, January brought the disgraceful local news that Midgley, a one-time Labourite, had become Minister for Education in the Unionist government—'the heel'. Towards the month's end, they visited Colin and Kate Middleton at Ardglass, County Down, where a fellow guest was Edward Sheehy, an occasional writer in Dublin's literary circle. John suffered a heavy cold, took to his bed for days, sleeping deeply. It was at this time that the idea arose of converting his work on the nineteenth-century Ulster poets into an academic thesis. Roberta shrewdly calculated that an MA degree would advance his candidacy when the gallery directorship fell vacant.[57] George Orwell died, and they recalled liking him at the Adelphi gathering of 1936.

In February 1949, Hewitt had struck up a friendship with Robert McElborough, an active trade unionist working in the gas industry and by background a Protestant. The McElborough family, though originating in County Tyrone, lived in the Sandy Row area of south Belfast, a staunchly Unionist, Orange working-class area. The two men corresponded as well as met to discuss politics, and Hewitt was entrusted with the older man's papers, which he subsequently deposited in PRONI. For the poet, the relationship brought a flare of Marxist optimism amid post-war austerity, though the persistent difficulty was an inability by any thinker to reconcile the rival claims of Britishness and Irishness.[58] The thirties were over; gone was the excitement of editing literary pages for *The Irish Democrat*. The austerity was mental as well as material. While chairing a public meeting in Bangor, recorded by the BBC, Hewitt spoke provocatively about 'The Ulster Character'. A member of the audience duly complained to the town council, and a resolution condemning BBC Northern Ireland duly passed.[59]

The big event was the UK General Election in February 1950. John and Roberta spent hours addressing envelopes on behalf of the local Labour candidate, though the British Labour Party never campaigned in Northern Ireland. The Short and Harland's Club on Ormeau Avenue was 'secretly' loaned to the Labour effort, some indication of discontent among Belfast's industrial workers (for the most part Unionist). Unionist bad habits spread among their opponents. In the Cromac Street tally room, Roberta met a 'tall blond girl of about 23, sucking her baby's

[56] From a hostile position, Ferris provides an exhaustive summary of the evidence concerning Hewitt and war service. See her *Poet John Hewitt, 1907–87*, p. 194 n. 6. Nevertheless, she confirms that he had not joined the Officer Training Corps at QUB, accepts that he did make efforts to enlist at officer level, but was not accepted.

[57] *Journal*, PRONI, D/3838/4/6, 17 October 1950. 'Secretly I feel if he gets his MA before Mr Stendall retires from Museum it would count with the City Fathers.' There is no evidence that Roberta, when encouraging the project, knew of her husband's academic difficulties as an undergraduate.

[58] See *Loyalism and Labour in Belfast: the Autobiography of Robert McElborough*, edited by Emmet O'Connor and Trevor Parkhill (Cork: Cork University Press, 2002).

[59] Gillian McIntosh, *The Force of Culture: Unionist Identities in Twentieth-Century Ireland* (Cork: Cork University Press, 1999), p. 184.

comforter... [who] had been round to vote three times [and said] she had voted for Betty Sinclair in the last election "the dear knows how many times"'.[60] Sinclair, a communist, had polled well in 1945.

Confidence in Mount Charles was at low ebb. Hewitt felt that he might 'with luck succeed in becoming a minor poet'. Up in Antrim a few days later, his emerging pet theory was jostled by Keith Millar, Roberta's nephew, who remarked that one could become a regionalist only by travelling elsewhere and, in that way, learning to know how one's region differed from others. Life at the cottage was simple, the neighbours very affable, gardening and drainage chores not too burdensome. Keith was becoming scientific in outlook and, while his rifle helped to fill the pot for supper, a dead pigeon was clinically examined—160 ivy berries in its craw.[61] His uncle approved science against superstition, but longed to apprehend nature without the interference of either. Despite the boost to war-related manufacturing in Belfast, Korea hovered behind every horizon. Never able to forget her recurring ailments, Roberta felt the Asian war's dreadful potential, 'I still want to hold that little life as many years as I can.' Local feeling in Belfast continued narrow and vindictive. Hewitt considered subscribing to the Dublin Red Cross Magazine for 1951, but such a gesture 'would be frowned upon here'. After an early autumn holiday, they 'left the cottage with the usual grief'.[62] In London, Frederick Muller, having reported dire sales of *No Rebel Word* and the imperative to burn remaining copies, then relented somewhat by foregoing the income he might have earned from them. In Belfast John Stewart learned his phone was tapped by the police.[63] As a further reminder of the conflict in Asia, Roberta joined a group in Queen's of personnel who had worked in postal censorship during the Second World War—'refresher course in readiness for the next war'. But the university had a less gloomy side; on the previous day, with Roy McFadden for extra cheer, the Hewitts entertained a new assistant librarian to tea—Philip Larkin seemed 'a nice, well-informed chap'.[64]

Post-war Belfast still relied on coupons for essential purchases. Entertainment was relatively plentiful, but domestic gatherings were hampered by a shortage of anything resembling exotic food. A New Literary Dining Club—all male, it seems, emerged from the gloom: Sam Hanna Bell, John Boyd, Hewitt, McFadden were the principals, with the genial Joe Tomelty the only notable Catholic participant.[65] Just before Christmas 1950, Sophie and Jim Stewart decided on a party late in the evening, and telephoned their friends from Newtownards. The mood did not quite lighten, even when Jim dressed up, with a net brassiere on his hairy chest and a short skirt. Roberta eventually succumbed to the attempt at fancy dress, taking off her skirt and jumper and substituting two head-scarves. No record of John's antics.

[60] *Journal*, PRONI, D/3838/4/6, 23 February 1950.
[61] *Journal*, PRONI, D/3838/4/6, 13 April 1950.
[62] *Journal*, PRONI, D/3838/4/6, 2 June 1950, 5 August 1950, and 5 September 1950.
[63] *Journal*, PRONI, D/3838/4/6, 3 November 1950.
[64] *Journal*, PRONI, D/3838/4/6, 16 November 1950.
[65] McIntosh, *The Force of Culture*, p. 182.

The New Year of 1951 was celebrated with a rearrangement of pictures on the Mount Charles walls, Hewitt polishing the glass as he took down and replaced each item, among them a Japanese print-drawing of Bertie Rodgers. Roberta, who was acutely susceptible to atmosphere, noted how the pictures changed 'the whole temperature of the room'.[66] Her journal generally offers a businesslike start to the year, in January 1951 recording details of income mixed with political difficulty. Her husband's monthly take-home pay came to £40. 14. 0. In the previous twelve months he had earned £21 for printed poems and about £24 for radio work. She urged him to persist with a certain kind of remunerative poem, but he protested that it only required inferior verse. She got a new coat, the most expensive garment she ever bought for herself.[67] Hewitt went to Edinburgh where the Scottish Arts Council was showing work from Frankl's collection of Ulster Artists; naturally the selection failed to please everyone at home. On the last Saturday of the month, Bertie Moffat dropped in, still full of wobbly faith in the Soviet Union, to deliver a party magazine which denounced Winston Churchill, T. S. Eliot, and Johnny Hewitt as bourgeois, trivial, and escapist. No doubt others were named too, but the listing of Hewitt was unwelcome, even if he appeared among the condemned. Roberta remained a Labour Party supporter.[68]

The thesis on Ulster Poets 1800–70 was submitted on 30 April. It opened with two curious 'preludes', the first a quotation from Samuel Ferguson reviewing *The Annals of the Four Masters* in March 1848, the second an extract from Geoffrey Grigson's *The Victorians* (1950). The latter passage concludes with a sentence Hewitt must have chosen with an eye to disarming the overcritical examiner: 'This preservation of castles and poems, this antiquarianism, is not kept to its bound, is not kept distinct, and is allowed to appear to be "taste"; so by prejudice it becomes a hindrance to the arts of the living.'[69] During May, the Hewitts were having one of their tiffs, with Roberta retiring early to bed in the back attic. When the phone rang late in the evening, she could hear John further down the house saying to the unidentified caller, 'I am sure we could put you up somewhere.' She hollered 'I'm not shifting, you can take whoever it is in with you.' He burst out laughing, because the caller was Brendan Behan, ringing from the Falls Road. She joined in. Hewitt's account of the event in *A North Light* has their guest in Belfast because of difficulties with the Dublin police. Roberta's contemporary record has Behan turning up at Mount Charles after midnight, his lips bleeding and badly cut, with tatters of lint stemming the flow, his shoes spattered with whitewash. 'I came up on business but it didn't turn out too well.'

Behan, despite his injuries, was in good form, though nervous, entertaining the Hewitts with his mother's account of meeting Yeats. Mrs Behan had been a servant to Maud Gonne MacBride and, when she brought in tea, Yeats would make a point of talking to her 'just to show the others how democratic he was'. Brendan

66 *Journal*, PRONI, D/3838/4/7, 2 January 1951.
67 *Journal*, PRONI, D/3838/4/7, 28 January 1951.
68 *Journal*, PRONI, D/3838/4/7, 28 January 1951.
69 J. H. Hewitt, 'Ulster Poets 1800–70', a thesis offered for the degree of Masters of Arts in the Faculty of Arts,[n.p.], p. [ii].

revealed a wide knowledge of writers and books although, at this date, he had published very little and was not the celebrity he became. Next morning after breakfast he suddenly gave Roberta a mighty handshake, 'You don't know what you did for me last night.' Later he phoned John to thank him, explaining that he was on a greyhound farm near Portstewart. Back in Dublin he couldn't praise the Hewitts highly or wildly enough—'sent round the car for me'.[70]

During the winter of 1951–52, Keith Millar stayed in Mount Charles for several months. Sometimes the knot of family became too tight for comfort. Then major external crises brought a welcome distraction. In February, George VI died. On the day, John was effectively in charge at the gallery as his superior, Stendall, was over in London. A visitor, J. H. Delargy, was due to speak on folklore in the evening. A native of Antrim, he had been a professor at University College Dublin since 1941. Belfast City Hall was unable or unwilling to advise: cancellation of all public events was inevitable, but a political edginess crept into Hewitt's afternoon, unable to locate his guest or to guess whether the regal news had reached him on his way north. A domestic solution was found, with Delargy and a younger folklorist, Brendan Adams (to whom *Rhyming Weavers* would be dedicated), invited to eat at Mount Charles. Maybins joined the party, together with young Keith who had been camping upstairs for some time.

On Friday 8 February, Robert Flaherty's primitivist film *Man of Aran* was shown privately at the museum. In the evening the Hewitts attended a *Lieder* concert—Brahms, Schubert, and others—by Kathleen Ferrier, who would die the following year aged forty. 'At the beginning Gerald Moore [the accompanist] came in and we sang "God Save the Queen" for the first time... although we in Ulster don't sing the National Anthem as a rule.' The Hewitts were by no means predictable in their reactions. In bed on the Sunday morning, they both read Orwell's *Nineteen Eighty Four*: 'awful—worse because it contains what could grow out of seeds that are being nourished now'.[71]

On the next evening, Hewitt was to speak to the Royal Society of Architects on the use of sculpture in building, or so he thought. The meeting was actually scheduled for the following night.[72] Art in public buildings, especially schools, was a topic which he would develop in Coventry. Though the prospect of 'escape' (Roberta's term) seemed remote, and indeed the possibility of promotion to the Belfast Gallery directorship was encouraged by their friends, they were already itching to move, despite his appointment as acting deputy director on 1 February. While John was busy with the Dublin art dealer Victor Waddington, Roberta impulsively phoned an estate agent about properties on or near the Malone Road, Valhalla, for the Belfast professional classes. Waddington planned to bring an exhibition by Daniel O'Neill to John's gallery, and the art-loving factory owner Frankl stood lunch for all concerned. It was a day of contrasting priorities. Domestic sparks flew that evening in the flat, which Roberta was rapidly tiring of. But they

[70] *Journal*, PRONI, D/3838/4/7, 18 May 1951; and *North*, p. 238.
[71] *Journal*, PRONI, D/3838/4/7, 10 February 1952.
[72] *Journal*, PRONI, D/3838/4/7, 8–12 February 1952.

went to bed, grumbled at each other, each getting up in turn, and each slowly finding the row internally comic. When they got back into the bed, things were close as possible. She had to remove protective gloves from her damaged hands, in order fully 'to strip'.[73] If there was friction between man and wife, she was always too ready to take the blame. But they had a capacity to divert tension into calmer channels. When they solemnly stood to attention in their own living room, with the king's funeral broadcast on the wireless, neither could work out how long two minutes' silence might be.

At the beginning of April, the Hewitts took a weekend up at the cottage in Antrim, Roberta arriving before noon on Friday to air the bedclothes, John following early in the evening. She was still recovering from surgery, and suffering from numbness in her hands and feet. After the evening Angelus—for the Hewitts used the traditional bell-ringing of the Catholic chapel to mark the day's progress—he set out for Cushendun to address a visiting group sponsored by the British Council. The cottage warmed up; she read alone, made tea, and studied the fire. On his return, Hewitt reported a good discussion among the students with many nationalities represented, but no Russians or others from that quarter. The next day, they went down to Cushendall, planning to have tea there after the routine shopping. Hewitt became distracted; Roberta felt slighted by his inattention, and stomped off on her own. Another row followed, and he chose a word which came closer to her recent feelings than he realized. He said she made him numb. Then she hit him, broke his spectacles, and made his nose bleed. Now she was a bitch (he groaned), and she began to panic. Back in the cottage, they discovered that no piece of the spectacles was missing. On the Sunday evening he wrote four poems, he and she having made up.[74] Characteristically, she blamed herself (not her recent surgery, menopause, or periodic condition). 'I hope it has taught me something—but I don't know what except that I was humbled unto dust.'[75]

By the weekend—Easter—Hewitt had been cheered by the appearance of 'Dichotomy' in the *Irish Times*. Country and town are its polar terms, the rolling landscape of one, the painted gables and marching feet of the other. These images of Belfast (never named) are unmistakably political and, against them, he cites 'the bell at noon, the gilt cup lifted up' of rural Catholicism. The poet's attitude towards his home town contains its own dichotomy or paradox:

> Yet till I name it, I must never speak
> the full truth that my heart is eager with.[76]

On the Sunday evening after the poem's appearance, the Lodge hosted a small party, including several young people and members of the Millar family. Keith Millar gave temporary offence by appropriating a new paraffin lamp and leaving the Hewitts with old ones. But Monday redeemed all. John and Roberta sat out in

[73] Roberta Hewitt suffered from a recurrent minor skin complaint, shared by other members of her family.

[74] None of these poems is readily identified in Ormsby, and may have been discarded.

[75] *Journal*, PRONI, D/3838/4/7, 5 April 1952.

[76] The poem was never collected in Hewitt's lifetime; see Ormsby, p. 505.

the garden reading, and imbibing the sun. On the same day in 1952 he wrote 'Easter Flock'; but revised it ten years later, and only published it in 1978. Much of its imagery is pastoral of the 'All in the April Evening' kind, though without reference to God. Instead, the poem moves round central lines which negate the poet's presence in the conventional landscape—'Were I to straddle fence and stride across / I should add nothing.'[77]

Hewitt's religious beliefs are mistakenly taken to be a zero sum. Perhaps in 'The Green Shoot' and 'Easter Flock' there is something to encourage consideration of *negative theology* as close to his unstatable position. In a volume of essays published to honour Hewitt in 1985, Lynda Henderson took the phrase 'The Green Shoot' to introduce a discussion of 'transcendence and the imagination in contemporary Ulster drama'.[78] The complicating factors are almost entirely local and circumstantial—the painted murals with their biblical figures and slogans, the conjoining of religious affiliation with political identity of a boulder-like, homogeneous kind, whether nationalist or Unionist. Southern Ireland managed to alienate with its Roman confessionalism, as much as it exhilarated with its little magazines and galleries. When the Hewitts moved to Coventry in 1957, they occasionally attended a Unitarian church and, through the Disarmament marches, associated with practising Quakers. Peter Peri, a Hungarian sculptor whom they would befriend, was Quaker *and* communist. Easter Monday 1952 in the Glens brought no epiphany; on the contrary, it showed how difficult it was to extricate certain pastoral words and images from conventional usage without self-denial. Indeed, the self-denial is the point, beyond convention. Hewitt's bon mot of the day referred to a well-to-do couple keen to sell bad pictures they had inherited—'Money can't be important', he observed to Roberta, 'look at the people who have it.' And she ended her journal entry for the day with another characteristic turning-upon the sharpened nib, 'I feel more forgiven after this lovely week-end, and I am near a compromise with myself, if not self-forgiven.'[79]

*

The war had pressed hard on the museum service of the United Kingdom, partly by drawing volunteers into the armed forces and partly by using up resources (such as paper) needed for scholarly publication. The *Belfast Museum and Art Gallery Bulletin* had only been one casualty among many. In March 1950, it resumed circulation, with the first issue containing notes by Hewitt on portraits of James Armstrong and the United Irishman Watty Graham. It was typical that he should advertise a personal loyalty to the radical politics of a past era, and typical of the city he lived in that this gesture should be thought subversive. If the thirties had been haunted by fascism and anti-fascism, the 1950s would quake under the threat of nuclear annihilation and/or the communist menace.

[77] Ormsby, p. 232.
[78] See Gerald Dawe and Edna Longley, eds., *Across a Roaring Hill; the Protestant Imagination in Modern Ireland* (Belfast: Blackstaff Press, 1985), pp. 196–217. JH's work is not discussed in the book, which examines plays by John Boyd, Brian Friel, Martin Lynch, and Graham Reid.
[79] *Journal*, PRONI, D/3838/4/7, 14 April 1952.

There was still a whiff of contemporary radicalism in literary circles. At the PEN Congress of August 1950, held in Edinburgh, the guests of honour were Austin Clarke and the short story writer Frank O'Connor, a formidable Irish team. The Dublin delegates were the novelist Maurice Walsh and the now-forgotten Sheila Pim (1909–95). Belfast was represented by Hewitt and May Morton. The usually mellow proceedings were interrupted by three communists, bona fide members of the Scottish centre of PEN who objected to political digressions made by the American playwright Robert Sherwood. Initial tolerance of the protests soon turned to impatience, perhaps an indication of how close to (or with) the prevailing wind PEN liked to sail.

In July 1951, an unexpected visitor arrived at the Ulster Museum: Bunting, who had been Muller's editor at time of *No Rebel Word*. In the evening, he went to Mount Charles where the presence of others—including Cherith Boyd, of whom we will hear more—inhibited his reflections on the way Hewitt's book had been handled, beyond saying that things had been 'very badly' done. He brought samples of the new Gannymede reproductions of painting which pleased both Roberta and John.[80] During the summer, she was advised by her doctor, Olive Anderson, to consult Mr H. Lowry.[81] They took her parents to a Festival of Britain 'Farm and Factory Exhibition', courtesy of the Welsh ethnographer Estyn Evans, who hung up a pair of his own socks as an example of the pure-spun wool produced on the exhibition farm. The next day, Thursday 5 July, Roberta saw Lowry, who 'says curette' and arranged for her to go into the Royal Victorian Hospital.

A number of crises were to gather about Hewitt's head in 1952–53. Directorship of the Ulster Museum and Art Gallery was sure to be advertised with the retirement of Stendall, the incumbent. Hewitt looked like a natural successor, at least in his own eyes, those of Roberta, and also of art-loving friends, practising artists, and Belfast's small band of 'progressives'. There were external complications. His involvement with the International PEN organization would acquire a different colouration when the congress for 1953 was scheduled for Dublin and Belfast. Hewitt had been an active PEN pal for years, but the prospect of an Irish-based congress raised political issues of a ticklish kind. The gallery was a purely internal matter, the congress inevitably a cross-border one. To this contretemps one might add, as prelude, a political crisis in Dublin during the spring of 1951, involving the fall of a Coalition government on the issue of Church–State relations with specific reference to the health services.

The southern crisis broke when the Catholic Church denounced a proposed 'Mother and Child' welfare scheme, championed by Noel Browne, the young Minister for Health. On 12 April 1951, Roberta's journal noted the 'great stir'. She and John thought the minister 'very courageous', and felt that his party leader,

[80] *Journal*, PRONI, D/3838/4/7, 25/6/1951. The present writer now owns Cherith Boyd's copy of *No Rebel Word*, dated June 1949, which carries no inscription by Hewitt.

[81] See Greta Jones, 'Marie Stopes in Ireland: the Mothers' Clinic in Belfast 1936–1947', *Social History of Medicine* 5, no. 2 (April 1992), pp. 255–77. See also Diarmaid Ferriter, *Occasions of Sin: Sex and Society in Modern Ireland* (London: Profile, 2009), p. 302.

Sean MacBride, had been shown up as a bogus radical. 'I am becoming more and more afraid of the R. C. Church.'[82] None of this impacted directly on Hewitt as poet or even as art-gallery administrator, though it intensified the suspicion, persistent in the North, of southern timidity in the face of the Roman Church militant. Browne was a native west of Ireland Catholic, but his wife was a member of the Church of Ireland. The Mother and Child crisis boded ill for mutual understanding between Protestants and Catholics, a social frontier across which Hewitt had been moving quite freely. As late as 1964, he could claim 'The only Irish political group I subscribe to is Noel Browne's.' This was no clear indication of firm commitment.[83]

Hewitt's relationship with Austin Clarke was inextricably bound up with the latter's dedication to radio broadcasting and his inclusion of numerous poems by Hewitt in his Radio Eireann programmes. Their wives had evidently met, and spousely greetings generally featured at the end of letters from one poet to the other. Though Clarke was imaginatively saturated in the rituals and mental formulae of Catholicism, he was profoundly aware of the tyranny exercised by the Irish Church in political, artistic, and sexual matters. His poems about women and about the negative prudery of the priesthood were wonderfully sympathetic, perhaps because his own early sexual experiences had been very painful. This was not a theme upon which Hewitt ever ventured. Clarke's language, though more intricate and formal, possessed a quietude Hewitt appreciated and indeed practised in his own work. Dissidents each from his religious background, they occupied similar positions of isolation and exposure.

In 1953, their common purpose was opposition to censorship as practised in southern Ireland. More exactly, they deplored the connivance in official censorship of an organization supposedly devoted to upholding freedom of expression, International PEN. Like many bodies operating in Ireland at the time, PEN functioned through a dual structure, with centres in both Belfast and Dublin. There was, however, just one president of Irish PEN. Proposed changes of various kinds did not please Clarke, who slyly drew an analogy to the pre-1937 status of the British monarch in southern Irish constitutional arrangements. 'I have always felt that the Presidency [of PEN] was a sort of symbolic link like the Crown!'[84] If the Belfast centre planned to look south-east to London, rather than directly south to Dublin, even more unsettling developments were plotted by the Dublin centre, which was due to host an international congress later in the year.

Clarke was aware of the extent to which the minor scribes who dominated PEN committees were pushing their own work for the benefit of visiting delegates, a harmless indulgence were it not for the existence of a state censorship keeping

[82] *Journal*, PRONI, D/3838/4/7, 12 April 1951.

[83] UU, Hewitt, Box 9, carbon copy of an undated letter to John Montague, annotated by JH, '1964 spring'. Between 1958 and 1963, Noel Browne led a very small radical party, the National Progressive Democrats, whose two parliamentary representatives unquestionably rocked the political boat in southern Ireland. However, in 1963, it had 'merged' with the Irish Labour Party under whose protection both men lost their seats in the succeeding election.

[84] PRONI, D/3838/3/6, Austin Clarke to JH, [no date].

better writers out of view. Naturally, the Catholic Church was happy to facilitate the congress in whatever fashion would demonstrate compliance with the moral teaching of Rome. The national seminary at Maynooth, outside Dublin, offered hospitality to the delegates. To Hewitt, Clarke confided, 'When I saw that a special luncheon party was arranged at Maynooth, I concluded that the liberal element was to be kept out . . . censorship is now a Civil Service routine, with a paid staff. . . . I hope you will be able to plan something for the sake of Liberty.'[85] Personally, he intended to boycott the whole charade, a tactic well suited to his reclusive character.

A week later, Hewitt replied at length. He shared Clarke's outrage but found himself—like McFadden—compromised by the religious identities imposed across the island:

> I myself would raise the Censorship matter & Roy would back me up. But that would look like the Northern Protestants having a crack at the R. C.s, and dismissed as sectarian bigotry. . . . I'm writing to some Scottish friends to find out if they are coming to the conference and to suggest that among them the business [of censorship] gets brought up. But if this fails—Roy and I have been talking it over—we would try to get hold of some English or Continental visitors to ask a question at an appropriate session. We shall certainly endeavour to make clear to some of the better PEN delegates that there are Irish writers kept outside because of the sycophancy of the Irish centres [. . .] Its a pity a Southerner wouldn't speak up, for it might be construed as bad taste for a visitor to rush in. . . . But even if it means shewing [*sic*] a corner of my sash and more misunderstanding I'll try something.[86]

Hewitt's letter-writing could not be praised for style, though nuances deserve close attention. The hint that a southern delegate might be more effective in a protest against southern censorship may have been intended as a mild rebuke. Clarke, in 1953, was not well known publicly, and his boycott might be read as the exercise in legendary shyness. The corner of Hewitt's sash is of course one of those ironic gestures which his foes often misunderstood—Hewitt was no Orangeman. The letter, promising action but leaving the details unclear, ends with greeting from Roberta, and a cheery 'see you soon'. The signature, however, remained full and formal—John Hewitt.

Hewitt remained a devoted supporter of Clarke's difficult poetry. He was grateful when the older man came in from his near-rural home in Templeogue to hear a talk Hewitt gave in Dublin. That, oddly enough, took place in December 1955, shortly after he had represented the Belfast centre of Irish PEN at a congress in Vienna. As Roberta's mother was ill, there was some domestic uncertainty about the Hewitts' liberty to travel. In the end, her relatives insisted they would cope with the old lady, and John and she travelled by air via Zurich. The closeness of these years, the mid-1950s, to the Second World War, was brought home to them by the unobtrusive and unmistakable presence of Russian troops at the tiny and crude airport. A British soldier accompanied the bus which drove them from the

[85] PRONI, D/3838/3/6, Austin Clarke to JH, 16 May 1953.
[86] NLI, Ms 38, 658/3, JH to Austin Clarke, 22 May 1953.

plane to the shed-terminus.[87] In stark contrast, Austrian PEN had its headquarters in a former ducal palace. At a reception in the Schoenbrunn, the Hewitts spotted two southern Irish delegates—the Marxist R. M. Fox, and his wife, the novelist Patricia Lynch. They were, Roberta decided, trapped 'under the weight of a talkative American woman'.[88] Characteristically, Roberta intervened.

In June, the Hewitts noticed the Russians still in Vienna. In August their friend Jim Stewart visited the Soviet Union, while his wife Sophie (d.1991)—who has left us the defining image of John Hewitt in her drawing of him—stayed in Mount Charles. She was the sister of Dorothy Livesay (1909–96), a distinguished Canadian poet with radical-liberal positions on various political and religious issues. The Foxes were ideologically far removed from the sycophants whom Clarke and Hewitt deplored as PEN delegates. Yet, as committed Marxists, any comment of theirs against Irish state censorship would have been counterproductive. Hewitt's left-wing politics was partly sustained by these evidences of a worldwide contrast between the socialist and capitalist worlds, and partly compromised. The Cold War was waged at every level. A year later, Clarke maintained his old theme:

> There are only a few liberal and literary links now between north and south. The Church has been busy drawing a Holy Curtain around us here and the silly students who raid the Border don't realise that every stick of gelignite they use means another statue of the B. V. M.! Clerical pressure is so intense now, that even my own reviews in the Irish Times, now, are blue-pencilled, whenever I venture to hint at conditions here.[89]

Just before Christmas 1955, Hewitt had sent Clarke a cheque for two copies of *Ancient Lights*, published earlier that year. Later he dedicated a long poem 'Those Swans Remember' (1956) to Clarke who, in acknowledgment, remarked that 'fortunately' he liked it.

87 *Journal*, PRONI, D/3838/4/7, 25 August 1955.

88 *Journal*, PRONI, D/3838/4/7, 25 August 1955.

89 PRONI, D/3838/3/6, Austin Clarke to JH, 17 December 1956. B. V. M. is the Blessed Virgin Mother, whose image in stone (or plaster) sculpture pervaded Catholic Ireland in the 1950s. An IRA 'border campaign', mainly conducted through raids on northern police barracks, had begun in December 1956, lasting until 1962, when a more left-wing 'political' direction was adopted.

5

In Search of Regionalism: Cushendall, 1946–50

Apart from *No Rebel Word* and occasional magazine appearances, Hewitt the poet held to an unflattering self-publication regime. The disadvantages were obvious—no independent critical judgement, extremely limited circulation, low design and production standards. In a different light, the benefits were significant—independence from standardization by metropolitan agencies, and a closer relationship between writing and its reception. For years Hewitt skittered between the two objectives—sending typescripts to Jonathan Cape, Michael Joseph, John Lehmann, Faber and Faber etc. in London and, with the other hand, feeding material to the scarcely global *Ulster Young Farmer* and to jobbing printers in Belfast. The double-track approach in many ways resembled his political interests, rarely but occasionally dreaming of office (or at least election), more steadily evolving a ground-level analysis linked to theories of regionalism. The same division affected his domestic ideal.

In the gradually relaxing condition of Belfast after the war, he and Roberta somewhat perversely decided to find a country retreat. They had long enjoyed hiking and knew a great deal of natural history. However, urban flats offered no opportunities for gardening, no time to stop and stare, while the little resort towns of north and east Down, from Bangor to Newcastle catered for summer trippers, not the reflective type. John and Roberta had found north Antrim by going to Rathlin in 1935, but the island was too dependent on small boats and uncertain weather to provide a regular place of retreat. In any case, retreat was not the main concern; in their long years as visitors and semi-permanent residents in Antrim, they would prove to be highly sociable.

While his affiliation to the Glens is perhaps the best known and happiest detail of Hewitt's life, its background involved some hard thinking. Yet John Hewitt should not be set up as an intellectual. He was primarily a poet who had to make his living through a career in the museum service. His thought cannot be tracked down to a large monograph or series of heavy volumes. It moves deftly through many brief statements, book reviews, essays, newspaper articles and—of course—poems. Its sponsor is never a powerful institution or publishing house. In one important professional area—his engagement with the visual arts—he was careful to describe himself as 'a gallery man' rather than the more imposing 'art historian'. His method was regular practice, not accumulated wisdom. If, as many have argued, his most original contribution to public debate in Northern Ireland was his advocacy of regionalism, then the way he went about his theme was entirely consistent with the project itself. He was not a solitary voice: John Boyd (1912–2002) and George Buchanan (1904–89) drilled similar ground, less publicly.[1] None of the three published any lengthy account of their ideas, and the absence of a book or substantial pamphlet by Hewitt may be regretted.[2]

There is a more abstract way of thinking about the endeavour undertaken. If we bear in mind the fluctuating evidence of Hewitt's religious/secular concerns in the juvenilia, and (for a moment) anticipate his later tentative but repeated contacts with Catholic and Unitarian congregations, and his final unambiguous refusal of any ceremony to mark his death, then a phrase from the era of Victorian doubt may serve. How 'to live in the world' was the challenge confronting those who could not accept the existence of a supreme being and a future world beyond the present one. Charles Lamb (1775–1834), a pre-Victorian, spoke against the tendency in 'Living without God in the World' and, by doing so, conceded its existence. The succession of crises about fossils (in Lyell's *Principles of Geology*, 1830–33) and evolution (Darwin's *Origin of Species*, 1859) was paralleled by declarations of agnosticism (the term was Thomas Huxley's) or atheism or moral dissent from Charles Bradlaugh, Mark Rutherford, Samuel Butler, and scores of others. The independence bravely earned often brought loneliness as its price, exacted through perpetual instalments. The loneliness which sympathetic readers have discerned in Hewitt should not be taken simply as a token of his 'planter identity' in an Ireland increasingly given to 'ancient nation' theorizing.

Regionalism was part of Hewitt's endeavour to tackle social and philosophical problems which, in Northern Ireland, were compounded by sectarianism and partition. To some extent, the Second World War gave him opportunities to extol the province's native resourcefulness. His approach was characteristically discrete, small scale, and suggestive rather than dogmatic. In August 1942, he reviewed Estyn Evans's *Irish Heritage* for *The Bell*.[3] Evans was the son of a Welsh minister, *The Bell* a Dublin-based journal. Privately, Hewitt recorded mildly satirical observations in 'On the Choice of Title, a Rime for Estyn Evans'. Stanza after stanza encapsulated unattractive but unmissable aspects of traditional rural life, each final rhyming line ending with 'the Irish Heritage'. Some time before the notice appeared, the archeo-anthropologist wrote expressing thanks for the notice, observing ambiguously 'I feel you have taken the meat out very adroitly.'[4] In the same year

[1] Boyd was a scholarship boy at the Belfast Academical Institution. He edited *Lagan*, wrote fiction and drama, and was involved in the Lyric Theatre. The second half of Buchanan's life was strongly determined by the Second World War and his extensive combat experience: after it, he retired to Limavady for ten years, during which he served on the Northern Ireland Town and Country Development Committee. He also spent much time in London. He published fiction, autobiography, and poetry.

[2] *Ancestral* includes 'Regionalism, the Last Chance' (*Northman*, 1947) pp. 122–5. For a thoughtful examination of the art critic JH's commitment to regionalism, see Riann Coulter, 'John Hewitt: Creating a Canon of Ulster Art', *Journal of Art Historiography* 8 (December, 2013), <https://arthistoriography.files.wordpress.com/2013/12/coulter.pdf>.

[3] *The Bell* 4, no. 5 (August 1942), pp. 371–4.

[4] UU, Hewitt, Notebook 46; and Box 13, E. E. Evans to JH, 17 May 1942. JH apparently sent a copy of the review in advance of publication.

Hewitt began an immersion in writings about regionalism abroad, especially work by the American, Lewis Mumford (1895–1990), but also by the 'wandering Scot', Patrick Geddes (1854–1932). Superficially, all three points of reference line up without a twist or squiggle. As influences on Hewitt, however, they require individuation. Evans treated rural folk customs grounded in historical continuity, whereas Mumford and Geddes came to focus on the place of cities in a larger social fabric (Roberta gave him Mumford's *Culture of Cities* for his birthday in 1944). The paradox of Hewitt's commitment to regionalism involves his deep attachment to the Irish countryside and his studious engagement with books ('foreign' books) about urban theory, while his regionalism can also be read as a broad investigation of what socialism more exactly ought to deliver. The notebook which preserves the mild satire of Evans also contains 'Salute to the Red Army, from a Script for a Celebration' (February 1943), running to five pages.

Evans was a geographer by training—by 1945, in Belfast, Ireland's first professor of geography—and an archaeologist. His field of operations might be described as the man-made landscape, historically conceived. Mumford had wide interests in the history of American literature, especially the work of Herman Melville. A strong philosophical curiosity runs through his many publications, though this did not impede a scientific concern with the environment and the radical improvement of urban–rural interfaces. The eldest of the three and sometime student of T. H. Huxley, Geddes had trained in biology, written about human sexuality, and pioneered urban planning. He demonstrated strong imperial commitments especially in India, yet also absorbed something of Prince Kropotkin's anarchism.[5] Closer to Hewitt's home, between 1911 and 1916 Geddes was heavily involved in tackling Dublin's chronic health-and-housing problems at the prompting of the Women's National Health Association.[6] In 1914, an itinerant Summer School of Civics was based in the Irish capital, opening on 27 July, under Geddes' personal supervision. By 1912, he had become sufficiently distinguished to be offered a knighthood—declined on 'democratic grounds', despite lacking a regular job. When Norah, his daughter, continued this kind of work in Ireland, Belfast was not overlooked; the Town Planning Exhibition had reached the Ulster Hall in August 1911. Norah Geddes (1887–1967) published a book of poems in 1944. Clearly both Geddes and Mumford shared much with Hewitt, especially on the literary side. But, by the time he came to read their work, Geddes was dead and the American had moved central to debates about the nature of the city, socially and environmentally. The one publication of the Scot's named by Hewitt is a popular study of evolution, written with J. Arthur Thompson and published in 1911. These are events or publications contemporary with his childhood.

[5] See Emily Talen, *The New Urbanism and American Planning: The Conflict of Cultures* (London: Routledge, 2005), p. 219. The seventh chapter (pp. 213–50) deals with 'Regionalism' as one of the four cultures investigated.

[6] Geddes assigned the origins of the environmentalist movement to Germany. See 'Town-Planning: Lecture by Professor Geddes', *Irish Times*, 13 April 1911, p. 7. At home, he was a pioneer of a culturalist Scottish nationalism. For a useful contextualizing of the Women's National Association, see Padraig Yeates, *A City in Wartime: Dublin 1914–1918* (Dublin: Gill and Macmillan, 2011), pp. 31, 33 etc.

In Belfast, he had at least one kindred spirit in the University—George Davie (1912–2007), a Scotsman who taught in the department of philosophy from just after the war until 1959. The Irish Philosophical Club, from a Belfast base, published Davie on his countryman, John Burnet's theory of education. Davie was indebted to Geddes, but ploughed his own furrow, memorably in his one book, *The Democratic Intellect* (1961), published when neither Hewitt nor Davie was still in Belfast. If regionalism could be travestied as a form of deliberately limited specialism—my region right or wrong—Davie strongly commended an educational system in which philosophy and science, the arts, and practical affairs were brought and kept together.[7]

Hewitt could look back to an inter-war moment when he had not been out of touch with the preoccupation with urban planning. In Britain, its notable product was the garden-city movement, which he encountered first hand at Welwyn during the Independent Labour Party's 1933 summer school. It aimed to create moderate-sized towns, geometrically designed for privacy and communicative ease, in which green zones (trees, lawns, hedges, shrubs etc.) were laid down at the outset. An overarching objective was 'the planned community', a phrase innocent enough at the time, compatible with G. D. H. Cole's 'units of social feeling' which Hewitt approved of. By 1940, the ILP was discredited, while the Luftwaffe took on a leading role in British urban design. The local world in which Hewitt turned to Geddes and Mumford offered few opportunities for garden-city dreams. Instead, Donegal was a possibility, Dublin easier to reach. Closer to Belfast were the Glens and what city dwellers termed 'the countryside'. It was the Millars, Andy and Peggy, who set the example of renting a cottage, for they had moved out of Belfast to avoid the bombing (German, not Irish at that point), settling near Ballynure.

What was the countryside? It included both open common land and privately cultivated farms; woodland and pasture and tillage; rivers and lakes, the shoreline. It was far from being a unified or simple alternative to the urban. The Hewitts knew parts of the Ulster countryside very well; the long poem *Conacre* (1943) provides a record, a commentary, and an itinerary of outings near Garron and other parts of Antrim, these all in contrast to 'excreted silt of mill and factory'. But the countryside could not be identified with nature. As the contrasting investigations of Evans and Mumford showed, the landscape (except in very remote 'wilderness' areas) was permeated with human activity, interventions and adaptations occurring throughout millennia. Every weekend, thousands of British and Irish hikers took to 'the countryside' for cheap holidays and an escape from congestion; they were a continuation of those historic and pre-historic interventions of which many bikers and walkers preferred to be oblivious.

Other short pieces followed the notice of *Irish Heritage*. Again for *The Bell* he reviewed John M. Mogey's *Rural Life in Northern Ireland* in April 1948, *Ulster Folklore* by Joanne Cooper Foster in September 1951, and Evans's *Mourne Country*

[7] See Mundo MacDonald, 'The Outlook Tower: Patrick Geddes in Context: Glossing Lewis Mumford in the Light of John Hewitt', *Irish Review* 16 (Autumn/Winter 1994), pp. 53–73.

in July 1952.[8] In all of these publications, the focus is on rural areas little affected by modernization.[9] It can surprise no one disinterring Hewitt's reviews that, behind them, a personal commitment or local odyssey was ongoing—post-war but not post-austerity. In the summer of 1946, John and Roberta first rented a cottage, sometimes called The Lodge, near the gates to a Saint Louis convent just north of Cushendall, sharing it initially with Hester Maybin. Previously they had once or twice rented a stable cottage owned by the Turnly family. In 1980 John Turnly, a landlord turned peaceful republican, was murdered by loyalists in the little Antrim port of Carnlough.[10] The escape from urban bitterness came with no guarantee of perpetual peace.

As they owned no car, the journey involved a bus from Belfast, sometimes having to switch mid-journey to reach Cushendall. Once they reached the coastal village with a sandstone tower at its solitary road junction and the bare hills standing back, the walk to the cottage was less than a mile long. The Sea of Moyle lay to the east, Scotland beyond that, but not far. At points in the upper Glens, if you look east on a good day, Kintyre appears to be part of the same landmass, with no intervening channel.

Between Mumford and Cushendall, the disconnects could not be ignored. The American dealt with huge numbers and vast areas, with the world's greatest megapolis just down the highway, and a few others (Boston, Chicago, Cleveland, Houston, San Francisco) mere hours away by aeroplane. In Cushendall, County Antrim, basic provisions were supplied by locals—milk, butter and eggs (4/- a dozen) by the McDonnell family of Cloughglass. Meat could be bought from the village flesher. These transactions inevitably resulted in close relations with neighbours who, when the Hewitts became habitual visitors, would go in advance to the cottage, light a fire, and ready the place for them. Over the years, the McAllister, McDonnell, and O'Loan households were woven into the fabric of John and Roberta's lives. Occasionally, a youngster from the village or nearby would travel back with them, eager to see the gantries over the shipyards for the first time and to spend a few days amid the clutter and noise of the city.

Mumford struck a note to which Hewitt could morally respond without having the resources for personal implementation. In *The Culture of Cities*, he declared that 'by making the dwelling house a *point of departure* for the new movement in architecture, William Morris symbolically achieved a genuine revolution'. And the American had no qualms in specifying the politics of these ideas—'implicit in them, as he realized in his development as a revolutionary socialist, was the concept of a new social order, oriented not toward mechanization and profits, but toward

[8] *The Bell* 16, no. 1 (April 1948), pp. 69–73; 17, no. 6 (September 1951), pp. 63–4; 18, no. 4 (July 1952), p. 246.

[9] An exception in terms of content was E. R. R. Green's *The Lagan Valley, 1800–1850: A Local History of the Industrial Revolution* (London: Faber, 1949) which JH reviewed in *Tribune on* 29 July 1949. Green had earlier published a monograph on the cotton handloom weavers of Ulster, which was proving useful to the poet in his work on the Rhyming Weavers.

[10] Roberta Hewitt's Diary 1944 (February). For John Turnly (1935–80), see David McKitrick et al., *Lost Lives: The Stories of the Men, Women and Children who Died as a Result of the Northern Ireland Troubles* (Edinburgh: Mainstream, 2004), pp. 829–30.

humanization, welfare, and service'.[11] Here, in a qualified sense and on a very distant horizon, was the objective of *The Irish Democrat* (1937). With the Communist Party of Ireland's decision in 1941 to dodge any embarrassing alliance with the British war effort, Hewitt (who had been no communist, Irish or Great British) found a political credo bolstered by Roosevelt and the New Deal, and yet sympathetic to small-scale human communities. His favourite phrase of Mumford's described a crazed imbalance of 'apoplexy at the centre and paralysis at the extremes', very different to the Irish condition diagnosed by Joyce or indeed Hewitt himself.[12] He appreciated Mumford's eye for amusing detail, as when a craftsman said of a colleague, 'he was quite splendid with an eighteen inch file'.[13] It is striking that, in middle age, Hewitt should admit that Geddes simply led him back to Morris, to whom Mumford frequently referred (not always with deference). Sources of inspiration acknowledged for his regionalism were often connected to that theme indirectly, for example Victor Branford on *Science and Sanity* (1923). In retrospect, he placed his regionalism 'somewhere in the rich realm of Socialist Utopias'.[14] As early as Bloomsday 1926 in *The New Republic*, Mumford had come to the conclusion that 'Utopia is the World War, carried on in a big way, long after the fighting is done. Everyone is registered; everyone takes intelligence tests; everyone is trained; everyone is shown his place'.[15]

In Antrim, at one of the many discreet entrances to the Glens and their uplands, the Hewitts were not the only urban seekers after quiet, nor the only adepts of the arts. Charlie McAuley in Cushendall was a painter of talent. Mrs Mary Stone in the shop read Rabbie Burns, William Cowper, George Crabbe and other Scottish and English poets of the past, but she couldn't stand MacNeice. From Belfast, David Kennedy came down to lecture on the Glens and their literature; Dr McSparron called to the cottage hoping to borrow Robinson Jeffers's poetry. Other friends acquired cottages in north Antrim, notably Jim and Sophie Stewart. By the end of 1947, the Hewitts were still renting what was still called the Porter's Lodge, and finding it difficult to put the rent together.[16] New Year's Eve 1946 did not see them at the cottage, though in the future Midnight Mass became something of a tradition. Patrick Maybin had arrived in Belfast with news of his medical progress—midwifery experience in the Rotunda Hospital, Dublin. He and Maureen McNeill had arranged to marry in the summer. ('She is rather preoccupied with guerrilla warfare on the subject of weddings', Patrick wrote to Roberta more than a year later.[17]) The Hewitts attended a Watch-night service conducted by the Revd Arthur Linton Agnew, a liberal Non-Subscribing Presbyterian, son of a farmer, and husband of a medical doctor. Thus it was early January before John and Roberta

[11] Lewis Mumford, *The Culture of Cities* (London: Secker and Warburg, 1938), p. 406.

[12] See Hewitt, 'Regionalism; the Last Chance' (1947), *Ancestral*, p. 123.

[13] Lewis Mumford, *Technics and Civilization* (London: Routledge, 1934), p. 210. JH marked the passage in his copy of the book.

[14] *North*, p. 144.

[15] Lewis Mumford, *Findings and Keepings: Analects for an Autobiography* (London: Secker, 1976), p. 160.

[16] *Journal*, PRONI, D/3838/4/6, 18 November 1947.

[17] UU, Hewitt, Box 14, R. P. Maybin to Roberta Hewitt 25 February 1948.

arrived in Cushendall to find the cottage or lodge 'not bad'. Roy McFadden and his wife Edith were staying in Cushendun, a few miles to the north, since Christmas, but heavy rain prevented them from reaching the Hewitts. Patrick and Maureen arrived for late Sunday lunch, and then the two couples set out on separate walks. The Hewitts ended up in 'the chapel' or Catholic church, focus of a theme which alternates between them for years:

> I was too conscious of the red light on the altar that blinked and brightened like in an effort to be the heart of Christ—and then [it] went out. I felt that it was bad... both for the worshippers and me and then I was only aware of the building man had raised to God.... The chapel I could pray in must be a beautiful building—with fine careful paintings—altars of fine lace—or else a whitewashed, plain, oak and scrubbed board affair.[18]

William Morris stands at the back of any church Roberta longed for. When the two sets of walkers reunited, they 'cracked till midnight'. Snow began to fall. At the end of the month, the rent was paid and polite complaint made about a leak in the roof. 'We love that place and the wee cottage and it is always worth while for us to be there.' Long devotion to Cushendall involved a number of not always congruent motives. Natural beauty and rural peace were high on the list, being merits or motives in themselves. Unquestionably Belfast, as Charles Lever had remarked of Ireland generally, was a great place to live out of; it provided a salary (but not two); it occasionally welcomed intelligent guests, but spent most of the time chewing its own bifurcated tail and spitting out the mess. The northeast coastal area, from Carnlough to Ballycastle, supported a predominantly Catholic population, and the ratio of majority to minority resembled conditions in the southern Irish state. The tensions and suspicions and (frankly) hatreds which marked south Armagh or east Tyrone did not feature to any extent. The little villages and outlying farms offered associate membership of a community, with little required in return through adaptation or conformity.

That no effort had been made to seek out an area of comparable size, where a large Protestant majority felt secure enough to welcome the stranger, goes without saying. Hewitt's attitude towards Orangeism and ecstatic unionism was unambiguous, and his long established good relations with individuals and institutions in the south bespoke dissatisfaction with the northern establishment. Peggy Black's shopkeeper husband Andy Millar, an independent (Labour inclined) activist with strong commitments to public health, privately wanted cooperation with the south in fighting tuberculosis (Noel Browne's crusade), an Irish scourge to which Geddes in his time had attended. However Millar, like Hewitt, was not wholly trusted by the powers that were. All these temporal matters aside, the religious life of Cushendall positively attracted both John and Roberta, always with major reservations.

'Regionalism, the Last Chance' appeared in *The Northman* during the summer of 1947. Sketching the physico-moral rubble left after the war, including tentative

[18] *Journal TS*, vol. I, p. 21, *c.*January 1946. The order of events is not entirely clear in these pages of the journal, and two or more visits to Cushendall may have been inadvertently conflated.

searches for notions to live by, Hewitt asserts that what is needed to pass beyond the individual and react on the community is a concept which 'must become flesh. This word is regionalism.'[19] Though he proceeds immediately to cite Mumford and to approve, with minor qualifications, the Tennessee Valley Authority (1933), Hewitt's central preoccupations are cultural, specifically literary. Regionalism, he suggests began with the Provencal writer Fréderic Mistral (1830–1914) who set out to revive local mediaeval culture in reaction against the Revolution, centralism and modernity. From a political angle, it is worth noting that, as this French movement spread, it reached Lorraine through the novelist Maurice Barrès, an anti-Semite and fervent nationalist. Avoiding this legacy of Mistral's, Hewitt turns to Scotland (Hugh MacDiarmid and Lewis Grassic Gibbon), to the (very interim) Scottish National Assembly of 1946, and the Labour government's apparent willingness to reform administration north of Hadrian's Wall.

Turning then to his native place, Hewitt avers that 'a number of alert people are aware of a stirring in the dry bones'. He instances the CEMA exhibition of architectural drawings and photographs, the magazine *Lagan* ('almost the recognised organ of Ulster regionalism'), and half a dozen writers including Sam Hanna Bell, John Boyd, Roy McFadden, Joe Tomelty, and himself. Much of this was an exercise in modesty for Hewitt had organized the exhibition committee, and was an associate editor of *Lagan* throughout its short life.[20] Praise came the way of the BBC, the City Museum and Art Gallery (another touch of modesty), and even QUB ('the extra-mural activities of its more responsible personnel'). But when a solution is at last sought, Hewitt soon finds the obstacle to be official parsimony. 'Artists receive a minute crumb of financial support through CEMA, but no paintings, plays or compositions have been commissioned, while the writers are ignored utterly.'[21]

Two bothersome features of Hewitt's proposed regionalism deserve attention here, for it will not win universal approval from his literary followers. One is the vague notion that artists (in the broad sense) and planners should hold the ring, without any reference to democratic institutions. The other is that funding would still require the services of a central government. His options as to the way forward—either 'a federated British Isles or a federated Ireland'—were bound to fall on the resistance of one religious minority or the other, the Protestants of Ireland or the Catholics of Northern Ireland.[22] The condition which made regionalism advisable was exactly the condition which would doom it. Such a judgement is not an endorsement of latter-day dismissals such as those of Barra O Seadhgha, though the reservations of Hewitt's fellow poets will deserve attention.[23]

Religious difference or anxious dithering could surface close to home. In November 1947, an unexpected country guest arrived at the Belfast flat, stayed for

[19] *Ancestral*, p. 122. [20] *Ancestral*, pp. 123–4.

[21] *Ancestral*, p. 125. Gillian McIntosh, *The Force of Culture: Unionist Identities in Twentieth-Century Ireland* (Cork: Cork University Press, 1999), p. 111.

[22] McIntosh, *The Force of Culture*, p. 111.

[23] Barra O Seadhgha, 'Ulster Regionalism; the Unpleasant Facts', *Irish Review* 8 (Spring 1999), pp. 51–64.

lunch and, when John had returned to work, opened up the topic of religion and politics with Roberta. Wesley Lutton had worked in Davy McLean's bookshop. Nervously, he told her she was wasting her time on secular concerns. She admitted a need for the Catholic practices, but disliked Rome Rule and what she called 'the dishonesty of the Organised Church'. He, in her view, seemed to be swallowing the Catholic Church whole. The following January, she heard a Monday guest sermon at All Saints Church, in Elmwood Avenue, delivered by a Moravian minister. 'It's a new business to exchange ideas and broaden Christianity', though she was unimpressed. Both the Hewitts admired Agnew, the Unitarian minister at All Saints, no distance from Mount Charles. However, as opportunities to reach Cushendall arose principally at weekends, any involvement in Sunday routines was steadily reduced.

That same January, John took part in a discussion on Christian morality led by Raymond Calvert (1906–59) whose wife was an independent MP for Queen's University and a supporter of the painter Basil Blackshaw. Calvert was a stockbroker who wrote the comic 'Ballad of William Bloat'. The whole occasion was too Freudian and materialistic in Roberta's eyes. John declared that he couldn't believe in progress, except material progress—we hadn't gained spiritually, and perhaps we couldn't. From this, he moved on to the Fall of Man, which prompted Agnew to tease him about windmills tilted at in youth. Would he soon worry about Predestination?

The cottage appears to have been neglected until well into spring; perhaps the rental arrangement had lapsed. The Hewitts travelled from Belfast on 2 April, finding the place very damp and in need of airing. Nevertheless, the local magic soon began to work. Charlie McAuley's painting had improved since they had last seen him. Pat O'Loan arrived on the Sunday evening, and helped to set a hedge. Later in the month, potatoes were planted and daffodil bulbs, suggesting a more determined occupation. In May, John and Roberta celebrated their fourteenth wedding anniversary. On the day, she carefully noted 'Our marriage has been a happy one. I am sorry we have had no children, but maybe Johnny would not have enjoyed such freedom [to write].'[24] Simultaneously, Patrick Maybin and Maureen McNeill were engrossed in courtship, planning to marry when his medical courses were completed.

Maybin had been known to the Hewitts before the war. John met him while they were students at Queens, and he contributed prose to magazines such as *Lagan* even during his war service abroad. He also wrote poetry, though loathe to publicize the fact. Maureen had spent time in France during 1939, managing to get away days before war was declared. In England she had worked with Alex Comfort (1920–2000), psychologist and poet; McFadden and Comfort had shared an anthology of *Three New Poets* in 1942. Plans for the wedding depended on Patrick finding a practice, somewhere in the countryside by preference. His career had been interrupted by the war, when he served as a captain in the Royal Army Medical Corps, and now he was trying to complete an MA degree and get a specialist

[24] *Journal*, PRONI, D/3838/4/6, 7 May 1948.

midwifery qualification. Their relationship made odd contrasts with the Hewitts', and sparked off moments of self-doubt in Roberta. She remembered Patrick as cool and self-possessed in former times, whereas he had now been so bowled over by Maureen that 'one cannot have an intelligent conversation with him'.

Intelligence, or sophistication, was a topic on which Roberta could deliver any amount of contradictory evidence. Applicant for a paid post in the Edenderry Nursery School where she did voluntary work, she was passed over without notification. 'It rubs in my lack of education and now the Committee must know that I have none.' Back home, she broke down and wept. John was promptly sympathetic, 'and took me to his heart'. Yet the same woman could make the most acute judgements about music and art. Hearing a record of Joan Sutherland, with Malcolm Sargent conducting, she neatly distinguished between the wonderful voice and the accompaniment—'unsound musically'. She could discriminate between the work of painters who were friends and retain their respect and affection. Maureen McNeill, soon to be Maureen Maybin, was younger than Roberta, who defensively argued that 'women as a race are not very intelligent'. On the day she recorded this dismal analysis, she sold a painting for Colin Middleton, and on the next day headed off with John to meet W. B. Stanford (a sleek Greek scholar at Trinity) and the tumultuous Joe Tomelty. Patrick Maylin was hoping for a GP practice at Castlewellan in County Down, but also thought that the impending Health Bill might change medical practice in helpful ways.

Hewitt did not agonise over predestination, but worried greatly about 'the bomb', writing a short story in undramatic response—its narrator is working in retirement on a revised Old Testament chronology.[25] He opposed research in atomic physics, even if designated solely for the peaceful generation of energy. This anxiety, widespread in the early 1950s, carried a degree of irony in Hewitt's case, for the technology which produced the bomb owed much to the work of another Belfast-educated Methodist, the Nobel laureate of 1951, Ernest Walton (1903–95), the first person to split the atom. (Walton's father, a Methodist minister, had on several occasions stayed with RTH and Elinor when John was a child.) Progress, questionable at best, was not an open-ended Absolute, and the intersection of technological advance with moral acuity was poorly lit. 'Mould' was Hewitt's only traceable pursuit of these implications, 'a queer, creepy story' in Roberta's opinion when she typed it up, about the steady invasion of the widowed narrator's house by grey mould on his bread, his books, his walking stick, the fall-out (it is implied) of the Bikini Island nuclear tests. She did emotionally invest in literature, thinking that the world created by the Scottish novelist, Neil Gunn (1891–1973), could defeat the bomb, if and when Gunn's world was fully achieved. But Gunn's fiction—for example, *Bloodhunt* (1952)—increasingly damned modernization, and celebrated the northern Highland community into which he had been born. A Regionalist, yes; but a match for the bomb, hardly.

An experimental timetable at the Museum and Gallery promised to free up two Saturdays per month for John, making the cottage more accessible. In May,

[25] 'Mould' was first published in *The Bell* 1952; see *Ancestral*, pp. 138–45.

Maybin stayed overnight in Belfast with the Hewitts, who visited Roy McFadden and his young wife in Lisburn. Edith was not looking well, the first signal of her mortal illness and a savage death. Progress, once again, was not all. Hewitt read 'Mould' to Maybin who said little in response. These were grim times; fat for cooking was still rationed, the invisible bomb loomed, and the certainties of youth had evaporated. When Bertie Rodgers and a BBC lady arrived unannounced, the Hewitts' only reserve was 'a precious tin of sausages'. At several levels, Cushendall offered not more but better.

Yet weekends elsewhere were possible. Professor Hugh Owen Meredith (1878–1963), retired from Queens since 1943, lived with his second wife near Ballyhalbert on the Ards Peninsula. In June 1948, John and Roberta spent an afternoon with H. O., an economist by profession but also a translator of Greek drama, with an interest in the Russian poet Essenin. They visited a local church to inspect its memorial window.[26] In the evening they walked to Rubane House, where Marie and Wesley Lutton lived on a rented farm. Marie was engrossed in ducks, chickens, and a young goat. Wesley, who had shown signs of going over to Rome, now looked less nervous and more capable of work. Their landlord (or, landlady, Freda Laughton, an English-born poet) was somewhat unstable, unhappy with life, likely to put the farm up for sale. A few decades later, it was an institution for difficult children, some of whom were abused by their religious (Catholic) overseers, and the object of official enquiry.[27]

Loyally, the following weekend (26 June) was spent in Antrim at the cottage. The Belfast Gallery had decided to buy one of Charlie McAuley's pictures which John had originally hoped Zoltan Frankl might like. He then wrote the appropriate letter offering the picture for £20, and left it for Charlie to transcribe. On the Sunday, Roberta cleaned up her sister's occasional cottage where John's mother would take a summer break. When the Hewitts got back to Mount Charles, Maybin and McNeill were already installed. They too were to have a McAuley picture, 'Wet Day in Cushendall', as a wedding present. John paid the artist £5 for it. The new week began with Roberta officially greeting the Sadlers's Wells Ballet Company at the railway station. She thought their 'Sylphides' (Chopin and Fokine) poor, but 'The Haunted Ballroom' (Toye and de Valois) good—she saw it again later. At the end of the weekend, two of the McDonnell women folk travelled back to Belfast and were escorted up the Falls Road to their part of a town they scarcely knew.

Division and divisiveness were everywhere. The Hewitt archive at PRONI contains the copy of a letter which the poet sent to an unidentified newspaper, responding to sour Unionist comment on political change down south. He specified

[26] Meredith had published *The Economic History of England; a Study in Social Development* (London: Pitman, 1939) and *Four Dramas of Euripides: Hecuba, Heracles, Andromache, Orestes* (London: Allen and Unwin, 1937). He had been part of the Apostles' circle at Cambridge.

[27] See Howley's *Follies and Garden Buildings of Ireland* (1993) for an account of the place. A poem by Laughton (born 1907) is included in Gerald Dawe, ed., *Earth Voices Whispering: an Anthology of Irish War Poetry 1914–1945* (Belfast: Blackstaff, 2008), p. 162. In an earlier generation, William Lutton (1807–70) had compiled *Montiaghisms* (Armagh: Armagh Guardian, 1923), a list of County Down dialect words and phrases of the kind Hewitt relished.

an editorial about Sean MacBride, in which the anonymous journalist sneered at the 'pseudo-republic of peasants and poets'. Hewitt's reply drew together his older radicalism and his more recent regionalism, with a spicing of tart irony:

> In Ulster our greatest industry is still that of agriculture, and this calling of agricultural worker, or "peasant", is in no sense dishonourable, in ours and in any other instance. The presence of poets is, I had thought, something to be desired in any community, save perhaps in Plato's Republic.... Criticise Eire politicians by all means, but not, I beg of you, in terms which might suggest that we imagine ourselves to be more Philistine than they.[28]

From an increasing engagement with the local community around Cushendall, he knew something of the farmer's life, toil in the fields, the skills of cultivation, the culture of farmhouse and village.

The church of Saint Thomas, Eglantine Avenue stood at the other side of Belfast from where the McDonnells were staying. On 7 July, Patrick Maybin and Maureen McNeil were married in this suburban bulwark of Anglicanism, though both came from Presbyterian families. The groom had stayed overnight at Mount Charles; the bride's parents lived on Wellington Park, close to Malone Road. Hewitt wore his somewhat ageing grey suit to the wedding, having refused to buy a new one. The McNeill family turned out in strength, as did the Maybins. John and Roberta were favoured with a pew near the front of the congregation, though they felt the service to be formal and impersonal. Other guests included Dr Tom Murphy of Sligo, and his wife Nora (a sister of Patrick Maybin), with whom John stayed when he attended W. B. Yeats's second interment in September 1948. After the reception, some of the guests retired to Mount Charles where the bride and groom were changing into tweeds for their motoring honeymoon in the south.

The McDonnell women were still up the Falls and, on the twelfth of July as around it did come, Roberta collected them from their lodgings, took them to the museum (presumably for a private viewing organized by John), and then back to the Hewitts' place for tea. Mrs McDonnell was overawed by the arty living room, books and pictures everywhere, but the kitchen was too small for entertaining. On their way back to the Falls, Mrs McDonnell observed the Orangemen in bowler hats following the kilted fife-and-drum bands—all very respectable provided there was no trouble. Anti-Catholic discrimination in Belfast employment arose in their chat, Roberta pointing out that the best-qualified librarian had been passed over several times while unqualified Protestants were promoted. There were faults on both sides, as with the Catholic refusal to integrate the Mater Hospital into the health services. More reflectively, she wrote 'I am afraid of the narrowness of the Catholic Church altho' as a religion it has a strong appeal.'[29] Three days later she and Mrs McDonnell were off on a shopping spree.

Later in July 1948, the Hewitts reached Cushendall once more, sunbathing and reading in the cottage garden. John cut his thumb with the shears. Mary McDonnell, aged twelve, travelled back to Belfast as reward for winning a scholarship to secondary

[28] PRONI, D/3838/7/24. [29] *Journal*, PRONI, D/3838/4/6, 12 July 1948.

school. She had never heard of a zoo, and was alarmed by the strange animals she met. The Hewitts bought her shoes at Andy Millar's shop. The first weekend of August brought Colin Middleton, Kathleen his wife, and their son to the cottage at the convent gates. Impressed by the McDonnell farm and home, Middleton struck a 'back to the land' attitude. The late and rainy summer had its rural duties and relaxations, the communal haymaking, and a hurling match with Hewitt attended. Even Arthur Agnew looked in.

This was the extended summer holiday which brought John and Roberta closer to the local economy than any weekend stay-over. A mixed party of Hewitts and Millars crossed over a viaduct into Glendun. They moved to no fixed pattern or timetable, pausing to look here or listen there, dallying and spurting in their progress. Scores of wild raspberries and fewer blackberries distracted them from the way ahead. Roberta was confident she knew a house where they could expect to get tea, but after several false turns admitted she was wrong. However, the sight of two men working turf on the mountain renewed their hopes. The older man welcomed them, pointed to his still warm fire, and handed over teapot and water. 'The sun came out and the world was a grand place.'

John struck up a conversation with their open-air host who, it emerged, knew who they were and where they stayed. He could even name the burglar of their cottage some time past. This may have brought more relief than localized anger, for the Hewitts suspected that occasional break-ins were more sinister, the intrusion of Special Branch or other nosy authorities. Roberta drily conceded that 'it might appear to them that our cottage could be used in some way for unloyal purposes'.[30] After tea, everyone moved on, surprised to discover an abandoned railway carriage in the middle of nowhere with, inside, a woebegone stove and table, one original carriage seat, and a tin for boiling water. This peculiar excess of provision struck them forcefully. All round in Glenaan, heather and heath thrived, but very few wild flowers. A farmer in the distance with a good dog rounded up sheep with a few silent gestures.

Back in Cushendall at about 4 p.m., they stopped for more tea with the Millars, then went home. John read aloud from R. S. Thomas's *The Stones of the Field*. She darned socks, and gradually heard noises of pencil on paper and the gurgling of his pipe that indicated the early stages of composition. 'When I lift my head his eyes are always fastened on me. It used to disturb me but now I know his old head is churning and I am a live anchor for his eyes.' This was the first new poem for months.[31] On the Sunday following, Keith Millar and a friend improvised a game of cricket. Then, after lunch and heavy showers John and Roberta went out and about for a dander, meeting Rose McDonnell on their way. Alice, her sister, was listening to a Gaelic football match on the wireless and could not be disturbed. Later, she brought in a spinning wheel—it had been her mother's—from the barn and the sisters demonstrated the old craft.

[30] *Journal*, PRONI, D/3838/4/6, 20 August 1948, where Roberta by naming the culprit, a local man, effectively scotches any theory of security services' involvement.

[31] *Journal*, PRONI, D/3838/4/6, 20–3 August 1948.

Alice McDonnell's farm at Ballybrack went to work the next day with a vengeance—lint-pulling, an arduous task requiring a large work force. Again tea. Eight men with their caps stowed under their chairs ate soda bread, butter and jam:

> The kitchen has a battered dresser with lovely old cracked plates, a wooden bench ran from door to fire with bags and ropes and what not, a pile of turf at the side of [the] large blackened hearth... full of chirpling crickets in the evening and a cement floor. Don't look at the Glen kitchen if your folio of Japanese prints is your standard of beauty—the only glimmer of colour is the bad religious reproduction—but these people are fine and I wouldn't change them for your aesthetes in a London pub.[32]

This scene and the Hewitt view of it could be taken as a late example of the Yeatsian dream of Innisfree, the contrast of an imagined Irish rural adequacy with gross metropolitan excess. Though John rarely introduces the theme of religious difference into the poems—or, rather, he avoids or fails to deliver any non-Catholic position—it concerns Roberta at repeated moments in her journal. Behind Yeats, the teaching of William Morris is traceable—'Have nothing in your house that you do not know to be useful, or believe to be beautiful', recently quoted by Mumford.[33] Morris's Guild Socialism had been in communion with Christian Socialism, but some of the implications of their implied mediaevalism had become tarnished in the twentieth century. There were deeper chasms between the Hewitts and their kindly neighbours than either side might admit. In the McDonnells' eyes, was the religious artefact useful or beautiful? But at least, the existence of a difference was conceded, even if in the form of envy.

The Glens had their solitaries, just like Wordsworth's Lake District. Having visited Ossian's Grave, the two Hewitts crossed swampy ground into mist and heavy rain. At a cottage, where they asked for a drink of water, an old woman assailed or greeted them, who shook hands at length, announced that her blind husband and an old aunt were 'bedfast', that her only son had drowned eleven years earlier coming home from 'the pictures', and her daughter had an illegitimate child. To cap all, she declared that the water was bad. Later enquiries established that the woman was 'simple'; that her husband had married her for the farm she owned and he was now drinking both of them out of it.

The evening of this encounter on the hillside, John's story 'Mould' was broadcast on the wireless. The text had been cut in the BBC by Rayner Heppenstal, with the loss of Hewitt's allusion to the atomic bomb, jeopardizing its underlying theme of society in terminal disintegration. Mrs Stone, however, was enjoying John's *Conacre*. Visiting Cushendun a day or so later, they found it distressingly full of Belfast people. The holidays were virtually over. Back at Mount Charles, John found proofs for *New Irish Poets 1948*, a New York anthology. Roberta turned down an invitation to speak about the novelist Joyce Cary; the Young Ulster Society would be better off, she declared, reading Cary than listening to her.

Hewitt was more responsive to the young. From August 1948 to January of the following year, he contributed a six-part series of articles to the *Ulster Young Farmer*,

[32] *Journal*, PRONI, D/3838/4/6, 23 August 1948.

[33] Mumford, *The Culture of Cities*, p. 407.

probably unaware that even the Ulster Young Farmers were, it seems, monitored at some level of state authority. The topic was poetry, and the trick was to slip it in among discussions of flax policy and ads for milking machines. He began by quoting 'The Auld Wife's Address to Her Spinning Wheel', written a century earlier. He invited readers to send him samples of their own work. He propounded folk wisdom and advised 'turning again to our own ways of speech and thought'. In a later instalment, he declared that 'the poetry of the English-speaking peoples has been, in every generation, a turning again to the life of the countryman, as a fresh starting point for the development of living and realistic thought'.[34] The last instalment began with a reference to his attempt at lint-pulling the previous summer, and the rest of the article was given over to the resulting poem. The tensions, perhaps even contradictions, underlying these pieces are evident enough—attachment to traditional speech and skills, commendation of 'realistic thought' and its development. Though he invoked William Barnes of Dorset and Robert Frost of New England, he kept his distance from local examples—Patrick Kavanagh, for example.[35]

Yet Hewitt's links with southern Ireland continued to grow. His poem 'Overture to Regionalism' was broadcast on the Athlone wavelength at the beginning of September.[36] Later in the month, he and Nelson Browne set off for Sligo as the northern PEN delegates at Yeats's second funeral. While he was away from home, Roberta encountered a fellow member of the Northern Irish Labour Party who advocated fighting the Unionists with their own (corrupt) tactics. Horrified, she was also self-critical for not playing a more active role. The occasion of this exchange was a nationalist celebration of 1798—150 years earlier—which the Belfast Corporation had tried to prevent. Police were called in, and onlookers pushed around.

John's pilgrimage to Drumcliff turned out to be a semi-comic affair. Austin Clarke wondered aloud if one was permitted to smoke in a Protestant graveyard; Hewitt and Browne failed to change trains at Omagh and travelled on to Derry, where they had to stay overnight. At the funeral, Valentin Iremonger made a point of introducing John to Sean MacBride, Dublin's newly installed Minister for External Affairs. He sensed the minister's intelligence but remained wary of republican overtures. Others whom he met from the republican side included Rob Graham, Patrick McCartan, and Ernie O'Malley. In Belfast, a letter from Frederick Muller's office in London arrived during his extended absence; this at last gave some reliable promise of the breakthrough: publication of *No Rebel Word*. Hewitt wrote up an account of the Yeats ceremonies, which later found its way into *A North Light*.[37]

Trips to the cottage had been infrequent during the autumn. In mid-October, a week fell free of gallery responsibilities. Blackberries were still to be found, and

[34] John Hewitt, 'Poetry and You', *Ulster Young Farmer* 2, no. 8 (August 1948), p. 21; 'Programme for Poetry', *Ulster Young Farmer* 2, no. 10 (October), p. 15.

[35] Hewitt later wrote on the Monaghan poet, 'The Cobbler's Song: a Consideration of the Work of Patrick Kavanagh', *Threshold* 5, no. 1 (1961), pp. 42–51.

[36] The poem went through several revisions, with as many changes of title. See Ormsby, pp. 661–2.

[37] *North*, pp. 181–8.

potatoes dug on McDonnell's farm. On the Monday, Roberta paid rent due to Sister Mary Oliver, getting some vegetables in return. That evening, John studied Burns at length while she read short stories by Tolstoy—'we would need to realize [his] attitude to life now'. Graham Greene's *Heart of the Matter* bored her at first, but gradually she found it 'impelling'. Post from some magazine editors was now addressed to Hewitt at the cottage. Shown the poem 'Lint', Mrs McDonnell held it up to the oil lamp and read it to the bitter end. Back in Belfast, the Hewitts fretted about the forthcoming collection of poems, which finally arrived in time for the poet's birthday.

Reviews were sparse. Roberta sniffed at *The Northern Whig*'s perceptive notice, which referred to 'descriptive writing, cool, detached, assembling phrases justly, appraising, examining, analysing but never affectionate even for the thing he cares for most'. She wondered if the reviewer, a Jewish woman, was 'rooted enough' to feel Hewitt's love of Ulster. Year's end was celebrated in Belfast with the McCanns (George and Mercy), Bertie Rodgers, his wife Marie, and a few others. That was 30 December. Somebody sang 'The Ball of Inverness', or a version of it, which Roberta silently deplored. She replied with 'Three Lovely Lassies from Bannion' and other pieces known from Delia Murphy recordings. Marie Rodgers, who had passed out on the couch, woke and sang 'The Soldier's Song' (southern Ireland's national anthem) 'any time she was allowed'.[38] The Hewitts got back to Mount Charles about 2 a.m. On New Year's Eve they took the familiar bus to Cushendall. John wished for snow, but it stayed on higher ground.

Division of the week into days spent in the Gallery and a weekend in the cottage was not always feasible. If Hewitt was wanted by the BBC, the appointment could eat into time allotted to the rural life. In June 1949, Roberta travelled ahead of him to Cushendall with Kate Middleton, who did not settle. The two women argued about regionalism, Kate regarding it as incompatible with her communist dream of one world united; Roberta wanted both options. The weather was dreadful, but a favourite pigeon she was mothering reappeared like a biblical sign. Apprehensive in the wake of a few break-ins, she stubbornly declined the offer of company overnight from one of the McDonnells. After the guest's departure, Hewitt took the Saturday bus northwards for what Roberta expected to be a long weekend together. 'He had missed me very much and had needed me physically and spiritually—at least I hope so. He was most unusually amorous[.] I was quite surprised—I have often felt neglected physically as weeks go by, but now I am sure it is partly my fault—I am exhausted at night.[39]

For once Belfast was now the interlude, and during their few days in the city John found a few books in a sale which he had been searching for. Roberta maintained her pottery practice though suffering from lumbago, and both visited Ann and Davy McLean. Still faithful vendor of *The New Statesman*, McLean had not weathered well the disillusions of Spain, Stalin's pact with Hitler, and the onset of

[38] *Journal*, PRONI, D/3838/4/6, 22 December 1948. The reviewer was Ray Rosenfield, one of two sisters who wrote extensively in Belfast newspapers.

[39] *Journal*, PRONI, D/3838/4/6, 4 June 1949.

a Cold War. Once idealist and socialist, he had become (in Roberta's view) a man who lived to make money which he spent on drink. At a Highway to Life exhibition, the Hewitts met Cherith Boyd, a young woman accompanied by Rowell Friers, who had done two years at art school. She hung on John's every word, seeking his opinion about painting, poetry, and the rest. Roberta initially wrote her down as 'a lovely child'. On the wireless, John listened to the poet George Buchanan expounding regionalism, and complained about other people getting fees for ideas which he, Hewitt, had urged for Northern Ireland back in 1942. But the weekend brought the Hewitts once again to Cushendall in glorious weather. Sunday 26 June was 'a really lovely day'. Roberta lay nude on her stomach behind the cottage, allowing the heat to ease her painful back, and reading Dan Davin on the topic of possessive mothers.

Early July served merely as prelude to The Twelfth. John was trying to mark Museum Association exam papers, fussing over much about results and averages. Roberta had begun E. H. Carr's intimate account of Alexander Herzen (1812–70) and his circles domestic, sexual, and revolutionary, only to discover a passage which brought her to a halt: 'It is said that only the young or the sick—sick in body or soul—keep diaries.'[40] On 9 July, she escaped to the cottage, and John joined her bringing his review copy of Rodney Green's *The Lagan Valley*. The Millars, Andy and Peggy, were also in summer residence, Andy convalescing. A carload of relatives drove up the avenue to inspect the Convent Gardens, as good a way to greet the Twelfth as one could safely devise. But the week brought everyone home to the city where Roberta needed to stock up with inhalable penicillin for stubborn catarrh. On the way home from the pharmacy, she met 'Johnny's lovely wee fan', and they talked. The Lord Mayor passed in his official car, and raised his hat, setting Roberta to worry about recognition and worth, and the vanity of wishing her husband better recognized for his achievements. 'God help us all, it is hard to resist laying up a little treasure and risking rust and decay.' Guests that week at Mount Charles had included Billy Adair (who had rhymed bits of the Communist Manifesto for the Russian Red Cross) and his wife.

Elsewhere in the extended Black family, shifts of emphasis were occurring. Lilian's husband, Norman Kirkham, had been an ordained Presbyterian minister who worked during the war in an aircraft factory, then for the Ministry of Pensions. For three years, he had been studying for the Unitarian ministry, and was now (in 1949) called to a church (Ballyhalbert) on the Ards Peninsula. Though officially Hewitt was the radical of their circle, others adopted positions which by Ulster standards were decidedly liberal. Public health acted as a post-war catalyst, provided by the Labour government in Westminster and resisted in Unionist dug-outs across the province. Campaigns to eradicate tuberculosis or to provide for children with special needs won practical support from Andy Millar and Roberta Hewitt. John Hewitt took some personal risk in regularly visiting a boy in Belfast, dying of tuberculosis but passionately interested in poetry. Dr Maybin pioneered the linking of social workers and medical practitioners. Dorothy Maybin was an almoner in

[40] E. H. Carr, *The Romantic Exiles* (Harmondsworth: Penguin, 1949), p. 285.

the Belfast City Hospital. Keith Millar would become a hospital-based doctor and radiologist.

Roberta's personal health had long been irregular, and fear of (or onset of) the menopause added urgency and pathos. The minor problems were highly varied—tingling or numbness of the fingers, infections generating pus, back pain, shingles, persistent heavy colds, and, in 1951, gynaecological factors requiring hospitalization. She repeatedly felt extremely tired. In her journal she often fondly acknowledges John's sympathy and support, but also points to difficulties between them. In mid-August 1949, Maureen Maybin qualified as a doctor, and called to Roberta's nursery school to deliver the good news. Back in Mount Charles that evening the Hewitts had 'a very serious row', and Roberta retired to the back bedroom 'and stayed all night'.[41] The next evening, they entertained guests, though Roberta was bilious during the night. Next day 'still very sick and have not solved the problem with Johnny, he is being very kind but won't discuss our one big problem properly, I feel, which is that of sexual relations, and I feel very neglected'.[42] A faithful Irish Protestant of the old school in this if nothing else, Hewitt made no traceable further comment either to his wife or to a confidant, professional or personal.

On 2 September her doctor diagnosed over-work and advised a good rest in advance of their Italian holiday. On the way through London, they took in 'Fading Mansions', adapted from the French by Donagh MacDonagh, 'lovely wee theatre but very vile play'. Afterwards, they met up with John's sister Eileen, her husband (Norman Todhunter) and their two daughters. Life outside Belfast seemed cheering, even if the London café offered little nourishment and the waiter was German. At their hotel, John and Roberta took to their separate beds and slept till seven in the morning. 'Then I went into Johnny's bed and slept till 9 o'clock.'

The Italian interlude came courtesy of the Belfast PEN club, for which Hewitt acted as delegate with Roberta always at his side. It takes its place among the other foreign holidays similarly funded. On their way home, they stopped off in Paris to look at galleries. At the *Orangerie*, Roberta particularly singled out Paul Gauguin's 'Jacob and the Angel'. A theme often treated by painters including Chagall, Delacroix, Maurice Denis, and (at home) Colin Middleton, it may have acted as a private symbolism for her. Hewitt, oddly enough, drew on it for a poem beginning 'I wrestled with my father in a dream.' The Delacroix fresco, in the Parisian church of Saint Sulpice, was familiar to him since the early excursions to Europe with R. T. Hewitt. It, more schematically than the Gauguin, presents the immovable human and the irresistible angelic figures, but the story came to all Ulster Protestants (even liberal ones) from the Book of Genesis. Delacroix' struggle between the two figures has an unmistakable dance-like erotic dimension, climactic but unresolved. Back in Belfast, Roberta soon quarrelled on Black family matters but also on getting her dreams interpreted (possibly by Marie Rodgers). In connection with the dreams, she noted severely how Peggy 'forgets that I went to Canada when I was young'. All in all, the autumn of 1949 brought up a great deal of traumatic

41 *Journal*, PRONI, D/3838/4/6, 17 August 1949; emphasis in the original.
42 *Journal*, PRONI, D/3838/4/6, 19 August 1949.

material from her life. Much of her forty-fifth birthday was spent in bed 'with old cold', John acting as nurse and cook. The old cold persisted for a month.

In November, John began a campaign to revive the reputation of a nineteenth-century evangelical poet Anne Lutton (1791–1881), a native of Moira, County Down. At the Smithfield market (a bookman's Mecca, firebombed in 1974), he had come across a collection of hers, published in Dublin in 1829. Academic work on Ulster writers provided the official context for his excitement, but Lutton in fact touched off half a dozen interests. She had been a Methodist like his own immediate line; she was largely self-taught; she preached exclusively to women in large gatherings, swollen (it was said) by men in drag anxious for her Alleluias. She played a part among the earlier kin of Wesley Lutton, sometime an employee in the Progressive Bookshop and sometime a pilgrim moving towards Rome. Roberta had mixed feelings—no, not really mixed. Of the regional poets generally she inwardly exclaimed 'God knows their poetry is unreadable.' And Lutton was terrible. Husband and wife responded in complementary ways. In her view, John 'believes that the spirits of the Ulster Bards know that he is caring for them'. Despite her greater critical acuity, she loved him for a devotion to their cause 'but my love is not strong enough to read these rows of poetry lining this room. He has been so kind since this last dose of shingles, I am ashamed. I hope I don't wear him out.'[43] On 22 November, she met a hospital doctor who had treated her in 1935. The next day her dwarfish, handicapped mother came to help in the flat—advice, nothing practical—and Roberta felt her own advancing old age, and recorded the first evidence of 'the change of life'.

She sent a copy of Patrick Kavanagh's novel *Tarry Flynn*, as regionalist as anyone could hope for, to Hester Maybin, and a cheque to Norman Kirkham for his Ballyhalbert church. She saw *The Third Man* in the cinema, directed by Carol Reed. John was on the air live, and the painter Paul Nietsche called to Mount Charles to listen, and fell asleep. Hewitt was talking about Ulster heroes—William Allingham, Francis Hutcheson, John Lavery, Robert Lynd, Forrest Reid, John Toland—not the hard-headed businessmen approved by government. The weekend was spent in Belfast. On the Saturday evening, Cherith Boyd turned up at the Hewitts' flat, delaying their departure for a party at George and Mercy McCann's. Roberta had begun to articulate (at least to herself) the discovery that Cherith ('lovely child') was 'very struck' on Hewitt. They finally got rid of her, and caught up with the party. MacNeice was blind drunk, but his wife, Hedli Anderson, sang. Others of 'the gang' included Sam Hanna Bell and his wife, Tomelty, Nietsche, and John Midgely, husband of Freda Laughton. Also present, as somebody's guest, was Pat Maguire ('the spiv detective') suspected by Roberta of keeping bohemians under surveillance.

The cottage in December took second place to festive preparations and overdue commitments. John Luke finished the under-paintings for a major project commissioned through Hewitt. These were wonderful; 'the horse is grand—a lovely group of three dancers to the centre left'. Gradually, Roberta's franker opinions

[43] *Journal*, PRONI, D/3838/4/6, 26 November 1949.

emerged, 'a horrid female with unreal hands and no reason to be there'. At the initial viewing, she kept quiet while John admired the drawing skill, the technical this-and-that. Alone together, they agreed it was 'beautifully dead'. Luke stayed the night, which compromised discussion. But afterwards in bed, the Hewitts admitted to each other their disappointment in the picture—'Johnny very sad, as he had pushed for this.'[44]

Next day (a Friday) Wesley Lutton dropped in expecting lunch while Luke returned from a formal meeting with J. E. S. Stendall at the gallery. The Director had liked the under-drawings, so the commission was safe. Lutton lingered till close on 6 p.m. That evening, Roberta and John were due at the Malone Avenue flat occupied by Cherith and her sister, a return-match for the lovely child's supposedly uninvited visit to Mount Charles. Mrs Hewitt's account of the event is a triumph of wifely reason:

> They are nice wee females with an awful drawl in the speech[. W]e talked for ages about two fat black cats on which they dote—Cherith is much better company away from her sister—she is very intelligent and we saw a picture of... hers which looked very good indeed. But she makes the most awfully fatuous remarks... 'Oh, Mr Hewitt, your feet look like an advertisement for shoes[. I]t must be lovely to have nice big feet—don't you think so Mrs Hewitt...'. She sat at times and just gazed at Johnny in close up film-like admiration—I think she is a bit of a humbug in flattery but Johnny really loved it... you never know your man. He said coming home it was quite a new experience and he liked it.... I must confess I have pangs of something akin to jealousy and wonder if this could develop—I tell myself it would be good for him and he was very long suffering with me when I was a bit infatuated with Robert McCoubrey in 1939. Robert came at a time when I was finding sheer intellectual life a bit of a strain and he took me out in his car and bought me nice meals, wine and boxes of chocolates and he was just good fun and never a serious thought.[45]

The year was winding down. Hewitt's disappointment with John Luke's great project sank deeper and deeper. Roberta had another hospital session for X-ray and an injection of her swollen finger. Christmas in Belfast was the usual family affair. On 27 December, they finally got away to Cushendall. The cottage porch was swimming, the ceilings inside flaked and partly fallen in, the grate full of soot, and everywhere the droppings of rats. Yet the magic still worked and, after a marathon of scrubbing and scalding, they sat down to a grand supper. Afterwards, John finished a paper on the Ulster Bards, and Roberta read Marjorie Bowen's *Glen of Weeping*, a novel about the Battle of Glencoe (1695) which 'white-washed' King William. And so to bed, together for close on twelve hours. Then, 'a good winter day, very grey, cold but dry—a healthy day for soil'.

They visited the O'Donnell household for 'tea and crack' on the evening of 30 December, grateful for the warm reception and part exasperated by the long

[44] *Journal*, PRONI, D/3838/4/6, 8 December 1949.

[45] *Journal*, PRONI, D/3838/4/6, 9 December 1949. Having been made a prisoner of war by the Japanese in Malaya, McCoubrey died in 1945.

rituals of gossip, a fresh pot of tea, and other repetitions. In her journal, Roberta made an unusually detailed report of her husband's late night work:

> Johnny writes a poem now about his planter ancestors taking the land from the Irish and says as he reads it that he only realises now that why we cling to Britain is because we are scared—he laughed and said 'Everybody realises that but me, only Johnny didn't know in the whole of Ulster.[46]

However casual her jottings may appear, Roberta pinpointed the commencement of a major reorientation in Hewitt's outlook. The emphasis on immediacy ('now... now') suggests that the poem in question had some origin in the somewhat over-long evening in the O'Donnells' kitchen. In part the contrast was between 'rooted' people and weekend visitors, between those who knew more about reading the weather and the subtle movements of beasts in a haggard than about novels or art history. On that basis, conventional wisdom gives first prize to the Hewitts. But, the O'Donnells were not merely rooted (in some 'Yeatsian' sense), they were now hereditary possessors of the land, however recent the legislation to that effect might be. A usurpation, or plantation, had been reversed, if not in terms of state power or social prestige (these might follow) then certainly in terms of local substance. The 'we' of Roberta's summary quickly declines into 'only Johnny', the solitude of an observer who knows he has missed the point.

On New Year's Eve, they walked in the district, taking note of some houses built by the local authority. Roberta felt a tug of new-home-making—'not really as long as we are allowed to stay on [at the cottage.] It would be very hard to give up this wee damp, rat-infested inconvenient little house.' Midnight Mass disappointed both of them. Roberta insisted that she was *interested*, but her god never came near her heart 'during the service'. John missed the cadences of the King James Bible. Having parted from their neighbours, he declared that they should have gone to 'the little non-conformist church where we belong. We hoped we would find something in the ritual that we could identify ourselves with those people, but it has made the cleavage evident—there can be no real communication between these hill farmers and ourselves.' Hewitt then began the poem first called 'The Colonists' and later famous as 'The Colony' (see 'Break for Text II').[47]

On Saint Patrick's Eve 1950, Hewitt and the painter-photographer Nevill Johnston (1911–99) recorded a discussion about regionalism. When he listened to the playback, he exclaimed 'The thing I enjoy most next to giving a talk is listening to myself.' While his reading of Mumford was serious, and his engagement with the *Ulster Young Farmer* more than just an outlet during the long delays before *No Rebel Word*, Hewitt later conceded that he had no ambition to launch a campaign. 'I laid down no rules, no chart or time-table for its realisation, content simply to make propaganda for the idea.'[48] Nor did he ever collect his writings and speeches on the regionalist theme. The latest experience of Midnight Mass had been disheartening even though the McDonnells and O'Loans were warm company, excellent

[46] *Journal*, PRONI, D/3838/4/6, 30 December 1949.
[47] *Journal*, PRONI, D/3838/4/6, 31 December 1949.
[48] *North*, p. 144.

neighbours. Yet Hewitt's attitude was not one of rejection. The gulf existed, no point in deluding oneself. Yet the desire to find 'something in the ritual' was not denied. The cottage was damp, but preferable to the new council houses. What his regionalism did for Hewitt was to provide a framework in which he could address the actuality and the desire together. The revision of 'The Colonists' into 'The Colony' enacted some of the implications. The colonists or planters or settlers constituted a single group marked off from 'the others'. A colony, on the other hand, requires and incorporates both, though on terms which demand scrupulous examination.

Could these ideas travel? In March 1950, PEN in Dublin gave Hewitt a platform to advance 'The Case for Ulster Regionalism in Verse and Prose'. His historical prelude was diplomatically negative—Ulster had largely missed the Norman Invasion and, when it came to the later plantations, not the English but the Scots provided the influx. The resulting social structure, he argued, was

> more democratic; the small-holder replaced the peasant, and the "big house" was of less importance [than in the southern provinces]. The literature of a large section of the people is Burns and the Bible, instead of Celtic myth and legend.... The land tends to be a main source of inspiration to the Northern writer, and Belfast has not the predominant position in intellectual life that Dublin has in the South.[49]

No doubt somebody in the audience challenged the implication that southerners had neglected the land as a theme, or queried the perspective of those in Ulster who were not descended from planters or outside settlers. The newspaper reported no disagreements. The vote of thanks was proposed by Seumas O'Sullivan, editor of *The Dublin Magazine* and, by background, a Dublin Methodist; seconded by Joseph Johnston, a northerner by birth who championed a national economics for Ireland. Hewitt's regionalism did not go unchallenged by artists remote from the national or unionist camps. Nevill Johnson, English-born but settled in Ulster since 1934, objected in the name of something much closer to modernism. Johnson had befriended John Luke at the beginning of the war, and thus was part of Hewitt's Belfast circle.[50]

Roberta was quite unwell, stomach upsets, pins-and-needles not only in her hands and feet but also her cheeks. The doctor confined her to bed for a week. John consequently went to the Glens on his own, having agreed to lecture students at Cushendun. The following weekend, they both stayed at the cottage. The McDonnell family had contracted measles—Patrick was 'clad with the spots'. Domestic arrangements in the farm kitchen did not impress the Hewitts. On Sunday 9 April, the weather turned stormy. They stayed inside the cottage, reading. It was a moment of decisive adjustment. Hewitt came up with a definition, 'Great poetry is the recurrent and personal discovery and phrasing of the commonplace.'

[49] *Irish Times*, 21 March 1950, p. 5. Three months earlier, in December 1949, Hewitt and May Morton had been guests of the Dublin centre of Irish PEN at a dinner in Jury's Hotel, representing the Belfast centre.

[50] See *Irish Times*, 24 March 1950. Johnson subsequently settled in Dublin, and left behind a valuable photographic record of the city in the 1950s.

Patrick Kavanagh would have agreed, but expressed himself more forcefully. A few weekends later, he told Roberta that, as he walked back from Cushendun, he felt himself really dedicated to poetry. A line from Wordsworth came to him 'I made no vows but vows were then made for me.'[51] She enquired if being alone in the cottage would help. At the end of the month, he stumbled on a reference to himself in Howard Sergeant's *The Cumberland Wordsworth*.

Cushendall was not simply a rural village, secluded from urban excess. It too had its days of popular celebration. First communion was a major event in the calendar of Irish Catholics, and processions were organized on the first Sunday of June. Virtually the entire population of the village assembled on the shore, with children ranked in age, and the priest under a canopy of papal colours pronouncing a benediction. John and Roberta looked on. The local flute band provided music, and she recalled a line of John's—'and sunburnt youth carrying the banners with singing into the temple'.[52] On the way back to their cottage, they met an old crippled woman on a stick who thanked John for references to Cushendall on the wireless. Roberta admired Miss Cochran's wee cottage, and she replied, 'I think I'm good for another six years, you might have a chance of it then.'[53] The hawthorn by the roadside was at its peak, 'every branch seemed a brance of foam'. To cap a splendid day, butter was locally available without restriction for the first time since the war.

Marjorie Bowen arrived in Belfast; she and Roberta discussed Kafka, persecution of the Jews, and the Catholic Church. The novelist was very bitter on the last topic, claiming that a Catholic could not have a free mind. Roberta thought the Church could be 'helpful' if it kept to its ideals. She and John went several times to the theatre—'A New Way to Pay Old Debts' (Massinger) and 'Volpone' (Jonson). Belfast could rise to the occasion, occasionally. John was due to broadcast on the Friday evening and, just before he set off for the studio, he told his wife that he would like to invite Cherith Boyd to the cottage. He was not in the most diplomatic frame of mind for, on the wireless, he took apart the proud Unionist claim that fourteen American presidents were of Ulster stock. Roberta's concerns might be gauged from her opening phrase of 16 June 1950—'our pigeon had its baby today'.[54]

In Belfast, routine family events slipped into place beside graver duties. On 21 June, the Revd Norman Kirkham, husband of Roberta's sister Lilian and a liberal presbyterian, came to lunch in Mount Charles. Afterwards, they spent the afternoon with Edith McFadden, probably in a nursing home. Roy McFadden, like his mother a militant pacifist, had practised a literary regionalism in *The Heart's Townsland* (1947), while continuing also to practise as a small-town solicitor. A few days later, Roberta took the early bus to Cushendall, so as to tidy the cottage, leaving

[51] Actually, parts of two successive lines in *The Prelude* Book IV. 'I made no vows, but vows / Were then made for me; bond unknown to me / Was given, that I should be, else sinning greatly, / A dedicated Spirit.'

[52] Cf. the final lines of 'Because I Paced My Thought' which read 'on the council of sunburnt comrades in the sun, / and the picture carried with singing into the temple' Ormsby, p. 60.

[53] *Journal*, PRONI, D/3838/4/6, 4 June 1950.

[54] *Journal*, PRONI, D/3838/4/6, 16 June 1950.

John to travel later with Cherith. The afternoon and evening went well, much of the time spend walking to Layde with its ancient church ruins, back to Cushendall, then talking to the painter McAuley and Dr McSparran. The McDonnells were visited. Back in the cottage John entertained by reading the whole of 'Conacre' aloud. Roberta thought everything quite pleasant; Cherith 'wasn't as bad' as she feared.

On the Sunday, she noticed how their young guest deliberately posed at the old tree stump, or against the skyline, or anywhere she could draw attention to herself. Cherith gazed long, and perhaps longingly, at the poet. Still applying wifely reason, Roberta cleared off after lunch to a nearby hayfield. She knew how mortally ill Edith McFadden (née Larmour) was, and reflected intensively on life and death. The balms of nature did not perform to the highest standards. Having heard, and then silently located, a corncrake, Roberta studied it from about three feet away. It craked, stopped, and resumed. Then suddenly it rose from the ground—shitting as it went.

Back at the cottage John was again reading poetry to Cherith, both theatrically framed by the doorway. All three set out walking to Tiveragh but, at the top of the hill, the young girl moved apart from the Hewitts, and took up a silhouette position. A little later, after a repeat performance, Roberta lost her temper, 'For God's sake take her off that damned skyline and rape her or whatever she wants, but get her out of my sight till I make the tea.'[55] The bus journey back to Belfast, via Ballymena this time, was no less awkward. Once in her own home, Roberta cooled down though the day had been 'no use'—apart from the corncrake. She 'tongued' John about being taken in by a vain, stupid youngster. For once finding the diplomatic tone, he admitted that he had been deeply embarrassed all weekend, and begged forgiveness. She fell asleep in his arms.

On waking, the language of this exchange became curiously ornate, 'and so throughout eternity—I forgive you, you forgive me'. More was to come. 'As the dear Redeemer said: this is the wine, this is the bread.' Roberta confessed that she would have been insanely jealous if an affair had developed, adding, for her own discomfort, that John had never said a word when she had 'a wee affair' in 1939 which went on for months. In some contradictory way, the weekend of 24–5 June changed the status of the Antrim cottage in the Hewitts' lives; its potential as another Eden was dissolved, yet its simplicity and lack of allure confirmed its worth. The day after the tumult and the reconciliation, they heard that Edith McFadden was to have both breasts removed; in May Morton's words it was the end. On the Wednesday, Edith died.

[55] *Journal*, PRONI, D/3838/4/6, 25 June 1950. Ten days later, Cherith Boyd called to see JH at the gallery. He told her off for 'over flattery' and posing, or so he informed Roberta; see *Journal*, 3 July 1950.

Break for Text II

'The Colony' (1949–50)

THE TEXT

First came the legions, then the colonists,
provincials, landless citizens, and some
camp-followers of restless generals
content now only with the least of wars.
Among this rabble, some to feel more free
beyond the ready whim of Caesar's fist;
for conscience' sake the best of these, but others
because their debts had tongues, one reckless man,
a tax absconder with a sack of coin.

With these, young law clerks skilled with chart and stylus,
their boxes crammed with lease-scrolls duly marked
with distances and names, to be defined
when all was mapped.
                    When they'd surveyed the land,
they gave the richer tillage, tract by tract,
from the great captains down to men-at-arms,
some of the sprawling rents to be retained
by Caesar's mistresses in their far villas.

We planted little towns to garrison
the heaving country, heaping walls of earth
and keeping all our cattle close at hand;
then, thrusting north and west, we felled the trees,
selling them off the foothills, at a stroke
making quick profits, smoking out the nests
of the barbarian tribesmen, clan by clan,
who hunkered in their blankets, biding chance,
till, unobserved, they slither down and run
with torch and blade among the frontier huts
when guards were nodding, or when shining corn
bade sword-hand grip the sickle. There was once
a terrible year when, huddled in our towns,

my people trembled as the beacons ran
from hill to hill across the countryside,
calling the dispossessed to lift their standards.
There was great slaughter then, man, woman, child,
with fire and pillage of our timbered houses;
we had to build in stone for ever after.

That terror dogs us; back of all our thought
the threat behind the dream, those beacons flare,
and we run headlong, screaming in our fear;
fear quickened by the memory of our guilt
for we began the plunder – naked men
still have their household gods and holy places,
and what a people loves it will defend.
We took their temples from them and forbade them,
for many years, to worship their strange idols.
They gathered secret, deep in the dripping glens,
chanting their prayers before a lichened rock.

We took the kindlier soils. It had been theirs,
This patient, temperate, slow, indifferent,
crop-yielding, crop-denying, in-neglect-
quickly-returning-to-the-nettle-and-bracken,
sodden and friendly land. We took it from them.
We laboured hard and stubborn, draining, planting,
till half the country took its shape from us.

Only among the hills with hare and kestrel
will you observe what once this land was like
before we made it fat for human use—
all but the forests, all but the tall trees—
I could invent a legend of those trees,
and how their creatures, dryads, hamadryads,
fled from the copses, hid in thorny bushes,
and grew a crooked and malignant folk,
plotting and waiting for a bitter revenge
on their despoilers. So our troubled thought
is from enchantments of the old tree magic,
but I am not a sick and haunted man…

Teams of the tamer natives we employed
to hew and draw, but did not call them slaves.
Some say this was our error. Others claim
we were too slow to make them citizens;

we might have made them Caesar's bravest legions.
This is a matter for historians,
or old beards in the Senate to wag over,
not pertinent to us these many years.

But here and there the land was poor and starved,
which, though we mapped, we did not occupy,
leaving the natives, out of laziness
in our demanding it, to hold unleased
the marshy quarters, fens, the broken hills,
and all the rougher places where the whin
still thrust from limestone with its cracking pods.

They multiplied and came with open hands,
begging a crust because their land was poor,
and they were many; squatting at our gates,
till our towns grew and threw them hovelled lanes
which they inhabit still. You may distinguish,
if you were schooled with us, by pigmentation,
by cast of features or by turn of phrase,
or by the clan names on them which are they,
among the faces moving in the street.
They worship Heaven strangely, having rites
we snigger at, are known as superstitious,
cunning by nature, never to be trusted,
given to dancing and a kind of song
seductive to the ear, a whining sorrow.
Also they breed like flies. The danger's there;
when Caesar's old and lays his sceptre down,
we'll be a little people, well outnumbered.

Some of us think our leases have run out
but dig square heels in, keep the roads repaired;
and one or two loud voices would restore
the rack, the yellow patch, the curfewed ghetto.

Most try to ignore the question, going their way,
glad to be living, sure that Caesar's word
is Caesar's bond for legions in our need.
Among us, some, beguiled by their sad music,
make common cause with the natives, in their hearts
hoping to win a truce when the tribes assert
their ancient right and take what once was theirs.
Already from other lands the legions ebb
and men no longer know the Roman peace.

Alone, I have a harder row to hoe:
I think these natives human, think their code
though strange to us, and farther from the truth,
only a little so—to be redeemed
if they themselves rise up against the spells
and fears their celibates surround them with.
I find their symbols good, as such, for me,
when I walk in dark places of the heart;
but name them not to be misunderstood.
I know no vices they monopolise,
if we allow the forms by hunger bred,
the sores of old oppression, the deep skill
in all evasive acts, the swaddled minds,
admit our load of guilt—I mourn the trees
more than as symbol—and would make amends
by fraternising, by small friendly gestures,
hoping by patient words I may convince
my people and this people we are changed
from the raw levies which usurped the land,
if not to kin, to co-inhabitants,
as goat and ox may graze in the same field
and each gain something from proximity;
for we have rights drawn from the soil and sky;
the use, the pace, the patient years of labour,
the rain against the lips, the changing light,
the heavy clay-sucked stride, have altered us ;
we would be strangers in the Capitol;
this is our country also, nowhere else;
and we shall not be outcast on the world.

COMMENTARY

In after years Hewitt was inclined to acknowledge or propose the influence of Edwin Muir on 'The Colony', for example in a letter to John Montague of 1984.[1] Certainly, he read Muir's work during the post-Christmas days spent near Cushendall at the end of 1949 reading and visiting, which reached an episodic crisis after New Year's Eve vigil. The poem had begun to form twenty-four hours earlier, without any critical mass except the poet's amused discovery of his own failure to appreciate the ignorance he stood in. The issue at one and the same time became sharper and sank deeper. There was a profound sense of disappointment in the spiritual experience in church—'We hoped we would find something in the ritual that we could identify ourselves with those people, but it has made the cleavage

[1] Quoted in Ormsby, p. 586.

evident—there can be no real communication between these hill farmers and ourselves.'[2] This local or social crisis was, however, only the first stage of a larger one—the composition of a poem initially called 'The Colonists', and soon renamed 'The Colony'. The second (compositional) stage of crisis was devoted exactly to overcoming a dismal recognition of the first. Whatever local opinion in the Glens made of the poem, it failed to win a Festival of Britain poetry competition in 1951, and reached print in *The Bell* (summer 1953) courtesy of Peadar O'Donnell, as doughty a republican as one could meet but no sufferer of church authority.

At several levels, 'The Colony' rewrites 'Once Alien Here' (March 1942), a much shorter poem (twenty-four lines) which draws on Hewitt's regionalist enquiries. A number of crucial words occur in both—'labour', 'shape', and 'use'—and all in close conjunction. But the earlier poem resorts to contrasting 'Irish' and 'English', 'Ulster' and 'ripe England' in a way quite inadmissible to the later. Douglas Sealy, reviewing *Collected Poems 1932–1967*, remarked: 'Is it not strange how so simple a device as writing "legions" for "militia" and "Caesar" for "Henry" or "Elizabeth" should have given the lines an ironic violence and a universal relevance. Change "Capitol" to "Temple" in [lines 138 etc.] and they might have been spoken by a Jew of the Diaspora.'[3] Of course, the poem of 1949–50 had *not* been conceived or written about militias or Tudor monarchs, nor does it derive from Edmund Spenser's *View of the Present State of Ireland* as implied by Terence Brown.[4] 'The Colony' should not be grossly translated back into the local conflicts of either the eighteenth century ('militia') or the sixteenth (Henry, Elizabeth, and Spenser), where the voices would necessarily be conflictive. Sealy does not indulge this local-history temptation, as his allusion to Josephus and the Roman-Jewish War makes clear.

Paul Muldoon has written how the speaker 'concludes that the colonizer and the colonist have much in common', which is to say unusually little. He refers to the poem as a dramatic dialogue which (formally, at least) it isn't. This form, he concludes, 'allows Hewitt to say what would be unsaid, or unsayable, in polite society' and treats this outspokenness as regrettable.[5] Rather than seek out dramatic speakers, we might consider grammatical voices. These may be said to emerge in Line 18 ('we planted little towns...'), and this first-person plural often recurs (see Line 21 etc) but it is also disrupted by a present tense which admits an active third person plural—'they slither down and run / with torch and blade' (lines 26–7). From this shift of person and tense, there emerges a dramatic-present in which a speaker's consciousness predominates—'That terror dogs us; back of all our thought / the threat behind the dream, those beacons flare, / and we run headlong, screaming in our fear...' (lines 37–9)—over its presumed moment of utterance. If there was a particular textual source it is likely to have been the mendacious and often reprinted *Irish Rebellion... in the Year 1641* of Sir John Temple (1600–77). Conscious or otherwise,

[2] *Journal*, PRONI, D/3838/4/6, 31 December 1949.

[3] Douglas Sealy, 'An Individual Flavour: the Collected Poems of John Hewitt', *Dublin Magazine* 8, nos. 1–2 (Spring–Summer 1969), p. 20. The author (d.2013), an acute reviewer of poetry and chamber music, was the grandson of Douglas Hyde, from whom he inherited a learned interest in Gaelic literature as well as contemporary European culture.

[4] Terence Brown, *Ireland's Literature: Selected Essays* (Dublin: Lilliput, 1988), pp. 10–12.

[5] Paul Muldoon, *To Ireland, I* (Oxford: Oxford University Press, 2000), p. 46.

Hewitt's echoing this sensationalist work draws the moment of reading into complicity with the phases of Protestant anxiety when the *Irish Rebellion* was republished during the eighteenth century, and thus marks his poem with a satirical coloration. The structure of 'The Colony' employs alternating voices and grammatical persons with the result that its subject is presented as narrative, fantasy, confession, history, drama, and fiction. The 'nettle-and-bracken, / sodden and friendly land' may be unmistakably Ireland, and not Gaul, but no such regional names are admitted.

The Roman idiom to which Sealy drew attention works to paradoxical effect. It is a cliché of Irish history that the Romans never reached Ireland; to some readers 'The Colony' substitutes for all-too-actual seventeenth-century planters an invasion which never happened. A complication of the failure of the legions and centurions to conquer Ireland lay in the arrival of Christianity by means very different from those obtaining in Britain and Gaul. Patrick, the national saint, is taken from his British home by Irish pirates and enslaved with many others. Traditionally, his captivity is associated with modern Antrim. In this primitive scene, the native Irish are pagans, the Roman Briton is Christianity's pioneering missioner. By using Rome as a transparent metaphor to connote invasion, dispossession, and a settlement by outsiders, the poem rearranges the impositions of history, allowing for overlaps of age upon age, and for positive *lacunae*, where what is missing is best left that way if mutual understanding is the objective.[6]

What is missing? Technically, 'The Colony' employs just one such break, halfway through the poem at Line 66,

> So our troubled thought
> is from enchantments of the old tree magic,
> but I am not a sick and haunted man…

where the ellipsis (…) is unusual in a poetry of generally determined closures. In these lines, two themes effect a suggestive transference. The planter/speaker acknowledges that the 'troubled thought' of his people owes much to an earlier and native (supposedly natural) religion, but that he (individually) has not been harmed physically or mentally by the relationship. Of course, for some readers there may well be implications of evasion or self-deception to be disinterred among the dots of the ellipsis, but these supposed implications require a strong theory of identity by which the twentieth-century poet and the sixteenth- or seventeenth-century soldier-planter are held in line. Yeats demanded such a theory, and met his own demands through a part-invented ancestry, 'we are no petty people' to which Hewitt replied in 'A Little People'. And if the theory is to make headway it requires some such biological notion of identity. Hewitt demurs.

The latter half of the poem contains harsh words and phrases, some characterizing the object-people ('they breed like flies', Line 96) and others the subject-consciousness ('the rack, the yellow patch', Line 102) of voices greater than the speaker's. But two larger themes flourish alongside. The first (like the ellipsis)

[6] Nicole Loraux has linked the concepts of amnesia and amnesty in an account of reconciliation in the foundation and maintenance of Athenian law; see Loraux, *The Divided City: on Memory and Forgetting in Ancient Athens* (New York: Zone, 2002).

depends on curiously potent, yet unstable, incompletion. Lines 86–90 have to undergo a temporary repunctuation in order to make absolutely clear what phrase is grammatical 'object' of the verb to distinguish:

> You may distinguish
> (if you were schooled with us) – by pigmentation,
> by cast of features or by turn of phrase,
> or by the clan names on them – which are they,
> among the faces moving in the street.

This certainly floats towards a biology (or physiognomy) of difference, an admission of what was/is propagated in the school-rooms of colonization. The individual, however, is here the voice of his people ('us') but not their advocate. It is vital to question who is the 'you' to whom these lines are addressed—the reader or them. By this means one comes to acknowledge that 'The Colony' is not a historical or even (in the narrow sense) a political text, but a literary and dialogic one. The second larger theme relates to perhaps the most vexed issue of twentieth-century Irish poetry, the nature of the symbol. Lines 118–20 read:

> I find their symbols good, as such, for me,
> when I walk in dark places of the heart;
> but name them not to be misunderstood.

The big philosophical question would be: what does 'good' mean in this statement—adequate, appropriate, authoritative, efficacious, fit, permanent, pleasing, revelatory, universal, or whatever? A question requiring Denis Donoghue for answerer. The immediate concern, however, is to refer positively to the symbolic realm of 'these natives' whose code, though 'further from the truth, / [is] only a little so'. The concession is a step towards acknowledgement, elsewhere assisted by the speaker's admission of guilt. The speaker finds the symbols good, 'as such', by which I take him to mean that the symbols have no transcendental power (as Yeats would insist). The symbols are good symbols for things to which they relate by way of resemblance or reference, not identity in equational or hierarchic mode.

Hewitt's friend Austin Clarke investigated this issue within a specifically liturgical context. In the poem, 'Night and Morning' (pub. late 1937) a contrast is made between 'appearances' and 'elements', where the first word relates to bread and wine before transubstantiation, the second to their transformed state. To the doubting or despairing Catholic 'the very elements remain / appearances upon the altar'.[7] Hewitt's poem makes more than a differentiation between churches or denominations. Their symbols are good, as such, 'for me', that is for one individual—nothing more can be insisted upon. Indeed, the circumstances in which they are 'good, as such, for me' are delimited—'when I walk in dark places of the heart'.

Biographically, this may refer back to the numerous occasions (e.g. New Year's Eve 1949) when Hewitt and his wife ventured into a Catholic church, where he found both the symbolic regimen of Catholicism and a physical dark interior—candles,

[7] See Austin Clarke, *Selected Poems*, edited and annotated by W. J. Mc Cormack (London: Penguin, 1992), pp. 81–2; 232–3.

images, and 'the crowding gloom' (cf. 'The Lonely Heart', Part II of *Freehold*). Additionally or alternatively, it may refer to the 'dripping glens' where the poem's 'natives' maintain their beliefs. The phrase, however, complicates the treatment of symbols 'as such' by adding a possible ambiguity to the line—'but name them not to be misunderstood'. Is it the symbols or the dark places which the speaker claims to name, so as 'not to be misunderstood'? And in either case, has he actually named them? This is a point in the poem where its elaborate polyphony of voices and tenses is touchingly shown to depend on an individual (not an actual) speaker. It takes up where the ellipsis left off.

In a long sentence running from Line 121 to the poem's end (Line 140) and punctuated with semi-colons, commas, and dashes, Hewitt places his second treatment of the symbol, as such. It begins with a tentative admission of guilt, expressed in a negative statement about the natives (or, in more immediately present terms, 'this people'): 'I know no vices they monopolise.' A willingness to make amends for the raw levies of usurpation and to 'admit our load of guilt' follows. The individual speaker remains in charge, perhaps complacently so, while announcing the modes of adjustment. But when in Line 129, we read of 'my people and this people' who may be convinced that 'we are changed', the first-person plural pronoun goes some way towards dissolving a distinction between these historically presented different peoples.

The shift is curiously introduced by words displayed between dashes: '—I mourn the trees / more than as symbol—'. Here, surely, Hewitt is alluding to an eighteenth-century Gaelic poem, translated by Frank O'Connor in 1932 as 'Kilcash'. The fall of a great house is commemorated by reference to the destruction of its woodlands, its Catholic proprietor obliged to marry a Protestant kinsman in order to preserve social dignity. The family (Butlers of Clonmel) are not Gaels but Normans or, in the historians' phrase, Old English. The importance of Irish forests as an impenetrable refuge from the invader goes back to Edmund Spenser, and the systematic destruction of woods and groves was not just symbolic but constituted an act of warfare. Hence Hewitt's phrase, 'I mourn the trees / more than as symbol', echoes the load of guilt or exemplifies it at several historic levels.

The observer of nature, the hidden watcher of badgers and corncrakes, knew trees as among the oldest living objects of human knowledge. Approaching the final lines of 'The Colony', the political uses of which he could not have imagined in 1950, Hewitt lays down a modest account of the symbol *as such*. It involves no claims to sacramental or visionary substantiation. Its author is a realist, much as Jonathan Swift was. His people, from whom he typically dissents, have been altered, not transformed. His people and 'this people' may be cohabitants, though the biblical prophecy of the lion and lamb lying down together is scaled back to field-sharing goat and ox. If 'we' shall avoid the fate of being strangers in the Capitol, one reason for this happy escape lies in the knowledge that history condemns Roman glory and all its imitators to destruction by others, barbarian or post-colonialist. And the trees, alluded to economically, serve as a diplomatic symbol for the transience of human ambition, their annual growth-rings only displaying the work of slow time after the axe or chainsaw has brought them down.

6

Disappointments: Stranmillis and Mount Charles, 1951–56

The 1930 advertisement which the young John Hewitt read in a barber's queue required no specialist training or formal qualification in curatorship. The successful candidate learned the job as he went, in due course taking his Museums Association diploma with a short dissertation on 'The Problems of a Provincial Gallery'. Hewitt became an increasingly busy man in the Belfast Museum. At the beginning of the post-war decade, any junior but relatively long-serving member of the staff found his influence to be intermittent and not unchallenged at times. With an MA added to his formal and substantial qualifications, he had moved one step up the ladder of promotion.

In the context of his longer career, professional and political, the MA thesis makes curious reading. With a starting date of 1800, its survey of Ulster poetry avoids 1798 and the preliminary enthusiasm of Presbyterians for French radicalism. The date has its obvious rationale, but the issue of discreet exclusion recurs in the body of the text. A number of major writers are not treated because, though Ulster-born, their careers were spent elsewhere. The largest of these was Samuel Ferguson (cited in the 'preludes') whose critical and literary output could hardly have been mentioned without involving the cultural nationalism of Yeats's generation.

The thesis has many substantial merits, not the least of them its attention to the lists of subscribers appearing in twenty-nine of the volumes discussed. For example, when James Orr's *Poems* appeared in 1804, its financial sponsors numbered 468, of whom only eighteen individuals had Belfast addresses. Hewitt's point, not laboured, is the strength of small-town-and-rural (amounting to regional) culture at the time. An occasional flash of non-academic wit—'the alarming efficiency of Robinson's metre'—breaks through, this one prompted by Romney Robinson's *Juvenile Poems* (1806) with Maria Edgeworth and the future Prime Minister George Canning amongst its subscribers.

While an accepted view presents *The Rhyming Weavers* (1974) as the published 1951 thesis, the earlier version is by no means focused on that social and economic constituency. The thirteenth chapter, amounting to fourteen pages, does attend to the weavers, and is also striking for the range and diversity of its critical sources—Aodh de Blacam, Daniel Corkery, Helen Darbyshire (on Wordsworth), the economic historian Rodney Green, and Eleanor Hull, among them. Equally striking is the minimal attention given to James Hope (1764–1847) whose name, when it occurs, helps in establishing kinship between this local poet and that. Hope's greater historical significance, as a military leader of the United Irishmen in 1798 surviving defeat, simply is not mentioned. Ten years earlier, Hewitt had published a lengthy article 'James Hope, Weaver, of Templepatrick', concluding that:

> It would be a good and gracious act if, on some date—say 25 August every year—socialists of Ulster should walk the straight road to Mallusk, enter the little gate beside the grey house, and stand in file by the plain stone, to the left of the yew trees, that marks Hope's grave, and make resolution that those ideas he spent a turbulent lifetime evolving become the very stuff and nature of their thought and activity.[1]

But 1951 was not 1941; the requirements at Queen's University were not the principles of *The Northern Star*. Hope's work is not listed in the academic bibliography and it must be doubted that the examiners complained.

The Festival of Britain made efforts to please Belfast. For an associated poetry competition Hewitt submitted 'The Colony', an offering too far perhaps. The winner was May Morton.[2] In the same summer of 1951, Stanley Spencer (1891–1959), the brilliant English visionary painter, made one of his periodic visits to Belfast where his brother Harold taught music. Uncle Stanley's portrait of Daphne Spencer, dating from this trip, is now in the Ulster Museum. On 18 June, the Hewitts and Stanley took part in a Festival Céilí, at which John got drunk to the point of swaying on his feet, and Stanley beamed so broadly Roberta thought his face would be damaged. The Lewinter-Frankls were also organizing a sixtieth-birthday party for the eccentric visitor, a small omen of gradually broadening horizons on the post-war scene.[3]

Early in the new year, Roberta typed up a collection of her husband's poems, under the title *Out of My Time*, and posted it to Faber and Faber in London, complete with a list of the magazines in which some pieces had appeared. This was to be the successor to *No Rebel Word*, if successor was the right term. Faber was a premier division publisher, managed by T. S. Eliot, and boasting Ezra Pound and W. H. Auden on its list. MacNeice, with whom Hewitt was on good terms, also published with Faber. On 11 February, the typescript came back duly rejected. Michael Joseph, a respectable first division firm, invited Hewitt (and, doubtless, others) to submit prose or verse. Hewitt, who was about to appear in a PEN anthology under Michael Joseph's imprint, hummed and hawed, but eventually Roberta was authorized to reparcel the typescript. After more than a month, it too returned, unwanted.[4]

[1] Originally published in *The Northern Star*; reprinted *Ancestral*, p. 137. Anyone returning to the paper would have found JH also published there 'Some Thoughts on Marxism and the War', *The Northern Star* vol 1, no. 2 (April 1941), pp. 4–6.

[2] *Journal*, PRONI, D/3838/4/7, 5 June 1951. Southerner Mary Elizabeth Morton's winning poem, 'Spindle and Shuttle', drew on linen industry motifs which complimented a northern Unionist smugness, whereas 'The Colony' raised questions uncomfortable in all camps. Her poem was published by Her Majesty's Stationery Office before the year was out.

[3] Stanley Spencer, *Letters and Writings*, edited by Adrian Glew (London: Tate, 2001), p. 237.

[4] *Journal*, PRONI, D/3838/4/7, early 1952 *passim*.

By January 1952, it was generally recognized that Alfred George, Hewitt's immediate boss, was unwell to the point where his promotion to the top of both museum and gallery could be discounted. On 1 February, Hewitt took over the older man's office, desk and duties, acting as deputy to Stendall. Earlier predictions and plots could be revised. In all such places, a certain conflict of priorities equally affected day-to-day activities and long-range objectives. Was the gallery within the museum to serve immediate popular needs, respond to contemporary taste? Museums were, in the early 1950s, regarded as decidedly past-focused displays, with research playing a gradually enhanced but still hidden role. Or was the gallery to scan the future and create something worthy of generations yet unborn? Staffing levels were low by today's standards, and the art professional doubled up on administrative tasks. Despite these factors, Hewitt's primary concern was twentieth-century art and its steady acquisition.

Until 1962, the institution was formally and effectively a civic one—the Belfast Art Gallery and Museum. In that year, its title and function changed; it would become the Ulster Museum and Art Gallery. Originally founded in 1890, it had acquired new buildings at Stranmillis in 1929, the year before Hewitt joined the staff.[5] The ensuing career was not a seamless advance in a constant or static professional environment, even though his years of service preceded the gallery's promotion to what was virtually national status. At certain levels, one can detect that the emergence of an Ulster (as distinct from Belfast) gallery was in part driven by, or made possible by, Hewitt's earlier activities.

A few personal case histories may illuminate the point. First, let us take Alicia Boyle (1908–87), an Irish painter (born in Thailand) whom Hewitt wrote about and who featured among the guests (in her red socks) at Mount Charles. In Eileen Black's catalogue, Boyle is represented by just three pictures: a) a west of Ireland scene purchased in 1950; b) 'Bull in a Boreen' purchased after Hewitt had gone to Coventry; and c) 'The Other House of Sharon', painted in 1946 and bequeathed by Roberta and John Hewitt in 1987, following his death.[6] The year 1950 was clearly a prosperous one for the gallery; of thirty-five items by John Luke listed in MAGNI, more than half were purchased that year—many of them drawings. Again, the execution of Hewitt's will in 1987 led to several further acquisitions of Luke's work, including an ink sketch of Hewitt from 1932 and a crayon portrait of Roberta Hewitt from 1935.

Other artists feature in contrasting profiles. Colin Middleton who, like Luke, had been closely associated with Hewitt since Unit days, is represented in MAGNI's listing by sixteen items, only two of which were accessed during Hewitt's time in Stranmillis. Both of these arrived in 1943, both were oil-on-canvas works: 'Coal Quay, Early Morning' (1940), donated by the artist, and 'Lagan: Annadale,

[5] Eileen Black, *Art in Belfast 1760–1888: Art Lovers or Philistines*? (Dublin: Irish Academic Press, 2006), pp. 211–15.

[6] Eileen Black, ed., *Drawings, Paintings & Sculptures: the Catalogue* (Belfast: The Museums & Galleries of Northern Ireland in Association with Nicholson & Bass, 2000) (Hereinafter cited as MAGNI.) Acquisitions after the compilation of the catalogue are not factored in to these comments, which have Hewitt as their central concern.

October', purchased. Six Middletons were donated after the artist's death in 1983, one presented by his widow, and three bequeathed under Hewitt's will. A younger artist with whom Hewitt was less familiar, Basil Blackshaw painted two portraits of him, one in 1956 and another in 1984. Together with a crayon drawing of Roberta, and a sketch for the 1956 picture of her husband, all this material was bequeathed to the Ulster Museum in 1987. Seen in the round, Hewitt's relationship with the institution spanned more than fifty years, and survived the bitterness of rejection in 1952.

Painters from beyond Ulster featured in quite different proportions. The dominant Irish painter of the twentieth century, Jack Yeats (1871–1957) has no work in the museum listed by MAGNI, though Hewitt organized an exhibition in February 1956 and got much local criticism for his trouble.[7] Sean Keating (1889–1977) has one, an oil-on-canvas of 1935 donated by the (Dublin-based) Thomas Haverty Trust in 1941. Harry Kernoff (1900–74, and a Dubliner by adoption) is represented by three, one of which arrived into the collection during Hewitt's years through the generosity of James Creed Meredith, a southern judge and translator of Immanuel Kant. All three of these artists might well have been regarded with suspicion by the city fathers—Kernoff a supporter of the 'hard left', the other two nationalists. If one were to include Maurice McGonigal (1900–79; briefly interned for IRA activities in his youth), the result is not very different—three pictures, one donated in 1941, one purchased in 1947, and a third accessioned after Hewitt's departure. Relations between North and South were uneasy in the immediate aftermath of the Second World War. Dublin was inclined to look down on, not up to, Belfast. Yet a distinguished art historian has written of Middleton and his northern *confrères* that they 'not only dominated the later Living Art exhibitions [in Dublin], but largely determined the development of Irish painting throughout the 1950s'.[8]

Hewitt's movements in this period were asymmetrical. He did quite a lot of business in Dublin as a writer, publishing in southern journals or newspapers, and broadcasting on Radio Eireann. Yet the art curator appears restrained in his purchase of contemporary work by southern painters. The restraint may have been imposed from above. Yet, if Yeats, Keating, and McGonigal might be roughly classified as Fenians, that is military-minded 'taigues', the same could never be said of Evie Hone (1894–1955) or Mainie Jellett (1897–1944), none of whose work entered the Belfast/Ulster Gallery during Hewitt's years, despite their abstract leanings. What one sees from the lists in the MAGNI catalogue is a distinction as much generic as territorial or political. For all the brave innovations of the Ulster Unit, abstraction was not yet to Hewitt's taste, and the choice between representation and abstract work would arise for him quite sharply in Coventry, though not immediately on his arrival there in 1957.

He was a well-known figure on the professional and social circuit, with visitors arriving (often unannounced) at the gallery. In mid-August 1949, a three-man

[7] *Journal*, PRONI, D/3838/4/7, 22 February 1956.

[8] S. B. Kennedy, *Irish Art & Modernism* (Belfast: Institute of Irish Studies, 1991), p. 130.

delegation turned up consisting of Denis Ireland, Lord Killanin (Michael Morris), and Cathal O'Shannon. They wanted to enlist Hewitt in a New Ireland campaign aimed at bridging the gaps between north and south. O'Shannon was a vigorous trade unionist, unmistakably left-wing, one of the very few who mobilized in Ulster at Easter 1916; Denis Ireland, though Belfast born and ex-British Army, had just been appointed to the southern Irish Senate, and his lordship (Eton educated) was president of the Olympic Council of Ireland. Visitors of this calibre could compromise a babe-in-arms. Hewitt suspected Killanin of being a 'MacBride man', that is, a crony of the short-reigning Minister for External Affairs.[9]

One should not deny the political (or sectarian) implications at work even in contemporary art. Two quite different bodies of Belfast painting deserve consideration here. For the first, the names of John Luke and (unlikely though it sounds) Romeo Toogood (1902–66) will serve. Luke, a native of Antrim, had worked in the shipyards until he fractured a leg and sought better employment. In his youth he had 'painted King William on a gable wall in the approved manner'.[10] Toogood was the son of an English stone-carver who had travelled to work on Belfast's monumental City Hall. Their training and progress need not detain us: both developed a highly formalized landscape image—not so much *plein air* as *sans air*—which has led Brian Kennedy to speak (in relation to Luke) of 'the extreme stylization which characterized his later work and which ultimately stultified his development as an artist'. (He treats Toogood in similar terms.)[11]

Roberta Hewitt had her own line on Luke's development as a painter, on one occasion prohibiting her husband from declaring in public that 'he is now introducing the human element into his pictures'. She was prepared to concede that Luke 'was introducing "figures" into the landscapes but they were not "human" in the sense that they were void of any emotion—and they are as abstract as his mountains'. In her own mind, she filed away the suspicion that Luke aimed to be 'self perfect'.[12] He and Hewitt had been close since 1934, and the large body of drawings purchased in 1950 by the gallery indicated the high regard in which he was still held, not to mention the work which came in after Hewitt's death. Toogood was less prolific, and the two pieces listed were acquired through donation.

In the anthology *Northern Harvest* (1944), Hewitt had compared these artists. Of Toogood he observed 'his colour is altogether quieter than Luke's, his shapes not so sharply formalised, his vision closer to normal representation'.[13] Yet in the little Unit catalogue of 1934, Toogood had given an unblinking, unaccommodating account of his project. 'The painter's aim, I think, is to find in nature some sense of formal order, and to translate the same in terms of form and colour into a

[9] *Journal*, PRONI, D/3838/4/6, 22 August 1949. Ristéard O Glaisne (an Irish-speaking, Cork-born Methodist) records several other encounters between Hewitt and Ireland, all of a formal nature; see his *Denis Ireland*. ([Baile Atha Cliath:] Coiscéim, 2000), p. 173.

[10] Theo Snoddy, *Dictionary of Irish Artists: 20th Century* (Dublin: Merlin, 2002), p. 351.

[11] Kennedy, *Irish Art & Modernism*, p. 77.

[12] *Journal*, PRONI, D/3838/4/7, 6 February 1951.

[13] Hewitt, 'Painting in Ulster', in *Northern Harvest; Anthology of Ulster Writing*, edited by Robert Greacen (Belfast: McCord, 1944), p. 145.

pattern which relates to the size and shape of his canvas, the degree of abstraction used depending on the individual painter.'[14] Despite this emphasis on form, and the constitutive role played by the pre-existent canvas, Toogood generally named his pictures after actual, visitable, and verifiable places—'Barge at Edenderry' or 'Glencoe, County Antrim' (both 1936), for example. In 1949 Hewitt privately admitted his fears that 'Luke's interest in technique [was] leading him into death in painting.'[15]

One could venture an ideological placing of this rigorously controlled depiction of the Ulster countryside by suggesting its *need to impose* order rather than any wish to elicit—or any confidence in finding—it. Of course, psychological factors may have been at work. But order, in this argument, easily takes on a political meaning. Both painters abjure movement—no blustery clouds or spattles of rain, few running or jumping humans. To be sure, dancers and horse-persons people Luke's 'The Rehearsal' (1950, commissioned by Hewitt) but they are closer to figures in the mediaeval Bayeux Tapestry, or to theatrical Noel-Cowardish set-designs, than to contemporary representation of active flesh in the hectic machine age. At their most effective, and they are highly accomplished, what these pictures suggest is evacuation or absence, concealment even. When they suggest one of these things perhaps they do it unconsciously.

If Luke and Toogood were working through experiments commenced in 1934, then the changing social constituency of Belfast painting deserves attention. Unit associates were decidedly Protestant in background, and the ideological notion ventured above sees the two painters as dealing with the problems of a radically divided society, dealing with it essentially from within the terms of a Protestant history of Ulster. Division, you might say, features as exclusion. The depicted scene is not *here* in the viewer's eye, but somewhere slightly else. It is not here-and-now but, with a hint of proffered consolation, *There Now*.

Hewitt was also in touch with younger painters whose origins were very different. For the moment, that second body of artistic substance can also be considered through one or two instances. Gerard Dillon (1916–71) came from the Catholic side of town, and was educated by the Christian Brothers. Daniel O'Neill (1920–74) developed a distinctive neurotic-blue palette from which sombre luminous images arose. Hewitt's familiarity with these artists can hardly have been regarded by the city authorities as more suspect than his pre-war association with *The Irish Democrat* and his mantra-like recommendation of progressive ideas. Yet when the crunch comes, local sectarian rather than global ideological judgements appear dominant.

The early 1950s brought much ceremonial reinforcement of Ulster's position within the United Kingdom. The Festival of Britain in May 1951 was, in the words of its principal sponsor, 'a tonic for the nation' at a time when bombsites and rationing kept the recent war constantly in view. The young Elizabeth II came to the throne in February 1952, her coronation following a year later. In September

[14] Quoted in Theo Snoddy, *Dictionary of Irish Artists: 20th Century*, p. 658.
[15] *Journal*, PRONI, D/3838/4/6, 19 December 1949.

1952, the British Association visited Belfast, with lectures and banquets to mark the occasion. Unionist permanence was reinforced at every level. In this climate, framed by a remote yet potent McCarthyism, the directorship of the museum and gallery would become vacant when J. A. S. Stendall retired.

Edith McFadden's funeral had greatly shaken John and Roberta. Roy, quite out of character, had physically leaned on his friend for support. By September 1952, however, he was walking out (to use a regionalist idiom) with a new girlfriend. They met the Hewitts at a film show, 'The Blue Light', an uncomfortable occasion for all concerned. Margaret Ferguson, who married Roy later in the year, struck Roberta as 'frigid', setting off a minor avalanche of judgements about Roy's 'rather sticky foreword' to the magazine *Rann* (a delayed spring 1951 issue!) in which she detected both insincerity and guilt about his late wife's death. Personally, she took the sensible view that a widower of thirty could and should remarry. She extended this reflection to provide for her own death, more than twenty years ahead—'Johnny could not live alone well'.[16] Against the stereotype of reticence imposed on him, Hewitt certainly engaged with McFadden, when Edith died and then when Margaret came into view, providing condolence, advice, and support. Perhaps Hewitt himself was a notable non-beneficiary of his own capacity for sympathetic engagement, with Roberta ahead of him in the queue.

The late-summer of 1952 provided the distractions of British Association field trips and receptions, while decisions about the gallery job remained unspoken. The director lingered in office to facilitate his presence when the great and the good descended. Yet Stendall also took an honorary MSc at Queens' summer graduation ceremony, signal of imminent ascension from office. He was behind Hewitt, the soon-to-be-former director confided. Asked to provide a reference, he naturally agreed but added 'you would be better to cast your net wider and I will be working for you on Council'.[17] A willing referee was Dame Dehra Parker, Minister for Health and Local Government—by Unionist standards an ultra-liberal. Others approached included S. D. Cleveland, president of the Museum Association and director of the Manchester Art Gallery, who provided a very good testimonial. The Blakean contemporary English painter, Stanley Spencer, provided 'a wee personal one'.[18] Not a Fenian in sight.

In his account of the affair, piously headed 'From Chairmen and Committeemen, Good Lord Deliver Us', Hewitt recorded that he took an hour or two out from ordinary concerns to 'listen to and partially comprehend that alarmingly clever man Dr [Jacob] Bronowski on "The Theory of Experiment" '. If he succeeded Stendall, perhaps Belfast could maintain this level of intellectual and cultural distinction. But 'the Director's silver-haired and naked-faced cronies were much in evidence as his office became a sort of head-quarters for their convivial consultations'.[19] It is some

[16] *Journal*, PRONI, D/3838/4/7, 15 September 1952.

[17] *Journal*, PRONI, D/3838/4/7, 26 September 1952.

[18] *Journal*, PRONI, D/3838/4/7, 6 June 1952.

[19] *North*, pp. 205–6. 'From Chairmen and Committeemen, Good Lord Deliver Us' has been published several times: in *Honest Ulsterman* 6, (Sept. 1968), pp. 16–22; *Ancestral*, pp. 48–55; and *North*, pp. 205–12.

measure of Hewitt's bitterness towards Stendall that the director is never named in these pages of recollection. Roberta noted that her husband harboured both ambitions and reservations. As early as late 1947, he had insisted, 'not IF I am Director of the Museum, WHEN', a confidence she thought masking a deeper pessimism. 'He did say at times perhaps it was wrong for him as he was interested first in writing and maybe it would be better to have a small job, live quietly and write. But nevertheless he planned many things that could be done at Stranmillis.'[20]

On 23 September, Hewitt took an anonymous telephone call at Mount Charles from a Councillor Holmes, formerly of the Northern Irish Labour Party but by then a Unionist, warning that rumours were going round the city. The two men arranged to meet at the King's Bridge, and then drove to a deserted roadside where the councillor could speak his mind. The gist of his disclosure was that Mary O'Malley (1918–2006), a member of the southern Labour Party, very recently elected to public representation, active in the city's theatrical life, had written to the Council indicating her support for Hewitt. In time, it emerged that she had been prompted to this action by a friend of Hewitt's, the poet Valentin Iremonger, a serving member of the southern state's diplomatic corps. In the idiom of the day, Hewitt was supported by 'wrong-footers', that is, Catholics, Fenians, Free-Staters or worse.[21] He was devastated, especially as O'Malley's letter had already got to Percy Tougher, chairman of the Libraries, Museums, and Galleries committee. Hewitt's cameo of his nemesis left few stones unthrown: 'golfer, shirt manufacturer, son of a once well-known pawnbroker'.[22] The chairman was unwell, and required the silver-haired and naked-faced cronies to wait upon him at home.

Interviews were scheduled for Friday 26 September. On the Tuesday evening, in response to the alarm bells, Zoltan Frankl and his wife visited the Hewitts, pledging their support. Frankl, in the eyes of the city, was an art-lover and clearly no fruit of the British planter tradition in Ulster; no doubt some regarded him too as a 'wrong-footer', and a Jew to boot. But he was a wealthy man, his wife a major employer who wielded influence even among hard-boiled councillors. So down those mean streets, this elderly man went, driven no doubt by his chauffeur. Roberta went to see Stuart Henry, a Unionist councillor and sometime High Sheriff, for whom Hewitt occasionally wrote speeches on topics relating to the arts. He told her plainly that, until he heard of the letter, he had intended to support her husband. Meanwhile Hewitt himself went to see W. R. Gordon (1882–1955), the only committee member whom he regarded as a friend of twenty years' standing. Known affectionately as Daddy, he was 'an old man of no political influence, suspect... for having been a play-actor in the past, a singer of folk-ballads, and an artist into the bargain'.[23] Though Hewitt does not mention it, Gordon had participated in

20 *Journal TS*, vol. I, p. 9. 21 *Journal*, PRONI, D 3838/4/7, 26 September 1952.

22 *North*, p. 206. John Percy Tougher had been principal owner of the Garfield Manufacturing Company, Adelaide Street, Belfast, since February 1939. He could be regarded as one of the lower-grade 'captains of industry' near-central to the Unionist political economy. The Tougher pawnshop, from which all this sprang, had been located on Agnes Street where Hewitt (and his father) went to school.

23 *North*, p. 208. In 1969 the Arts Council of Northern Ireland acquired Gordon's 'Looking Up the Glen' (watercolour); it was subsequently sold in the United States (1993).

the Ulster Unit exhibition of 1934 which, in Hewitt's opinion, should have been accommodated in the Belfast Gallery. He, though genuinely down with flu, promised to attend the interviews and do his duty. Andy Millar, an independent in party-political terms, even telephoned the chairman, Percy Tougher.[24] These actions, taken in response to Councillor Holmes' frightened revelations about the O'Malley letter and the Tougher use of it, have been indicted as improper canvassing.[25]

It is as well to clarify the sources for an understanding of what happened that autumn of 1952. Beyond a minuted decision, no official record is available, mandarins being cautious of the written word. Why leave records behind; in Sir Boyle Roche's formula, 'what has posterity ever done for us?' However, there is no dearth of evidence. As early as 1968, when the Troubles were breaking out (again), Hewitt published it in *The Honest Ulsterman*, edited by the poet James Simmons. Its appearance at that moment constituted a deliberate political act, exposing the chicanery of the entrenched Unionist regime under pressure from the Civil Rights movement. While it is likely that he discussed these matters with Roberta in 1968 (and no doubt earlier), her journal constitutes a secondary, if not wholly independent, contemporary source. There are, or were, a few eyewitnesses, none of whom challenged Hewitt's basic account of events. Edna Longley and Declan Kiberd concur, though dissenting noises have been heard from Sarah Ferris and Adrian Smith. Some months after the fiasco, *The Irish Times* pointedly noted Hewitt as the only Belfast-based professional 'who has any qualifications whatever for membership' of the Art Critics' Society.[26]

Some retired or disengaged clergymen applied for the job, to no avail. Only two candidates were to be interviewed, Hewitt and W. A. Seaby, curator of Taunton Castle in Devon. Hewitt was also aware that the director (in which Kafka-esque idiom he continued to indicate Stendall and all his works) had visited Taunton in recent days, supposedly to vet the castle for a development grant. Meanwhile Tougher, struggling with (was it?) the flu, insisted that interviews be held over until he was fighting fit. On the morning designated for these, Mrs Stendall telephoned to wish John luck—Roberta took the call.[27] 'By chance', Hewitt found himself 'travelling to the City Hall in the same bus as the Director.' They spoke about the weather. And the weather had its part to play. Though everyone failed to inform Hewitt, his rival was delayed by fog preventing the Liverpool boat from berthing; so, out of consideration for Seaby, interviews were postponed till the afternoon. This was to prove a material factor, because one of Hewitt's supporters had shifted an important appointment to the afternoon, and so would now be unable.

Eventually, when the candidates met, Hewitt found Bill Seaby a pleasant and intelligent man with whom (as it turned out) he was able to work harmoniously

[24] *Journal*, PRONI, D/3838/4/7, end of entry for 24/9/1952.

[25] Sarah Ferris, *Poet John Hewitt (1907–1987) and Criticism of Northern Irish Protestant Writing* (Lampeter: Edwin Mellen Press, 2002), pp. 187–8.

[26] Nichevo, 'An Irishman's Diary', *Irish Times*, 25 July 1953, p. 7. Nichevo was the pseudonym of R. M. Smyllie, long-serving editor of the paper.

[27] *Journal*, PRONI, D/3838/4/7, 26 October 1952.

after the Englishman's appointment. But, due to the change of timetable, the too-finely balanced committee was locked on a 50/50 indecision. The chairman, no longer unwell, cast his vote for Seaby. When Hewitt, exiting through a swing door, bumped into 'Daddy' Gordon, the old man blurted out: 'It's a bloody scandal.' When a non-Council member of the committee Dr McDonald (no friend of Hewitt's) brushed past, Gordon added 'That bla'guard should be ashamed of himself.'[28] Blackguards rarely are.

To conclude that McDonald, or Tougher, or 'the Director' behaved badly is not a matter of special pleading. Belfast was notoriously partisan with appointments in the 1950s, and the gallery job was a civic gift made by the city fathers through their Libraries Etc. committee. The Unionist Party had been in control of province and capital ever since the establishment of Northern Ireland at the beginning of the 1920s. It does not seem that any impartial, external arbitrator was involved. With only two candidates shortlisted, the decision was immediately politicized—do we want the 'wrong-footer' (Hewitt in every respect, except tribal origin) who has twenty-two years' knowledge of the institution, good relations with contemporary artists and cultural life generally, two university degrees, professional diplomas and publications? Or do we want an English castle-custodian with a fraction of these qualifications? In more recent idiom, a 'no brainer'.

While informed opinion has always condemned Hewitt's rejection, it is as well to review the circumstances which made that rejection possible. Unionist hegemony or City Hall philistinism is no sufficient or complete explanation in itself. Mary O'Malley's letter foolishly provided data easily turned into a political rationalization. She belonged to a (somewhat) left-wing party with headquarters outside the United Kingdom. Until May 1998, Dublin did not concede *de jure* recognition of Northern Ireland's status. The Hewitt business was only her second 'little brush with the authorities'.[29] Within Northern Ireland she represented a Belfast ward (Smithfield) known for its hostility to the regime and for its wonderful book market. That she had been prompted to her indiscreet action by a 'foreign' diplomat made things worse, though that detail may not have been widely appreciated.

There is then, at least in the average Unionist councillor's worldview, the question of Hewitt's allegiance to the regime. In the 1930s, he had assisted a London-based Council for Civil Liberties in its critique of policing in Northern Ireland, a highly political issue. In 1937, under the flimsiest of disguises, he had contributed to a newspaper published in Belfast by communists and left-wing republicans. This involvement probably breached the Civil Service prohibition on its employees' engaging in politics, laughable if one looks at the hegemonic smooch of Orangeism, the Unionist Party, and the maintenance of provincial law and order, but nonetheless citable against an applicant hailing from outside that embrace. The veteran Labour politician, independent-minded and locally attuned, Paddy Devlin held that the Unionists saw Hewitt as 'an intractable enemy' ever since the 1930s.[30]

[28] *North*, p. 210.
[29] Mary O'Malley, *Never Shake Hands with the Devil* (Dublin: Elo Press, 1990), p. 64.
[30] Paddy Devlin, 'No Rootless Colonist', *Threshold* 38 (Winter 1986/87), p. 22.

Two straws are worth winding together: (1) Hewitt's decision not to post stuff to *The Irish Democrat* office in Great Victoria Street in 1937, and (2) Councillor Holmes' insistence in 1952 that he rendezvous with Hewitt in a deserted area. Holmes may have been more cowardly than careful—hard to tell after so many years. But we shall hear from him once more. The clear implication is that a meeting could have dire consequences for either of them, or both. Add the passing observation that John D. Stewart's phone was tapped, and one has an accumulating if rough measurement of the extent to which dissidents were treated as dangerously unreliable, if not actively subversive. Postal surveillance, political victimization, covert phone tapping, and rumour-mongering all bolstered the status quo. Would it be worthwhile, even now, in making a formal request for publication of Hewitt's Special Branch file?

The rumours were contradictory—Hewitt was a communist, or communist-sympathizer, and he was au fait with the Catholics. In any liberal seminar, the contradiction would be patently clear. But Ulster Unionism was never liberal and had no time for academic seminars devoted to its critics. In the best tradition of rumour, the allegations shifted almost on a daily basis. When it had been categorically demonstrated that Hewitt was not a communist (but a socialist), interested parties told each other that he was in with the Tomelty crowd. Joseph Tomelty (1911–85) was a playwright, novelist, film-actor, theatre director, and Jack of most cultural trades. He came from a County Down Catholic background, lived in the Falls, and genially failed to match the desiderata of Belfast propriety. His play 'The End House' (1944) openly mocked the Special Powers Act and, through the Group Theatre, he collaborated with the Jewish director, Belfast-born Harold Goldblatt. In 1945, Tomelty had played a taxi driver in the film version of *Odd Man Out*.

This poisonous campaign could only function in a radically divided society lacking any refuge or cordon sanitaire. Not only Hewitt was damaged by his alleged complicity in Tomelty's circle, so was everyone else in the circle. A bonus. The rumours continued to shift, and it was time to highlight Hewitt's supposed lack of ability as an administrator. Here, the campaign against him finally sank venom into its own veins. For, if Hewitt was a poor or incompetent administrator in the very institution where he was now a candidate, why was he promoted Keeper of Art in or before June 1951, and why was he shortlisted for the top job? Why was only one modestly qualified rival listed for interview, if it was all-important to prevent an incompetent becoming administrator of both gallery and museum?

The bones of an administrative error could be disinterred, if only to check their sectarian odour. Hewitt got on well with the non-professional staff in Stranmillis, especially the carpenter Herbie Young. He and Young boasted they were the only two in the place who read *The New Statesman*. Social relations went beyond the workplace, even to the extent of the Youngs joining the Hewitts at the cottage above Cushendall. Closer to base, Herbie and his wife occasionally visited Mount Charles for supper; did so early in January 1952 when the lines of battle were redrawn with Alfred George's effective withdrawal from the contest. Only a day or two earlier Hewitt had brought home to breakfast his junior colleague

George Thompson, after a trip to London where Stendall had distanced himself from the party at large.[31] And, did they but know it, the City Fathers would have frowned on the Hewitts' lending their Antrim cottage to Miss Connolly, who cleaned the stairs in the Mount Charles building. Fraternizing with 'other ranks' alarms all mandarins, especially when practised by someone with talents above their average.

It is hardly surprising that Hewitt performed poorly on the day, though the account he gave Roberta afterwards spoke of 'a good and pleasant interview'.[32] For a week, he had been running a gauntlet of allegations, double-edged warnings, and office shenanigans. In a late memoir of the occasion, Mary O'Malley recalled considerable prejudice against him even in the course of the meeting. She had to admit that 'he had not made such a good showing at the interview', but proceeded to add what must seem now to be an entirely irrelevant point—'did not have army service'.[33]

O'Malley (née Hickey) deserves further consideration. Born in County Cork, and educated by Loreto nuns, she had married the psychiatrist Pearse O'Malley in 1947, and worked strenuously in Belfast to advance modern theatre. Before moving north, she had been an active member of Dublin's New Theatre Group, with which Owen Sheehy Skeffington and his French wife were involved. The Dublin Group's policy was 'the presentation of plays of a working-class nature: "plays with a purpose"'. Roddy Connolly, son of the executed 1916 leader and a card-carrying Red, moved in the same circle.[34] Not a background or profile likely to see military experience as a requirement in gallery or museum directors, but certainly an unhelpful link between Hewitt's 1937 associates and his too open supporter in 1952. (His shunning of the OTC while at Queens was no doubt recorded in some file somewhere.) What her later memoir discloses is the importance of Hewitt's martial deficit in the eyes of other councillors and members of the interview board. As with the allegation about administrative shortfallings, any facts were well known before the interview list was drawn up.

This was the sectarian idiom at its most refined, with no awkward reference to Catholic or Protestant differences. He had been disloyal or cowardly and, if that was not enough to convince a waverer, evidence of Hewitt's consorting with Peadar O'Donnell or Joe Tomelty (or indeed, Herbie Young) could be cited—reluctantly, of course. If the waverer insisted on pointing to Hewitt's recent internal promotion, then the answer by a nod if not in so many words consigned him to the inferior

31 *Journal*, PRONI, D/3838/4/7, 5 January 1952.

32 *Journal*, PRONI, D/3838/4/7, 26 September 1952.

33 O'Malley, *Never Shake Hands with the Devil*, pp. 246–7. O'Malley's account of the interview arrangements differs somewhat from Roberta Hewitt's. According to the former (a member of the selection panel), the initial time of meeting was changed because she could not be present. This may strike veteran Belfast watchers as unlikely (a changed schedule just to *include* a Hewitt supporter?). In the event, a different Hewitt supporter was unavailable when the meeting finally took place. Roberta, writing close to the action, has the two times of meeting set within the same day—i.e. morning and afternoon. O'Malley, writing long after the event, confirms the tied vote, and the chairman's decisive action. (See O'Malley, *Never Shake Hands with the Devil*, pp. 64–5.)

34 Andrée Sheehy Skeffington, *Skeff: a Life of Owen Sheehy Skeffington 1907–1970* (Dublin: Lilliput, 1991), p. 84.

role (no matter how elevated) in which authority over an entire institution was never to be his. So far but no further would he go. And if the waverer still harped on the pointlessness of interviewing a candidate so heavily stigmatized, then the answer was, 'Now he knows his place.'

As if to confirm such a fantastical scenario, when the result (by secret ballot) was announced, Councillor Holmes rose and thanked Chairman Tougher for his efficient conduct of the meeting. The city council's approval was a formality—Hewitt called it 'party routine'.[35] Stendall, director for a few more weeks, instantly suggested that the defeated candidate might attend a London auction where some Irish silver was on offer. While the city appointed Seaby, Hewitt boarded the Liverpool boat. He stayed restlessly on deck, watching the lighthouses round Belfast Lough pass on port and starboard—Carrickfergus, Bangor, and the more distant Copeland Islands. Even when the vessel was 'pulsing away into the darkness', and the crew had retired, he could not go down below:

> I still marched on, round and round the deck mechanically. Once I stopped at the rail and looked down at the troubled waters, sliding, folding over, and turning past, and, for a minute or more, I was nearer suicide than I hope I shall ever be again.[36]

Gaining his cabin at last, he suffered bouts of intense claustrophobia during the night, but travelled on by train the next morning. At the auction, he made no bid for the silver mug. London had other consolations. Tomelty was acting in the Strand Theatre and, after the performance Hewitt joined him in his dressing room. The actor-playwright expressed no surprise. The next day Hewitt met up with his English acquaintance Howard Sergeant, editor of the poetry magazine *Outposts* and sometime lover of Muriel Spark. In 1950, Sergeant had published *The Cumberland Wordsworth*, a study of the great romantic which chimed with Hewitt's regionalist ideas and made generous reference to Hewitt's verse. Sergeant had been a welcome guest at Mount Charles. Over lunch, the north-countryman advised his guest, 'get out of that God forsaken hole'. Instead, Hewitt wrote to Dame Dehra Parker, his local referee, to apologize for associating her with a candidate thought disloyal to the state. She phoned to reassure him that, while fully aware that he was no Conservative, she recognized he had made regionalism his position and 'disloyalty was nonsense'.[37]

The local press noted the result. *The Irish News* (a nationalist paper) used the headline, 'Museum Job Given to Englishman instead of Belfast Applicant'. *The Belfast News-Letter* (a Unionist paper) scarcely differed: 'Belfast Museum Director; Casting Vote for Englishman'. *The Northern Whig* (liberal in some respects) added a detail, 'Casting Vote in "Tie" Ousts Belfast Candidate'. The matter would not simply lie down. Friends of the Hewitts, the sisters Judith and Ray Rosenfield contributed regular articles to both the *Whig* and *Newsletter*—Ray became a significant drama critic in the province. Challenged by O'Malley, Tougher replied through the same medium; in a letter published in *The Northern Whig* on 2 October 1952 (a week after the interviews), to the effect that he 'knew a year and a half ago

[35] *North*, p. 211. [36] *North*, p. 211. [37] *Journal TS*, vol. II, p. 114.

[he] would not be able to agree to Mr Hewitt's appointment'. Even if the chairman had divined Alfred George's imminent retirement, the Mao of City Hall had entered the committee room with his mind fixed months earlier, and supervised an entirely fraudulent comparison of the two candidates, one of whom (Seaby) had no experience of curating art. Alfred George's non-availability may have led the powers-that-were desperately to spy out another candidate, and the fact that Seaby was an outsider unquestionably wounded Hewitt's justifiable pride in what he had done for Belfast. To have lost to Alfred George could have been rationalized as biding one's time a little longer.

The Hewitts were steeply inclined to blame Stendall, understandably outraged by telephoned good wishes which, in retrospect, rang hollow. Stendall, like the new man Seaby, occupied the Unionist equivalent role of Lenin's 'useful idiots'—call them Belfast Linen-ists, English appointees valued for a decorative-obstructionist function. Villainy of a more local stripe deserves closer attention. A highly ingenious attempt has been made to find a rationalization for Tougher's dating of his advance decision against Hewitt. Sarah Ferris calculates with pardonable laxity that the declared year and a half takes us back to the summer of 1951, which she argues 'is coincident with Hewitt's Griffinesque review of Lavery'.[38] Hewitt, it is alleged, had crudely or arrogantly treated the work of Sir John Lavery, an Ulster painter dead since 1941. In so far as a review of Lavery by Hewitt can be identified, it had appeared back in 1934, and it had indeed brusquely treated the great man and upset the Libraries Etc. committee at the time. (It does not seem to have bothered Lavery.) To tie her research to Chairman Tougher's position of 1951/52, Dr Ferris has to invoke a survey article by Hewitt published in 1951, 'Painting and Sculpture in Ulster'. Of its twenty-five pages, less than two are devoted to Lavery, beginning with the words, 'the greatest name so far in our record, John Lavery…'. In a lengthy passage to which Dr Ellis does not refer, Hewitt dealt with a painting in his own gallery, comparing Lavery's 1920 portrait of Cardinal Logue to the usual run of sitters: 'faced with a subject who refused to be flattered and who commanded his deepest respect an altogether more mature and searching portrait resulted, and a greater depth of human understanding was revealed'.[39] Unless the most fervent anti-Catholicism had overtaken Percy Tougher, the chairman could hardly deem these comments unworthy of a future director.

In the interregnum, on 10 October Belfast welcomed another English visitor, E. M. Forster, arriving as the British Association carnival wound down. The author of *A Passage to India* had been invited by Samuel Knox Cunningham (later Unionist MP for Antrim South at Westminster), to honour Forrest Reid (1875–1947),

[38] Ferris, *Poet John Hewitt*, p. 11. 'Griffinesque' refers to the character Griffin (based on Hewitt) in J. L. Green's novel, *Odd Man Out* (1945).

[39] Sam Hanna Bell, Nesca A. Robb, John Hewitt, eds., *The Arts in Ulster* (London: Harrap, 1951), p. 83. John Montague recorded his first meeting with Hewitt in the Belfast Gallery. Both poets were somewhat tongue-tied as they toured the collection. In front of Lavery's portrait of Cardinal McRory, the younger man blurted out 'he's my second cousin; his mother's name is Montague'. The gallery-man replied, 'It's a bad painting.' John Montague, 'Spiritual Maverick', *Threshold* 38 (Winter 1986/87), p. 17. Hewitt made some deprecating remarks about William Conor in 1945: 'unclarified by a sharp political philosophy…sentimental…'; see 'The Bitter Gourd', *Ancestral*, p. 116.

Belfast-born novelist and one-time student at Cambridge. Reid's former home on Ormiston Crescent brought together a strange medley of celebrants. Homosexuality, still a crime (though not so condign as mixing with the Tomelty crowd or sharing *The New Statesman* with a carpenter) united Cunningham, Forster, and the dead man. Stendall, enjoying British Association bun-fights and side-shows, attended; likewise the Hewitts, determined to play the brave card. Among northern writers, George Buchanan and John Boyd were to the fore. Slouching from the south came Lennox Robinson. Lunch at the Grand Central Hotel was a tricky occasion, with Roberta seated close to the sirector. A relatively unfamiliar but sociable Mr Gotto generated huge crack around the table.

In the evening, Mount Charles rang with the clatter of perhaps its most distinguished party. Forster was the toast, with Philip Larkin, the McFaddens, and Michael McLaverty adding youth and levity. Evidently it was no dry 'do'. Writing up her journal, Roberta could not remember the name of George Buchanan's new wife—'Shocking'. A week later, relations with the director had eased. After a committee, Stendall told Hewitt that he would be appointed deputy director under Seaby. Hewitt asked for a reference before Stendall retired, and the latter agreed, this time adding 'you should get out—go to England, it would be better for you'.[40]

To Austin Clarke in May 1953, Hewitt wrote about his fate at the hands of committeemen. 'I've no illusions about this country. Last autumn I missed the Directorship of the Belfast Gallery because I was suspected of sympathies with the South.' He felt compelled to balance his complaint with another, more sharply worded. 'Last Monday at a party in a Chelsea pub [the Irish poet] Anthony Cronin attacked me for my bigoted verse, my deliberate sneering at his people, my Orange attitude to the rest of Ireland.' And five years later, he told the same correspondent that another southern poet, Donagh MacDonagh, had called him 'an Orange bastard' to his face, 'because he heard me read verses which referred critically to the theology of the majority of my fellow-countrymen'.[41]

There were at least one or two positive developments in the Hewitts' lives during 1952—Roy McFadden's marriage to Margaret Ferguson, and the arrival from Newtownards of Jim Stewart and his Canadian wife, Sophie. James Uprichard Stewart (1904–74) came from a Presbyterian background in Dundalk, just south of the border, where his father had been a church caretaker. Helena Sophia Livesay (1912–91) was a Canadian painter, the sister of Dorothy Livesay (1909–96), who had become a communist in 1931, and later was Canada's poet laureate.[42] Jim and Sophie had attended the Marx Memorial Library Summer School at Swanage (Dorset) in 1936, the year they married. (Lecturers included J. D. Bernal, Harry

[40] *Journal TS*, vol. II, pp. 116–17, 17 October 1952.

[41] NLI Ms 38,658/3, JH to Austin Clarke, 22 May 1953; and JH to Clarke 4 November 1958. John Kilfeather averred that Hewitt was accused of mocking Cronin's grandmother in a poem about the Famine, but that the two were apparently friends when they met later at a party given by Michael and Edna Longley; see Kilfeather, 'Remembering John Hewitt', *Threshold* 38 (Winter 1986/87), p. 31.

[42] For a lively account of the Stewarts, see John Boyd, *The Middle of My Journey* (Belfast: Blackstaff, 1990) pp. 82–4. For Sophie's family background, see Dorothy Livesay, *Beginnings: a Winnepeg Childhood*, rev. ed. (Winnepeg: Peguis, 1988); and *Journey with My Selves; a Memoir 1909–1963* (Vancouver: Douglas, 1991).

Plate 1. The poet's parents, Robert and Elinor, in old age.

Plate 2. At the statue of François Coppée, in Paris, July 1929. The knickerbockers later concealed a copy of Joyce's *Ulysses* as Hewitt returned through UK customs.

Plate 3. John and Roberta (née Black) at their new home, Fortwilliam Park, Belfast, 1934.

Plate 4. John and Roberta in the Glens, 1950s (courtesy of Philip Flanagan).

Plate 5. The historian David Beers Quinn with Hewitt somewhere in the Glens of Antrim (courtesy of Brenda Stewart).

Plate 6. Official parade in Dresden, May 1959. Hewitt was one of Coventry's two civic representatives at the 10th anniversary of the German Democratic Republic's formal establishment.

Plate 7. Edwin Muir, Roberta Hewitt, and Willa Muir in Edinburgh.

Plate 8. Chinese poet and political activist, Shelley Wang.

Plate 9. Terence Flanagan as a young painter, with Roberta and John Hewitt (courtesy of Philip Flanagan).

Plate 10. Fellow Ulster poet, John Montague, with Hewitt outside the Herbert Gallery, Coventry, September 1969.

Plate 11. Hewitt with Zoltan Frankl and his wife, Annie Levinter.

Plate 12. The widowed poet in his home at Stockman's Lane, Belfast, *c.*1984.

Pollitt, and John Strachey.) This was the Spanish moment and, in response to the fascist uprising, many on the Left stiffened their political allegiances. The Stewarts were members of the British Communist Party, and Jim additionally joined the Soviet Friendship Society. With Frank Edwards (a Copper-Bottom Bolshevik, in eyes less blinkered than his own) and Stephen Wynburn, he visited the Soviet Union on three occasions. But the invasion of Hungary in October–November 1956 appalled them, and both Stewarts resigned from the party.[43]

Throughout the years when Hewitt was trapped in Belfast, the Stewarts provided a new surge of energy and high spirits. They lived in Camden Street, a short walk from Mount Charles. Jim was committed to technical education and an optimistic view of science; Sophie, though she almost abandoned painting once settled in Ireland, painted a fine portrait of Roberta and drew the image of a seated John Hewitt, which is now the Hewitt Society's icon. In time, they too acquired a cottage in Antrim, and their guests included the Hewitts, George and Molly Hill, and other dissenters from Belfast's double-barrelled orthodoxy.

Arriving in January 1953, the gallery's new director had his own interests, closer to the museum than the gallery, and including trams, dolls, and early Irish farthings. The initial arrangements were stiff, though Seaby went out of his way to be friendly with everyone. Roberta continued to speculate about ultimate responsibility for her husband's humiliation—'Professor [Estyn] Evans of Queen's is somewhere in it, as he has not been able to be friendly to Johnny lately…'. Then she proceeded immediately to record the great fulfilment she gained by once again having children to stay in the flat, noting their speech habits, choice of breakfast, and neighbourhood friends.[44]

On a Sunday in mid-March, Frankl and his wife entertained the Hewitts and the Seabys, with Art School people for leaven. Roberta voted it a nice evening. Spring opened up the Glens as the ideal foil to city manipulation and blandishment. A watercolourist drove them from Belfast to the cottage, talking constantly—'his tongue never lay'. When they arrived at 9.30 p.m. on a Friday, darkness had long fallen, but their neighbour Mary McDonnell had the fire lit and the place warmed. For Sunday lunch, Roberta invited the Seabys and their two children, and the whole party walked to Layde churchyard, north of Cushendall. The children pleased her as children always did. Of their father, she noted simply, 'I like him very well.' Before dusk the Seabys drove back to Belfast, and steadily gained a reputation for amiability and devotion.[45]

A local man died and the Hewitts got involved in the wake, men and women segregated in different rooms. The endless talk rarely if ever related to the dead man who lay abed under the window. Cigarettes on a dinner plate were offered to the men, but no whiskey appeared before midnight, by which time the Hewitts had left. There was much easy praise of the good old days, though John put in a word for the welfare state and educational opportunity. Later Mrs McDonnell let

[43] I am grateful to Brenda Stewart for these details of her parents.

[44] *Journal*, PRONI, D/3828/4/7, [no day given] January 1953. These were the children of Jim McKinlay, whose work JH had published in *Forum* (1937).

[45] *Journal*, PRONI, D/3838/4/7, 8 March 1953.

Roberta know that, as wakes went, that had been 'a poor wan'. The old dialect lingered—'he that failed' was now a *corp*, not corpse.[46] The little ports below the Glens were not immortal communities of spiritual resource.

The funeral took place on Saint Patrick's Day. While John went off for a primer in McCollam's pub with a man from Glenarriff, Roberta attended an auction. The two then advanced up the shore road to meet the cortege, and took another drink. 'They eventually picked up the funeral on the Layde Road and fell in at the back of the men but in front of the women.' Having bought a towel rail, Roberta visited Mrs Stone who put on her hat (for respect of the dead) and the pair stood on the street with the door 'till' (nearly closed). Down the street came the funeral, its mood fairly cheerful—'many the smile I got'. This was a Protestant funeral and with less than ecumenical charity, Roberta conceded that some Catholics did enter the red sandstone Church of Ireland. The officiating cleric doubled up as organist, playing 'Abide with Me' faster than Roberta had ever heard it before—'a few grace notes and it would have made great swing music'. John felt obliged to sing and 'strangely enough did keep the general direction of the tune'. He returned to the pub with friends, then got home about 6 p.m. with a headache.[47] This was not quite Utopia.

Recovered from the spells in McCollam's, the poet wrote a good deal in the days after the funeral. Two poems composed in late March 1953 place the Glens between contrasting points of reference historical and geographic—Denmark of mediaeval times, and contemporary Belfast. In the first stanza of 'The Braes o' Layde', he wrote

> The Danes were here. The forts above the road
> are still called after them, and down by Layde
> you can point out the port their longships used
> when they left Ireland after their last raid.[48]

'The Belfastman', in contrast, appears to discount the possibility of leaving, while also emphasizing intransigent differences, as much between the title (Hewitt himself?) and the lines that follow:

> In this my valley how should I revolt
> against the stream that is the pulse of it,
> against the great hills rounded to the north
> and the wide east from which each dawn is lit?
> Should I go there, the sea would change my tongue
> and the lip hardly know its syllable;

[46] *Journal*, PRONI, D/3838/4/7, 15 March 1953.

[47] *Journal*, PRONI, D/3838/4/7, 17 March 1953. JH provides a complementary account (without the headache) in 'The Sun Dances', an unpublished essay in UU, Hewitt, Box 5. The deceased, of mixed denominational background, was Daniel Hyndman. Learned in traditional lore, he had once seen the miraculous dancing of the sun at Easter. This belief is central to Austin Clarke's 'mediaeval' novel of 1952, *The Sun Dances at Easter*, banned in the Irish Republic.

[48] Ormsby, p. 125. This may relate back to 'The Red Hand' #LXXI which concluded with a reference to the Danes made by 'an oul man and grey' to the poet—It was better for the country/before they went away.'

west lies the sod we sought and travelled from,
its falling petals always spell farewell.
This then is home; its clay has clenched my foot,
its angry factions jangle in my heart,
and I must wait until the bells clash past,
before I hear the patient birdsong start.[49]

Back in town by midweek, the Hewitts suddenly realized that they were due at an 'at home' hosted by Lady Wakehurst, wife of Northern Ireland's recently appointed Governor. This required a new dress for Roberta, advised by May Morton. The Seabys picked up the Hewitts and all drove to the official residence at Hillsborough, where they mingled with 'Good Works' (Maurice Boyd's term), those who have performed for the general benefit. Hewitt was inclined to a similar view, tersely attributing the change of attitude to the welfare state. It was the first time people of their low level (Roberta's phrase) had been included. But, she added, she was there because she had married Culture.[50] The next day, they struck back to Cushendall.

Hewitt's father had died at the end of the war, in July 1945. Yet it was in April 1953, within weeks of the Cushendall funeral and the Hillsborough reception, that he wrote 'My Father's Death in Hospital' and 'My Father's Ghost'. The first is a too-heavily freighted reconstruction of the last hours, achieving an unexpected definition when (lines 15–16) the poet writes 'Can this rough death, / wombed in his being, be his closest heir?' The implied denial of the son's existence, in favour of death itself, may echo those cold hours on deck between Belfast and Liverpool and the beckoning waves. The shorter poem almost celebrates a long departed parent, 'My father dead, the prince among my dead, / has never come again except in dream...' It is altogether a more resolved piece, in which son and father both find rest in their hermetic firmaments, the one permanent, the other riddled with time. If the first of these poems is distressed (in some fundamental sense of the word) by the rustic jocularity of a Glens funeral the previous month, then the second moves to acknowledge what had been gained or given at Hillsborough:

yet, when I since stood in some famous place,
I've always thought I'll tell him he must come.[51]

John and Roberta were not revolutionaries, either after the war or before it. Intelligent and energetic individuals with no stake in the establishment, they wanted and worked for something better than the dispensations of Brookeborough Unionism administered through the dislikes of Percy Tougher. And they wanted it for all, the mill girls painted by Conor, the Catholic unemployed, eccentric geniuses with brush or chisel, and homely glensmen above Layde and Cushkibb. John had avowed the dialectic, Roberta lamented dialect's slow collapse. They had sworn no allegiance to Orange orders or Republican brotherhoods.

[49] Ormsby, p. 505.
[50] *Journal*, PRONI, D/3838/4/7, 22 March 1953.
[51] Ormsby, pp 208–9.

On 25 March 1953, the widow of George V died. In her journal, Roberta who would sing the praises of Robert Emmet, Jimmy Maxton and George Orwell, noted the event:

> She was a good Queen. As a mother she had many sorrows. As a woman whatever tears she shed were very private but her body was well cared for and she was well housed and servanted. I saw her in 1921 with the king and thought she looked nice—we all thought they were brave to come to Ireland during the Troubles.[52] We [ie the Black family] were in a Mrs Coopers house in Great Victoria Street and they passed there. Soldiers were lined all the way along and Mrs Cooper sent them out tea and sandwiches.... Later one of the soldiers came... and asked for me; but I was away home. He said he had never seen any wee girl he liked the look of so much... I talk of the Queen but I talk of me.[53]

Clearly this passage arose from more than political or constitutional issues; it transcended its own sentiment, moving from high state ceremonial to the most intimate reflection. Neither comrade to comrade, nor plebeian to potentate, Roberta's words reflect and respond between two women. Only a few days had elapsed since the Hillsborough 'at home' and the Hewitts' return to Cushendall. On that Sunday, John had left for Belfast, their friend Norman Carruthers staying for another day. Alone, she opted for the soft bed in the smaller room, not the shared hard bed Johnny preferred. Her thoughts about this brief interlude were not self-indulgent. 'I have so many sleepless nights now, when I get exasperated I start to bring all the blame [for] anything on Johnny's sleeping head. When I get unhappy he cannot talk to me at all and cannot help me. He is a good husband but no lover. I feel I would be better alone.'

The entry in her journal for Tuesday 24 March suggests that, in part at least it was written mid-journey, perhaps on the Larne train, 'The weather was lovely at the cottage but somehow I was not so sad to leave as usual although I don't particularly want to go home.' Not for the last time, she longs for a room of her own. The motives, concerns, implications inevitably remain opaque. Her criticism of John is sharp, but hardly more cutting that her self-criticism. 'I cannot see things roundly and I am as nothing going blindly nowhere and no reason to be asked of me why I sit or stand—I need not stand—I need not do anything. No one would even think of blaming me.'

The queen's death next day provided an external focus but with a discernible backward scrutiny of Roberta herself. The queen had been lavishly cared for, perhaps to the point of arousing trivial jealousy. Yet the queen doubtless shed private tears. On the occasion more than thirty years earlier when they were a street's breadth from each other, a young soldier had taken appreciative notice of Roberta, still a teenager. 'I talk of the Queen but I talk of me. I am more important to me. But as the Queen who was head of my State dies, I die an inch—inches of me die

[52] George V opened the Northern Ireland parliament in Belfast on 22 June 1921.
[53] *Journal*, PRONI, D/3838/4/7, 25 March 1953.

with every noted death. Thousands of inches of deaths are in between the dates of birth and deaths of Kings and Councillors—we poor inches.'[54]

John's double commemoration of his dead father after eight years, Roberta's dissatisfaction with her domestic life and her reaction to Queen Mary's death (linked to a teenage moment of potential romance) do not merge to present a clear account of the couple's relationship in 1953. She had been anxious to get out of Belfast for some time. The disappointment which he suffered at the hands of Tougher and McDonald contributed to her anxiety but did not make up even half its sum. The ease with which the Seabys and Hewitts came to socialize casually, in Belfast, Hillsborough, and even in Cushendall, cannot have been entirely reassuring for her. If they could never quit Stranmillis and Mount Charles, where would she find a room of her own?

They are halfway through their married life together, he professionally frustrated yet secure, she active in the Edenderry Nursery School project yet unrewarded, committed to painting the radiators or changing soiled bed clothes. She has written down her disappointment at his bedroom performance, from which act of hers it may be fairly deduced that he did not have (or sneak) access to the journal when (for example) he put together 'From Chairmen and Committeemen, Good Lord Deliver Us'. She could write without evasion: 'No word, no gesture is real, he never makes love to me and I am sure this is my main trouble.' Yet the issues between them also take on a literary-critical mask; 'I am getting tired of so many poems of trees and leaves and wish a small trace of passion could creep in and less description.'[55] Their secular wedding had taken place a few days less than nineteen years earlier: no children, a topic indirectly addressed by Roberta, never by John, not at least in documentation traced so far. Back in 1951, she had gone into the Royal Victoria Hospital on the day after his MA conferring. The Matron recognized the wife of a man who had written 'Painting and Sculpture in Ulster'; a few privileges came Roberta's way. The consultant, Lowry, dealt in gynaecology or, as the patient expressed it 'another shove for poor wee Fanny'.[56] No surgery altered the Hewitts' condition in this respect. In April 1953, Roberta's problems seem comparatively minor—extremely sore fingers (one medical mandarin said they weren't sore enough) with pus oozing from under the nails.[57] Anne, a niece, is having a similar problem 'and it proves to be emotional... unfortunately a boy she was very fond of—a young medical student in England[—]was called up for National Service, was sent to Korea and was killed'.[58]

On Hewitt's medical or psychological chart, little can be traced, because the charts (if anything of the kind existed) do not survive. The confident apostle of progressive ideas lampooned in *Odd Man Out*, the eloquent dispenser of aesthetic verdicts, is tongue-tied on private, intimate topics. He is far from unique in his time and place. Bertie Rodgers constructed a quasi-ethnic schema of Protestant

[54] *Journal*, PRONI, D/3838/4/7, 25 March 1953.
[55] *Journal*, PRONI, D/3838/4/7, 4 April 1953.
[56] *Journal*, PRONI, D/3838/4/7, 11 July 1951.
[57] *Journal*, PRONI, D/3838/4/7, 8 April 1953.
[58] *Journal*, PRONI, D/3838/4/7, 12 April 1953.

taciturnity and Catholic garrulousness (at least in Ulster), but Bertie was a living refutation of his own theory. Or, perhaps, Bertie had escaped from the underlying cultural dichotomy; trained as a Calvinist minister and called to the cockpit of Loughgall, he had discovered poetry and the exuberance of poetic language. Ironically, he had learned of this alternative world from John Hewitt. Hewitt had not been tongue-tied when the Council for Civil Liberties investigated Ulster's B-Special policemen, nor when George Padmore denounced fascism. Nor was his pen shy in declaring the relative merits of John Luke and Colin Middleton. It was on the one issue of marital relations that words failed him, according to Roberta. Her anguished sincerity cannot for a moment be doubted, especially when it carries within it a strain of self-blame. John kept no journal, and no second perspective on the situation of April 1953 is available. But when, years later, he put together *A North Light*, one glaring feature of incompleteness is its avoidance of any deeply personal theme.

Cushendall provided balm yet also offered the privacy for domestic rowing that a flat in Mount Charles did not. After 12 July 1953, various friends arrived by invitation or accident. Jim and Sophie Stewart were down to stay in their own cottage. To visit them, John and Roberta walked over Lurig Edan through dismal scenery, she striding ahead, both tormented by midges. 'When I got to the top and looked back to where J. was my heart turned over[.] It looked awful. The top was uninteresting, it is shallow like a saucer and very wet and we had to walk over four miles.' Yet after coffee and something to eat at the Stewarts', and a lift home, it became 'a good day to remember'.[59]

A few days later, they met Tomelty in Cushendall, looking more than usually exotic with his hair 'long, in a bob to below his ears and side locks, growing across his face to reach the mouth', an effect required for his role in a film. A get-together at the Hewitts' cottage was planned for the next evening, with the Stewarts, the folklorist Michael Murphy, George Hill and his wife (who were staying with the Stewarts). 'The Dust Under Our Feet', a play designed by Murphy to show up Irish intolerance, had just opened to howls of outrage. Tomelty denounced attempts at propaganda on stage, and went further to denounce the Irish in London—their downfall was drink, never women or crime. On the sexual issue, Roberta took note; Joe declared his compatriots 'too mean to <u>take</u> a woman... not so pure, but they are without passion'.[60]

Hewitt evidently played little or no part in this discussion. Though drama had been central to the evening's excitement, an underlying political concern was unmistakeable, not only in Murphy's concern with the fate of an illegitimate girl in Irish society, or Tomelty's analysis of the London-Irish. John D. Stewart had been under a kind of surveillance, and Hewitt had written loudly for the Workers' cause in a paper to which he had been introduced by a trio of men including George Hill. Tomelty, who now deplored propaganda on the stage, and took to

[59] *Journal*, PRONI, D/3838/4/7, 12 July 1953—middle of long entry, probably written over several days.

[60] *Journal*, PRONI, D/3838/4/7, 12 July 1953. The emphasis is Roberta's.

writing a 'soap' for television, had dealt with the excesses of the police and the law in 'The End House'. If it had been a political file from that period which doomed Hewitt at the interview of September 1952, his nemesis (Percy Tougher) died in July 1953, less than a year after casting the chairman's harpoon.

Towards the end of the month, Hewitt went to Dublin on personal business. The timing was awkward, even odd, because Bertie Rodgers's first wife, Marie, had just committed suicide.[61] In the evening after the funeral, Roberta wrote John a long letter, providing many details—but did not post it. Looking at Marie Rodgers in the open coffin and touching her hair, Roberta had murmured, 'God rest your soul', not a Protestant sentiment. Angry at herself, she asked rhetorically in the letter if she could do the same for Percy Tougher. 'I must confess it is easier for me to say "Damn him", but I suppose God will not be influenced and I do not wish to bring pressure on God—I need prayer for me.'[62] The depth of humiliation and frustration which the Hewitts had experienced after the interview defies measurement, even if reasons of state might offer an explanation. Marie Rodgers' funeral brought other sombre emotions and anxieties to the surface. There was the question of religious belief, tentatively reopened with recourse to the traditional Catholic phrase/prayer for the dead. There was also grief and guilt about the fatal illness and suffering of the departed who died of a deliberate overdose. Roberta knew that much of her own torment in the summer of 1953 was caused by persistent colitis, strangely complicated by coldness in the feet. At the funeral of a woman reduced to seven stone in weight by the ravages of cancer, these minor ailments were laid aside. Roberta, however, attended on her own, Johnny being down south. Separations of husband and wife took many forms—a short business trip or, at the other extreme, death. In between lay the possibility of divorce or a second (non-licit) union. Bertie would remarry within months, and at his first wife's funeral had bravely declared 'Mayne was the one Marie loved and Marie was the one Mayne loved.' Roy McFadden had remarried, and Colin Middleton also had a new (second) wife. The Hewitts, for all the intensity of Roberta's disappointment in bed, stayed together until her death in 1975.

At the string of refuellings which followed Marie's funeral, the actor James Boyce declared that revolutionaries ended up with a smashed chin, for all their flamboyance, citing Winston Churchill as an unlikely example. Roberta countered with Beethoven, Cézanne, and Rilke, adding that 'dust to man and rib to woman was revolutionary'. It was not a sober occasion. The following month Milly Morton died, unaware that her sister had cancer. In October Kathleen Ferrier died of the same cause. The early 1950s, dominated by fear of the bomb and the implications of war in Korea, heaped individual griefs and losses on top of the *Zeitangst*.

In the autumn after the deaths of Marie Rodgers and Percy Tougher, Hewitt found additional opportunities to write. *The Irish Times* wanted art and theatre reviews. Ruby (as she signed on this occasion) asked Bertie if he would supply poems for a project *The Belfast Telegraph* had put to her husband—it was trying to

[61] John Boyd, *The Middle of My Journey* (Belfast: Blackstaff, 1990), p. 92.
[62] *Journal*, PRONI, D/3838/4/7, 20 July 1953.

turn itself into a liberal paper.[63] The editor asked Hewitt to contribute to a Saturday half-page on literature on a retainer fee of five guineas, plus occasional pieces under the name McArt. This was a clever pseudonym, familiar to all Belfast readers through McArt's Fort, on Cave Hill, overlooking the town: here, in the 1790s, the United Irishmen met to plan a Jacobin republic. Considered as an amalgam of Gaelic and English words, it meant Son of Art. He was also elected to the board of CEMA. In the general election of October 1953, both he and Roberta addressed envelopes for Samuel Napier who contested for one of the Queen's University's four seats. Representing the Northern Ireland Labour Party, Napier came last in the poll.

John Betjeman lectured at the Stranmillis museum early in December, entertaining but not entirely convincing. Hewitt had been trying for years to wring an invitation for him, but only succeeded in the dying days of Stendall's regime. Betjeman also did a poetry reading at which he endearingly lost his place or his programme several times. Betjeman's copy of *No Rebel Word*, inscribed by the author, ended up in Essex University. The Hewitts visited Dublin, saw Shaw's 'Saint Joan' at the Gate Theatre, inspected the two Protestant cathedrals, and 'called in to see Mass at St. John's Chapel'. New paintings by Gerard Dillon were on view in Victor Waddington's gallery.

In January 1954, W. A. Seaby proposed an exhibition of paintings, drawings, and book illustrations of British birds, which provoked a comic southern protest—'Surely that's taking partition too far? I can't help wondering if all our native birds are classified as "British" or only those that stray into the six northern counties.... Even though the birds of Ireland may not be true-blood Republicans, I don't quite see why they should be classified as British.'[64] The following year, with a new interparty government installed in Dublin, the southern Minister for Education (General Richard Mulcahy) offered to lend some Old Master paintings from the National Gallery for display in Belfast. Hewitt promptly and publicly welcomed the initiative.

He recognized Roberta's anguish during these years, and acknowledged his inability to respond adequately. A series of five sonnets, commenced in August 1954, attempted to address the situation, none of them published until 1979, four years after her death. The Shakespearean form scarcely helped, and one senses that the texts were written communications offered when word of mouth would not come to him. Her journal for 1954 opens with a brief summary (written in June), and only gets down to detail for the final two months of the year. If the depth of their unhappiness cannot be measured or denied, the tenacity of each deserves as much attention.

In June 1954, they had travelled to Amsterdam through London, taking in a performance by Edith Evans in Christopher Fry's 'The Dark is Light Enough', a play which did not impress. At an open air exhibition in Holland Park, they bumped into the Frankls, who provided an *entrée* to various private galleries. The

[63] PRONI, D/2833/C/8/8, Roberta Hewitt to W. R. Rodgers, 1 November 1953.
[64] *Irish Times*, 16 January 1954, p. 13.

poet and architectural historian, Maurice Craig, took them to lunch. Amsterdam involved another PEN conference, the conferring of an honorary degree on 'wee Morgan' (that is, E. M. Forster) and Jean Schlumberger at Leyden, and inevitably the great Van Gogh exhibition. John bought Roberta a ring made in Bali, treasured because it had been 'made by someone who is near the origin of making things for love'.[65] Five years later, while settling in to Coventry, Hewitt observed to Bertie Rodgers that Amsterdam was somewhere he could live in—'a decent clean Protestant place'.

On the way back through London, they spotted Joe Tomelty reading his paper; after coffee all three walked to Princess Gardens where, as guests of the Hills, they ate lunch, drank two bottles of wine, 'and only had time to fall into a taxi and get the train home'.[66] Straw in the wind though it may be, reference to the Hills following less than a year after the Cushendall discussion of Michael Murphy's play goes some way towards confirming the identity of George Hill (in 'The Brown Horse', 1937) with George Hill (guest, with his wife, of the Stewarts, 1953). In *A North Light* Hewitt never named the three men in the pub but did observe that two of them shortly moved to England for work.[67] Never a revolutionary in the sense that Frank Ryan or Malachy Grey could claim the honour, Hewitt did not dissociate from the companion-comrades of his youth.

The post-war establishment in Northern Ireland slowly changed, though not in its operative methods. The Wakehursts in Hillsborough brought a promissory note of reconciliation into their engagement with the Ulster community. Margaret, Lady Wakehurst (1899–1994), came from such long-lived English liberals that her father had marched as a boy in support of the Great Reform Bill (1832). Both the governor and his wife called into the gallery quite often, and came to like Hewitt. On 25 February 1954, Hewitt gave a copy of *No Rebel Word* to Lady Wakehurst, inscribing it 'with the author's respectful compliments'. The connection cannot have done the deputy director any harm with his municipal employers. Lady Wakehurst acknowledged the pitfalls everywhere throughout Ulster politics, and chose to 'work on the bridges like Art and Nursing and Welfare'. She agreed to visit Roberta's nursery school where she took photographs of children on play-slides and swings. Roberta began to review novels for the *Belfast Telegraph*.[68] But Jim Stewart stuck to at least one old interest, travelling to the Soviet Union in August 1955.

The Hewitts' first motor car arrived in September. The following March, it skidded on the road between Dundalk and Drogheda, and overturned. Both ended up in the Lourdes Hospital with head, neck, and arm injuries in her case, high blood pressure in his. (Was this cause or effect of the accident?) They couldn't

[65] *Journal*, PRONI, D/3838/4/7, 24 October 1954. The Schlumbergers were a notable French Protestant family, some of whom had moved in André Gide's youthful circle.

[66] *Journal*, PRONI, D/3838/4/7, 24 October 1954. The train took them to the boat, either at Liverpool or Heysham.

[67] George Hill's name, together with Edward Boyle and Joe Sherlock's, is given in Ormsby, p. xxxii. George and Molly Hill were particular friends of Jim and Sophie Stewart, still members of the Communist Party at this date.

[68] *Journal*, PRONI, D/3838/4/7, 24 October 1954.

express how kind they had found the nuns to be. In the immediate aftermath, as they recuperated at the cottage, Basil Blackshaw painted John's portrait, and worked on at least seven preliminary sketches of Roberta. The summer holidays of 1956 were spent in Donegal with the Maybins, for whose children the Hewitts served as godparents, first Roberta, then John, shaky though their religious commitments were. Patrick Maybin was one of those unnoticed, unambitious poets whom Hewitt, occasionally embattled with Laurie Green, Percy Tougher, or Anthony Cronin, sometimes longed to join.

There were triumphs or mixed triumphs along the way. In February 1956, Jack Yeats finally reached the northern capital with an exhibition of forty-five paintings, most of them loaned by private collectors or public institutions, and some provided by the artist himself. This latter category was offered for sale, but the Libraries Etc. committee wasn't having any. Hewitt inevitably wrote the catalogue, observing dryly that it was a little late in the day to say anything in general terms about Yeats's art. To Rodgers he conceded that his opinion of Yeats needed revision. Some of the private loans came from northern collectors, including two owned by Zoltan Frankl, the Hewitts' highly supportive friend.[69]

His last big exhibition at Stranmillis featured the veteran Ulster painter William Conor (1884–1958). The occasion was complicated by a lightning strike in the Belfast shipyards which left much of the city paralysed. Politics brooded everywhere: the resignation of Dame Dehra Parker, on grounds of ill-health, added to a mood of uncertainty; would the young Brian Faulkner (Dublin educated) be taken into the cabinet? Of aristocratic background and president of CEMA, Dehra Parker was well known to the Hewitts; in February 1951, she had presided at the opening of a regionalist English Contemporary Painting exhibition, at which John had introduced Roberta to her. Indeed, she had written in his support for the directorship. Conor was scarcely a controversial artist, though a richly talented one. Nevertheless, a southern correspondent noted that 'his qualities have been little enough recognised by bourgeois Belfast, for his most characteristic works have dealt with such uncommercial subjects as mill-girls in their skirts and shawls…'. And an Ulster *émigré* lamented Hewitt's imminent departure for Coventry: 'if someone is visiting Northern Ireland and wants an introduction to the place, who can I send him to when John Hewitt's gone?'[70]

[69] See the review signed G. H. G. in the *Irish Times*, 23 February 1956, p. 3.
[70] *Irish Times*, 19 March 1957, p. 4.

PART II

HOME THOUGHTS FROM ABROAD

7

An Irishman and -Woman in Coventry, 1956–66

In her journal for 1956, Roberta Hewitt recalled divided hopes of the future. When John was called for interview in Coventry, she was convinced he had the job within grasp, while also

> afraid we would never get the chance to leave Belfast. All our married lives I wished he would get a job elsewhere... but he always gave me his talk on the 'rooted man' and I have repeated 'Roots should be under your feet, not around your neck.'

John's defence borrowed a crucial term from the eulogy of J. M. Synge in 'The Municipal Gallery Revisited' (1937); by the autumn of 1954, he had borrowed the poem's title *tout court* (together with the ambulatory structure of Yeats's) for his own 'The Municipal Gallery Revisited, October 1954', written two years after his rejection by the Belfast gallery authorities. Hewitt's efforts to get out of Belfast had never been energetic, though he was interviewed in Manchester and Norwich. In 1949, while passing through London, he had been urged to apply for the Whitechapel Gallery directorship. He was not interested; his mission in London was to visit the *Tribune* office, headquarters of the Labour Left in print.[1]

Whatever the 'security' dimensions of his rejection at home may have been, the issue of political unreliability does not seem to have been a factor in Britain. One of Hewitt's referees for Coventry was Thomas MacGreevy, by now director of the National Gallery in Dublin, but also a noted Gaeilgeoir and pious Catholic.[2] Hewitt had reviewed MacGreevy's little book on Jack Yeats without sentiment. Things were not simply to be revisited, but triumphantly relocated. The Coventry interview over, he telephoned Roberta to break the good news. 'It's a most interesting place and it is growing—they don't seem to be afraid of ideas and I like the committee that appointed me.'[3] He beat five rival candidates for the job.

Shortly after John settled into his adopted English home town in April 1957, he was quick to note pre-existing good omens. Hewitt was a common enough name in Warwickshire. Indeed, he proudly noted that an eighteenth-century John Hewitt had been senior alderman of Coventry in the 1770s, who left behind a valuable *Journal* of his career as a justice of peace, dealing with 'riots, coiners, murder, highway robberies', and other social disorders. The Irish poet and man of the Left did not dwell on the kind or quality of the social order defended by his namesake,

[1] *Journal*, PRONI, D/3838/4/6, 15 August 1949. [2] *North*, p. 249.
[3] *Journal*, PRONI, D/3838/4/7, 12 September 1956.

content to find a degree of continuity between past and present. But a major, more urgent, factor in Hewitt's assessment of the mediaeval and wartorn Warwickshire city lay in its emphatically *not* being Belfast. Here was no sulky or downtrodden aboriginal minority biting at the heels of civic order; here was no arrogant philistine majority turning such order to its own narrow advantage.

Coventry was located near the centre of what Ulster Unionists were wont to call 'the mainland', but in September 1956 (when he was interviewed) its cultural, political, and social make up was as far removed from the Unionist ideal as that of—say—Berlin. For a start, the Labour Party held the reins of power, both in the parliamentary and municipal spheres, having taken control of the council in 1937. Second, the city characterized itself by reference to international parallels, establishing relations with numerous continental 'twins' on either side of the Iron Curtain. Third, culture featured prominently in the city fathers' plans for urban renewal—through a school-building programme, social housing, the commissioning of a wholly new cathedral to replace the mediaeval structure destroyed under the Blitz, and the development of museums and art galleries. In the words of one latter-day, and somewhat condescending, reviewer of the situation in 1957, 'it seemed that the Age of the Common Man was about to dawn'.[4] The new director would happily throw his weight behind this future.

The recent past had been decidedly grim. In Hewitt's own account, forty acres of the city's heart had been totally laid waste under the bombing, with a proportionate loss of human life, and intense anxiety about the outcome of the conflict.[5] Later, with a parliamentary majority of 180 seats over the Tories in the general election of July 1945, Labour inherited a vast post-war debris. Even earlier, Coventry had displayed a rugged militancy to which we will have to return in considering Hewitt's response to the city's traditions and ambitions. The Great War had enormously boosted the Midlands' industrial capacity, and Coventry was to the fore in manufacturing motor engines, aeroplanes, munitions, and other comestibles of destruction. Certain famous names—Dan Rudge's bicycles (since 1884), Daimler cars (1896), Courtaulds' artificial silk (1904)—summarize the range and depth of inventive applied science of which Coventry boasted, even without the wars. Industry and labour did not so much go hand in hand as demand cooperation each of the other. Hence the union militancy here as elsewhere, and also a remarkable local initiative in industrial relations, which had a profound bearing on Hewitt's career.

As he well knew, Hewitt's home town had also experienced rapid industrial development, the growth of trade unionism, and the consequent political divisions and clashes. The English Midlands had been saved the divisive effect of ethnic particularism and the exploitative religious campaigning which had assailed Scotland

[4] Brendan Flynn, in notes prepared for the opening of a retrospective exhibition, 'Pictures for the People: British Life and Landscape Collection 1957–2000', which ran for most of 2004. These notes are preserved in the Herbert Art Gallery archives. Flynn was a curator at the Birmingham Museum and Art Gallery.

[5] Signed introductory essay to a book of photographs, *Coventry; the Tradition of Change and Continuity* (Coventry: Coventry Corporation, 1966), p. 9.

and Ulster's working-class movement. In the late 1920s, the young poet had studied James Connolly, readily embraced the cause of labour only to find—again and again—that nothing was black and white (or permanent red) in Belfast politics, where orange and green demanded allegiance from 'their' share of the workforce. Now, Coventry offered an uncomplicated spectrum, and his preferred allegiance was dominant in the council chamber.

There was one area of resemblance between the new Midlands environment and the older world of his grandparents in Ulster—Methodism. Although Hewitt Senior had adopted an occasional stubborn independence from the Church, and his son retained little or nothing of the egregious jollity of that persuasion, the historic role of Methodism in Warwickshire was not easily avoided. Apart from the (reduced) presence of Wesleyan believers in the mid-twentieth century, there was an additional factor appealing to John Hewitt. The social constituency of Victorian Methodism in the city was craft-based, and weavers in particular were numerous in its ranks.[6] These craftsmen (and women) were forerunners to the industrial skilled worker within a proletariat regimented through the car factories of the twentieth century, but they were also kin to the rhyming weavers of Antrim and Down whom Hewitt had researched in depth and would later celebrate in print. In 1953, he had already written that the bards of Ulster, 'particularly the "Rhyming Weavers" were Freemasons, members of book clubs or reading societies, and often radical and democratic in their politics and liberal in their Presbyterianism'.[7]

E. P. Thompson has famously described how English Methodism fitted into counter-revolution in the 1790s and after, a notion not wholly different from the Irish historiographical wisdom about 'killing Home Rule with kindness' a century later.[8] In Coventry, Alfred Herbert Ltd practised a self-interested paternalism towards its staff which seemingly reduced union complaints. In its early days, Herberts manufactured machine tools rather than finished products, and consequently was less driven by mass demand for conveyor-belt delivery of identical items. For whatever reason, the company's industrial relations were harmonious compared to those prevalent in the car factories and suppliers of wartime materials.[9] And one reason certainly was the personality of its founder and long-serving chief executive [Sir] Alfred Herbert (1866–1957). He was patron of the new gallery where John took up his post on 1 April 1957.

Herbert had long debated with himself whether to give Coventry a planetarium or an art gallery. Before the war, he had even thought of sponsoring a museum in

[6] Michael J. Harris, *John Wesley and Methodism in Coventry; the First Century* (Coventry: Historical Association, 2003). See in particular Appendix 4 (p. 72) where, among the membership of twenty-five listed for the Lockhurst Lane circuit in 1839/41, only three were not weavers.

[7] JH, 'The Course of Writing in Ulster', *Rann* 20 (Spring 1953), pp. 43–52; see *Ancestral*, p. 67.

[8] See E. P. Thompson, *The Making of the English Working Class* (London: Penguin, 1991), pp. 194–5 etc. For his comments on Methodism among weavers in the early nineteenth century, see p. 395 etc. JH owned a copy of the first edition (Gollancz, 1963) of Thompson's classic, signed by the author.

[9] John McG. Davies, 'A Twentieth-Century Paternalist: Alfred Herbert and the Skilled Coventry Workman', in *Life and Labour in a Twentieth-Century City; the Experience of Coventry*, edited by Bill Lancaster and Tony Mason (Coventry: Cryfield Press, [n.d.]), p. 99.

Scotland, and was well informed about new cultural facilities in Europe. One of his supporters, an official in the Leicester city museum service, was advised in September 1938 that 'it is probably out of the question entirely to suggest visiting Europe at a time like this'.[10] Herbert was no dabbler in these matters. His final choice was made in favour of balance—Coventry had enough science already, and work on the museum/gallery was sufficiently advanced by wartime for the nucleus to provide air-raid shelter. Sir Alfred was neither a self-made man nor a Methodist. Even if the firm's reputation for good conditions and worker-loyalty was something of a myth—'If gaffer told us to jump in the river we'd do it'—maintenance of the myth was itself a factor. Drama and cycling clubs provided an extension and a mitigation of the workplace collectivity. Health and safety were sedulously promoted in practice and in public discussion. The *Alfred Herbert News,* a quarterly magazine which ran for decades, mixed articles dignifying labour and technical skill with features on entertainment and recreation. In the mid-1950s, it ran several articles by 'Arkle' on holidaying in Europe, Italy in particular. Covering the gallery's formal opening in 1960, the A. H. N. made no mention of the new (indeed, first) director, though Sir Anthony Blunt's presence was proudly noted![11]

The son of a small landowner, Herbert had advanced rapidly in local industry, first in partnership with his brother, who had connections to French manufacturers. During the Great War, he had been attached to the Ministry of Munitions, but continued as the driving force in the family firm. His personalized regime was not all beer and skittles; on the contrary, some rules were harsher than those applying in other Coventry factories. But whereas the car firms often worked six months, and then laid off men for the next six months, Herberts tried to maintain continuous employment. The sense of an organic relationship between the employee and the enterprise, the boss's repeated emphasis on *character* as the basis of technical skill, his wife's ministrations to the families of sick employees, all served to create a bond of moral fervour which built satisfactory profits. On this accumulated wealth Hewitt would draw—through the medium of civic administration—developing the Herbert Art Gallery from 1957 until his retirement in 1972.

Most of this was past history when he took up his post—Herbert died a few months later at the age of ninety, without ever meeting his first art director in office. But the legend and the paternalist outlook continued to resound, partly through the firm as an important Coventry employer, partly through Lady Herbert's influence and the pervasive circulation of the *A. H. N.* With its celebration of the industrial craftsman and his integration through football, dances, and amateur dramatics into the system which used him, the journal inscribed a successfully ambivalent philosophy of work into the city's everyday discourse—'the Herbert spirit'. Hewitt remained sufficiently a socialist to recognize the

[10] COV, PA 2567/23, S. F. Markham (Museum Association) to E. E. Lowe (Leicester Museums), 28 September 1938. 'Nevertheless, the Museum of German Art at Munich is a remarkable design, and the Boijmans Museum at Rotterdam… [is among] the best of the Dutch ideas.'

[11] *Alfred Herbert News* 34, no. 2 (March–April 1960), pp. 25–9. JH certainly met Herbert on at least one occasion in December 1956, before he took up his appointment, when he and Roberta visited Coventry on a preliminary house-hunting mission.

exploitative base of capitalism even when it dispensed charity and bluff good humour. But he shared with Alfred Herbert a respect for the craftsman, the practitioner of a skill acquired with patience over time, the man who could handle and produce material things of benefit to his fellows. In all his fifteen years at the centre of Coventry's web of cultural-industrial life, he never abandoned the fundamentally rural idiom of the poems collected in *No Rebel Word* (1948). His skilled artisan remained a countryman or a worker directly with natural materials, often a solitary in the Wordsworthian manner. This tension in Hewitt's outlook came to the fore in Coventry.

There is little surviving evidence that he had sought other posts after the humiliation of 1952. Nor is it possible to reconstruct the competition he faced when he applied for the Herbert directorship, nor the expert opinion consulted in the process of selecting him. There were five rival candidates, whom he felt were backed by the Arts Council in London or the commercial galleries. In Roberta's account of things, this prompted John to speak plain. He even told the committee that they had made a mistake in a recent acquisition by purchase—and got the job.[12] The town clerk, Charles Barratt, played the role of convenor and intermediary.

Surviving documents indicate that the appointment was central to a much wider initiative in the cultural sphere. In 'Particulars of Appointment of Art Director' (dated 5 May 1956), it is established that the new gallery would come under the control of the Libraries, Art Gallery and Museums Committee, the chair of which was E. Simpson, city librarian and chief administrative officer. In the light of his experiences applying for the Belfast Museum post, Hewitt would have been gratified to know that the second paragraph of the particulars read:

> In order to encourage the development of the Art Gallery and Museum services the Art Director though subject to the general administrative control of the Chief Administrative Officer of the Department, will be professionally independent, and will be directly responsible to the Committee on all technical aspects of that work[13]

The distinction between professional and technical judgement, and the guarantee of 'independence' in the former, promised to give him a kind of freedom which did not exist in the Belfast service to which he was still attached when applying to Coventry. The requirements sought did not particularly faze him: applicants were expected to have a British degree or equivalent; it was also desirable to have the Diploma of the Museums Association, or a degree or diploma in History of Art. A foreign language was desirable, as was experience of lecturing, knowledge of other galleries, home and abroad, public and private collections. The phrase 'wide cultural interests' pleased. Applications were due by 16 June 1956.

Various factors drove the timetable of appointment. Sir Alfred was more than elderly, the city's existing art collection was still largely in storage since the war, the building programme was under way. The city council wanted the new facilities to open in the spring of 1958—just twenty months later—with a sculpture court in

[12] *Journal*, PRONI, D/3838/4/7, 12 September 1956.
[13] COV: CCA/3/1/11671.

the surrounding grounds. The location was central to historic Coventry, in the immediate vicinity of the ruined cathedral beside which Sir Basil Spence worked on the splendid new building. The expected total cost of the Herbert Art Gallery was given as £420,000, with more than half of that sum (£250,000) provided by Herbert.

The scale and determination of Coventry's renewal programme were evident, but the minor details were equally important to a new director. Applicants were informed that the council aimed to provide a minimum of £2000 per annum to buy art, and that during 1957 a cumulative £4000 would be available. 'In addition the City Council has credited the art fund with a sum of £5,000 under the terms of a private bequest.' The successful applicant's income would be £1307. 10. 0 per annum, increasing by increments of £52. 10.0 to a maximum of £1,517. 10. 0: the scale was under review. At the time Hewitt's annual salary at the Belfast Museum was £955. A bureaucratic summary of the successful applicant's career and accomplishments neatly demonstrated how close a match he was to the job description. He was forty-eight years of age, married, currently deputy director of the Belfast Museum and Art Gallery. He held two degrees from Queen's University (the BA of 1930 and the more recent MA of 1951). Between these he took his Diploma of the Museums Association in 1939, and in 1952 had been elected an association fellow. The account of his extra-mural activities stressed long involvement with CEMA and his membership of the International Association of Art Critics. There was no reference to hill walking or countryside pursuits. Under publications, he had highlighted three items in the *Museums Journal*—'Aesthetics in the Museum' (September 1936); 'Multi-coloured Block Mounting' (with J. A. S. Stendall; January 1937); 'Recent Developments in Gallery Display' (May 1952) plus many reviews. To demonstrate his familiarity with other galleries, he listed places visited in this pursuit—Belgium (1927), Paris (1928, 1929, 1930, 1934, 1949); Venice and Padua (1949); Holland (1954), Vienna (1955). Finally, there was the question of leisure interests. He had broken these down into two groups—(i) writing, and (ii) broadcasting. For the first he listed 'verse [*sic*], articles, art and drama criticism, reviews, mainly in Irish journals'. The poet in Hewitt had almost been submerged.

The preliminary trips to Coventry inspired Roberta to be more confessional in her private writing, an objective she felt that she had shirked. The move came at the end of a phase in their lives together when she felt that her youth had gone and that she had not amounted to anything in herself. 'I was hurt by his interest elsewhere', she admits, without elaboration. But her first visit to Coventry was 'intensely interesting', though not without its unredeeming features. 'The place is full of workmen and looks tatty.'[14] During December 1956, they were promised a council flat for six months, were entertained in the home of the city's chief librarian with his wife, his two sons, and the German wife of the eldest son. All in all, 'Coventry has a great social sense and loyalty that I think [John] will be able to identify himself with it. However we will see.'[15]

[14] *Journal*, PRONI, D/3838/4/7, 15 December 1956.
[15] *Journal*, PRONI, D/3838/4/7, 15 December 1956.

One of the most curious features of Roberta's journal at this period is the absence of any reference to events in Hungary, the attempt at reform and neutrality, the popular support for Imre Nagy's government, and then the Russian tanks. It is true that she recorded very little for the year 1956, but the impact of the Soviet intervention was enough to drive the Stewarts (Jim and Sophie) out of the Communist Party, and dominated the newspapers for weeks. Hewitt's wartime enthusiasm for the Red Army had waned by the beginning of the fifties, but his new appointment in Coventry would bring him positively into contact with Eastern and Central Europe, specifically with the 'satellite' states. By contrast, he and Roberta were invited to dinner at Government House, in Hillsborough, on 5 December. Other guests included a judge, an army man, a secretary to the governor, with wives. One can only regard the Hewitts' presence as a congratulations-and-farewell gesture. It was a formal occasion, long dresses and dinner jackets. 'Johnny washed his hair and his feet and his Co-op white evening shirt.'[16]

On appointment in Coventry, Hewitt was responsible for the Temporary Gallery and for advising on the furnishing and equipping of the new one. He had been in harness months before he joined the payroll or hunted for accommodation. In October 1956, the Libraries, Art Gallery and Museums Committee observed with concern that, while 530 pictures had been recently checked in some eight different temporary stores, more than thirty remained to be examined in the Old Peoples Homes where they were housed. Consequently, Hewitt returned to Coventry on 18 October for a two-day visit during which he inspected the Temporary Gallery, the picture store at Foleshill, and—with especial interest—the building under construction. He saw detailed drawings for its completion, and undertook to provide comment. Oh yes, the committee had one or two other questions for him. Material offered for sale or by donation was speedily assessed: he advised against the purchase of three pictures offered by a Mr Sillitoe, declined the steel engravings offered gratis by Mrs Fielding, and further declared against Kodak's offer of an exhibition, Best of Both Worlds, made up of British and American photographs. The Ramblers' Association were also sent packing with their proposed exhibition, while the Society of Aviation Artists got his one positive vote.[17]

A more significant decision surrounded a painting by Luca Giordano (1634–1705), a Neapolitan painter, and the most important Italian decorative artist of the second half of the seventeenth century. The matter had come up at the committee's 6 June meeting (that is, before the interviews), offered for sale at £200. The picture was in poor condition, removed from its stretcher and rolled into a column. Coventry declined to buy, a decision later supported by Hewitt, who may have had no part in the discussion. He was against Old Masters generally though not absolutely; the committee had limited funds for conservation. Nevertheless, Giordano's 'Rape of the Sabine Women' is today hailed as an important picture, now owned by the

16 *Journal*, PRONI, D/3838/4/7, 5 December 1956.
17 COV, CCH/3/1/4.

National Gallery of Australia.[18] A special meeting on 4 July had discussed offers of a 1926 Triumph motorbicycle and a 'collection of bird skins'.

*

The old guard in Belfast had been enlivened by the arrival of the O'Malleys, even if Mary's political inexperience had contributed to the debacle of September 1952. To celebrate the Coventry appointment, her Lyric Theatre mounted a simple production of Hewitt's historical verse drama, 'The Bloody Brae', which investigated themes of violence and forgiveness in seventeenth-century Antrim. Many years elapsed between his writing (in 1936) of these events and first publication of the text (in *Threshold*, autumn 1957), a further instance of the poet's reluctance to invoke divisive histories even when trying to nurture an inclusive understanding.[19]

The Hewitts left Belfast on 27 March 1957, visiting relatives of Roberta's in Liverpool, and then driving on to Coventry in the 'wee Austin'. On 1 April they became the first tenants in No. 320 Purcell Road, a new council property. Neither gas nor electricity had been connected, so they cooked on a primus stove and used a lamp brought from their Glens of Antrim cottage. The view was also surprisingly rural. An elm and an ash tree stood outside near a stream which flowed into the Avon River. 'The Blackthorn came out white on the bushes by the stream and we have thrushes nesting around and magpies and chaffinches and sparrows—it was a great relief... it was good to see the fields beyond being ploughed.[20]

Once in post, John's most pressing task was to begin a collection worthy of the new gallery. He had three years to assemble a coherent body of work with which the gallery would open its doors in 1960—the 1958-deadline quickly became impossible to meet. An immediate decision—more recognition of necessity—was to ignore largely the art of the past as too expensive and available only through minor and random instances. A Cézanne was brought to Coventry's attention, but, as Hewitt wryly noted, it would have meant 'one and two pence on the rates'.[21] While much of the Herbert Gallery's liveliness would draw on temporary visiting exhibitions, the need for a core collection was strongly felt by both the director and his ultimate employers on Coventry City Council. After comparatively little debate, the theme of British Life and Landscape was agreed.

This was not entirely without complications. Arguing that 'as the owners of the gallery are average citizens, more interested in their fellows and the world around them than in the convolutions of aesthetic theory', he felt 'some attention ought to be paid to their present and potential levels of response'. The political condition of

[18] See Brian Kennedy, 'A quintessential Baroque painting: Luca Giordano's "The Rape of the Sabines"', *Artonview* 22 (Winter 2000), pp. 9–12.

[19] 'The Bloody Brae' is included in W. J. Mc Cormack, *Ferocious Humanism; an Anthology of Irish Poetry from Before Swift to Yeats and After* (London: Dent, 2000), pp. 230–44. When Hewitt included the poem in *Freehold and Other Poems* (1986), he directed the reader to D. H. Akenson, *Between Two Revolutions* (1979) for 'an informed reference to the legendary and largely fictitious event which provides the background for the play and which is supposed to have taken place in Islandmagee, Co. Antrim, in January 1642'.

[20] *Journal*, PRONI, D/3838/4/7, 6 June 1957.

[21] COV, 'A Permanent Collection for the Art Gallery'.

Coventry, so very different from Belfast, encouraged concessions to English Midlands public taste he would hardly have risked for the burghers of his native city. Among the objectives detailed in his policy document were:

> (c) the fostering of a wise sense of local patriotism through familiarity with such art objects as worthily record the history and topography of the area; (d) the attempt through the arts to assist personal and social integration, by demonstrating the fit adaptation of means to ends, by showing the accurate accomplishment of emotionally necessary tasks such as the successful decoration of spaces, the satisfactory organisation of forms, colours and rhythms, the statement of psychological truths, the recording of human character.

This was the year of Samuel Beckett's *End Game*, Francis Bacon's 'Screaming Nurse'—to mention two marginal Irish artists in words and paint who hardly shared Hewitt's faith in psychological reintegration—the year also of Richard Hoggart's *The Uses of Literacy* with its loving yet unsentimental account of working-class south Leeds as it disappeared.

Even with the elm and the sparrows nearby, the Hewitts found their changed surroundings exhilarating and disturbing. For some time before they left Belfast, John's mother, Elinor, had been increasingly difficult to manage, and her daughter Eileen—who did most of the caring—was herself unwell. Mrs Hewitt had undergone a mastectomy some time earlier and, after an apparently full recovery, had begun to decline mentally. Decisions were taken to put the old lady into Hollywell House, a traumatic step for both son and daughter, but additionally so for the happily exiled son. Roberta reflected on her mixed feelings about leaving Ulster, her fluctuating confidence in what John had been able to do in Belfast, and other less easily formulated concerns. 'Many things were difficult in personal relationships for a while.'[22]

His reception in Coventry revived both of them. The *Coventry Evening Telegraph* of 1 November 1957 quoted Hewitt to be keen for an art collection appealing 'to the factory worker and his family whose thought will seldom if ever be caught up in the complicated tangle of aesthetic theory'. The influence of Alfred Herbert still lingered. At the Libraries, Art Gallery and Museums Committee meeting of 19 June 1957, Hewitt had presented 'A Draft of Policy for the New Art Gallery'. He was less than three months in post. He began by characterizing Coventry in exact terms—'a provincial city with no strong tradition, as yet, in the visual arts; a city with a rich and varied history, which has now become unique in these islands as the pioneer of mid Twentieth Century civic development'. If this was plain talk, he offered a remarkably soft profile of the future gallery visitors' experience. The institution should make available 'comfortable and decorous opportunities for satisfaction and pleasure to the community'.

Roberta's advice about roots had borne fruit, whether or not her husband acknowledged his compliance with it. There were, of course, complex other factors. If the factory worker's response was taken as a norm, echoing Sir Alfred's salute to the industrial craftsman as a species of artist, the risk persisted of imposing a doctrinaire

[22] *Journal*, PRONI, D/3838/4/7, 6 June 1957.

recipe for art's content. Consequently, a defence against possible allegations of ideological bias was cautiously raised. He would not slavishly [*sic*] follow any variant of academic socialist realism. The committee's agreed policy statement, however, reveals greater concern about the possible advance of modernism—'elements of abstraction and distortion are permissible, provided the content remains visibly communicable to a normally intelligent view after a fair scrutiny'.

The antipathy towards the modern in particular echoed local prejudice. Delivering the Eighth Annual Alfred Herbert Lecture late in 1956, Ronald Ossory Dunlop (1894–1973) inveighed against Picasso—'Jewish and Spanish and has a certain ruthlessness—a black magician rather than a white magician but certainly a magician.'[23] An insistent jingoism supported this judgement; impressionism for Dunlop descended from Constable and Turner and was not essentially French in origin. Dunlop, one might add, was the Dublin-born son of a theosophist-turned-anthroposophist. Sir Alfred's advisers had a Catholic taste in Irish Protestants.

If the zebra is a horse designed in committee, Hewitt's draft policy makes similar concessions and contrasts. His own decidedly (also confusedly) left-wing attitudes of the 1930s are clearly visible, though now the challenge is to nurture them in a milieu broadly sympathetic rather than defend them in one narrowly antagonistic. In addition to the Labour Party, the politics of Coventry was home to a resilient if numerically small Communist organization. Its status depended less on the pioneer achievements of the Soviet Union in the early 1920s, more on the tenacious defence of Stalingrad from July 1942 until February 1943 under siege by the German army. Equally potent in the self-image of Coventry was its resemblance to the experience of Dresden, carpet-bombed by the RAF and the USAAF from 13 to 15 February 1945. Coventry's own blitz (in November 1940) was re-inscribed in the popular consciousness by these later, larger but remote wartime events in which the contribution of the Soviet Union (and Western communists) was acknowledged. In November 1941, the Coventry Anglo-Soviet Unity Committee had been formed, on the initiative of three leading members of the local Labour Party, and supported by individuals of all persuasions. In January 1942 an Anglo-Soviet week took place in Coventry, with a civic parade and church service, an exhibition illustrating life in the Soviet Union, and a concert given by the London Philharmonic under Malcolm Sargent. Even before Stalingrad, the links had been forged; after the Red Army's repulse of the Wehrmacht, the Coventry committee organized an exhibition of the sword forged in London and presented by King George VI to Stalingrad; in return, the city was presented with a book of greetings signed by 30,000 Stalingrad women.[24]

However, by mid-1957, this association had already gotten a sweet-and-sour taste: Hungarian refugees in Coventry gave visible evidence of a darker Soviet contribution to peace in Europe. The author of *The Making of the English Working Class* began his disaffiliation from 'the Party' in the aftermath of Budapest 1956, as

[23] 'Some Aspects of Modern Art', *Alfred Herbert News* 31, no. 1 (January–February 1957), p. 6.

[24] Kenneth Richardson (assisted by Elizabeth Harris), *Twentieth-Century Coventry* (Coventry: City of Coventry, 1972), pp. 95–6.

did the Stewarts in Belfast, and hundreds elsewhere. In the 1961 local elections, Labour won ten of the sixteen Coventry wards; the Communist Party contested seven wards, its highest poll amounting to just 413 votes.[25] Nevertheless, the objective of the CPGB was not formal power but influence, and the Stalingrad legacy affected Hewitt's early decisions as director of the Herbert Art Gallery, his warm tolerance of visiting exhibitions from Eastern Europe.

The most obvious statement of this fact was the choice of towns with which Coventry had an agreement in cultural affairs. Head of the list was Stalingrad (1942) followed by Lidice, the Czech village more than decimated in SS revenge for the assassination of Reinhard Heydrich in June 1942; then Kiel (West Germany), Arnhem (Netherlands), Graz (Austria), Dresden (East Germany), Warsaw (Poland), Caen and St Etienne (France), Belgrade and Sarajevo (Yugoslavia), and Toronto (Canada). At the time of drawing up this list (summer of 1959), 'through the Irish ambassador, a link with an Irish town is being sought'.[26] Of the twelve names already twinned with Coventry, exactly half lay in the post-war Soviet sphere. As late as 1960 Hewitt's new abode preserved the wartime concept of a United Front against the fascist enemy.

In 1957, he was at once the appointed arbiter of the new gallery's future and the necessary inheritor of wartime associations. The 1956-report of the (general) director of museum services for the borough referred to the exhibition in the city of work designed for Stalingrad later in the year, and to contacts with the British-Czechoslovak Friendship League about folk costumes. There was no quick way out of these bonds of friendship, even if he had wanted one. Between 25 February and 2 March (seven days), 1993 people had visited the display planned for Stalingrad, compared to 3595 who saw an Arts Council sponsored exhibition of stained glass in a two-week period.[27] The factory worker, or whoever actually constituted the average visitor to Coventry's temporary exhibition space, approved of links with the East, tacitly at least. More was to come, exhibitions of Czech Graphic Art (December 1956) and of Modern Yugoslav Paintings (March 1957).

The new director found ways of accommodating himself. His emphasis on communication in art implied more than a preference for realism of whatever kind. As a value enshrined in a civic museum, it involved recognition of the local, both as a theme in painting and in the relations between artist and viewer. Here, Hewitt devised an ingenious double-track programme which gave non-realist art more freedom than the Permanent Collection might allow it. For the Collection of Local Art, he guaranteed that 'if there is good abstract, expressionist or surrealist work from local hands, efforts will be made to secure it'. To some degree this dual approach acknowledged a reality which, in its most potent aspects, was new to Hewitt and perhaps only half-evident to him—the ever-changing nature of social and cultural life. Irish affairs had been bogged down in antagonisms which, no matter what their recent origins might be, were dipped in the aspic of historical immutability. Ulster Unionists sneered at southern conservatism while insisting on

[25] *Coventry Civic Affairs*, June 1961, p. 4. The Liberals contested only one ward (coming third).
[26] COV, CCA/3/1/14358. [27] COV, CHH/3/1/4.

their own permanent right to power. Catholic hated Protestant and had always done so; Protestant responded in kind, and would always be justified. Coventry had felt the force of this explosive parallelism when, in August 1939, the IRA detonated a bomb in Broadgate, killing five people and injuring many others. While emigrants' organizations hastened to dissociate themselves, 2000 aircraft workers marched into the city as part of a wider anti-Irish demonstration of feeling. Strikes were threatened against the continued employment of Irish workers.

Though happy to be out of Northern Ireland, Hewitt diligently kept in touch by contributing reviews and art notes to the *Belfast Evening Telegraph*. (For southern balance Michael Murphy sent the *Irish Times* on a regular basis.) Journalism suited his day-to-day routine. When a Jack Yeats exhibition upset the Ulster plaster cast of mind, Hewitt contributed to the discussion through several newspaper pieces written under several different pseudonyms. Among artists he encouraged was Gretta Bowen (1880–1981) who took up painting at the age of seventy, inspired or provoked by the example of her sons—George Campbell (1917–79), the best known. In 1977, when he had retired and she was ninety-seven, Hewitt wrote about Bowen with great warmth and appreciation, describing her as 'a genuine primitive of the Grandma Moses kind'.[28]

Psychologically, the move to Coventry involved a severe challenge to Hewitt's inherited modes of thought and response. What he could most readily embrace was the city's wartime endurance, a stoicism not unlike the personal style he had evolved in Belfast. But the war was twelve years over when he arrived in England, and commitment to a planned urban environment involved changes which inevitably altered the social and political agencies which made the commitment. In words Derek Mahon borrowed from Auden, 'we are changed by what we change'.[29] One notices in Hewitt's early statements of policy the recurrence of terms which semi-consciously reflect an urge to preserve—art is (valuably) an illustration, it provides a record, it documents the present for the benefit of future viewers.

In their early Coventry years, the Hewitts explored the Midlands and the Cotswolds, and saw a magnificent performance of 'Julius Caesar' at Stratford-upon-Avon—though Roberta thought Alec Guinness 'too much of an elocutionist' and too refined in movement. Still without a home of their own, though renting a council house, they visited stately homes and ancient churches. They called on Bertie Rodgers and his new wife, Marianne Helweg.[30] Terry Flanagan (1929–2011), a young Belfast painter, visited Kenilworth Castle with Roberta in January 1958; late in March, the Hewitts took a trip back to Belfast where John spoke at the opening of an exhibition of Zoltan Frankl's collection. At Windsor Castle, John was reluctant to go into the state apartments, but not his wife. On 24 August, both Hewitts marched against 'the bomb' in Cambridgeshire. The forms of radical politics were changing, and the Campaign for Nuclear Disarmament (CND) quickly

[28] John Hewitt, *Art in Ulster 1557–1957* (Belfast: Blackstaff Press, 1977), p. 137.
[29] See 'Beyond Howth Head', in Derek Mahon, *Lives* (London: Oxford University Press, 1972), p. 37.
[30] See Jon Stallworthy, *Louis MacNeice* (London: Faber, 1995), pp. 393–4.

came to the fore. In Belfast, the younger Stewarts Brenda and Jill took the initiative before their parents. But not all was politics. In October, John's mother was weakening, and he flew home to see her. She died on 22 October 1958. The Irish links were not breaking, even if relief from their once adamantine grip continued to please. On 17 November, Hewitt spoke in Leamington Spa on the poetry of Yeats—'Inisfree to Byzantium'.

In September 1957, they had moved to No. 27b Radford Road, still not a permanent home, just as the new gallery had yet to reach completion. The modern house—containing several flats—belonged to an architect, whose wife became a friend of Roberta's. They often took coffee between 11 a.m. and noon. 'The various females of the four flats meet and it has been useful to keep me in touch with ordinary things.'[31] One finds less evidence of Hewitt's social life or private feelings. What Roberta wanted was 'an old small place with one large room with a bit of space round it'.[32] But they couldn't get a mortgage on older property.

The less than serenely stable condition of Coventry politics in the two decades following the war can be gauged by brief glances at the lives of some public figures whom Hewitt worked with or knew personally. Take, for example, William Callow, who was elected lord mayor in June 1961. Born 1905 in Sutton Coalfield, Callow had joined the Independent Labour Party at the age of sixteen; became an active trade unionist (dismissed twice from the Humber car works); also acted as chair of the local Left Book Club on its establishment; took a Workers' Educational Association course in local and central government. 'He well remembers taking the chair at a meeting addressed by Victor Gollancz on the perils of fascism abroad and in this country.'[33] A stalwart of the labour movement, the mayor had reached the pinnacle of his career, and could describe it fully in colours drawn from the heroic past.

Compare the local members of parliament—notably Elaine Burton (1904–91), Richard Crossman (1907–74), and Maurice Edelman (1911–75.) Burton, who had published *What of the Women; a Study of Women in Wartime* (1941), lost to the Tories in 1959, but not before becoming a friend of Roberta Hewitt's. Crossman also lost his Coventry seat, though he was re-elected elsewhere and went on to a distinguished ministerial career under Harold Wilson. Edelman, a prolific novelist and a writer on historical topics, had come into Parliament in 1945, but never abandoned his journalism and research—he died in democratic harness in December 1975. In the *New Statesman* of 12 June 1948, he had strongly urged the party to recognize its need of (not just dependence on) the middle classes (he insisted on the plural.) The post-war victory was not achieved on a working-class franchise. In so arguing, he indicated how Labour had either been changed in the processes of election to power or was doomed to lose any chance of retaining power. (And, in due course, after thirty years of invincibility Labour lost control of Coventry's municipal government in 1967.)

[31] *Journal*, PRONI, D/3838/4/7, 1 January 1959.
[32] *Journal*, PRONI, D/3838/4/7, 6 June 1957.
[33] *Coventry Civic Affairs* 156 (June 1961), p. 1.

This uncomfortable insight into the constancy of change is not distant from tensions evident in Hewitt's early decisions at the Herbert. His first purchase was effected before 1957 ended. James Fitton's 'Café' (1948) met the criteria proposed for the core or permanent collection, but also exposed them to questioning. Depicting a couple in a bright interior with a view to the street, it was peaceful, urban, beautiful in its coloration, and a marked contrast to the recent chaos of war. Painted while rationing and 'austerity' persisted throughout Britain, the picture retained something of the egalitarian mood of 1939–45. Hewitt's commitment to factory-worker appreciation sounds in retrospect like doctrinaire socialism, but its emotional roots might be traced back to the war years, where class differences were diluted. His relationship with Coventry was not one of identification with its ambitions if, by such a notion, one meant indifference to its suffering under the bombs. But his desire for permanence would involve an acceptance of change.

Fitton (1899–1982) had been born the son of Oldham mill hands in Lancashire, moving with his parents to London in the 1920s. His was a genuine popular art in the pre-war years; he was active in the Labour movement, providing cartoons for the *Daily Worker* and *Left Review*. During the war, he worked for the Ministry of Education. Hewitt visited his studio during his first six months at the Herbert, and showed several works to the Art Gallery and Museum Committee. 'Café' would occupy a prominent place in the formal opening show in 1960, alongside work by Cézanne, Rembrandt, and Van Gogh. The appearance of Stanley Spencer brought memories of the drunken ceilidh in June 1951. Admiring some amateur work, Spencer declared 'I do hope he doesn't get any better.'

Completion of the new gallery remained to be seen. Naturally, the project outran its budgets, a state of affairs certainly encouraged by the new director's energy and appetite. The city's funds were never likely to bridge the gap between the late Sir Alfred's donation and the actual cost of finishing and furnishing the gallery named in his honour. There were amusing distractions. Tyrone Guthrie was directing a modern-dress production of 'All's Well that Ends Well' in Stratford; the Hewitts got tickets and especially enjoyed the waving of 'Irish Free State flags' in a crowd scene. But there were less positive experiments—a kind of spiritualist therapy in Birmingham which Roberta described at length in her journal:

> Nothing startling or greatly moving was said [by Bapak], but that was all right and when he got up every one rose to their feet and stood while he walked from the platform down the passage between the chairs—I didn't like this but rose—Johnny sat—the only one.[34]

Hewitt's response was largely negative. After he had been 'opened' and had attended further sessions, he seemed to get a kind of release, 'Johnny moves around and swings his arms and hums and even laughs out loud.' Recollection of his early Methodist background, though it was far from indoctrination, is clearly evident. He liked Bapak, 'the little man', but complained that 'if his message is true and

[34] *Journal*, PRONI, D/3838/4/7, 10 May 1959.

he is a prophet he shouldn't behave like a bishop—he would be really among us, like Christ'.[35]

Easter brought the first Aldermaston march, and John felt strongly opposed to nuclear weapons. The Hewitts drove to Maidenhead, and thereafter marched, slept on floors, and generally made do with the rest. They noted the presence of Harold Steel and his family, marching in their Rolls Royce, but supportive. Saturday was a bleakly wet day and, though only 300 stuck to the march, Hewitt walked every foot of it. At a hotel, he took a bath, and was so weak Roberta had to lift his legs into bed. The next day he spent mainly driving and picking up supplies. 'It was a great experience—there was a wonderful feeling of good nature but deep unity for a single purpose. The man behind you was a Stalinist, [the next] a Friend.... A great man, an Irish chap, who sold the [Irish] Democrat... shouted in a rich brogue 'we are walking to preserve your beautiful English villages...'.[36]

Though both Hewitts later attended a mass CND rally in London, took part in the Brize Norton protest, and teamed up with Terry and Shelagh Flanagan for yet another event, they did not join the second Aldermaston march. 'We felt we were picnicing [*sic*] for peace.' Locally it was possible to do work at least as useful. When the poet, sexologist, and anarchist Alex Comfort spoke at a Coventry peace meeting, the Hewitts put him up. In May, the local Peace Council met national leaders including Pat Arrowsmith, Gordon Schaffer, and D. G. Arnott. Arnott stayed with the Hewitts. 'But the Bomb is still with us and Bevan has still his atomic Fig Leaf, my own phrase.'[37]

If Hewitt the professional man hit the ground running, there were slower adjustments on the domestic front. Accommodation in the English cities was in short supply, and the Hewitt household experienced its own unique difficulties, some of which grew with time. At the beginning of 1952, Roberta had longed to escape from the flat in Mount Charles, perhaps even reaching as high as the Malone Road, again.[38] In Belfast, their financial—or was it emotional?—circumstances appeared to tie them into rented property, whatever John's prospects might be. The Belfast prospects of 1952 came to nothing, though Frankl offered to put up a deposit, and their removal to Coventry five years later initially brought them shelter within the public housing sector. A kind of socialist pride in this endured for some time. No. 5 Postbridge Road, where they finally took up their English possession on 1 March 1960, was a small thoroughly mortgaged house in new suburbs, very different from what they had enjoyed in Belfast's university district.

[35] *Journal*, PRONI, D/3838/4/7, 10 May 1959. Bapak Muhammad Subuh (1901–87), an Indonesian religious teacher, was invited to England by J. G. Bennett, whom the Hewitts also met, though they disliked him.

[36] *Journal*, PRONI, D/3838/4/7, 10 May 1959. This is one of JH's minor encounters with the new-style *Irish Democrat* which he failed to distinguish from its namesake of 1937.

[37] *Journal*, PRONI, D/3838/4/7, 10 May 1959.

[38] *Journal*, PRONI, D/3838/4/7, 12 February 1952. Roberta inspected several houses, including one close to the home of Estyn Evans—'none suitable... I suppose I was envious—I got cross with Johnny and started a yap about him not allowing me to buy a house ages ago—not being interested in furniture or where we lived'.

The weeks before the Hewitts took over the house were tense. At their temporary Radford Road address, Roberta had worked to the end womanfully 'to keep the living room undisturbed' while John zigzagged between deliveries of pictures from central Europe, the local issues of décor in the Herbert, and lighting for their first private home. She was enormously relieved to get into it. Neighbours lent a willing hand in the transfer, whose names are lovingly recorded—Margarite Burgonstall scrubbed out the old place, Connie Wright painted bookcases for the new one.[39] The result of these Warwickshire neighbours' womanly efforts was to create a domestic base which complemented the male Hewitt's great project at the gallery. And yet, the suburban remoteness of Postbridge Road from the Herbert Gallery fractured all those aspirations of cultural unity implicit in the Labour policy of civic development—'a shower and no bath which [would have] cost us more'. Nevertheless, there was a rural prospect even in Midlands England—'now (July) we are eating [our own potatoes] and they are good. We have had already lots of spinach, some peas, lettuce enough, lots of raddish....'[40]

The earliest visitors at their long-term Coventry home were decidedly cosmopolitan—the Hungarian sculptor Peter Peri, and the Polish artist who arranged one aspect of the Herbert's inaugural exhibition. Ulster was not far behind, and indeed the foreign/local distinction was not easy to maintain. The naturalist Norman Carruthers, turned up; also Pearse and Mary O'Malley. Then 'Siegfried Alexander who was a German refugee we met in Belfast over twenty years ago'. When Roberta recalled Jim and Sophie Stewart in the same breath, she added Laura Huezek who 'lived with us for about six months in around 1940...a refugee from the Spanish Civil War'. All of this may sound like displaced Belfast radicalism, unsupported by any political judgement in the English Midlands where the Hewitts were settling down. 'The mixed population has given rise to a cheerful friendliness & we have found everyone helpful.'[41]

John travelled in the English countryside, occasionally reporting happy discoveries. In the summer of 1958, he reached the village of Thaxted in Essex. Noting the restored church, he particularly remarked the chapel dedicated to a fourteenth-century peasant insurgent, John Ball, familiar through William Morris's *Dream of John Ball*. 'It's a place I could live in, I think, happily, for there's a legendary air about it.'[42] Irish visitors turned up, many of them family. In the spring of 1961, the folklorist Michael J. Murphy arrived for over a week. A trip to London was proposed, as if to counterbalance Murphy's essentially rural preoccupations. As the Hewitts and their guest approached Westminster, seat of the imperial Parliament, centre of the vast metropolis, 'a lorry passed with a steaming load of dung & a graip [four-pronged fork] standing up in it', which all three took as a good omen.[43] Generally speaking, Hewitt was aware of the Irish community in Britain, and

[39] *Journal*, PRONI, D/3838/4/7, [no day] July 1960.
[40] *Journal*, PRONI, D/3838/4/7, [no day] July 1960.
[41] PRONI, D/2833/C/1/13, JH to W. R. Rodgers, 21 April 1957.
[42] PRONI, D/2833/C/1/8/18, JH to W. R. Rodgers, 7 April 1959.
[43] PRONI, D/2833/C/1/8/20, JH to W. R. Rodgers, 27 March 1961 (The incident had occurred in February.)

broadly sympathetic to it. In his early days at Coventry, he could, however, refer to 'the Irish' as if he and his wife belonged under some other heading—'we meet them without the scenery'.[44] This did not prevent him from applying his mind while in England to the work of perhaps the most difficult Irish poet of the time, Austin Clarke. To Rodgers, he remarked '[Clarke's] best single poem is, in my opinion, "Loss of Strength" in his last little book but one. That is, for layers of sense and facets of character. But objectively, his purest is of course "The Blackbird of Derrycairn"... He's a poet you need to talk about or quote and try reading at different speeds and so, ill-adapted to the diagram of the critical essay.'[45]

The magazine *Threshold* (first issue February 1957) provided a link with Belfast and Irish writing. Hewitt acted as poetry editor but advised on wider topics. Material came from far afield, including a short story, 'Big Annie', from Yugoslavia. Hewitt was enthusiastic, telling Mary O'Malley how he would 'love to go over this and smooth out the rough edges and keep the simplicity consistent'. He did not intend any additional rewriting. In the end, the story, by Mira Buljan, appeared in the autumn 1958 issue. The author, born in Serbia but of Croat nationality, was a Marxist.[46] *Threshold*, though it was a lifeline, also brought news of expanded literary activity in the city from which Hewitt felt expelled. The Lyric Theatre in 1956/57 produced plays by Chekhov, Lorca, and Yeats, as well as work originating in English. The latter included Hewitt's own 'Bloody Brae'. John Jordan of Dublin lectured on Shaw, and Nelson Browne is credited with a talk on Hewitt's plays.[47] Mary O'Malley, director of the Lyric, had splendidly risen above her faux pas of 1952.

At Christmas of 1961, the Hewitts were asked if they would take in an African guest. He stayed for three weeks, regaling his hosts with accounts of his father dying while the lad was studying medicine in Dublin. As a consequence he had been obliged to work on the railways in Britain before getting a teacher-training grant at Oxford. John bought him shoes, and gave him spending money. Roberta bought a coat and other items of clothing. Then he disappeared. A fellow student responded to the Hewitts' enquiries, but was cagey in his replies. Gradually, the facts emerged—the man was married with a wife and two children in Africa whom he had deserted. Then, a year after staying and disappearing, he resumed contact, looking for a reference. Roberta suggested that, if he got a job, perhaps he could repay something of what they had outlaid on him. Nine years later, he turned up with a new wife and three children, all seemingly prosperous.

Once again, children entered the Hewitt house, this time at the behest of a probation officer. They came one by one in the early 1960s, but their background was the same—youngsters living rough, sleeping in public lavatories at night, the

[44] PRONI, D/2833/C/1/17, JH to W. R. Rodgers, 13 February 1959.

[45] PRONI, D/2833/C/1/8/20, JH to W. R. Rodgers, 27 March 1961. 'The Loss of Strength' appeared in *Too Late a Vine* (a private publication of 1957) and collected in *Later Poems* (Dublin: Dolmen Press, 1961), pp. 61–8. 'The Blackbird of Derrycarn', based on an early Irish text, was published in *Ancient Lights* (1955); see *Later Poems*, p. 51.

[46] Mary O'Malley, *Never Shake Hands with the Devil* (Dublin: Elo Press, 1990), p. 119.

[47] See the list of productions etc., in *Threshold* 1, no. 3 (Autumn 1957), pp. 85–6.

products of broken homes. First there was Norman, who looked about twelve years old though he was seventeen. He was handy with electrical things, and helped in Postbridge Road with new switches and repairs to the kettle. His aunt eventually took him under her wing, to Roberta's evident dismay, though the lad phoned regularly for months. Then there was Tony, a late-teenager with the sense of a seven year-old. The Probation Service found him a job, and Roberta routinely got him up at 6.30 each morning until one evening, when he failed to return, she found his working clothes under the bed. Later he went to jail.

These occasional young visitors clearly brought fulfilment—however temporary and heart-wrenching—to Roberta, though John's attitudes remain less accessible. When Shelagh and Terry Flanagan went up to London for a few nights in March 1961, they left their young son at Postbridge Road. Philip and Hewitt got on very well: in Roberta's words 'he was so very good and Johnny adored him and still does'. But her vulnerability is more palpable than his responsiveness.

> I took on a Mrs [blank]—and a wayward family of husband, wife and four children that became five—I tried for two years to help her with her money and with the children but she only looked on me as good for money or clothes or food. I got nowhere—I did like the wee boys but I had to drop it. They will be wee rogues, they are marvellous liars at the age of four and look like angels.[48]

In September 1961, Hester Maybin made a trip to the Soviet Union as part of a study-year programme at Bristol's Institute of Education. Kathleen Maybin had disappeared from her family's ken, as a consequence of becoming Palme Dutt's secretary. From Coventry, things appeared less black and white, less orange and green, than at home. Hewitt had written little in 1961–62, nothing at all from August 1961 until 15 July 1962. The following year, in November, he revised three poems composed much earlier. One of these, 'The Green Shoot', opens with evocations of his Belfast childhood and aggressive confrontations with a Catholic priest and an errand boy, only to slip further back in memory to a frosty Christmas Eve when, being bathed by his mother, he heard carol-singers 'somewhere in the dark'. The infant likes the singing until he notices his mother's tear-filled eyes:

> Out of this mulch of ready sentiment,
> gritty with threads of flinty violence,
> I am the green shoot asking for the flower,
> soft as the feathers of the snow's cold swans.[49]

Writing her journal on 20 February 1963, Roberta recalled an alarming moment of two years earlier. One winter's night John had woken with a huge swelling on his lips, 'it was frightening[,] really like elephantiasis [*sic*] except his skin was not discoloured'. A doctor offered two diagnoses—allergy and nervous reaction. Dr Joe Spears, a rotund Scot who remained a steady friend even after the Hewitts had returned to Ulster, advised rest. The swelling moved downwards across his chin until he looked like a mumps patient. Inflammation continued at intervals

[48] *Journal*, PRONI, D/3838/4/7, [no day] July 1960.
[49] Ormsby, pp. 63–4.

throughout 1961 and '62 with slighter swellings of the tongue, then an affliction in the scrotum, several times in the thumb, hand and arms. Hewitt's condition made him extremely anxious about lecturing in public. More than a dozen tests in Birmingham Hospital appear to have established only that he was allergic to the tests themselves. The problem persisted into early 1963, despite efforts at home to monitor his diet and eliminate suspect foods.

During this long period of occasional but recurrent ill health, he lectured at the Yeats Summer School (15 August 1961) on the Victorian Irish poet William Allingham, and travelled (7–18 June 1962) to Warsaw for the centenary of Poland's national museum. He visited Auschwitz. In the summer of 1963, he and Roberta holidayed in Czechoslovakia, by which time his health seems to have improved.[50] Central Europe was now a holiday destination, not just a (remote) political destiny or useful source of borrowable art, though the old interests lingered. Hewitt's localized illness may well account for the relative paucity of his writing in these years, but is it possible to account for the illness? Joe Spears's advice would tend to confirm a psychosomatic diagnosis, of symptoms occurring at a time when the issue of childlessness was played out in Postbridge Road through the pathos of short-term custody.

'The Green Shoot', revised in late 1963 or very shortly afterwards, had been originally written in 1946, and published in *The Bell* of March 1948. Revision principally took the form of reduced length, from nine stanzas to seven, with a more dramatic juxtaposition of the incidents recalled, and less narrative detail. The final (unaltered) lines—'I am the green shoot asking for the flower, / Soft as the feathers of the snow's cold swans'—cannot be attributed to the nervous ailments of the early 1960s, but the poem's deliberated re-emergence, revision, and (eventual) retitling draw attention to the poignancy of those final lines.[51] The original title, 'The Frozen Sod', was retained when the shorter version appeared in *The Bell* (and several other publications), only achieving its final title in the *Collected Poems* of 1968. The change of emphasis effected in the change of title clearly, if very slowly, signals a coming-through, perhaps as decisive as the ultimate publication of *No Rebel Word* twenty years earlier. Of the thirty-six poems in the volume of 1948, only fourteen were collected in 1968.

The longest engagement with pen and blank page undertaken during the Coventry years was *A North Light*, partly a collection of essays on events and personalities, and partly an autobiography. It was never completed, and only a few excerpts appeared in print before the edition of 2013. Receipts preserved among his papers establish that much of it was typed up between November 1963 and April 1964. The business of emigration had threatened the poetic impulse, this in a man who

[50] For an acute survey of JH's interest central and Eastern Europe, see Guy Woodward, '"We must know more about Ireland": John Hewitt and Eastern Europe', in *Ireland West to East: Irish Cultural Connections with Central and Eastern Europe*, edited by Aidan O'Malley and Eve Patten (Oxford: Peter Lang, 2013), pp. 101–13. Woodward discloses the extent of Czech reading matter in Hewitt's library at the time of his death (though I must protest at the suggestion that the Mandelstams were Czech).

[51] I draw here on Frank Ormsby's extensive account of the poem's development: see Ormsby, pp. 63–4, 557, 583–4.

had often written three or more poems a night. The typescript preserves a few memories of the Belfast which he cherished—notably 'Men My Brothers, Men the Workers', an account of Bob Molyneux the nightwatchman, including vignettes of several craft workshops on Agnes Street.[52]

John's surname nearly but not neatly rhymes with poet, and his vocation often seemed under pressure from day-to-day urgencies and obligations. Even poets have to live. Frank Ormsby's valuable chronology of Hewitt's composition lists no poems commenced or revised in 1957, names just eight for 1958, and only two for 1959. But of these, several deserve immediate attention. 'Lines on the Opening of the Belgrade Theatre' (February 1958) has Hewitt dutifully recording an event in Coventry's post-war recovery, acting the civic laureate and, in doing so, inscribing in verse one of these central European places which figure so prominently in the annals of the Herbert Art Gallery. First published in the *Birmingham Post* of 28 March 1958, and never collected into a volume, 'Lines on the Opening' marks Hewitt's acceptance of his new abode, his exploration of its inadequately known past:

> This is no upstart town: in ancient days
> the Corpus Christi guildsmen roared the lines;
> from Gosford Street to Bishop Street their plays,
> in vivid pageant, smote the Philistines.[53]

The tug from beyond the Irish Sea and North Channel drew his hand back to the ever-present notebooks. Cryptic, where the Belgrade Theatre piece was doggedly accessible, 'Jacob and the Angel' (written 11 April 1958) conjoins Hewitt's loss of his father (died July 1945) with the painting of Colin Middleton, RHA (1910–83). The poem is readily quoted in the short version published in *Poetry Ireland*, no 1 (autumn 1962):

> I wrestled with my father in my dream,
> holding my ground though he strove powerfully,
> then suddenly remembered who we were,
> and why we need not struggle, he and I;
> thereat desisted. Now the meaning's clear;
> I will not pause to struggle with my past,
> locked in an angry posture with a ghost,
> but, striding forward, trust the shrunken thigh.[54]

The biblical account of Jacob's encounter with the angel (Genesis 32: 4–32) ends with Jacob's survival despite a mysterious injury to his thigh, which relates back to the episode of cheating his brother (Esau) of their father's blessing, and links up with the equally cryptic dream of the ladder reaching heaven. Apart from his unavoidable saturation in biblical knowledge, Hewitt knew of the incident from Eugène Delacroix's great mural in the church of Saint Sulpice, Paris. Middleton's picture, 'Jacob Wrestling with the Angel', had been exhibited in Gothenburg, Sweden, in 1952. Both Hewitt's poem and the strangely blue portrait present a

[52] UU, Hewitt, Box 5. [53] Ormsby, pp. 513–15. [54] Ormsby, p. 96.

struggle easily resolved, without epic or metaphysical implications—Middleton's Jacob has a butterfly resting on his thumb. Yet it is such burdens which try us, and sometimes break us. Years later, when Martin Dodsworth (also an enthusiast for Austin Clarke's work) reviewed Hewitt's *Loose Ends*, he alluded to the same biblical scene in titling his review—Jacob Wrestling with His Angel.[55]

On the theme of relations with the past, 'An Irishman in Coventry' (2 July, revised in September 1958) deserves particular attention:

A full year since, I took this eager city,
the tolerance that laced its blatant roar,
its famous steeples and its web of girders,
as image of the state hope argued for,
and scarcely flung a bitter thought behind me
on all that flaws the glory and the grace
which ribbons through the sick, guilt-clotted legend
of my creed-haunted, godforsaken race.
My rhetoric swung round from steel's high promise
to the precision of the well-gauged tool,
tracing the logic in the vast glass headlands,
the clockwork horse, the comprehensive school.

Then, sudden, by occasion's chance concerted,
in enclave of my nation, but apart,
the jigging dances and the lilting fiddle
stirred the old rage and pity in my heart.
the faces and the voices blurring round me,
the strong hands long familiar with the spade,
the whiskey-tinctured breath, the pious buttons,
called up a people endlessly betrayed
by our own weakness, by the wrongs we suffered
in that long twilight over bog and glen,
by force, by famine and by glittering fables
which gave us martyrs when we needed men,
by poisoned memory, and by ready wit,
with poverty corroded into malice,
to hit and run and howl when it is hit.
This is our fate: eight hundred years' disaster,
crazily tangled as the Book of Kells;
the dream's distortion and the land's division,
the midnight raiders and the prison cells.
Yet like Lir's children banished to the waters
our hearts still listen for the landward bells.[56]

[55] *Guardian*, 18 August 1983.

[56] In P. W. Joyce's influential version, he notes that 'the children of Lir had some obscure foreknowledge of the coming of Christianity'. In JH's Coventry situation, he implies a desire to return to an Ireland in which some acceptable, non-schismatic faith has been introduced during his exile. See Joyce, *Old Celtic Romances* (London: Routledge, 1879), p. 16. In an authoritative recent study, Caoimhin Breatnach regards the tale as primarily religious; see Breatnach, 'The Religious Significance of Oidhreadh Chloinne Lir', *Eriu* 50 (1999), pp. 1–40, esp. p. 20.

It is risky to take apparent biographical fact out of a literary text; nevertheless we are led to believe that Hewitt has spent a little time among the 'enclave' of his nation who toil in Coventry on building sites and in construction gangs. Perhaps at some topping-out ceremony or in a local pub this limited encounter encourages identification. Simultaneously, however, the poet marks off as a distinct historical reality, 'my creed-haunted, godforsaken race'. Three terms are employed to graph the overlappings and non-congruities of the situation—nation, people, and race. We have one firm detail of affable contact across some of these divisive unities; at an Irish Club in the city, Hewitt overheard a Catholic priest speaking in a familiar accent; on enquiry, it turned out the man hailed from a village the poet knew well.[57] 'An Irishman in Coventry' remains one of Hewitt's best-known poems, repeatedly anthologized, yet it also deserves recognition as a statement of irresolution, a disinclination to merge. Family, and commitments in European affairs, even his beloved visual arts, are left aside. Unfortunately, for the dates when the poem was being written and revised, Roberta's journal amounts to nothing more than a skeletal list of summer details. It is perhaps significant that, between the original composition and the revision in September, the Hewitts were in Ireland for nearly three weeks (31 July to 19 August). Immediately after their return, they spent much of their time with the Flanagans, marching against the bomb and visiting Kenilworth again.[58] In the mid-1990s when her enthusiasm for Hewitt had waned, Edna Longley's declaration that '"An Irishman in Coventry" appears blind to its own political unconscious' appears blind to what a political unconscious might be or could see.[59]

Threshold provided the surest link with home, while Coventry provided a useful distance between its poetry editor and the hubbub of literary Belfast. The spring/summer issue for 1960 carried a lengthy article by Roger McHugh about the diaries of Roger Casement, recently deposited in the Public Record Office, London. McHugh, who lectured on Irish drama at University College Dublin, held strongly republican views which led him to insist that the so-called Black Diaries were forged. Mary O'Malley, like her husband Pearse O'Malley, was also of republican outlook. She and McHugh also shared an enthusiasm for the plays of W. B. Yeats, which she produced at the Lyric Theatre. But McHugh's thirty-page article, demonstrating to his own satisfaction that the evidently homosexual diaries were concocted to discredit Casement in 1916, drew an immediate response from Letitia Fairfield (1885–1978), an Irish doctor and barrister who had known Casement in her youth. Fairfield's letter, printed in the succeeding issue of *Threshold*, ruthlessly exposed McHugh's sloppy analysis. Though Hewitt officially acted just as poetry editor, it is unlikely that O'Malley

57 *North*, p. 94. The man was Fr Arthur Diamond; the village Kilrea.

58 *Journal*, PRONI, D/3838/4/7, note for 26 August 1958. In July Alfred George, whose early retirement appeared to clear the way for JH's promotion at the Belfast Gallery, visited the Hewitts with his wife Ella.

59 Edna Longley, 'Progressive Bookmen; Left-wing Politics and Ulster Protestant Writers', in *Returning to Ourselves: Second Volume of Papers from the John Hewitt International Summer School*, edited by Eve Patten (Belfast: Lagan, 1995), p. 20.

published McHugh's article without consulting him. When Fairfield (who had admired Casement) entered the fray, Hewitt was certainly implicated because she had published a report on the trial of the IRA men who had lethally bombed Coventry in August 1939. Casement and the executed bombers—Peter Barnes and James McCormack—had also been unhelpfully linked in an appeal for repatriation of their remains made by the Scottish Communist MP, Willie Gallacher.[60] This was the kind of paramilitary politics which liked 'to hit and run and howl when it is hit'.

At the end of May 1958, the new offices were ready. On Sunday 31 May, the Hewitts went to the Unitarian church. Spiritualist therapy, anti-war demonstrations, and occasional attendance at church lightly outline a sense of expanded horizons, or of need. Comparing their own situation to that of a young recruit, John Morley, to the Herbert Gallery staff, Roberta noted his good taste, interest in Victorian things—'a bit precious'. His fiancée hated work in a comprehensive school, lacking, in Roberta's eyes, any sympathy with lusty Midland girls ready to hop on the pillion seat of a motorbike but without interest in poetry or grammar. 'Our young roughs are criminals in Edwardian trousers and our young intellectuals are Victorian. It is left to the middle aged like us to be modern.'[61]

In July, the Hewitts were introduced to the novelist and art critic John Berger ('a good man') by Peter Peri whose work John encountered in a survey of Coventry schools. Berger had curated an exhibition of young British artists in the Temporary Gallery, before Hewitt's arrival. They saw Brendan Behan's 'The Hostage' and the first production of Sheila Delaney's 'A Taste of Honey' in London, but on their return to the Midlands Roberta (if not also John) resumed the therapy in Birmingham. It was a summer of relatively free time, thanks in part to delays in opening the new gallery. On a Scottish trip in the autumn, they saw O'Casey's fantastical play 'Cock-a-Doodle Dandy' (1949) in Edinburgh, went to the Abbotsford pub with the poet Sidney Goodsir Smith, and visited an aunt of John's. There was gallery business to be done also. Pictures by Joan Early and MacLaughlin Milne were bought for Coventry. In Ayr, they teamed up with Norman Todhunter, one of the old Belfast circle, married to John's sister, Eileen. Family and career, Britain and Ireland, art and poetry kept popping up side by side.

In February 1959, Hewitt with Coventry's Lord Mayor flew at short notice to East Berlin, by way of the Polish airline, en route for Dresden. Their joint purpose was solidification of the wartime bond to ensure cooperation in the Herbert Art Gallery's opening show the following year. Off his own bat, Hewitt was keen to trace a young Belfast-born artist, Elizabeth Shaw (1920–92), whose work he had seen in a London exhibition of 1958 devoted to contemporary German art.[62] She was otherwise unknown to him. The account of his trip, published in *Threshold*, deftly moves from complimentary observations on East German policy, to sardonic asides

60 See W. J. Mc Cormack, *Roger Casement in Death; Or, Haunting the Free State* (Dublin: University College Dublin Press, 2002), p. 166.

61 *Journal*, PRONI, D/3838/4/7, 1 June 1960.

62 See Theo Snoddy, *Dictionary of Irish Artists: 20th Century*, 2nd edn. (Dublin: Merlin, 2002), p. 599.

about bureaucracy, and generous sketches of personalities and unofficial events.[63] Among artworks he saw in Germany was a recent triptych by Heinz Lohmar (1900–76) with a central panel depicting an Egyptian mother and dead child, with the sky trail of NATO bombers overhead. 'When on various occasions', Hewitt wrote in direct response to this detail, 'I remarked that their [i.e. the East Germans'] painting was much better than the Russian [examples], it was politely suggested to me that this was not so'. He complied with no orthodoxy in politics, while endorsing a social realist perspective. 'I began by announcing that I was a bureaucrat and asked them how I might save my soul alive. After a moment of silent shock their laughter indicated that they knew that I was only joking.'[64] Shuttled rapidly out of Berlin for his official business in Dresden, Hewitt never managed to meet Shaw or her husband, the Genevan sculptor, René Graetz (1908–74). However, she got in touch later, and the two met in London. He described her work as 'goodnatured, whimsical, shrewd in observation, expressed with a deceptive simplicity'.[65]

On 14 July 1959, Barratt, the town clerk, wrote to the Gulbenkian Foundation proposing to bring Hewitt up to London two days later. The Coventry delegates evidently made a positive impression for, on 21 July, Barratt wrote again to W. A. Sanderson at the Gulbenkian summarizing their situation: 'As Mr Hewitt and I explained, the City Council at the beginning of the financial year voted a sum of £2000 to cover the cost of the opening of the new Art Gallery, but the Exhibition which the Art director now has in mind is clearly beyond such a limited vote.'[66] Coventry, he pointed out, was 'the first municipality to build post-war an art gallery and museum'. The director's plans for the opening consisted almost exclusively in an international loans exhibition in which his dislike of Old Masters (if that is really what it amounted to) played second fiddle to his interest in the art resources of Eastern or central Europe. After some careful humming and hawing, the Foundation agreed to contribute £2000, by which point Coventry was in need of a little more. The Isaac Wolfson Foundation was unwilling to help, but Coultaulds Limited (an industrial giant with its origins in Coventry) handed over £1000 on 24 September 1959. Associated TV gave £250, the good news conveyed by Norman Collins who had been an editor in Gollancz when Hewitt's poetry was rejected. In October 1959, he was represented in *The Guinness Book of Poetry,* and in December he flew to Belgrade to choose pictures for the Herbert's opening.

In practice, the Gallery was only part of Hewitt's responsibilities—officially, he was city art director. Consequently, the Finance and General Purposes Committee of the council's Education Committee had commissioned a report on 'Works of Art in the City Schools Used for Embellishment of the Buildings'. Hewitt's eight-page report positively whizzes through one school after another, noting murals, free-standing sculpture, paintings, and the rest. Though the document is undated, the gallery's archivist has assigned it to the 1950s, and so it must have been written

[63] John Hewitt, 'A Dresden Notebook; Some Aspects of Art Under Communism', *Threshold* 3, no. 2 (Summer 1959), pp. 46–60.

[64] Hewitt, 'A Dresden Notebook', pp. 51, 58.

[65] Quoted in Snoddy, *Dictionary of Irish Artists: 20th Century.*

[66] COV, CCA/3/1/14358.

in the earliest days of Hewitt's appointment, while he was still working towards the formal opening and the inaugural loan exhibition. His enthusiasm for the task is evident as he records not just formal works of art but, for example, curtains in the city's five comprehensive schools. 'Each set has been designed independently so that there is no tedious repetition of devices.'[67]

A list of the artists represented in the schools indicates a strong reliance on native English work but not, in Hewitt's view, on immediately local artists. Fred Millet won his repeated praise. At Wyken Croft Nursery he was less impressed by Colin Browning's painted panel based on the ballad of Sir Patrick Spens:

> an exercise in what might nowadays be called Abstract Impressionism. . . . I find its composition restless, and the texture of the pigment, while fashionable just now in the Bond Street galleries, is of no great interest. I cannot imagine its having much appeal to the pupils of this school. A mural in this school should surely be related in some way to the old painting in the fairly adjacent church, even if only as an exercise in local history.

Characteristically blunt in his assessment of individuals, Hewitt was also willing to inscribe a few political observations into his report. These are not inevitably mere personal opinions. His approval of murals in schools chimed with views expressed in an anonymous article—probably by E. P. Thompson—in *The New Reasoner* of autumn 1958, illustrated with a photograph of Millet's treatment of the seasons in Wokingham Secondary Modern School. Hewitt was in favour of an opinion poll among pupils. 'This is not to suggest that every work must be geared exactly to fit the taste and win the approval of all its viewers at any given instant. There must always be the pedagogic desire to train and elevate that taste'. Taking the argument into a historical direction, he averred that 'the painters of the Middle Ages and the Renaissance accepted as a matter of course the strictest specifications and frequently achieved masterpieces within the most rigorously imposed limits and nobody worried about freedom of expression'. Still under GENERAL REMARKS, he commended legislation in Scandinavia and proceeded more expansively to record practices he had recently observed in the German Democratic Republic:

> A definite percentage of the building costs of any state or civic project must be devoted to the integration into the building of the skills of decorative artists as a fundamental part of the total intention, design and effect; so that those buildings which serve the community should not merely be functional in a utilitarian sense, but contain, by their very nature, the finest expression of human skill and imagination possible in each instance.

The condition of primary schools inevitably raises the question of children, and the Hewitts' childless home. At one point in her journal, during the Coventry years, Roberta lamented their condition, but added that a child might have disturbed John's concentration. Late in 1959, something of a storm blew up in the city's administration about so-called ineducable children. In October Councillor T. L. K. Locksley wrote sharply to the Medical Officer of Health, 'I regard the situation relating to

[67] COV, CCA/3/1/13604.

E[ducationally] S[ub] N[ormal] children as so serious as to request you to place on the Agenda of the next Health Committee an item for discussion under the title "The Procedure for Ascertainment of E. S. N. Children"'. This description was later modified, apparently by the town clerk, to read 'Dealing with Ineducable Children'. The councillor was insistent, 'I understand that a medical member of your staff told the mother of an E. S. N. child that "it was no use seeing her Councillor about the child." I should like your assurance that such comments will not be made by members of your department in the future.'[68]

Hewitt's vision of the primary school as the first stage in culture, not just in economic survival, had its complement in his wife's life-long engagement with schools, often in the capacity of committee- or board of guardians member. The existence, or the stigmatization, of children who were 'ineducable' challenged his political assumptions, both as to the character-forming capacity of art and the rightness of progressive theories in urban planning, housing etc. The war's legacy, and the post-war optimism of the Left, might for some cancel each other, giving rise to a paralysis no better than that locking Belfast's antagonists together. Coventry was to be good for the Hewitts, but it was not without major complications.

Purchase of No. 5 Postbridge Road, Styvechale, did not happen in time for the general election of 1959, and scarcely happened for the Herbert Art Gallery opening. Elaine Burton's loss of her Coventry South seat was an omen of Labour reversals in local government, but it provided the defeated candidate with an opportunity to acknowledge Roberta Hewitt's active support. From London she wrote,

> What a sad time for us all but what wonderful friends I had to help all the time. The result would have been a great deal worse without them—and you. I am looking back on my team that gave such unstinted service—every day. Nobody could have done more or given more.[69]

Significantly, there was no reference to John, then up to his eyes in preparations for the gallery's physical completion and fitting-out, and for the international loan exhibition to mark its formal opening. Perhaps his professional engagement with the Labour-controlled administration inhibited direct involvement in politics. Perhaps his politics was not so simply defined. The deliberate reporting his trip to East Germany once again drew attention to his interest in the Soviet sphere. As Sarah Ferris has demonstrated, Hewitt's comments on the subject were inconsistent. To John Montague in 1964, he wrote 'I have never been a Communist...I should best be described as a Utopian Socialist.'[70] In *The Planter and the Gael* (1970), a project shared with Montague and sponsored by the Northern Irish Arts Council, he presented himself as 'too much an individualist' for any such allegiance, though he went on to offer Trotskyist as a possible identification.[71] To Geraldine Watts some years later, he admitted (or boasted) to having used the Marxist dialectic as

[68] COV, CCA/3/1/13604, Locksley to Medical Officer, 13 October 1959.
[69] PRONI, D/3838/4/1, Elaine Burton to Roberta Hewitt, 12 October 1959.
[70] UU, Hewitt, Box 9.
[71] Hewitt and Montague, *The Planter and the Gael* (Belfast: Northern Irish Arts Council, 1970).

a 'handy if not all-purpose tool'.[72] These inconsistencies should not be taken as culpable; in part, they provide cover for sniping at his enemies, especially those in Belfast. But they cast an odd light on Hewitt's steadfast respect for the soviet satellites of Eastern and central Europe—notably Poland, Czechoslovakia, and the German Democratic Republic (as he named it punctiliously in his 1959 report.) The same document's jocose dismissal of an artist's right to free expression, its low-key contempt for abstraction, and emphasis on 'pedagogic desire' can be read as a decidedly anti-romantic stance when planning was the need of the hour, though Stalinist echoes are audible too.

The opening exhibition of 1960 was to make or break the new director. Based largely on art borrowed from galleries abroad, it was to involve complex negotiations about insurance, especially where material owned by state institutions in Eastern Europe was concerned. Dresden was willing to send impressive items, even if the sums given as insurable values were in a few cases fantastic—Cranach the Elder, 'Paradise ($50,000 value); Rembrandt, 'Saskia with a Red Flower' ($625,000); Van Dyck 'Portrait of Thomas Parr' ($38,000); Ostrade, 'Artist in his Studio' ($150,000); Belotto 'View of Dresden' ($20,000); and Rubens 'St Francis de Paul [*sic*] besought by Victims of the Plague' ($100,000).[73] These names cannot but have impressed the Gulbenkian and other sponsors. The Herbert Art Gallery was determined to launch itself under an impressive array of Old Masters' flags. In the event, the French contribution of nineteenth- and twentieth-century pictures was equally impressive—'The White Church' by Maurice Utrillo and 'Place de Theatre Francais' by Camille Pissarro, together with works by Boudin, Cézanne, Corot, and Gauguin. Goya and Poussin were also represented. These great figures were tactfully juxtaposed with British artists, including Fitton and the sculptor Jack Greaves (b.1928).

On 9 March 1960, Lady Herbert unveiled an exhibition which, in several respects, did not comply with priorities set out by Hewitt in his early drafts and reports. Beforehand, a civic ceremony including lunch took place in Saint Mary's Hall. For the afternoon event with Lady Herbert in the gallery, both John and Roberta were invited. Three days later, an informal gallery 'at home' gave guests a chance to enjoy the art at closer quarters. Once again Roberta was included. The official opening had been covered in the local press at gratifying length, but its national impact was limited.[74] In Roberta's recollection, 'the committee just refused to have the Queen to open the Gallery…and the London papers didn't give it as much publicity as usual'.[75]

Hewitt believed in what might now be called proactive publicity. His eye was caught by an advertisement in the London *Times*: Lilian Bomberg, widow of the painter David Bomberg (1890–1957), sought a gallery willing to host a retrospective

[72] Geraldine Watts, 'John Hewitt, the Non-Conformist Conscience of Northern Ireland', MLitt thesis, TCD, 1987, p. 140.

[73] Listed by the Staatliche Kunstsammlungen Dresden in a letter dated 17 October 1959.

[74] COV, CCH/5/1/10. See *The Coventry Evening Telegraph*, 9 March 1960, pp. 4–5. But see also the magazine *Sphere*, 19 March 1960, for a photograph of Hewitt (not identified) in the gallery.

[75] *Journal*, PRONI, D/3838/4/7, [no day] July 1960.

exhibition. It went down very well at the Herbert, so much so that Mrs Bomberg donated a picture to the permanent collection. The poet Stephen Spender reviewed the show, and in January 1961 the elegant bulletin of British Insulated Callender Cables Ltd used a colour photo of the Herbert opening.[76] Hewitt had passed the test with honours but without royal approval. About the same time as the Bomberg gift, Lord Iliffe presented the gallery with a collection of Graham Sutherland's working cartoons, drawn for the early design of his huge tapestry now hanging behind the altar of Coventry Cathedral.[77]

In the longer perspective, the succeeding twelve years in Coventry were satisfying, fruitful, and even happy, though the writing of poetry did not come easily at first. Some of the most exciting occasions involved conflict and a change of heart on aesthetic priorities. The Herbert acquired Ben Nicholson's 'Two Forms' three years after the gallery's formal opening, this adding to the suspicion (evinced at the time of the Bomberg show) that contemporary British art was gaining ground in far from realist modes. During 1964, Hewitt commissioned a F. E. McWilliam bronze figure of the artist Elizabeth Frink. His thinking was strategic; by familiarizing the committee to these names, he could 'at the ripe moment' lead it to more advanced work. Local commotion suggested that local opinion held more faithfully to the realist creed than its apostle of 1957. Conflicts of opinion between gallery and public (or a section of the political public) were renewed with prejudice in 1966 when Hewitt bought a piece by the distinguished British sculpture Barbara Hepworth. Coventry was no socialist utopia.

The general election of October 1964 had brought Labour and Harold Wilson to power. No. 5 Postbridge Road served as a centre for canvassing based, as Hewitt learnedly reported to John Boyd, on the Reading System. In local terms, it was satisfying to win back a constituency lost in 1959. The Hewitts' home was thrown open to forty or fifty Labour canvassers, including the newly arrived professor of English literature George Hunter, author of a book on the Elizabethan dramatist John Lyly, and an enthusiast for European literature.[78] Anecdote and archive suggest that Hewitt's left-wing interest were more diverse. Several 1967 issues of *Newsletter*, the weekly organ of the Socialist Labour League's central committee, are preserved among his papers. One veteran of conversations from the years 1964–67 places the poet at meetings of Northern Ireland Labour Party in a pub on Belfast's Dublin Road: these presumably occurred during holidays largely spent in Cushendall. As the 1960s reached their Irish crescendo, he maintained a critical balance—between a cutting from the *Pyongyang Times* ('the mission and role of revolutionary literature') and an *Irish Times* supplement marking Dáil Eireann's fiftieth anniversary (January 1919).[79]

[76] For Spender's review, see *The Listener*, 8 December 1960, p. 377.
[77] COV, CCB, Ian Hollick, 'John Hewitt in Coventry: Brief and Distant Memories', p. 5.
[78] LINEN, JH to John Boyd, 11 January 1965.
[79] UU, Hewitt, Box 20.

8

Defending Barbara Hepworth before the Ratepayers; *Collected Poems* (1968)

The 1960s brought a modestly higher tide of prosperity. Air travel eliminated the long train-and-boat journeys back to Northern Ireland. In July 1960, Roberta went on holiday to Paris with Sophie Stewart. On the way back, they met up with the Stewarts' daughter, Brenda, in London. Hewitt, in a rare and oblique allusion to their childlessness, classified Roberta and himself as providers of second generation hospitality, 'a pleasant state implying a certain stability'.[1] The old Belfast gang found itself at some greater ease, though the province's long-term political stability was beginning to crack. In 1965, the Hewitts gave up renting the cottage north of Cushendall, signalling their acceptance of Coventry as home. However, before ten years is up, an employee has either internalized the job and its demands or become increasingly restless. Hewitt's job suited him in ways unimaginable when he applied. It gave him professional authority and it recognized his own innate authority. It provided reassurance and security, yet opened up unsuspected novelties. Having noted an eighteenth-century namesake while walking by memorials before his interview, he discovered a far longer past below the half-rebuilt modern city. Mediaeval history figures at proper length in the long introductory essay he wrote for *Coventry; the Tradition of Change and Continuity* (1966), an elegant collection of photographs with captions in English, French, German, and Russian. Though published in 1966, it seems that an earlier printing was circulated to visitors by the City Council; identification of its text as Hewitt's work of that period is an important addition to his bibliography.[2] But a question remains—in writing this anonymous essay for the city fathers, years after his appointment, was he kingpin or dogsbody, was he settled or restless?

The book was designed for presentation to important visitors. Eventually issued in a commercial edition, it unexpectedly constitutes Hewitt's longest single prose essay (about 8000 words), embodying a history of Coventry and its earliest origins, and taking in a good deal of architectural comment. The poet is active on the first page, quoting Alfred Tennyson's 'Godiva' to introduce the famous mediaeval legend of a lady who, to shame her husband into an abatement of taxes, rode naked through Coventry. The social motivation, expressly mentioned by Hewitt, is often forgotten and, in another effort to scrutinize the legend's hypnotic aspect, he notes

[1] Linen, JH to John Boyd, 8 May 1965.

[2] I am grateful to Rae-Ann Byatt of the History Centre, Herbert Art Gallery, for bringing this material to my attention.

the very late addition of peeping Tom to what is by now more myth than legend. The poet Philip Larkin, born in Coventry and sometime based in the library of Queen's University Belfast, is also quoted.[3]

The foreword's subtitle—'tradition of change and continuity'—is manifestly the work of a subcommittee, though it uncannily links two directions or urges in Hewitt's vision—progressive social concern and retrospective curiosity. Writing about Coventry at the end of the seventeenth century, he moves in two short paragraphs from a cameo of King James II being mobbed in Saint Michael's Cathedral—by folk believing in miraculous curative powers—to the moment

> when that robust octogenarian, George Walker, bishop of Derry, whose courage as governor of that city during its tremendous seige [*sic*] by the army of James and his French allies had won him national fame, passed through [Coventry] on his way to London [and] all the bells rang out and he was given a hero's welcome by the roaring populace in the narrow streets.[4]

Hewitt's interest in history rarely looked back so far. He was more confident in pointing out that the phrase Christian Socialism was first put into print by a local Coventry schoolmaster, Joseph Squiers, and that the Irish radical Feargus O'Connor 'harangued a Chartist rally on Greyfriars Green'.[5] Inevitably, the essay attends to events of his own lifetime and experience, providing an insight into Hewitt's revised opinion of his new home after a decade. Writing to John Boyd during this period, he noted astutely and prophetically that '[Ian] Paisley is making the wee North notorious, only partly redeemed by the West Belfast result.'[6] Any confidence in the Northern Ireland Labour Party was to prove sadly over-ambitious. In the post-war English landscape, he places

> the foursquare Herbert Art Gallery and Museum, token of our mixed economy, of private benevolence and public enterprise, the Museum with its cars and ribbons and antiquities, the Art Gallery with the challenge of its changing exhibitions; this diapered-brick building being the first art gallery and museum built in Britain since the war.[7]

But the cathedral is unavoidable, 'presenting the Ideals of the Good City to the people of Coventry, and by giving witness to the world of the necessity for reconciliation and mutual forgiveness among men of every belief and colour'. He is clearly moved more by the art than the creed, by 'Basil Spence's bold, flanged design…the leaping [Jacob] Epstein bronze'. And two artists with German names—Hans Feibusch (1898–1998) and Georg Ehrlich (1897–1966), the latter making 'an unsectarian contribution' to the civic crematorium in the shape of a recumbent bronze figure—are pointedly mentioned.

[3] *Coventry, the Tradition of Change and Continuity*, rev. edn. (Coventry: Coventry Corporation, 1969), pp. 1–2.

[4] *Coventry, the Tradition of Change and Continuity*, p. 5. Walker was never more than bishop-designate.

[5] *Coventry, the Tradition of Change and Continuity*, p. 7.

[6] Martin McBirney, later assassinated by the Provisional IRA, polled well. See Linen, JH to John Boyd, 21 April 1966.

[7] *Coventry, the Tradition of Change and Continuity*, p. 10.

The homeward tug persisted. In November 1965, Hewitt had received a student magazine from a teacher in Derry. Replying, he chided Alan Warner for neglecting a notable figure in the city's public life. Professor Tom Finnegan had been president of Magee College whom Hewitt revered as a spokesman for liberal views in the late 1940s and 1950s. 'I didn't always agree, but I saluted his right to speak out.' Magee, in those days, was a Presbyterian establishment associated with Trinity College Dublin. Indicating some ambition to teach, he admitted recurrent feelings that he should have liked to have been 'somewhere within his ambience'.[8] Hewitt had been commissioned by the southern Irish Arts Council to edit a selection of poems by the Donegal Victorian, William Allingham (1824–89), which appeared under the Dolmen Press imprint in 1967, a year after the essay in Coventry history.

Prose written for office purposes never flowed in such quantity again. Hewitt's best-known poem of his English years is 'An Irishman in Coventry' (already examined), and it has found its way into such influential American anthologies as Anthony Bradley's *Contemporary Irish Poetry* (1980). Far from being another exercise in the long tradition of emigrant yearning, the poem works between two never reduced claimants to an exclusive identity. There is 'my creed-haunted, Godforsaken race', itself an internally disturbed unresting place. And then also, 'a people endlessly betrayed' who, in retaliation, like 'to hit and run and howl when it is hit'. Any recollection of the IRA's bombing would implicate recollection of *The Irish Democrat*, sponsored in 1937 by a very different aspect of republicanism yet manifestly still in bitter communion with the parent body. That had been pre-war Belfast. In Coventry, probably in the late-1960s or very early 1970s, he committed his recollections of this attachment to the paper, concluding:

> By means I have never been able to understand, *The Democrat* became the monthly organ of the Connolly Club, a Communist-inspired Irish Association in London and continues to this day. It seems to me now an altogether deplorable production, its pages well padded with the words of sentimental Irish songs which most Irishmen anyway know by heart and ear. Wildly wrong in its interpretation of Irish affairs, foolishly supporting the reactionary I. R. A., lacking in frankness, blatantly opportunist, it has nothing to do with what we intended. Yet when, on the fringes of an open-air meeting in an English city, a young man with a thick brogue invites me to buy a copy, I always experience a momentary thrill of emotion for those far off days of the Left Book Club, The Popular Front, Aid for Spain and the snug in *The Brown Horse*, and take my copy and, turning its pages, rage at the betrayal of our dream.[9]

The gallery-man found compensation in his work. Yet the exhibition planned for the autumn of 1966 turned out to have more than an aesthetic impact. Gone were the Old Masters, the old reliables. Perhaps the scale of the thing determined the nature of some responses. Fifteen artists were represented, some of them sculptors whose work occupied large areas of public space. A show not easily ignored. In addition, the material on display was unmistakably modern, new, contemporary, unmediated by the familiar pieties of art history. The painters were Merlyn Evans

[8] Private collection, JH to Alan Warner, 29 November 1965.

[9] *North*, p. 69.

(1910–73), Terry Frost (1915–2003), Michael Fussell (1927–74), Alfred Janes (1911–99), William Gear (1915–97), Rodrigo Moynihan (1910–90), Ben Nicholson (1894–1982), Victor Pasmore (1908–98), John Piper (1903–92) Ceri Richards (1903–71), John Plumb (1927–2008), and William Scott (1913–89). This was a powerful mobilization of British art for any provincial gallery, and if the names which endure are Nicholson, Pasmore, Piper and Scott, the others contributed range and relative value. The town of Swansea was particularly well represented by Janes and Richards, whose circle included the poets Dylan Thomas and Vernon Watkins.

Manx by birth, the youngest participant, Bryan Kneale (b.1930), was both painter and sculptor. The two remaining artists were the sculptors F. E. McWilliam (1909–89) and Barbara Hepworth (1903–75). The only woman to be included in the show, Hepworth was to prove the most contentious of the lot. Yet by 1966, she was a pillar of the cultural establishment. What is noteworthy in retrospect is Hewitt's diplomatic omission of his own Ulster painting friends—Terence Flanagan, John Luke, Colin Middleton—or the emerging Wicklow-born and Dublin-based abstractionist Cecil King. Ireland was 'represented' only by McWilliam (born Banbridge, County Down), and to a lesser extent by Scott (born Greenock, of Scottish and Irish parents). If there was a glaring British absence, it was the sculptor Henry Moore.

Hewitt had not been the sole activist in putting the exhibition together. He drew on the expertise of two close associates, Mervyn Levy and Ian Hollick, the former a staunch ally in the London art scene, and the latter a dedicated member of a Herbert Gallery committee and unofficial spokesman for Sir Alfred's point of view. In a useful memoir written after Hewitt's death, Hollick suggests that Elisabeth Frink (1930–93) was included (or was to be included) in 'Metamorphosis'.[10] If he was wrong, as the catalogue would indicate, his mistake may arise from the inclusion of McWilliam's bronze statue of Frink, which the Herbert Gallery had bought. Aged thirty-five at the time, she would have been the youngest exhibitor. Her work, however, lay outside the declared concerns which Hollick and Levy articulated in their contribution to Hewitt's big tribute to contemporary British art. Frink stuck to naturalistic forms, and remained a figurative sculptor even though she elided surface detail.

The show emerged within a remarkably tight schedule. Levy had visited Coventry for an exhibition of housewives' art in January 1966. In conversation, the two men could not fail to be struck by the huge changes which had occurred within a decade or so. The war had sidelined the arts but also transformed them. To assess and appreciate what was happening in its aftermath, especially what Hewitt termed 'the swinging-over or leap from representation to abstraction', required courage in both viewer and curator.[11] The centenary of Sir Alfred Herbert's birth was approaching, and something worthy of a generous patron was essential. Hewitt consulted Hollick about a proper title for the occasion, and 'Metamorphosis' was

[10] COV, CCB, Ian Hollick, 'John Hewitt in Coventry; Brief and Distant Memories', p. 5.
[11] John Hewitt, 'Foreword', *Metamorphosis*, p. 3.

the reply. In turn Levy used the old classical notion in his introduction (completed by June) to the catalogue. But it would be a mistake to relegate Hewitt to third place in the team. Of the thirty works of art on display in September, mainly loans, two had already been purchased by Hewitt as director of the gallery. These were Nicholson's 'Two Forms', an oil on canvas dating from 1946/47, and McWilliam's seventy-two-inch-high bronze statue of Frink. At the close of the Exhibition on 2 October 1966, he bought from it Hepworth's 'Figure: Walnut', a bronze cast in 1965 and supplied on loan by the Gimpel Fils Gallery. It was not an inch shorter than McWilliam's 'Frink', and the two pieces drew attention to each other, the female nude and the abstract work of a woman.

Later in the year, the purchase became the subject of heated public debate in Coventry during which Hewitt once or twice lost his cool. 'Metamorphosis' constituted a turning point, or at least marked one, in the city's post-war evolution, politically and culturally. Labour hegemony, and international solidarity with bombed Continental towns and galleries, were going into decline. Nine years earlier, as if to greet the refugee from Belfast, the prime minister had declared to a large Conservative rally in Bedford,

> Go around the country, go to the industrial towns, go to the farms and you will see a state of prosperity such as we have never had in my lifetime—nor indeed in the history of this country.... Indeed let us be frank about it—most of our people have never had it so good.

The message even got through to the long traumatized people of Coventry, where the motor industry was thriving. Ironically, the newly secure Tory minds had been happier with Old Masters borrowed from communist regimes, or with representational work produced by local artisans than they were with William Scott's 'Up and Across' (1962).

Personally, Hewitt too had enjoyed the links with central and Eastern Europe, where the language of socialism was still a political vernacular. His doughty attachment to socialist realism had not been concealed in his early English years. It was ironic that, as he gradually developed an aesthetic outlook sympathetic to abstraction and experiment, the city altered too. Levy's introduction to 'Metamorphosis' could hardly be regarded as provocative. He began by questioning the usefulness of 'non-figurative' as an art-critical term. 'As a matter of simple semantics, none of the figures or motifs of painting and sculpture can in fact be non-figurative—a contradiction in terms.' If this was an exercise in wooing the public, perhaps he was courting too slow. The reassurance offered in the argument that 'curves, undulations, rhythms, suggest the organic movements and growths of nature' was bound to provoke some demand for an even more reductionist art—no art.

The selectors had attempted to include both representational and abstract work by most, if not all, of the participating artists. For example, numbered items 1 and 2 (both by Merlyn Evans) were (1) a pencil sketch 'Portrait of Giorgio di Chirico', and (2) 'Time King, Vertical Abstraction', tempera on canvas. Like most artists, Victor Pasmore was represented by four works, including (42) 'Beach in Cornwall' (1950) and (44) 'Red Development No. 7' (1964). Abstraction, viewers were led to believe, was a matter of personal development, not revolutionary change. During the exhibition's month-long run its public reception appears to have been relatively positive; Hewitt could even observe that the art subcommittee had proposed the Hepworth purchase 'unprompted by me', whereas the earlier acquisition of Nicholson's oil had been a 'struggle'. Like so many of his projects, Hewitt had imagined 'Metamorphosis' having a subtle educational role within the full complexity of a modern urban community.

Harold Macmillan's vaunted prosperity was equally complex, driving art prices up and encouraging a metropolitan concentration of dealers and agents. The 'struggle' for Nicholson had begun in London, 'on the steps of Burlington House', no less. A very high proportion of the work in 'Metamorphosis' was lent by the artists themselves—all four of Gear's pictures; three of Kneale's four and of Pasmore's four. Mervyn Levy and his wife loaned Plumb's 'Man Drinking Tea' (1954), and Plumb provided two others. These gestures wonderfully increased the personal tone of the exhibition not only by demonstrating the artist's direct engagement with the Herbert Gallery but also by indicating the director's standing among professional artists. Yet a subtext murmured: paintings loaned by the painter were paintings which were, for whatever reason, unsold.

Sculpture raised different concerns. Though Kneale loaned two works in steel, Hepworth was professionally represented by the Gimpel Fils Gallery, which loaned three works by her, two of them bronzes. (A fourth item belonged to the Arts Council of Great Britain.) As her dealings with the canon of Coventry Cathedral would reveal, she was generous but tough in negotiations. By the mid-1960s, her work fetched top prices; she was in demand. The completion of Basil Spence's new cathedral offered a complementary venue for modern art close to the Herbert. Quite apart from the intrinsic quality of the building, Graham Sutherland provided the colossal tapestried Christ above the altar, John Piper was responsible for much of the window glass, and Jacob Epstein's 'Archangel Michael and Satan' leaps and falls outside the west door. For Hewitt's 'Metamorphosis', Piper loaned a large (117-ft × 82-ft) model in glass for the baptistery window. The regeneration of Coventry was itself a metamorphosis, in which the past was not easily recognizable in the new forms and idioms.

Following the closure of 'Metamorphosis' early in October, disagreement between the Herbert Gallery and the city's altering political dynamic gradually broke the surface. Labour would shortly lose control of municipal government, and an augury of the new dispensation appeared as the Federation of Coventry Ratepayers' and Residents' Associations. In his recollections of 1987, Ian Hollick observed that Sir Alfred Herbert's gift of the gallery had not been 'universally welcomed' by councillors, who saw it as a future drain on their resources.[12] In his earliest days, Hewitt learned that a painting by Paul Cézanne might be available. Apart from his acquisitions policy which did not favour big names, he noted wryly that such a purchase would burden the rates. The federation certainly shared that view. Though their public disagreements were delayed, Hewitt indicated that trouble

[12] Hollick, 'Brief and Distant Memories', p. 1.

was brewing and that the effect on his planned acquisitions had already registered. Levy, who acted in a variety of unofficial roles (adviser, dealer, friend, advocate), had offered 'just the Moore for Coventry' in late September 1966. The phrase is ambiguous: did he mean that, of a larger collection of works, he could extract and offer just one piece by Henry Moore; or did he mean that he had found *exactly the right* Moore for Hewitt's permanent collection? Either ways, Hewitt was brutally frank—the art subcommittee would be publicly lynched by the Ratepayers' Association.

His difficulties did not crystallize until after Christmas. On 28 December, the Association president (Mrs J. Mitchell) asked the town clerk to make arrangements for her members to visit the gallery and meet the director, on a date agreeable to Hewitt.[13] The clerk, who was by now *Sir* Charles Barratt, had no difficulty in obliging, and 30 January was agreed by all. However, the involvement of Sir Charles demonstrated the extent to which Hewitt fell short of being fully master in his own gallery. Prior to his arrival, Coventry's small collection of art works had been in the care of the museum director, who in turn took orders from the city librarian. Completion of the Herbert Gallery had not prompted any modification of this hierarchy, even though it rapidly became one of the most important exhibition centres outside London. Throughout his fifteen years, Hewitt was not authorized to sign his own correspondence, and the office designed for the holder of an entirely new post (art director) was in practice occupied by the city librarian. Most of the time, harmonious relations between the various administrators endured, but the altered political colouration of municipal politics introduced a note of friction.

Mrs Mitchell and her fellow Ratepayers knew they were dealing with a man who did not fully command his own specialist field of operations. They wanted to see 'the exhibits' in private and, in Hewitt's perspective, put him on the spot. As early as 2 January, the town clerk indicated that the Hepworth sculpture was top of their agenda, more as recent purchase than as enduring work of art, though abstraction in general clearly did not please them. (There had been loose talk about paying good money 'for a hole'.) Within two days of the Federation's visit, Hewitt chose to publish his account of it in *The Coventry Evening Telegraph*.

He had been glad of the opportunity to conduct members of the Ratepayers' Association round the Art Gallery. Thereafter, his letter disclosed what a small degree of mutual understanding had resulted. He had spent 'an hour and a half explaining the Committee's policy in forming its various collections'. He complained, perhaps unwisely, about the smallness of the budget available to him, adding that some acquisitions had increased in monetary value since their purchase. He 'indicated with almost tedious reiteration' that abstract works formed only a minute fraction of the gallery's accessions. Spurred on by his own courage, he dropped all pretence of diplomacy:

> Of course, I did not expect Mrs Mitchell, the Federation President, easily to surrender her prejudices; but I considered it possible that she might grasp the relation of the

[13] COV, VA 1966.49.

Hepworth sculpture to the Committee's overall plan for the cultural enrichment of the community which claims her loyalty and mine. What I do find difficult to understand is that, in referring to the cost of the bronze, she disregards the fact that the Council received a 50% grant towards the purchase, from the Victoria and Albert Museum, the nation's arbiters in these matters. The actual cost was £2,480 2s 6d.

Clearly, this was a conflict at once personal and political. Hewitt's dander was up, as his fellow Ulstermen might express it. He did not intend to reach an accommodation with the Ratepayers, complaining in his final paragraph (when he reached it) of Mrs Mitchell's use of the royal 'We' in her public pronouncements. Determined to go down fighting, he informed *Telegraph* readers that none of the federation visitors could assure him that they had seen the Kinetic Art exhibition of the previous May. Game, set, and match to the Philistines.

Within a few weeks, John reached the tenth anniversary of his appointment in Coventry. The tenor of his letter, as much as its material content, reveals the unease which still remained. Nominally the art director, and phenomenally successful in attracting good material of all kinds to the collection, he stood third in a bureaucratic hierarchy. He was aged fifty-nine; there was, frankly, nowhere else to go for the remaining few years before retirement. In the summer of 1968, Ian Hollick retired from the arts subcommittee. Hewitt tried to accept the loss of his ally with good humour:

I too have felt the change as the end of an epoch, an epoch in which we had our victories, and in which firm bases were established, impossible to liquidate. End of chapter, but only that. Even my old battered hat—something of a supernumerary appendage to the Art Sub Committee—has given up, and I have been compelled to seek its replacement, for battered new hats are hard to come by.[14]

The row about Hepworth had been spooky from the outset, perhaps compromised by the Hewitts' absence on a Greek holiday during part of the exhibition's run.[15] (From Athens, they sent a postcard to Norman Carruthers, complaining of bogus and mass-produced antiques. And 'the resinous wine is a bit too much'.[16]) Bureaucracy may have taken offence or advantage, but the specific subject of the row was no push-over. In 1966, Hepworth had been a Companion of the British Empire (CBE) for eight years, appointed a trustee of the Tate Gallery in September 1965. Her place in the St Ives (Cornwall) artistic colony was central to the entire panoply of the post-war British cultural achievement. Yes, she was a typical Yorkshire character, warm and cussed, who liked a glass of whiskey and smoked in bed. (In 1972, she died in a fire at her cottage-studio.) She exemplified true grit, plain speaking, hard work, and the highest integrity, values one might have thought important to Mrs Mitchell. Hepworth's abstraction certainly did not fit easily into Hewitt's long-established aesthetic, and his defence of the purchase was overheated in part

[14] COV, CCB, PA 2563/23/3, JH to Hollick, 18 June 1968 (copy).

[15] A senior art assistant, Norman Pegden, appears to have been in charge during the director's absence.

[16] PRONI, D/3838/5.

because it marked a shift in his own view of art, a shift all the more significant in that it occurred near the end of his professional career.

On the specific issue of spring 1967, his antagonist managed to have the second-last (and gracious) word. The *Telegraph* was her natural ally or, at worst, hers to commandeer. In response, Hewitt admitted 'It would be churlish of me to ignore Mrs Mitchell's kind remarks in her reply to my rather indignant letter. One does not expect commendation for what one is employed to do, but any degree of approbation is always welcome.' The editor chose not to publish this, but forwarded it to Mrs Mitchell. The Tories achieved their city council majority the following year. Privately Hewitt had the consolation of a new interest in his work among the associates of his old university. The pamphlet, *Tesserae*, was published through the QUB Festival office in May 1967, taking its name from a Latin word for the component pieces of icon-mosaic and thus affirming his concern with shape as a quality in verse as well as the plastic arts. While mainly given over to poems arising from holidays in Greece, *Tesserae* opened with an image from photographs of spaceman manoeuvres—'this billowing freedom threatens to / smother me with euphoria. / Hand over hand eagerly I crawl / back to uncertainty.'[17] The astronaut mirrors X-rays of the foetus, by which resemblance 'Hand over Hand' leads back to poems recalling childhood and then forward to the Greek snapshots. In 'Old Corinth', the speaker recalls how among 'the synagogue knee-high, the shop turned church / with the crumbling fresco, like an open byre, / we endured the harsh breath of Roman authority'.[18] Here, surely, is fractured culture, better termed history.

Back in England, a longer perspective brought results. From June to August 1968 an exhibition of contemporary British sculpture, set in the ruins of the old cathedral, included work by Hepworth, McWilliam, and Henry Moore. The Hepworths on temporary display were 'Square Form with Circles' (1963) and 'Dual Form' (1965). On 15 August 1968, Canon S. E. Verney reported that 'some five thousand people a day are visiting', a success due in no small part to the controversy eighteen months earlier involving the Herbert Gallery and the Ratepayers. In his public contention with Mrs Mitchell, Hewitt had made no reference to Basil Spence's radically innovative cathedral with its soaring tapestried Christ by Sutherland, window-glass by Piper, and the sombre bronze figures by Epstein outside the west door. Whereas Hewitt, with the support of his art subcommittee, had bought a Hepworth piece in 1966, Canon Verney was content to negotiate a loan of 'Square Form' limited by the business-like sculptor to a period of one year (renewable).[19]

Late 1966 had also its private side. Writing from Coventry to Sophie Stewart in October, Roberta Hewitt addressed her principal concern directly and at sympathetic length:

> I am sure it was a bit of a shock about the cervical smear—& I am sure you couldn't help worrying a bit, but I suppose it is splendid you found out before it became a major complaint—this is a splendid service for women—Montgomery House [in

[17] Ormsby, p. 51. [18] Ormsby, p. 56. [19] COVC, PA 2506/1/3/S.

> Belfast] is not a bad place... I was on [the] Committee that built it or adapted the building. It was all to the good you had your holiday—& it sounds a marvellous one.

Consoling and reassuring her friend, she drew on her own recent experiences:

> I went too—the Med[ical] D[irector] of Health in Coventry started a public service & I nipped in with the first lot [aged] 55–60. I was clear but they found an infection of something else—I don't know what—I have been complaining for years & D[octor] gave me ointment for it by Lady Jane. I am having treatment for a week to investigate that & may go into hospital for a week to investigate that and old bladder weakness. This could prove more difficult to treat & remain a nuisance until I get "between boards" as Cushendall would say.

After this shadow the letter delivers sunshine. She couldn't begin to recount the wonders of their Greek holiday unless she 'wrote for a day & a half'.[20] No reference to the Hepworth bother.

At the beginning of December, Roberta could proudly report that her husband 'has given birth to many poems—it is nice after a dry year'. Under the positive veneer, it is not merely possible but obligatory to discern an awkward balance, cordial yet unresolvable, between the lives of poet and wife. Fertility, it would seem, was his, not hers. The hope of pregnancy had long ago faded with the onset of middle age. The prospect of hospitalization, the need to apply ointment 'by Lady Jane' (that is, through the vagina), and the threat of a lifelong condition added gall to the immutable condition of childlessness. Coventry had brought much in the way of artistic, intellectual, and political companionship. Their English years had given some compensation for what had been at times the abrasive mood of Belfast, its official vindictiveness in refusing John Hewitt directorship of the Belfast Museum. Roberta had her own intellectual or emotional needs. To Sophie in Camden Street, Belfast, a sometime painter, she confessed how she 'would love a room of my very own & a key for it'. Then the pendulum of her feelings swung to the other side; Coventry brought them into active contact with large issues and capacious minds—'We were at a marvellous Party with E. P. Thompson (History of English Working Class) a lovely man you & Jim would enjoy them—His wife & family perfect.'[21]

The modern English disease—perpetual interference with ways of doing things, despite good results—was catching on in post-Labour Coventry. The gallery was not immune. In May 1968, Hewitt complained to Mervyn Levy that, as committee reconstruction was afoot, 'we shall be grouped in with Swimming Baths, Parks and Allotments'. Even the membership of his committee was uncertain for at least a further month, frustrating his plan to lead them on an inspection of work by Gaudier-Breszka.[22] An art curator can take more than one avenue to the sort of

[20] PRONI, D/3838/4/1, Roberta Hewitt to Sophie Stewart, 14 October 1966. After Roberta's death in 1975, Mrs Stewart returned the letters addressed to her, so that the correspondence could be complete.

[21] PRONI, D/3838/4/1, Roberta Hewitt to Sophie Stewart, 1 December 1966.

[22] COV, CCB 5/1/1/2.

pictures he wants to acquire—the commercial galleries, the wealthy patron, the well-disposed artist him-or-herself, and the friendly middleman. Levy, who lived at Richmond, just outside London, played the latter role to perfection. In March 1967, he was able to send Hewitt a photograph of a small Picasso. Hewitt did not go out of his way to placate a useful friend—'I must say that it has been our practice to avoid collecting autographs. It is a very slight thing; its only interest being its association with the Master.' In November of the same year, Levy could offer a male nude by Edward Burne Jones and 'a superb William Mulready drawn . . . 1846–50'. Hewitt's interest in Victorian painting was limited, though not so limited as his appreciation of Picasso. In March 1969, Levy is again offering a snip, this time a Wyndham Lewis drawing of a seated woman, dated 1935, for £195. These relatively big names might obscure the fact that Levy championed 'The National Exhibition of Housewives Art'; indeed he hosted a television series dedicated to the genre. Hewitt, returning a favour, suggested that the woman newly appointed to the Hugh Lane Gallery (he did not know her name) might agree to host it in Dublin. In 1970, The Housewives returned to Coventry, a great success with 117 people at the formal opening. One project may finance another very different one. When, in June 1970, Hewitt was offered a portrait of D. H. Lawrence (by Frederick Carter, 1924) for £50, he consulted Joe Spears, perhaps hoping for a donation. (In August, 'our funds have been very seriously run-down'.[23]) Indeed, during Hewitt's final years, financial support from the City Fathers had declined substantially from the heady levels of 1957.

Levy (1914–96), it should be admitted, was part of a Welsh bohemian mafia with whom Hewitt did a variety of business at the Herbert. Born in Swansea, he had been a fellow pupil of Dylan Thomas's at the school where Thomas Senior taught English, just as Hewitt Senior had been a benign parent/teacher in Belfast. With the painter Alfred Janes and the future Marxist scholar Bert Trick, Levy and Thomas participated in lively gatherings at the Kardomah Café, Swansea. Later when Thomas moved to London, he and Levy passed drunken hours discussing how many mice it would take to pull a train from London to Glasgow. It is difficult to imagine John Hewitt joining in these revels, and Thomas's lamentable death in 1953 preceded Hewitt's arrival in England by a safe number of years. Apart from his own art, Levy wrote on Gaudier-Brzeska, D. H. Lawrence, L. S. Lowry, and a number of other figures who appear on Hewitt's Coventry agenda.

The years 1967–68 were particularly active for Roberta as a woman with decided political commitments. The situation in Northern Ireland slid towards disaster at the end of the decade, but, from her permanent home in Coventry, she saw the issues in a wider context, ranging from adult education, to Ban the Bomb, and the Vietnam War. The records suggest that it was she, rather than Hewitt, who conducted their political correspondence. In February 1967, she wrote to the Foreign Office about the war, and received the customary postcard in acknowledgement. It is clear, however, that she initiated several correspondences through the same concentrated medium into which she could squeeze a good deal of political advice,

[23] COV, CCB/5/1/1/2.

opinion, and moral fervour. On 25 February, the left-wing Labour MP Anthony Wedgewood Benn replied by letter to one of Roberta's densely packed postcards, thanking her for positive comment on raising the school-leaving age, on industrial training, and what was then envisaged as a University of the Air (later the Open University). 'Like you', he concluded, 'I desperately want to see the end of the Vietnam War.' The Left was the natural home, so to speak, of the Hewitts, and a month (or less) after lobbying Tony Benn, she was in touch with Jenny Lee, whose secretary insisted that 'there is no question of the Government supporting the bombing of North Vietnam, and in fact the Prime Minister has protested against it'.[24]

Hewitt's politics, though instinctively 'of the left' (to use John's own words), derived less from political theory than non-conformist moral conscience. Affiliation to the Labour Party, and a good deal of constituency work on Roberta's part, remained constant commitments—she acted as secretary to the Cheylesmore Ward branch. But when the issues which moved them required approaches (and compliments) to other political organizations, she was happy to spread her wings. The Liberal Party Assembly of September 1967 impressed her, especially the attitude of Young Liberals. So she despatched a card to Jeremy Thorpe congratulating all concerned. Less predictably, she wrote a 'friendly & encouraging letter' to the Tory Quintin Hogg in October 1969, by which time the Ulster situation had loomed larger and less bright on her horizons.[25] During these years, the Left heard from her periodically; in addition to Benn and Lee, Michael Foot and Maurice Edelman were in receipt of communications from Postbridge Road. Stuart Holland of the political office in Downing Street assured her than Harold Wilson had studied her postcard, noted its contents, and 'very much appreciated your taking the trouble to write'.[26]

She was realistic about the value of bulk-lobbying. More than two years earlier she had spent another (nine-day) period in hospital, writing postcards to politicians. 'I have a reply from George B[rown] saying nothing, [and] a poor reply from Jennie Lee. It breaks my heart when I remember the young rebel at Summer School of 1933.' The working coincidence of illness and political endeavour, of anxiety in the personal realm and rebuffs or disappointment in the public one, recurs in her story. In local politics, differences could not always be relieved by committing them to the Royal Mail. At the beginning of 1968, Roberta Hewitt resigned from the Coventry South Constituency Party, for reasons as yet unclear. The sitting MP, William Wilson, expressed polite regret and hoped that she might return to the fold some time in the future.[27]

It may be that the causes were not political in any strict or exclusive sense. Roberta's temperamental reaction to a minor traffic spat in Coventry in the first half of 1968 reached an unsustainable level of complaint when, in September of that year, she began to draft a reply to Sir Robert Mark, who was nothing less than commissioner

24 PRONI, D/3838/4/1, Dana Andrew to Roberta Hewitt, 16 March 1967.
25 PRONI, D/3838/4/1, Quinton Hogg to Roberta Hewitt, 14 October 1969.
26 PRONI, D/3838/4/1, Stuart Holland to Roberta Hewitt, 15 January 1968.
27 PRONI, D/3838/4/1, William Wilson MP to Roberta Hewitt, 7 February 1968.

at Scotland Yard. Though the notes are sketchy, and it is unlikely any letter based on them was ever sent, the surviving documentation—preserved by both Roberta and John in turn—suggests a temporarily oversensitized personality. The original incident appears to have involved Roberta driving on the wrong side of a policeman on point-duty, whose reprimand or warning she felt to be excessive. Having pursued a complaint to the highest authority in the entire British police system, she concluded despairingly, 'we are no further[,] I in my distrust or you in understanding'.

Though glumness could return, politics did have its entertainers. The unconventional Labour backbencher Andrew Faulds was the son of Presbyterian missionaries, who escaped the manse to begin a radio career as Jet Morgan of 'Journey into Space'. It is said that he joined the Labour Party on the advice of Paul Robeson. Roberta Hewitt liked 'In All Directions' a show in which the fiercely anti-racist member for Smethwick was involved. She wrote to congratulate him, and he—always the ladies' man—replied by suggesting that an appreciative letter from her might lead to a revival.[28] He ended by complaining about the metropolitan tripe served up in 'the regions' in the name of culture.

Birmingham and Coventry did not amount to a region in the Hewitts' sense of the term, which owed a great deal to Mumford's work on urban life, its variants and alternatives, not to mention the tugs of origin and upbringing. Their own region was beginning to assert itself again in aggressive ways. Though Hewitt held an influential and senior post in the Herbert Gallery, and Roberta had found much fulfilment in the city's social and political life, Coventry could not be home in the vital Irish business of demanding attention and inflicting pain. By the beginning of December 1968, she had mended some bridges to the local Labour Party. Her MP, William Wilson, declared that he and Gerry Fitt were 'good comrades' and that he would provide the MP for West Belfast with whatever help he might need.[29] Four days later, Maurice Edelman wrote in reply to John Hewitt in much the same terms—'I needn't tell you that my sympathies are wholly with those who claim their civil rights.'[30]

In autumn 1966, the Hewitts holidayed in Greece. The clarity of natural colours stunned them. The amphitheatre at Epidaurus impressed them. They paid two separate visits to Delos, birthplace of Apollo and Artemis, at the centre of the Cyclades archipelago. On the second occasion, having disembarked in the glittering harbour, they made their way to the village by keeping to a path behind the ancient slave market.[31] John raged against the evil which the entire slave system had been. Less than a year later, and after the Colonels' seizure of power (which she does not mention) Roberta resumed her account of Delos. She had experienced a slippage in time which she found difficult to record in words. 'Suddenly doing a right turn

[28] PRONI, D/3838/4/1, Andrew Faulds MP to Roberta Hewitt, 26 September 1968.

[29] PRONI, D/3838/4/1, William Wilson MP to John and Roberta Hewitt, 12 December 1968. Gerry Fitt (1926–2005) was a left-wing republican Belfast politician, who sat in the House of Commons from 1962 to 1983. His distaste for nationalism exposed him to intimidation from both sides in Northern Ireland; his election agent was murdered, and his house attacked on several occasions.

[30] PRONI, D/3838/4/1, Maurice Edelman MP to JH, 16 December 1968.

[31] *Tesserae* (Belfast: Festival Publications, 1967) included six poems arising from the Greek holiday, plus 'No Second Troy' which, to deny both Yeats and Homer, deal with a childhood nurse who drank.

I was transported' to a 'peculiar moment in time' when the village seemed to be at once an ancient settlement, a museum, and yet inhabited. 'I feel I saw a young dark man with a drape of dark cloth over his arm . . . I wanted to be alone there to listen.' Johnny was still denouncing the slave market, which irritated her. 'Such a pity, there was a great beauty—I'm afraid I didn't want to hear of the evils, we live with such evils every day.' The moment of transportation could never be recovered. 'I write this [the journal entry, "5/6/" 1967] almost a year after the visit.' Should she communicate her experience to J.P. Priestley (1894–1984)?[32] The reference to Priestley was itself a minor incident of transportation back in time: his play, *I Have Been Here Before* had been first performed in 1937. Moreover, the journal was becoming intermittent, and occasionally uncertain about dates.

Hewitt made a selection of William Allingham's poems for the Dolmen Press in 1967, and contributed an introduction. The idea had been John Montague's, and Mervyn Wall, director of the southern Arts Council and a novelist, found official sponsorship. The renaissance of Ulster poetry, dated generally from Seamus Heaney's *Death of a Naturalist* in 1966, had actually begun earlier and had not been exclusively a northern achievement. Montague had been educated at University College Dublin; *Forms of Exile*, his debut collection, appeared in 1958 from Liam Miller's emergent Dolmen Press. He sought a wider readership through a new London imprint, McGibbon and Kee, publishers of William Carlos Williams in the UK and of Flann O'Brien's lost novel, *The Third Policeman*. Montague suggested to the editor Timothy O'Keefe that Hewitt might be ready with a new collection.

In 1964, Montague had boldly entitled his account of Hewitt's project 'Regionalism into Reconciliation'. Carefully noting the glaring omission from *The Oxford Book of Irish Verse*, he ventured a wry explanation:

> To a generation slowly escaping from a morbid emphasis on nationality, Hewitt's position must often have seemed not merely reactionary but absurd. To be Irish was bad enough, but to insist on being Ulster as well seemed to drag literature to the level of a football match. But . . . Hewitt's instinct was right: the Ulster question is the only real outstanding political problem in this country: to live in the province and ignore it would be like living in Mississippi without questioning segregation.[33]

In keeping with his high estimate of Hewitt's work, he set out to have a *Collected Poems* issued in London.

This was not to be a lightning success at any stage. The failure of *No Rebel Word* rankled even as its author protested a stoic indifference. To Montague he offered a somewhat disingenuous explanation—'the title, a quotation from a sonnet of mine, was deliberately ambiguous meaning no word leaping or tugging out of the consigned order, and at the same time no word by a rebel, asserting as it were that

[32] *Journal*, PRONI, D/3838/4/7. The lengthy account of the Hewitts' holiday in Greece (22 September to 7 October 1966) extends into a telescoped treatment of 1967 commencing with Roberta's 'transportation' in time and ending with JH taking 'his small collection' (the typescript which becomes *Collected Poems 1932–1967*) to London.

[33] John Montague, *The Figure in the Cave and Other Essays* (Dublin: Lilliput, 1989), p. 148.

I was no rebel whatever folk might think'.[34] Here certainly was a recantation of 1930s politics if, in the Ulster fashion, all radicalism was treated as nationalist rebellion. The sonnet in question presumably had supplied a title for the ghostly untraced pamphlet of 1945, and was associated with a poem written in December 1942 containing the lines 'the rebel always carries on his back / the roaring master or the prim-lipped aunt…'.[35] This had found its way into *No Rebel Word*. The assembling of material for a second full collection required careful return visits to the archival past. Both Roberta and Montague have testified to Hewitt's refusal in the early 1960s to send poems to magazines or remotely contemplate a full-sized collection.

In early spring of 1967, Hewitt took about twenty-five or thirty poems down to O'Keefe at McGibbon & Kee. The editor demanded more. Back in Coventry, the poet sifted through his accumulated drafts and final versions, but tended all the time to cut back or reduce what he considered worthy of inclusion. Roberta advised letting O'Keefe make the final choice. John countered by asking the firm to leave final decisions to Montague, though the latter complained afterwards about the selection being too safe.[36] By the end of August a typescript was despatched to London, recalling the long delays and frustrations of twenty years earlier. The previous month John and Roberta had travelled to Belfast, already contemplating permanent accommodation there. Seamus and Marie Heaney entertained them, with Michael and Edna Longley as fellow guests—and a young man who fell asleep. Roberta thought them 'a nice group'. They visited the Flanagans in Marlborough Park North, Jim and Sophie Stewart in Camden Street, and John D. Stewart in Stranmillis Road. They were back on old turf, close again to Mount Charles, but close also to the Ulster Museum and Gallery.

McGibbon & Kee offered publication quite promptly, and undertook to get the book out within a year. Just before Christmas 1967, the poet was able to report that the formal agreement and an advance cheque had arrived, with proofs due the following month.[37] A background of growing discontent in Ulster, and muscular resistance to demands for reform, is invisible to readers of the *Collected Poems 1932–1967*, published in August 1968. The book opens with 'Ireland', an early poem which Frederick Muller's advisers had kept out of *No Rebel Word* (1948). Despite a distinctive edge of self-mockery, it reads like a very late contribution to the Celtic Twilight. August was the month of a major civil rights march in County Tyrone, followed six weeks later by violent clashes in Derry between the police and defiant marchers. In early October, Belfast students demonstrated for political reform, and what became known as The People's Democracy emerged as an energizing radical ginger group, challenging not only the Unionist establishment but also the accepted forms of dissent, nationalist or socialist. In the (Stormont) general election of February 1969, the mildly reformist premier Terence O'Neill won a pyrrhic victory, and the Northern Ireland Labour Party clung to its last two seats.

[34] UU, Hewitt, Box 9. [35] 'The Happy Man', see Ormsby, p. 41.
[36] John Montague, 'Spiritual Maverick', *Threshold* 38 (Winter 1986/87), p. 18.
[37] Private collection, JH to Alan Warner, 17 December 1967.

Two months later, Bernadette Devlin was elected to Westminster and, two days after that, a civil rights march was attacked in Derry and driven into the Bogside. Sammy Devenny was severely wounded by police and died some months later. Petrol bombs were first used in Derry during these incidents. O'Neill resigned.

The Hewitts found most of the reviews—and they were not many—extremely disappointing. In this they were not entirely fair: Seamus Heaney and Douglas Sealy published thoughtful and approving notices, each with a tincture of reservation or qualification, proper to the critical task. Heaney, recalling Hewitt's own practice as a reviewer in *Threshold*, his occasional castigations and exhortations, went on sympathetically to examine the *Collected Poems* 'against the standards [Hewitt] applied to other poets'.[38] By the end of 1970, John was resigned to the fact that the book had not taken off; it was in print, nothing more than that. In January 1971, he came upon two copies remaindered at £1 each, and bought them. In the interim, Northern Ireland had descended further into communal violence. Rioting occurred in Derry, Dungiven, and Belfast throughout July and early August 1969, with the B-Special Constabulary (condemned by Hewitt thirty years earlier) playing a vanguard role. Nothing on this scale had happened since the early 1920s. The Ulster Volunteer Force attacked the Dublin headquarters of the national broadcasting station, revealing the potential for an All-Ireland conflict.

For the latter stages of these northern disturbances, the Hewitts were travelling by bus towards Hungary, arriving in Budapest on 9 August 1969. They had spent time at one of the Lake Balaton resorts, admiring the scenery and noting shrewdly that the collectivized agriculture was 'in good heart'. Little or no foreign news would have been available to them. Waitresses ignored them unless bribed. 'We felt sad that a socialist country should be so tied to the old tip.'[39] Budapest was far better—the food excellent, the bath towels large, the rain positively Irish. Though they were package tourists, their trip had been assisted in advance by a Hungarian curator who had written to the Herbert Gallery for catalogues. László Vörös' wife, Rózsi Vályi, was finishing a book on dance; the two couples found they shared many interests.[40] Contacts through International PEN also opened doors. Among others whom they met was Klára Kárpáti (1914–86) the widow of Lajos Kassák (1887–1967), a writer and painter of working-class origins, and Agnes Gergely (b.1933), a Jewish poet who would later write a book about Yeats, acknowledging John Boyd's assistance. While lunching one day, Roberta heard her name called out—a young art teacher from Coventry hiking across Europe spotted her. She maintained her journal in Budapest while a supply of notepaper could be found; she wrote it in the form of a letter to friends at home, and because 'I was wailing.'[41]

In fact, the most striking occurrence of the holiday was Irish. In 'Conversations in Hungary, August, 1969', Hewitt records how his host 'Miklos, a friendly writer'

[38] Seamus Heaney, 'The Poetry of John Hewitt' (first published in *Threshold* no. 22, Summer 1969), reprinted *Threshold* 38 (Winter 1986/87), pp. 38–41.

[39] *Journal*, PRONI, D/3838/4/7, 9 August 1969.

[40] Valyi's 400-page illustrated book, *A Táncművészet Története*, was published at the end of 1969, and the author dispatched a copy to John and Roberta.

[41] *Journal*, PRONI, D/3838/4/7, 10 August 1969.

told them of a radio bulletin reporting 'Riots in Northern Ireland yesterday: / and they have sent the British Army in.'[42] In point of historical fact, British troops were first deployed in Derry on Friday 14 August and in Belfast on the following day. By that date, the Hewitts had left the Balaton area (cf. 'In a back garden at Lake Balaton . . .', the poem's first line) and had reached Budapest. It is possible that they had made an unofficial or private return with their host, Miklos Vajda, a literary journalist and translator, later editor of *The New Hungarian Quarterly*—he had a summer cottage at Tihany, on the lake's northern shore. Alternatively, the poet has created a semi-fictional scene in which the bad news from Ireland reaches him at a quiet garden table in the company of 'keen friends'.[43]

On several counts, Hungary was an appropriate place in which to learn of an Irish crisis. Numerous Western visitors would discover that the country enjoyed a more relaxed social ethos than any of its neighbours in the Soviet bloc. Nevertheless, the summer of 1969 was not relaxed—post-Paris, post-Prague, the satellite countries were made palpably aware of Soviet dominance. Civil society was not entirely eliminated in the name of Marxist orthodoxy and, in particular, a truce of kinds was emerging slowly between the Socialist Workers' government and the cultural sphere. More helpfully still, comparisons between Hungarian and Irish history had a long history. It is this latter conversational trope which rounds off the poem. New friends at the table know that the English overran 'your little isle', whereas more numerous invaders took the broad Hungarian plain—'Tatar, Hapsburg, Ottoman'. The list curiously omits both the Nazis and the Soviets. Equally implicit are comparative exercises neither side of the table can propose—(1) comparison of the Magyars as invaders (the first Magyar king reigned from 1001 to 1038) with the Anglo-Normans who arrived in Ireland in 1169; (2) comparison of the socialism Hewitt has long avowed in Ireland and England with that implemented under Soviet dominion.

Hewitt had ached for change in Ulster, not simply out of socialist principle but also out of his personal experience of victimization. When change loomed, it bore little resemblance to his ideals. 'I've had an unprecedented rush of verse these past weeks. . . . I feel it's all I can do to here at a safe distance, to ease my guilt & frustration'—this in October 1969.[44] Perhaps Morris's rebel, John Ball, had a point: when the thing men fought for comes about, it appears as something they never intended or even envisaged. Does the Ulster situation of 1969 exemplify Hegel's cunning of history, or Murphy's Law? Whatever the objectives of the People's Democracy, whoever the real masterminds of the Northern Ireland Civil Rights Association were, the response to these movements in 1969 was sectarian, primarily because 'the state' in Northern Ireland was sectarian. The dynamic in practice does

[42] Hewitt, *An Ulster Reckoning* [Belfast: privately printed, 1971], p. 14; see Ormsby, pp. 129–31. For an extended account of *An Ulster Reckoning*, see 'Break for Text III'.

[43] For an assessment of the poem, and its relation to JH's efforts at a comparative understanding of Northern Ireland, see Guy Woodward, '"We must know more about Ireland": John Hewitt and Eastern Europe', in *Ireland West to East: Irish Cultural Connections with Central and Eastern Europe*, edited by Aidan O'Malley and Eve Patten (Oxford: Peter Lang, 2013) esp. pp. 111–13.

[44] Linen, JH to John Boyd, 18 October 1969.

not lie with the insurgents (however persuasive), but with those (however discreet) who have long held power. Once back in Coventry, Hewitt wrote to Vajda apologizing for the delay, 'I have been so concerned about the tragic happenings in my own country—my leisure hours crammed with verses urgent to be written—that I have failed in courtesy.' The perception of Northern Irish affairs as *tragic* is virtually an admission that they are irredeemable.

Roberta never really kept a journal during 1969–70 as the Ulster crisis deepened. Perhaps the topic was simply too painful, too bewildering. She and John had bought No. 11 Stockman's Lane, Belfast in April 1969, though much work remained to be done before the little urban cottage became habitable—there were, however, three tenants in place. Steps towards repatriation were afoot, notably the Arts Council project known as *The Planter and the Gael* (see Chapter 9). Though no one can know these things at the time, Roberta was well advanced into the final decade of her life. There is no disguising the divisions which afflicted her in contemplating the Ulster situation and John's approaching retirement. These had implications for her own self-reflection. Just before Saint Patrick's Day, 1969, the television dramatist Jim Allen wrote thanking her for appreciative remarks about his latest play, 'The Big Flame'. The two clearly were on reasonably long-standing friendly terms. Not only did he use her Christian name, he mischievously quoted parts of her own letter back, in an attempt to refute her glum self-assessment. Aged sixty-four at the time, Roberta Hewitt had called herself 'a semi-detached semi-intelligent semi-old aged woman'.[45] Her correspondent was forty-two, Irish by background, Liverpool-Catholic by birth, and Trotskyite by strong inclination. A note of Roberta's weariness, perhaps envy, can be detected through the mirror of Allen's response.

In June, Willa Muir, the seventy-nine-year-old widow of the Scottish poet Edwin Muir, wrote to Roberta from rural Cambridgeshire about the *Collected Poems*.

> I am so much out of things nowadays that I don't know how to advise you & John for your letter sounds as if John were having bad luck with his poetry. He may well be, for today's poetry had not seemed to me to be poetry at all for some time.

In an undated letter, probably written in mid-autumn, Roberta summarized her attitude to Northern Ireland at this time:

> What is there to say now about Ulster that is worth saying or repeating [?] We have been thinking about you & know you must be sick. Johnny was greatly distressed & now we are in grey despair. I feel there is no hope. J wants to come [*sic*] over & I say he should go—I don't want to go & feel we were trapped there long enough.

The last Coventry phase was in practice determined by John's retirement date, an issue on which he had some room for manoeuvre, but not much. Roberta's resistance to going home to Belfast took the practical form of having central heating

[45] PRONI, D/3838/4/1, James John Allen (1926–99) writing on BBC headed stationery but using the address, No. 73 Rounthorn Road, Middleton, Manchester.

installed in the Postbridge Road house. But her diary for 1971 is eloquent in less assertive ways:—four hospital appointments in July, and numerous dental appointments throughout the year. She was back in action for the Labour Party, and attended a candidate selection board in November. During John's poetry-reading tour of Ulster small towns with John Montague, she stayed in the Stewart cottage near Cushendall, and also briefly at the Lodge near the convent avenue, though the Hewitts no longer rented it. The options were gradually reducing for Roberta, in ways she could not anticipate.

Years after the Hewitts left Coventry, years after the death of both, the gallery mounted 'Pictures for the People; the British Life and Landscape Collection 1957–2000', running from February to October 2004. The organizers sought the opinion of visitors. 'This exhibition examines John Hewitt's policy [which] continues to influence the character of the Herbert collection. Was he right in pursuing his policy and in the pictures he chose... We would welcome your comments on the cards provided.' Tom Paulin spoke at the formal opening where about twenty pictures and one or two pieces of sculpture were on view. A later speaker thought the achievement hopelessly outdated. Brendan Flynn, curator of the Birmingham Gallery, found the landscapes too exclusive—no scrapyards, no Black or Asian people. Perhaps he missed Goswami V. Patel's 'Factory Workers' which Hewitt had bought for the Herbert in 1968. By 2004, it was clear that the strictures of a cultural studies perspective rendered his acquisitions 'extremely dated pictures'; worse still, 'cultural imperialism' was at work through an unambiguous if unconscious racism.[46] The magazine *Avocado*, tempered these absolute judgements, referring to 'a democratic (and now, rather quaint) vision of a high culture for the common folk'.[47]

John Hewitt's long retirement at home in Belfast brought closer encounters with the ethnically charged radicalism which cultural studies encouraged—unconsciously, of course. His involvement with John Montague in *The Planter and the Gael* project was based on affinities rather than difference.

[46] From notes preserved in the Herbert Museum and Gallery.

[47] *Avocado* (Autumn 2004), pp. 12–13.

Break for Text III

An Ulster Reckoning (1971)

An Ulster Reckoning (1971) remains one of Hewitt's most important publications, and yet poses difficulties for the biographer keen to give critical analysis its proper place. Among his pamphlet collections of verse, it is distinguished both for the number of items included and for the details of 'publication' recoverable from one source or another. It was composed to meet a crisis, whereas the earlier and longer poems of *Conacre* and *Compass* had emerged from contemplation and reflection. On the inside of the pale-blue cardboard cover, it is stated that 'This Brochure was printed for the Author and may be obtained from his address: 5 Postbridge Road, Coventry, CV3 5AG for Fifteen New Pence a copy.' Hard to beat that for privacy in publication, especially when the twenty poems respond to essentially public events. It is decidedly an exile work. A 'foreword' is signed off 'Coventry, April 1971'. The dedication, 'To John Montague, a practical friend', was a tribute to the younger man's assistance (and insistence) in the publication of Hewitt's *Collected Poems 1932–1967*.

The most substantial poem, 'Conversations in Hungary, August 1969' had already appeared in *The Planter and the Gael*, the programme of an Arts Council sponsored reading tour of the province (see Chapter 9). Having shared the limelight with Montague in an official publication, he was reverting to the well-tested practice of job-printing and non-commercial distribution. In part, the arrangement arose out of a new northern acquaintance, George Johnston, whom he met in 1970, and whose wife was English. For much of the year, Johnston was the only young person within reach of Coventry with whom he could discuss the Troubles on equal terms. Roberta recognized that both exuded the same 'Ulster-man-ism'. Johnston she regarded, without any sense of contradiction, as 'very left politically' and 'extremely well balanced'. But the initial impetus to gather the poems arose from the conversations in Hungary.

During a visit to Belfast in late 1970, connected with the Hewitt-Montague tour, Roberta arranged with a Miss Johnston, a printer in Great Victoria Street, to fund a small pamphlet. It is not clear whether Roberta, or Miss Johnston or some third party was to supply the funds, though Roberta must be the benign prime suspect. A seven-week strike by British postal workers early in 1971 held up the proofs. Roberta flatly refused to sanction delivery by 'the black leg post', and eventually George Johnston delivered the packet, indicating that he and the printer were perhaps kin. (In the 1940s, Thomas Johnston had printed both *Conacre* and *Compass.*) Of *An Ulster Reckoning*, two bookshops in Belfast took a dozen each—Erskine Mayne and Mullan—and the latter reordered a further three dozen.

Jack McCann, founder in 1987 of the John Hewitt Society, got nine dozen (paying the full cover price of 15 pence). Back in Coventry, Hewitt sent out about seventy to friends and potential reviewers. Most of the press, especially in southern Ireland, ignored *An Ulster Reckoning*. Personally, Hewitt was satisfied. The booklet became a measure of how things had become as bad as they were.

Though responding to crisis, the contents had been written during a relatively long period of almost a year. With the delay caused by the postal strike, *An Ulster Reckoning* finally appeared two years after some of its constituent parts. These individually belong to 1969, with the Battle of the Bogside (12 August) and the sending in of British troops later in the month. But the tone of the Ulster crisis is best caught in the words of a figure whom Hewitt feared and detested. The Revd Ian Paisley, speaking to a crowd of 5000 in Loughgall on 13 July, had declared, 'I am anti Roman Catholic but, God being my judge, I love the poor dupes who are ground down under that system.'[1] While anticipating publication of the pamphlet in 1971, we should treat the poems in the chronology of their provocation. A simple list of the contents is shown in Table 1.

The period of writing for what became *An Ulster Reckoning* began on 23 April and closed on 11 December 1969. Curiously, two notebooks were employed, a detail which may reflect the Hewitts being in Hungary for a crucial period in August 1969. The order of composition is of less interest than the order of publication in newspapers and journals before the appearance of the brochure (Hewitt's own term). Only six items appeared in the brochure for the first time. On 2 September, 'An Ulster Landowner's Song' appeared in the British independent left-wing *Tribune*, which had been founded in 1937, the year of Hewitt's involvement with *The Irish Democrat*; a second featured on 26 September. 'Parallels Never Meet' was twice pre-published, first in the University of Calgary's *Ariel: a Review of International English Literature*, and then in a textbook published in Glasgow. Three items achieved print inside Northern Ireland, via *Threshold* (of which Hewitt was poetry editor), the Belfast BBC's educational service, and the Arts Council's *The Planter and the Gael*. It is striking that the *Belfast Telegraph*, which had long provided him with a platform for comment on artistic matters, did not fancy Hewitt's new political reckonings. The rest were published in a variety of Dublin papers—*Hibernia* (four in the same issue, plus one later), the *Irish Press* (two on the same page), and the *Irish Times* (two).

These represented a range of ideological constituencies. The *Irish Times* had traditionally been the voice of southern Protestant middle-class opinion, sympathetic but not uncritical of the Northern Ireland regime. In 1970 its editor was Douglas Gageby, a northerner born into Christian Science who served as an intelligence officer in the southern army during the Second World War, and was privately termed a 'white nigger' by one of his own directors. The *Irish Press* belonged to the De Valera family; it espoused constitutional republicanism but, by 1970, was edited by T. P. Coogan, a shrewd and (then) revisionist popular historian.

[1] Quoted in Paul Bew and Gordon Gillespie, *Northern Ireland, a Chronicle of the Troubles 1968–1992* (Dublin: Gill and Macmillan, 1993), p. 16.

Table 1. *An Ulster Reckoning* (1971): Publication History

Poem	Copied to notebook (Nk 00 etc.)	Prior publication	Comment
'An Ulsterman'	23 April and 12 October 1969; Nk39	BBC schools booklet (*Here in Ulster*), spring 1971	Nk39 alternative title, 'Birthright'
'The Dilemma'	2 September 1969; Nk38		Nk38 title, 'Ulsterman's Dilemma'; text later revised for *UR*
'An Ulsterman in England Remembers'	28–31 August 1969; Nk38	*Tribune*, 26 September 1969	Nk 38 title, 'Inheritance'; *Tribune* version had four lines later dropped
'In this Year of Grace'	25–6 August 1969; Nk38	*Irish Times*, 3 January 1970	
'Street Names'	11 December 1969; Nk39		Also ms. loose copy with title, 'The People of the Shankill Road'
'Ulster Landowner's Song'	2 September 1969; Nk39	*Tribune*, 2 September 1969	In his copy of *UR*, JH wrote [James] 'Chichester-Clarke'
'Fables for Stormont'	1 September 1969; Nk38		
'The Coasters'	15 September 1969; Nk39	*Threshold*, No. 23 (summer 1970)	
'Memorandum for the Moderates'	27 August 1969; Nk38	*Irish Times*, 31 January 1970	Nk38 title, 'Advice to the Moderates'
'The Tribunes'	13 September 1969; Nk39	*Irish Press*, 1 November 1969	In his copy of *UR*, JH annotated the phrase 'young men / who had spoken for freedom' with the initials P. D., for People's Democracy.

'The Well Intentioned Consul'	13 September 1969; Nk39	*Irish Press*, 1 November 1969	In his copy of *UR*, JH identified 'the ailing aged consul' as Lord Brookeborough, and named Sean Lemass among the 'received emissaries'.
'Parallels Never Meet'	5 September 1969; Nk39	*Ariel* vol. 1 no. 3 (July 1970); *Exercises in Practical Criticism* (ed. John O'Neill), 1971	
'Prime Minister'	25 September 1969; Nk39	*Hibernia*, 10 October 1969	Nk39 title 'James Dawson Chichester-Clark'
'Demagogue'	26–8 September 1969; Nk39	*Hibernia*, 10 October 1969	Nk39 title 'Rev Ian Paisley'
'Minister'	28 September 1969; Nk39	*Hibernia*, 10 October 1969	Nk39 title 'Brian Faulkner'
'Agitator'	26–7 September 1969; Nk39	*Hibernia*, 10 October 1969	Nk39 title 'Bernadette Devlin'
'Conversations in Hungary, August 1969'	21–2 October 1969; Nk 39	*Hibernia*, 1 May 1970; *The Planter and the Gael* (1970)	In Nk39 interim section titles are used.
'Exile'	14 September 1969; Nk39		
'A Belfastman Abroad Argues with Himself'	26–8 August 1969		
'The Iron Circle'	26 August 1969; Nk38		Revised in Nk39, 30 April 1970

An *Irish Press* literary page, edited by David Marcus, flourished during these years. *Hibernia* (1937–80), a weekly paper originally attentive to conservative Catholic thought, became more progressive under the editorship of John Mulcahy who, in 1970, was assisted by the American poet Tom Tessier at the literature desk. As in the war years, Hewitt drew strength from the support of Dublin's literati.

The evolution of a coherent pamphlet- or brochure-collection from these scattered appearances was complicated by personal, political, and industrial-relations factors. It remains to be seen what its political thrust was. Not all twenty of the poems were satirical or even reflectively political. 'The Dilemma' (second in the contents list) is largely historical/autobiographical: the speaker has steered clear of 'that ailing church [i.e. the Catholic Church] which claims dominion' but also has 'denied / all credence to the state by rebels won / from a torn nation' where the rebels are Edward Carson's followers of 1912–14. 'The Iron Circle' (last in the list), though it commented on the nature of Ulster's violence, was dedicated 'to the memory of the late W. R. Rodgers', who had ministered to the Presbyterians of a village where now Paisley ranted.

The crisis of 1969 had faintly dawned four years early when, in January 1965, the northern premier Terence O'Neill (1914–90) had invited the southern Taoiseach Sean Lemass to Belfast for amiable talks. (O'Neill had succeeded Lord Brookeborough.) Surrounded by hard-headed rivals in his own party, including Dublin-educated Brian Faulkner, O'Neill was in turn succeeded by James Chichester-Clark. These names feature in *An Ulster Reckoning*, either in the poems themselves or in alternative titles preserved in Notebook 39. Except O'Neill's. Ormsby is right in supposing that 'The Well Intentioned Consul' was O'Neill. Though Hewitt himself privately identified 'Prime Minister' as Chichester-Clark, the portrait seems a little too concessive simply to represent that unimaginative, inflexible, aristocratic dunderhead. Is it a split-portrait of both O'Neill and his successor? When Brookeborough's retirement raised questions about the succession, Northern Ireland's Governor General, Lord Wakehurst, had thought O'Neill the best prospect.[2] In the early 1950s, between Hewitt's rejection by Belfast Corporation and his appointment to the Coventry gallery, he and Roberta were guests at several receptions and formal events at the governor general's residence in Hillsborough; indeed she and Lady Wakehurst had further contact through the nursery school project. Had Hewitt met Captain O'Neill on one of these occasions? Certainly the educated and relatively liberal MP for Bannside knew of Hewitt's humiliation by the 'crooked masters' in City Hall, a style of Unionist cronyism he kept at fastidious length. Whatever answers, if any, may emerge to this question, 'The Well Intentioned Consul' adopts an imperial metaphor deployed in 'The Colony' of 1949–50, the poem in which Hewitt sought to present grounds for mutual understanding between the historic communities. Planter and Gael, Protestant and Catholic, Unionist and Nationalist, these pairings-in-antagonism were now in 1969 volubly represented by equally loud spokespersons—Ian Paisley and Bernadette Devlin. O'Neill had attempted some degree of bridge-building—he attended a Gaelic Athletic Association hurling match, at which nuns were present!—inadequate and condescending though it seemed to the Catholic minority. By May 1969, he had been ousted from the premiership.

On the positive side, Hewitt admired both Devlin (in 'Agitator') and the People's Democracy (PD) (see 'The Tribunes'). A psychology student at Queen's University, she had joined the PD, and took part in public demonstrations for radical reform.

[2] See Mark Mulholland's article on O'Neill in *The Dictionary of Irish Biography* (Cambridge: Cambridge University Press; Dublin: Royal Irish Academy, 2009), vol. 7, p. 802.

In 1969 at the age of twenty-two, she was elected to Westminster for the Mid-Ulster constituency, and published *The Price of My Soul*. Though unquestionably a social radical, Devlin reflected traditional republican and nationalist positions; in 1974 she helped to establish the Irish Republican Socialist Party (with an Irish National Liberation Army attached.) People's Democracy, which developed a Trotskyite view of revolution, gradually lost members to Provisional Sinn Féin. Although, in the months when *An Ulster Reckoning* was written piecemeal, Hewitt regarded Devlin and the PD with favour, respected their courage and energy, he quickly revised his position. The larger Northern Ireland Association for Civil Rights, with Official IRA and Communist Party support, maintained a broad active membership including numerous individuals whom Hewitt knew personally—Paddy Devlin (1925–99: Labour; not related to Bernadette Devlin), Gerry Fitt (1926–2005: republican socialist), and Betty Sinclair (1910–81: Communist). The investigation of 1935–46 into the Special Powers Act (1922) which he and Roberta had actively assisted remained a benchmark for civil liberties in Northern Ireland.

The naming of poems can effect subtle distinctions. If Ms Devlin is applauded as an agitator, Dr Paisley is condemned as 'Demagogue'. Hewitt was not the first to cast a gemstone in that direction. W. R. Rodgers had observed 'there but for the grace of God goes God'. Derek Mahon, closer to home, ironically addressed the master, 'God, you could do it, God / help you, stand on a corner stiff / with rhetoric, promising nothing under the sun.' A repeated or double god, it seems, was necessary in confronting Paisley. Hewitt makes no such concession to authority; *An Ulster Reckoning* does without God in any of his three persons or under earthly names. Instead 'a Samson self-ordained' holds the ring, with 'ordained' neatly pointing at Paisley's dubious ordination as a man of the cloth. When *Hibernia* printed 'Prime Minister', 'Demagogue', 'Minister' and 'Agitator' on 10 October 1969, they appeared as 'Four Northern Portraits'.

'Conversations in Hungary' allows Hewitt a briefly privileged vantage point from which he both receives bad news from distant Ulster and provides commentary for sympathetic acquaintances uninvolved in the Irish Troubles. With this uncommon balance, it appeared admirable for *The Planter and the Gael*. For the fourteen lines in each of its three numbered sections, it employed something like the sonnet form to which he was devoted throughout his career. And the effect is again to provide strength in perspective, a balance within a collection where immediacy of detail and feeling might otherwise overload the craft. Between comparisons of Irish and Hungarian experiences down the centuries, a rare classical interpretation is tentatively proposed:

So failing there, we turned to history;
The savage complications of our past;
Our luckless country where all old wrongs outlast,
In raging viruses of bigotry,
Their first infection; certain tragedy
Close-heeled on hope, as by the Furies paced;

Blight in the air, and famine's aftertaste,
Frustration, guilt, and fear, and enmity.[3]

In some respects, the 'Conversations' rewrite (in the sense of writing again) 'The Colony'; but the other sense of rewriting (that, is *altering* what has been written) is also present, for the history invoked is less that of the seventeenth-century plantations and the 1641 Rebellion, and recognizably more that of the 1840s and after—potato blight producing famine, and famine generating frustration and guilt. The Furies, who pursued Orestes for his mother's murder, were in the Greek myth transformed by Athene into the Eumenides, or kindly ones; from which cessation of violence and punishment it is possible for earthly justice and the city (Athens) to come into being. Hewitt does not indulge this possibility in relation to his own society in his own time. Nor does he concede to contemporary political violence—as Yeats did—anything of the sublimity or dignity we associate with tragic action.

[3] Ormsby, p. 130.

PART III

SLOW TIME

9

Return of a Native

Le vieux Paris n'est plus (la forme d'une ville
Change plus vite, hélas! que le coeur d'un mortel).

Charles Baudelaire (1861)

'The work is done', grown old he thought,
'According to my boyish plan;
Let the fools rage, I swerved in naught,
Something to perfection brought';
But louder sang that ghost, 'What then?'

W. B. Yeats (1937)

Now that Northern Ireland has reached what is widely accepted as 'post-devolution', it is tempting to read the forty or so years commencing in 1968 as a single narrative which, despite reverses and atrocities, moves towards innovation and resolution. This may perhaps be a valid political (or, administrative-managerial) analysis, but it ill accords with the nature of Hewitt's thought and art, his engagement in slow time as theme and medium. Nor does it adequately account for the situation at the moment of his death (27 June 1987), almost twenty years into the Troubles. In April 1987, the Lord Chief Justice of Northern Ireland and his wife were killed by the IRA; in May, eight IRA men were killed during an attack on the police station in Loughgall, County Armagh, a place Hewitt knew well through the Revd W. R. Rodgers, poet.

Instead of linear congratulation, a tour of the biographic kaleidoscope may be more revealing. In that configuration, adjacent or associative material, not a sequence of events, can be assessed. The material is for the most part verse, poetry, literature, fiction, writing of one kind or another, though 'the outer life of telegrams and anger' (E. M. Forster's phrase in *Howards End*) will not be avoided. The final phase of John Hewitt's life, amounting to fifteen years from his Coventry retirement to that death in Belfast, almost exactly equalled time spent in the English Midlands. Back home living under emergency conditions he was prolific, yet old patterns re-emerged, especially the publication of work long after the date of writing. There was no lack of urgency in the 1970s and 1980s. He had mocked Ulster's middle-class complacency during the brief suzerainty (1963–69) of Terence O'Neill as northern premier. Diligently following the electoral fortunes of the Northern

Ireland Labour Party in 1966, he was delighted by Martin McBirney's 45 per cent of the vote in East Belfast.[1] Thereafter, Hewitt did not fail to address a deteriorating situation.

Poetry had become an active ingredient in public discussion of Northern Ireland's woes, as a platoon of troublesome writers (consider Sam Thompson, a working-class Protestant; Seamus Heaney, an 'uppity' Catholic; and Jimmy Simmons with his 'handbook for revolution') proved.[2] In 1968, Heaney took part in a reading tour with the poet Michael Longley (culturally a Protestant) in what can now be seen as a prototype for *The Planter and Gael* (Hewitt and Montague) two years later. The Heaney/Longley project had been diplomatically entitled 'Room to Rhyme', suggestive of an aesthetic—some might say, tasteful—accommodation *between and for* two antagonist traditions.[3] No harm in that, at the time. At the beginning of 1968, delicate inter-governmental talks between north and south had used non-contentious topics such as foot-and-mouth disease and cultural exchange as a screen to hide more desperate problems. There was harm in that, unintentional perhaps but rapidly inflicted, by official deception and the use of sedatives. Unemployment in Northern Ireland was rising (7.8 per cent); sectarian prejudice in the allocation of public sector housing had attracted radical direct action. The charismatic Eamonn McCann admitted that the 'conscious, if unspoken, strategy was to provoke the police into over-reaction'.[4] Born in excess and matching folly with folly, the Unionist authorities attempted to ban all protest marches in Derry and other flashpoints, thereby providing the best occasions on which the Royal Ulster Constabulary could overreact. In October 1968, the People's Democracy was formed by QUB students, its demands including repeal of the Special Powers Act, which Hewitt had critically analysed in 1936. The stage was set, and the brutal restlessness is history repeating itself.

In January 1969, an ongoing correspondence in the *Coventry Evening Telegraph* provoked him to repeat a much used formula 'I belong to Ulster, to Ireland and to the British Isles, and no disruptive influence from Mr. Paisley's or anyother [*sic*] sectional faction can alter [that].' The culmination of the letter looked further afield. Wherever the ugly mask of reaction might appear, he would declare his solidarity. 'I think of that lad in Prague, of the students in Tokyo, in Mexico City, and those young men and women who marched in Londonderry the other day.' On 4 January 1969, a civil rights march heading for Derry had been attacked by a loyalist mob at Burntollet Bridge, leaving more than a dozen protesters in need of

[1] Linen, JH to John Boyd, 21 April 1966; Boyd Papers.

[2] Launched in August 1968, *The Honest Ulsterman* was initially 'a handbook for revolution', but the subtitle disappeared after a police raid on the editor's home in Portrush. The second issue fired an early salvo in Hewitt's re-invasion of the colony. 'From Chairmen and Committeemen Good Lord Deliver Us' struck at the moral pretensions of a politicized bureaucracy keen to paint its critics red, alien (cf. 'Once alien here…'), and potentially violent. See *Ancestral*, pp. 48–55.

[3] The resultant publication also included traditional folk song; see *Room to Rhyme; an Anthology of Poems by Seamus Heaney and Michael Longley and of Ballads Collected by David Hammond* (Belfast: Northern Ireland Arts Council, 1968).

[4] Eamon McCann, *War and an Irish Town* (London: Pluto Press, 1974), p. 35.

hospital treatment. Serious rioting in the city resulted, with the Catholic Bogside area enduring aggressive police incursions.[5]

This was a public commitment, albeit in a provincial English newspaper. A day earlier, Hewitt had written to the *New Statesman*, addressing a wider and more politicized readership, while focusing on provincial (Ulster) affairs. True to his non-conformist background, he resorted to Bunyan's *Pilgrim's Progress* (1678), casting Parliamentary Secretary Roy Bradford (1920–98) as Mr Plausible and Premier Terence O'Neill as Pilgrim. These worthies promised reform, but the agenda had in reality been decided by the marching students. Nor can the reformers in Parliament disown Ian Paisley, who simply articulated 'the very ideology which has activated Unionist mental and emotional processes for years and, by reverse action, the ideology of the Nationalists too'. Hewitt was not, however, looking for middle ground. 'Those most blameworthy are the moderates in both... sectors. They drifted with the tide, ostentatiously stayed out of politics [then] quickly paid their subscriptions to the appropriate addresses. Now they accuse the marchers of stirring things up.'[6] His poem, 'The Coasters', mocks the suburban morals of those who drift along the coast of looming crisis.

By far the most telling of these responses was *An Ulster Reckoning*. Later the new poems, when collected, often appeared alongside quite old ones. Willa Muir had observed after *Collected Poems 1932–1967* was issued, 'John is always waiting.' It is a remark deeper than it seems at first glance. Inside or alongside the poet of today, there is always a substantial attendant—at times co-existent—past. Contemporary events are never purely contemporary, nor are they wholly new. Those who want instant or total change often mistake what Mrs Muir called waiting for what Hewitt called drifting or coasting.

The Hewitts were committed to returning home, John more willingly than Roberta. Before the actual move, a reconnoitering expedition was advisable, as in the days of Vikings or Cambro-Normans. The banner under which it advanced was 'The Planter and the Gael', a phrase loosely modelled on 'Room to Rhyme' for, in popular cliché, the planter had long had the best room even if the Gaels were rich in rhyme. In the latest venture, two scouts, Hewitt and John Montague, represented opposite sides of earlier divisions and conflicts. The resultant extensive publicity copper-fastened Hewitt's early strategic term of self-description, 'planter', more thoroughly than he may have wished.

Though the venture sought a working partnership and reconciliation between the named identities, a less immediately resolvable issue arose on the historiographical side. For both amiable participants, it presupposed direct access to the

[5] UU, Hewitt, Box 13, JH to *Coventry Evening Herald*, 21 January 1969 (copy). Jan Palach (1948–69) committed suicide by self-immolation on 19 January as a protest against Soviet suppression of 'the Prague Spring' in 1968. In opposition to the Vietnam War, Japanese students protested against the continued presence of American troops in their country. In October 1968, demonstrators in Mexico City were fired on by government troops, with many casualties. Strangely, Hewitt makes no reference to the events in France of 1968 which had a decided impact on government policy, however non-revolutionary.

[6] UU, Hewitt, Box 13, JH to the *New Statesman*, 20 January 1969 (copy).

seventeenth century (and, for Montague, earlier) through which one could meet up with ancestors and their neighbours (including their enemies). 'The Bloody Brae' (1936) had ingeniously addressed the problem, but Hewitt delayed in releasing the text until, in January 1954, it found its medium—the radio. Ironically, Hewitt blurred the date of the central action evoked in the play, though in 'The Colony' the 1641 uprising is clearly delineated (in lines 29–36) without, however, any territorial specifics. The notion of spontaneous invocation of the past is far from simple, for it usually seeks to identify *speaking-for* a particular historical entity with *speaking-from* it, a dangerous but popular assumption in Northern Ireland.

More broadly yet potently relevant in the Ulster crisis, it bears comparison with the insistence of the Protestant Reformers that they were returning to biblical Christianity, by-passing and even annulling the accretions of tradition and church practice to establish a (spiritual and unmediated) communion with Jesus, the gospel authors, and St Paul. The sixteenth-century Reformation, so vital to the English plantations in Ireland and elsewhere, achieved this aim to its own satisfaction by internalizing the religious life (denying temporal measure, whether slow or otherwise) and creating what some Roman opponents regarded as subjective belief. However that comparison may stand up to a more thorough scrutiny, it remains certain that 'the planter' is entirely absent from Hewitt's most renowned and (in the 1970s) most celebrated poem. That is to say, easy familiarity with earlier Hewitts and Redpaths contributes nothing to the poem, though the earlier history thus signalled is far from being a truism.

Sponsoring their provincial tour, the Northern Ireland Arts Council published a selection of poems by the pair. Hewitt was represented by 'Once Alien Here', 'The Green Shoot', 'The Glens', 'An Irishman in Coventry', 'The Watchers', 'My Grandmother's Garter', 'Betrayal', 'No Second Troy', and 'The Colony'—all taken from the recently published *Collected Poems* (1968)—and some poems later collected.[7] Montague, who had been instrumental in advancing Hewitt's cause with the London firm of McGibbon and Kee, was in many ways the lead-man on the road, though twenty-two years the younger. Born in New York in 1929, a sometime resident of Paris, and proud of his family's republican tradition, he was also the better known at the time as both poet and short-story writer.

The tour occurred in November 1970 and, while the two Johns took to the byways of rural Ulster for Ballymena (Adair Arms Hotel), Coleraine (New University of Ulster), Derry (City Army Hotel), Omagh (Royal Arms Hotel), Enniskillen (Portora School), Armagh (the County Museum) and—crucially—'schools in these centres', Roberta stayed with her sister Peggie Millar in Belfast. The small bungalow near Musgrave Park Hospital, at No. 11 Stockman's Lane, had already been bought in 1969. When Roberta examined the place closely, she realized its damp condition, the leaks and stains, and a tiny kitchen blue with condensation.

Ray Rosenfield, for the *Irish Times*, reported stages of the poets' progress. In Omagh, the audience was puzzled and then annoyed by Hewitt's line 'the lifted hand between the mind and truth', though she noticed that a Catholic priest

[7] See Ormsby, pp. 592–3.

warmly applauded. In Armagh, they detected a slight to a famous British regiment in Montague's 'Clear the Way'.[8] Montague remembered fewer Planters in the audience than Gaels, and declared that he could not have had a better travelling companion. Between engagements, the two visited prehistoric and early Christian sites in west Ulster. In Dungannon, Hewitt 'danced at an old girlfriend's house... sporting a flashy weskit'.[9] He had just passed his sixty-third birthday.

'The lifted hand' opened up several interpretations and revisions, indicating Hewitt's delicate and sensitive position between the warring factions of Ulster Christianity.[10] In *No Rebel Word* (1948), the contentious line had read exactly as Rosenfield reported it twenty-two years later. That it should be taken as exclusively a swipe at Catholic practices and attitudes was perhaps inevitable in Ireland though, from Roberta's journal, we now know more of their cautious but persistent interest in visiting Catholic churches and even attending mass. Outside the social location specified for the poem, 'The Glens', the lifted hand might be thought symbolic of Christian authoritarianism generally—Anglicans and other Protestant clergy also lift the hand imposing benediction on the compliant faithful. When Alan Warner was preparing *The Selected John Hewitt* in late 1980, the poet tussled about the line, confirming that the clearest statement of his intended feeling was 'the lifted hand against unfettered thought', less arrogant than the original. Warner had evidently thought the phrase 'vainer faith' no less likely to offend, but Hewitt defended the adjective for its alliteration with 'violent' in the succeeding line.[11] He was not always delicate.

Hay-foot-straw-foot, by alternate steps *The Planter and the Gael* was a remarkable success, and augured well for the Hewitts' repatriation. The Arts Council was highly professionalized, beyond anything CEMA had dreamed of, yet also employed so gifted a young poet as Michael Longley. However, a note of sympathetic caution was recorded by Liam de Paor, archaeologist and author of *Divided Ulster* (1970), reviewing the tour programme. We would not, he thought,

> learn a great deal about the origins of the political culture of Ulster by studying the seventeenth-century plantations (although we will learn something.) But by studying the myth and saga into which seventeenth-century history has been transmuted in the traditions of the North, we may learn a great deal about the present-day political culture.[12]

Here was a sophisticated distinction which Hewitt might have added to his Planter argument—but didn't.

The elegant programme issued by the Council says much about Hewitt's position within official Northern Ireland. Poems by the touring writers alternated in

[8] 'Ulster's Two Cultures in Poetry', *Irish Times*, 3 December 1970, p. 10.

[9] John Montague, 'Spiritual Maverick', *Threshold* 38 (Winter 1986/87), p. 18.

[10] See Gillian McIntosh, *Force of Culture: Unionist Identities in Twentieth Century Ireland* (Cork: Cork University Press, 1999), p. 198 etc.; Sarah Ferris, *Poet John Hewitt 1907–1987 and Criticism of Northern Irish Protestant Writing* (Lampeter: Edwin Mellon Press, 2002), p. 194.

[11] Private collection, JH to Alan Warner, 21 November 1980.

[12] 'Roots', *Irish Times*, 6 January 1971, p. 10. The previous year, JH had expressed a preference for Rayner Lysaght's *Making of Northern Ireland and the Basis for its Undoing* over de Paor's *Divided Ulster*; see Linen, JH to John Boyd, 1 June 1970.

blocks of two, three, or four. Montague appears first with 'The Sean Bhean Vocht', 'Like Dolmens Round my Childhood', 'A Lost Tradition', and 'Old Mythologies'. The very titles proclaim a distinct cultural history, in terms not so much religious or political as, by implication, linguistic (Gaelic). The first Hewitt selection opens with 'Once Alien Here', closes with 'An Irishman in Coventry': the implied emphasis is on movement, arrival, and departure both within a lifetime and over the centuries. Among the texts in the final selections, an excerpt from Montague's 'A New Siege' acknowledges the immediate conflict. Hewitt is represented by 'The Colony' (written decades earlier) and by 'Conversations in Hungary, August 1969', composed after the recent holiday. The programme was illustrated with woodcuts from John Derrick's *Image of Irelande* (1581), which Montague and his Dublin publisher (Liam Miller of the Dolmen Press) had been studying.

Elizabethan prints sprang from a violent phase of history midway between Montague's archaeological imagery and Hewitt's visits to central Europe. The poems do not line up in rival formations, though they offer contrasts which help to illuminate the Troubles already unfolding in Ulster. The natural world is present in Montague's poetry, but in Hewitt's it is pervasive and invasive. One apparently non-political element—the love poem—is Montague's terrain, not Hewitt's. In the latter's case, the issue is not emotion or lack of it; the issue is expression or reticence. Or, better, *reserve*, a manner of not saying, in the service of a later, better saying.[13] Northern Irish divisions exploit these spectra of proportion: those with a leaning towards the Paisleyite view of Catholicism often repeated the biblical injunction 'use not vain repetitions, as the heathen do'. Or, with greater precision, St Paul's 'let your yea be yea'.

'The Watchers' (1950), included in *The Planter and the Gael*, draws several of these concerns together:

> We crouched and waited as the day ebbed off
> and the close birdsong dwindled point by point,
> nor daring the indulgence of a cough
> nor the jerked protest of a weary joint;
> and when our sixty minutes had run by
> and lost themselves in the declining light
> we heard the warning snuffle and the sly
> scuffle of mould, and, instantly, the white
> long head thrust through the sighing undergrowth,
> and the grey badger scrambled into view,
> eager to frolic carelessly, yet loth [*sic*]
> to trust the air his greedy nostrils drew;
> awhile debated with each distant sound,
> then, settling into confidence, began
> to scratch his tough-haired side, to sniff the ground
> without the threat of that old monster, man.
> And as we watched him, gripped in our surprise,

[13] Frank Ormsby has insightful things to say about JH's gradual and late admission of love; see Ormsby, p. lxx.

that moment suddenly began to mean
more than a badger, and a row of eyes,
a stony brook, a leafy ditch between.
It was as if another nature came
close to my knowledge, but could not be known;
yet if I tried to call it by its name
would start, alarmed, and instantly be gone.[14]

Between the writing in 1950 and the public reading in November 1970, the poem is among the many things that changed. Fatuous to say it had become 'politicized' like a fresher at Queen's. The sixty minutes 'we' had assigned to waiting for sight of a badger has quantitatively expanded into two decades. But, qualitatively within the poem, it had already changed to a moment, one which 'suddenly began to mean / more than a badger, and a row of eyes / a stony brook, a leafy ditch between'. The 'we' is not to be facilely identified as Jack and Ruby, for identity itself is given no privilege. There is *another* nature, where the adjective may indicate something additional (and complementary) or something radically alternative (and incompatible). This other and implicitly different nature can be apprehended, but it cannot be named. It is accessible through reticence. Waiting for the badger, rewarded with 'another', any effort to name will lead to a reversion and a disappearance. No poem by Hewitt more comprehensively takes the reader inside his slow time. Any attempted political reading of 'The Watchers' must surely deal with 'that old monster, man' before jumping to identifications of the badger as a resurgent once-underground force of innocence or as an invader of the open air. It is not alone. Other poems which disclose a preoccupation with slow time are 'Mykonos', 'The Frontier', and (with some humour) 'The Covenanter's Grave'.

*

A twist or gyre of the kaleidoscope brings Yeats into view, a master poet whose funeral Hewitt had respectfully attended, writing it up later in a mood of affable independence. His profession, in the strict sense, put him more in touch with Jack Yeats. His attitude to the painter never warmed to anything higher than tepid acknowledgement, though the role of judicious art curator provided cover for an alleged lack of patriotic gore in his response. Jack Yeats died in March 1957 when the Hewitts were packing for the move to Coventry; no question of John attending that funeral. His attitude to his fellow poet and playwright was, naturally, more complex. Hewitt belonged to a generation later than Yeats and 'the last romantics', and so was freer to draw upon the first generation of romantic poets, especially Wordsworth, a poet Yeats could never tolerate. Among the inducements to warmer approval was the Lyric Theatre's championing of Yeats's plays, and Colin Middleton's rugged stage sets. Besides, Hewitt genuinely admired Yeats's writing, and said so. His echoes (cf. 'Easter Tuesday', 'Nineteen Sixteen, or The Terrible Beauty', and 'No Second Troy') were never to be mistaken for clumsy tributes. Tuned to an

[14] Ormsby, pp. 80–1.

ironic key, they were a lesser (but less combative) writer's sparring with the anxiety of influence.

The most extensive engagement took place in 'The Municipal Gallery Revisited, October 1954', which Hewitt wrote between October and December of that year. Yeats's great poem of similar title dates from his final years, collected in *New Poems* (1938), written in the autumn of 1937. It announces itself among the images of thirty years. Hewitt's poem qualifies the title it borrows by adding 'October 1954', a point in his life between rejection in Stranmillis and escape to Coventry. Hewitt had more than thirty years to live, Yeats less than eighteen months. The Nobel Prize winner concludes that his glory was 'I had such friends'. Or, to be more exact, having named patrons, poets, and politicians from Roger Casement to J. M. Synge, he *requires* the reader to 'say my glory was I had such friends'.[15] The younger poet does a little naming too, showing that he is true to what he copies, even as he cunningly divagates. But the consequences in Hewitt's work never confer glory, nor require it. He is aware of names casually omitted from the gallery's lists and labels, and he indirectly records how Antonio Mancini's portrait of Augusta Gregory—'greatest since Rembrandt' in Yeats's phrase—is affected by time, mechanical and human. Like Yeats, focused upon canvas, Hewitt concludes with a stage direction for the reader:

> for, see, before me, threatening, immense,
> the creeping haircracks of indifference.[16]

Haircracks had become all too evident in the portrait celebrated in Yeats's poem. A reaction of cool emotion, using the same concluding term, finished off Hewitt's versed remembrance of his early fiancée—'occluded by a vague indifference'—written in April 1985.[17]

He may still have had Yeats in mind when composing the 'Hesitant Memorial', for indifference (in a higher sense) informs one of Yeats's most incisive poetic interrogations of historical stability and political turbulence. 'Nineteen Hundred and Nineteen' surveys the unfounded optimism of the late Victorian realm, an era of 'ingenious lovely things', of 'pretty toys' but also of 'a law indifferent to blame or praise'. The legal concept of impartiality encapsulated in these three terms could draw on authorities who used similar terms, from Aristotle to Milton and beyond. Yeats's poem faced into the Troubles of 1919–23; Hewitt faced into an even longer spell of communal violence intensified by state brutality. If the earlier occasion had become associated in the popular mind with Easter 1916 as lighting the fuse (as one might light a torch), Hewitt queried the length of the fuse and the duration of the conflagration:

> It took those decades crammed with guns and ballads
> to sanctify the names which star that myth;
> and, to this day, the fierce infection pulses
> in the hot blood of half our ghetto-youth.[18]

[15] W. B. Yeats, *The Poems*, edited by Daniel Albright (London: Everyman's Library, 1992), p. 368.
[16] Ormsby, p. 91. [17] 'Hesitant Memorial'; Ormsby, pp. 394–5.
[18] 'Nineteen-Sixteen; or The Terrible Beauty' is reprinted in Gerald Dawe, ed., *Earth Voices Whispering: an Anthology of Irish War Poetry* (Belfast: Blackstaff, 2008), pp. 180–1.

Written in March 1973, 'Nineteen Sixteen, or The Terrible Beauty' echoed a letter Hewitt had written to John Boyd before he had retired from Coventry—'Where's "the terrible beauty" now? A seven [actually seventeen] months old child carried dead in a blanket on the Shankill Road.'[19] In turn the letter had resulted from a meeting between Hewitt and a group of Birmingham lay Catholics in October, at which he had found it difficult to overcome his audience's predetermined sympathy with republican violence. During an earlier phase of the Troubles, Yeats's regret at the dissolving of 'a law indifferent to blame or praise' had its immediate origins in brutal incidents near Lady Gregory's home for which Black and Tan units were to blame. It was not unqualified regret because the law was part and parcel of a culture valuing superficiality, triviality, and display above substance and understanding. Yeats's instancing of 'parliament and king' as daftly euphemizing all military affairs as 'trumpeting' may have revived Hewitt's (and Roberta's) memories of George V at the opening of Stormont. Hewitt had no sympathy with Yeats's extreme politics, and took steps to ensure that he was not seduced into any association with one violent faction or another in Northern Ireland.[20]

*

In early December 1971, Peadar O'Donnell travelled down from London to stay with the Hewitts for a few days. The two men of the Left, differing in many ways, talked for four hours, preoccupied by the unfolding disaster in their native province. Hewitt described a recently broadcast TV play by John Boyd in which the author evidently made a cameo appearance:

> I was telling him of that play of yours, and how I felt that you stood in my mind as representing how my generation and kind should act. When we [i.e. JH and Roberta] glimpsed you in the shot of the Botanic Gardens Rally it seemed inevitable and just. I felt that you were there for me too.
>
> As events have worsened, although we persuade ourselves that we know what it's all about, there is always the empty sensation that the facts, sensations, reactions, moods are utterly beyond our comprehension.[21]

The assumption that Hewitt would return primarily to confront Ian Paisley neglects the journalistic context in which such a possibility or obligation had been mooted.[22] John Hewitt was not *that kind* of political thinker or political actor. He would certainly support his friends, of all sorts, Boyd and O'Donnell among them. He would be 'Bifocal in Gaza'—despite or because of failing sight—the poem's

[19] Linen, JH to John Boyd, 11 December 1971. The child, Colin Nicholl, was killed in his pram by a no-warning IRA bomb outside a furniture shop on the Shankill Road, at lunchtime, Saturday 11 December 1971. See David McKittrick et al., eds., *Lost Lives: the Stories of the Men, Women and Children Who Died as a Result of the Northern Ireland Troubles* (Edinburgh: Mainstream, 2004), pp. 129–30. The incident, which claimed four lives in all, provoked instant and widespread revulsion, with extensive television coverage in Ireland, Britain, and France.

[20] See Edna Longley, *The Living Stream: Literature and Revisionism in Ireland* (Newcastle upon Tyne: Bloodaxe, 1994), p. 116. 'Despite his hostility to Yeats's politics, Hewitt accepts Yeats as the public voice to beat'.

[21] Linen, JH to John Boyd, 11 December 1971.

[22] *Coventry Evening Herald*, 1968.

title a deliberately skewed biblical reference Paisley could not miss. He would aim to avoid Samson's fate in the struggle between 'his' people and the Philistines.[23] Hewitt's most trenchant literary contribution to an informed consciousness of Northern Ireland's crisis was executed through private publication—an odd but conventional term. His recovery from the limited success of *Collected Poems* would be boosted by the physically slight *Ulster Reckoning*, to give notice of his intentions.

European travel, though rarely amounting to much more than a holiday, gave him a sense of perspective and, in so doing, encouraged his contact with southern Ireland. His friendship with Sean O'Faolain had begun in the 1940s under wartime conditions. In troubled 1970, it survived. Hearing the short-story writer in a radio broadcast, the Hewitts found the tone lacking in reverberation; John would have liked more of a 'chaunt'. He also regretted O'Faolain's avoidance of Daniel Corkery as an influence to be acknowledged, 'after all both he and [Frank] O'Connor came out of his pocket'.[24]

Nevertheless, he still remained an Irishman in Coventry while Belfast was firebombed. The experience was traumatic and indefinable. He felt that he was watching a theatre stage bogusly emptied of real people by his own distance from the place. On 9 August 1971, internment without trial was introduced by the Stormont authorities on a massively partisan, sectarian (and incompetent) basis. Riot and counter-riot broke out across the province, but especially in Belfast and Derry. The Hewitts sat in Postbridge Road listening to nightly bulletins about the burning out of streets and factories, casual and deliberate killings. 'We step from pool to pool of depression.' On 10 August, they phoned Peggy and Andy Millar—his shoe shops boarded up to avoid looting and vandalism. They spoke also to the Todhunters who were watching a row of houses on fire in the nationalist Ardoyne. No. 5 Postbridge Road was on the market—the current plan was to reach Belfast by November. Part of Roberta wanted to scamper abroad, but she knew John would feel a traitor even though 'his voice would go unheard by the two factions who create most of the trouble'.[25] The implication that Hewitt stood between contending forces is present in the foreword (dated April 1971) to *An Ulster Reckoning*: 'As I could not readily walk among the barricades with my white flag, I found release for my sense of frustration in verse.'[26]

Apart from 'Conversations in Hungary', the most enduring of the poems is 'The Coasters', a scathing (because understated) indictment of the complacent and compromised middle classes:

> You coasted along
> to larger houses, gadgets, more machines,
> to golf and weekend bungalows,

[23] For the text of 'Bifocal in Gaza' see Ormsby, pp. 395–9; for the story of Samson, blinded by the Philistines and set to work 'eyeless in the Gaza at the mill with slaves', see Milton's *Samson Agonistes* (1671), line 40; and in the Old Testament, *Judges*, ch. 13–6.

[24] Linen, JH to John Boyd, 1 June 1970 (original emphasis).

[25] *Journal*, PRONI, D/3838/4/7, 10 August 1971.

[26] See Ormsby, p. 593.

caravans when the children were small,
the Mediterranean, later, with the wife.[27]

Initially, John and Roberta had expected to fund the Belfast cottage by mortgaging their Coventry home and renting it out. But he kept changing his mind about an exact date for retirement. In the end, the house on Postbridge Road was sold outright, making a clean break with the English Midlands. The return was emotionally less clean, involving old scores, old sores, and the fear of recurrent miseries. From a spring holiday in 1971, they had despatched a postcard to the now invalided Norman Carrothers, 'The Greeks left interesting ruins. What will the Stormont oligarchy leave?'—a sardonic and hardly confident glance at the future, taken under the rule of a military junta.[28]

*

Apply a southern twist to the kaleidoscope. John Montague, who had studied at University College Dublin, became guest editor of *Threshold* for a special issue devoted to 'The Northern Crisis'. He was sharply critical of the magazine's lack of political interest during the previous decade and, in his foreword, he urged all and sundry to confront the problem not to ignore it, 'as previous generations (with a few honourable exceptions) have tended to do. For the time being to be an Ulster writer is, in a sense, to be a revolutionary writer: *old moulds are broken in the north.*'[29] Though the magazine itself went steadily into decline, Montague's seven words struck home more effectively than he could have anticipated. A civil servant friend of his, Eamon Gallagher of Donegal, had recently been transferred to the Department of the Taoiseach (or prime minister), Jack Lynch. On 11 July 1970, Lynch addressed the nation on television. The date was significant, the eve of 'the Twelfth' when Ulster Orangemen marched to celebrate historical and mythical victories. Within his own party, Lynch was uncomfortably placed between the sacking of two cabinet members for deviance from agreed 'northern policy' and their trial for conspiracy to import arms. The address lasted just five minutes, and its rhetoric was founded on a quotation from Montague's foreword in *Threshold*, 'old moulds are broken in the north'. Gallagher had been instrumental in drawing the Taoiseach's attention to this lambent phrase.[30] The address was circulated through the Department of External Affairs in an edition of 10,000 copies.

If Gallagher had supplied his leader with a copy of *Threshold*, Lynch would have been presented with a rich choice of literary material. Apart from his foreword, Montague contributed a portion of his long poem, 'A New Siege'; Seamus Heaney contributed 'Tollund Man', and Thomas Kinsella a section from *The Táin* ('The Pangs of Ulster'). Hewitt was represented by 'The Coasters', and a prose memoir 'The Family Next Door'. Colin Middleton designed the cover. It is worth noting that the lambent phrase did not come from the powerfully atavistic texts of Heaney

[27] Ormsby, pp. 135–7. [28] PRONI, D/3838/5/11.

[29] *Threshold* (Summer 1970), p. 1. Emphasis added. On *Threshold*'s decline, see the postscript to Frank Shovlin, *The Irish Literary Periodical 1923–1958* (Oxford: Oxford University Press, 2003), p. 184.

[30] Information supplied by John Montague, in a letter to the present writer, May 2013.

and Kinsella. Perhaps Gallagher had, in effect, limited the Taoiseach's options to one author, his friend Montague.[31]

This was a time of speeches and quotations, as the politicians had little talent for original thinking. On Saint Patrick's Day 1971 in Philadelphia, Jack Lynch quoted lines from 'The Colony' despite the fact that Hewitt was scarcely known in the United States, never having visited the place. (In contrast, Montague and Mary O'Malley hammered out the final shape of *Threshold* No. 23 while in Carbondale, Illinois.) On 12 July, Irish newspapers gave top billing to another speech by the Taoiseach and leader of the Fianna Fáil party. The previous day, on the fiftieth anniversary of the truce between Britain and the Irish insurgency, Lynch had unveiled a statue in Dublin's national Garden of Remembrance. The sculptor, Oisin Kelly (1915–81), came of Protestant stock. His subject was the Children of Lir, a mythic tale closely associated with the North Antrim coast. Lynch abjured violence, protested against partition, pleaded for a British initiative, and sought to characterize Northern Protestants sympathetically. 'Do we agree', he asked the invited attendance, that, as John Hewitt writes, they '"have rights drawn from the soil and the sky" which are as good as any title held by any previous migration into Ireland?'[32] Without saying as much, he was echoing both the closing lines of 'An Irishman in Coventry' and 'The Colony'. Once again, Gallagher had been instrumental in suggesting that the earlier citation of Montague might be effectively augmented by citing Hewitt from the other side. A week later, the *Irish Times*'s Backbencher was sneering at Honest Jack Lynch and, by extension, at John Hewitt too.

Oisin Kelly's choice of subject adroitly linked persecution and exile with religious faith, but did so by reference to a safely pre-Reformation era. The story generally known as 'The Children of Lir' opens in pagan Ireland but includes elements familiar from more recent European tales (e.g. the cruel stepmother). It had been published in *Atlantis* (1863) by Eugene O'Curry, who drew on manuscripts none of which predated the eighteenth century. This late source-history, together with the story's conclusion in Christianized Ireland, indicates a far from classic Celtic provenance, though the persons of the action all pre-date the arrival of the Celts in Ireland. Gerald Griffin and Thomas Moore knew of it, but it became popular for Hewitt's generation through paraphrase in P. W. Joyce, *Old Celtic Romances* (1879) and a version in *More Celtic Fairy Tales* (1894), and thus found its way into the repertoire of Yeats's Celtic Twilight.[33] 'The Children of Lir' can be read as narrating an orthodox relationship between Christianity and native paganism, by commencing in cruelty and expulsion (sin instigated through a number of women whose names are variations of Eve) and ending in return and resumed full humanity (redemption). A resistant, unorthodox counter-narrative is given in Yeats's 'The Wanderings of Oisin' (1889). As poet, Hewitt relates to the Lir story in intermittent, complex ways.

[31] Other contributors to *Threshold* No. 23 included Seamus Deane and Derek Mahon.

[32] *Irish Times*, 12 July 1971, p. 1.

[33] See Eugene O'Curry, 'The *Tri Thruaighé na Scéalaigheachta* (i.e. The "Three Most Sorrowful Tales") of Eirinn II: *"The Fate of the Children of Lir"*', *Atlantis* 4 (1863), pp. 113–57.

In March 1972, when the British premier Edward Heath shook the Ulster establishment by announcing a one-year suspension of the Stormont system, the *Irish Times* (edited by a northerner) sought to reassure more reflective Unionists that they were not thereby thrown to the wolves. This exercise emerged through an editorial headed NOT OUTCAST ON THE WORLD, which concluded with the last lines of 'The Colony':

> this is our country also nowhere else;
> and we shall not be outcast on the world.[34]

This may have been gratifying to John and Roberta as they gradually packed their bags in Coventry, but it scarcely proved Hewitt a radical or a dissenter. Paddy Devlin felt that, even after he retired from Coventry, John 'confined his political activities to attending talks with outside speakers and encouraging us... generally to clear up the mess left by earlier efforts at organisation and to get a united Labour Party organised for people like himself to support'. He and Roberta did, however, attend meetings of the NILP as members of the branch for the Windsor/Cromac district of Belfast, she being the more frequent speaker of the two.[35] For the years after her death, he maintained a particular interest in the trade union movement, evidenced by various conference cards and invitations preserved in the archive. In March 1984, he was invited to attend a Belfast Worker Writer's Group, organized under the auspices of the Ulster People's College.

*

The 'Children of Lir' is a myth, not a history, but it is a myth with a history of its transmission, accretion, and reception. As de Paor noted in connection with *The Planter and the Gael*, we learn more from the latter processes than from the *ur*-events, taken as symbolic facts. Similar dynamics have been noted within the psychic life, or along the dotted (not continuous) line, which lies between the psyche and the physical. Surveying his career from a basic suburban house in Coventry, John observed how interesting it was 'to search back for the clues, the determinants'.[36] He had come far, he had achieved much. Was all of this preordained, as Calvin or Marx might have put it, though in contrasting idioms? Of the two, Marx was closer to Hewitt's heart, or at least more often on his tongue. In the disjointed autobiographical chapters to which he gave the non-resonant title, *A North Light*, he reverted on several occasions to issues of guilt. On one of these, the tone is light-hearted: officially exempt from military service because of his civil service employment, he had lectured to troops in camps across the Six Counties, even speaking once from a boxing ring. But the avoidance of war experience could not always be glibbed away. 'May be in that loss

[34] *Irish Times*, 25 March 1972, p. 13. The editor was Douglas Gageby (1918–2004) whose anti-Unionist positions included unwarranted admiration of Charles J. Haughey.

[35] Paddy Devlin, 'No Rootless Colonist', *Threshold* 38 (Winter 1986/87), p. 23. For the Hewitts' NILP membership, I am grateful to Neil Faris (via Connal Parr), sometime chairman of the branch. See also James W. McAuley on the Labour Party and Northern Ireland in the 1980s, in *Culture and Politics in Northern Ireland*, edited by Eamon Hughes (Milton Keynes: Open University Press, 1991).

[36] *North*, p. 4.

I have suffered a serious deprivation which has left me perhaps less adult than my years require.'[37]

Nothing comparable in the several manuscripts and typescripts assembled for *A North Light* addresses deprivations or shortcomings in the sexual area, hardly surprising perhaps in that day and age.[38] Where could his determinants be sought? In 'The Bitter Gourd' (in *Lagan*, 1945), he approaches the problem from two directions, having begun with two discouraging observations. 'The Ulster ideology' of mechanical inventiveness and active devotion to the imperial economy 'offered the writer no inspiration'. Perhaps this contains an uncomfortable truth, but the German contemporary parallels (admittedly large, *almost* beyond comparison) gave us impressive instances of creative dissent—Theodor Fontane and Thomas Mann, to go no further. Two paragraphs earlier, Hewitt had adverted somewhat confusedly to the paradox 'that the very inarticulateness of the Protestant block' resulted in the latter finding articulation through non-Ulster voices—Randolph Churchill, F. E. Smith, and Edward Carson.[39] Here too one detects an incomplete truth, for the leaders of Ulster Protestantism—notably 'Roaring' Hugh Hanna (1821–92) and Ian Paisley (b.1926)—were never at a loss for words in denouncing popery and its dupes. 'The Bitter Gourd' never fully returns to the problems of the Ulster Writer, but instead deals with happier American cultural circumstances. Curiously, in a man intrigued by regionalism, Hewitt does not seem to have read much by William Faulkner, creator of Yoknapatawpha County, and dedicated student of oppressive divisions in society.[40]

'The past is never dead. It's not even past', Faulkner wrote in *Requiem for a Nun* (1950), one of those novels Hewitt evidently did not read. The society of his growth to manhood was established in 1920 (he was thirteen, his future wife sixteen) as the product of armed intransigence, violence, and violent resistance, occurring before and after the Great War. Veterans of the trenches were renowned for a reluctance to speak about their experiences, a reaction easily accommodated in Northern Ireland where, for other political reasons, it was often advised that 'whatever you say, say nothing'. Gillian McIntosh has suggested that the contrast of Protestant reticence and Catholic volubility, and the association of reticence with loyalty, was effected by Unionist writers in the 1920s, perhaps drawing unconsciously on the trauma of war service.[41] Against this, Hewitt's capacity for

[37] *North*, pp. 127–8.

[38] Hewitt never seriously considered publication of *A North Light*, and came to regard it as a quarry from which he might dig out occasional gems. In its published form (2013), the text omits some of these (but not all).

[39] 'The Bitter Gourd; Some Problems of the Ulster Writer', *Ancestral*, p. 114.

[40] Hewitt's library, as it passed to UU after his death, contains none of Faulkner's novels, though it should be remembered that some stray volumes ended up in secondhand bookshops instead of remaining with the collection.

[41] Gillian McIntosh, *The Force of Culture: Unionist Identities in Twentieth-Century Ireland* (Cork: Cork University Press, 1999), p. 195. See pp. 194–9 for extensive treatment of W. R. Rodgers' contrast of Catholic and Protestant attitudes to speech, which amounted to a racial theory or at least a 'racial difference'. Hewitt entertained no such theory. She also quotes Tom Clyde: 'Hewitt's antipathy to Catholicism was based, not on Ulster Protestant bigotry, but on a blind spot common to most socialists of his generation, particularly those who had been involved with communism.... Since this generation experienced first hand the Catholicism of the Lateran Treaty, of symbolic relationship with

public speech was unquestioned; indeed, it provided a platform for F. L. Green's lampoon in *Odd Man Out*. His particular reticence on intimate (especially sexual) matters may be attributed to the suburbanized Puritanism of 'the whole Protestant community', even though he marked himself off from that body at virtually every other point. Joyce's Mr Duffy, in 'A Painful Case' (written 1905/6), suffers and inflicts a greater breakdown of the affections, without a Protestant alibi. The lives of Yeats's Pollexfen relatives in Sligo, or of MacNeice's parental households, amply testify to a widespread phenomenon. Nor were the victims of this Victorian prudishness disproportionately Irish, as biographies of Edmund Gosse, Thomas Hardy, and a hundred others can demonstrate.

His experience of the Troubles in 1919–22, for some a triumph, for others betrayal, was more sheltered than Roberta's. His temporary engagement to Dorothy Roberts, and thoughts of foreign mission fields, indicate a high degree of conformity within his Methodist inheritance, evidently as late as 1930. Nothing so helpful as *the* formative experience leaps out from the records. Yes, Roberta and her sister were once shot at impersonally; yes, he saw a man with a gun partly concealed. How, exactly *how*, does the past matter; or how does it most potently (damagingly?) materialize? If we were to draw on Freud's notion of 'the auxiliary moment', would it be possible to spot an event—remote, trivial, or innocent in itself—which alters the force, direction, or significance of much earlier experience, rendering it powerfully traumatic in the personal domain?[42] Can the kaleidoscope be twisted anti-clockwise?

*

In the summer of 1953, the Hewitts occupied various middle points. They were roughly at the middle of their life together—twenty years done, twenty-two to go. He was mid-career, perhaps beached. She was, in a phrase of the time, at a certain stage of a woman's life, a concern she had first registered to herself in late 1949. Her anger at his inadequacies (in her assessment of the relationship) gradually reached near-boiling point. Then a seemingly unrelated event: old Queen Mary (1867–1953) died, someone utterly remote from Mount Charles, Cushendall, and the entire social and mental landscape they lived in. Allowing for a little sentimental effusion, Victoria Mary Augusta Louise Olga Pauline Claudine Agnes of Teck meant nothing to these self-conscious middle-class radicals. (Roberta's mother positively hated Elizabeth and Philip.) Yet news of the royal widow's death set off a secondary, prior self-consciousness, which took Roberta back to 1921, with the royals in Belfast for the opening of a Parliament bent on legitimizing Unionist defiance. The psychic structure to bear in mind is that which unites the inchoate private anger and the sudden public announcement.

the dictatorships in Portugal and Spain and the anti-communist propaganda disseminated directly from the pulpit, their attitude was understandable, if a little simplistic' (pp. 198–9). This seems to me confused, and certainly does not meet the Hewitt case.

[42] For Freud's use of the term, see 'Miss Lucy R.', in *Studies on Hysteria* by Freud and Josef Breuer, in *The Standard Edition of the Complete Psychological Works*, edited by James Strachey (London: Vintage, 2001), pp. 123–4, 133–4 etc.

Roberta embraces this sudden recollection and resists it. She recalls the young soldier who came back to see her; she insists that her focus is not the queen, who made that near-meeting nearly possible, but *me.* There is simultaneously the reopening of sexual allure at a promisingly blank page, with the inch-cluttered tape lashing her to an aged woman pronounced dead—in German romantic terms, Death and the Maiden. Opposites merge, and a thing sought is to be found not where it is. Or, to quote a passage by William Morris highlighted in the journal: 'Men fight and lose the battle, and the thing that they fought for comes about in spite of their defeat, and when it comes it turns out not to be what they meant, and other men have to fight for what they meant under another name.'[43] Those with a taste for Hegel might see this as 'the cunning of history' in a worker's smock. Hewitt himself illustrated something like this model by observing in one of his public talks,

> In the old days, the lady was white and pink and the worker was sunburnt and weather beaten—then came the factories and the worker became pale and delicate looking and the lady collects sunburn to show her leisure—so much so that now workers buy their sunburn in bottles.[44]

The political context of 1921 is not external to the conjuncture of hope and desolation felt by Roberta in 1953; they are vectors in the kaleidoscope, co-tempories in the psyche. When George V (with his wife) insisted on travelling in person to a still much disturbed city in June, he declared that he did so in the name of a wider reconciliation to follow. 'Few things are more earnestly desired throughout the English-speaking world than a satisfactory solution of the age-old Irish problem . . . I appeal to all Irishmen to pause, to stretch out the hand of forbearance and conciliation'.[45] Hewitt in the 1960s conceded the monarch's courage in travelling to a city 'astir with civil disturbance'—and he too had watched the royal procession.[46] Of course the king was to be disappointed, not least by the rapid collapse of Unionist rhetoric into a narrowly defensive policy executed through 'a Protestant parliament for a Protestant people', eventually closed down by a Tory prime minister. But for some months, hopes of a peaceful and equitable settlement ran fairly high. Percy Tougher lay in the distant future (cf. 'Lines for a Dead Alderman', written in late 1953 and only published in 1968).

Of course political wisdom over nine decades has rubbished idealistic expectations of this kind, cynically or clinically detailing the low motives of this faction, the treachery of that, and the self-interest of all. Monarchs don't count, and the particular royal personages briefly active on the Belfast stage were known incidentally as George and His Dragon. Good Queen Mary was, to an extent, the creation

[43] William Morris, *A Dream of John Ball [and] A King's Lesson* (London: Reeves and Turner, 1888) p. 31. I have restored Morris's original words which Roberta misquoted in one or two unimportant details.

[44] 'The Place of Work', talk given to the Standing Council of Women's Organisations (Belfast), March 1950.

[45] See, for longer extracts, Patrick Buckland, *Ulster Unionism and the Origins of Northern Ireland 1886 to 1922* (Dublin: Gill and Macmillan, 1973), p. 144.

[46] *North*, p. 26.

of her sons' later and contrasting careers—Edward VIII who caused a crisis, abdicated, and married a divorcee, and George VI who first laboured with a stammer and then contracted cancer. Her long viduity (to borrow from Beckett) also helped. In the fairy-tale version of hierarchical (power-riveted) society, the poor man under the lash would be righted, if only the Czar knew. The inaccessible pinnacle is righteous. And so Roberta reflected, in her misery. But, Yeats coldly observed, 'the lash goes on'. Responding to John's enigmatic poem, 'The Ram's Horn', in May 1950 Roberta made a remark which indicates a more characteristic attitude to social stratification, 'there is an aristocracy about evil'. He asked her to write it down, though she may have intended something less overtly political—a gradation or gradations of evil.

*

The political situation when they finally reached Belfast in October 1972 was dire. Killings by the Parachute Regiment on Bloody Sunday (30 January 1972) had hugely exacerbated nationalist alienation, while loyalist organizations were seeking to wag the government dog ever more violently. Republicanism (which embraces militant nationalism) had split into Official and Provisional wings of both the IRA and Sinn Féin. The larger Provo movement relied on bomb and bullet; the Officials on dialectics, mostly but slowly. Betty Sinclair, still a communist, had played a leading role in the Northern Ireland Civil Rights Association, helping to quell 'ultra-leftism' among the People's Democracy. Bloody Sunday converted the situation into a contest among several sets of terrible twins. The killing peaked that year (497 victims in all, an average of almost ten per week), but did not decline below 260 (ten per fortnight) until 1977. In September 1974, Martin McBirney was murdered at home by the Provisionals. Sometime chairman of the Northern Ireland Labour Party, a barrister and playwright, he had been a friend of Sam Thompson and Louis MacNeice. The Hewitts' friend, Terry Flanagan, painted 'Victim' in response to McBirney's death; in it, 'a pure-white figure reclines like a loose-limbed sarcophagus'.[47]

When John informed the local Coventry press in 1968 that, if he retired home, he must oppose Ian Paisley, he was indicting the same system. The final sentence of Patrick Buckland's scarcely radical analysis of Northern Ireland in 1969 provides more than a summary of political failure; 'the 1920s mentality had produced a 1920s situation'.[48] The kaleidoscope defied the apparent passage of time. What deserves attention in this final assessment is not the implication of a deep and self-damaging conservatism in Northern Ireland but, to revert to a more Freud-nuanced analysis, the discovery of an elision of time as in the workings of the unconscious. More abstractly and implicitly, Buckland proposes a mathematical/time equation—1920 = 1969 or, to put the implications more plainly 49 = 0. The cancellation of intervening years, not so much claimed as achieved by the Stormont mentality, takes its toll in the lives of real people. Within an influx of 1921 memory,

[47] Fionola Meredith, *Irish Times*, 19 April 2014, reviewing 'Art of the Troubles', an exhibition at the Ulster Museum, Belfast.

[48] Buckland, *Ulster Unionism and the Origins of Northern Ireland 1886 to 1922*, p. 178.

Roberta, in 1953, struggles desperately to maintain trust in her own ego. Not the queen but me becomes a possible solution for (by distraction from) the difficulties of her domestic life. But, with that possible solution, comes a reversion to abolished history, all the years and alterations of 1921–53, a sort of depersonalized hysteria. This is not simply a diagnosis of the individual but, potentially at least, of the fractured collective. We exist and survive, triumphantly, but only where and what we have always been.

10

1974, and after Roberta

The indifference which had turned its back on Hewitt or sneered at him for half a century morphed into mild public acknowledgement. Loneliness by habit still warmed his shoulders. Like the visitor among statues in October 1954, he found himself 'facing disarmed the stone and metal men'. Life, including the years to come, was not a steady march through difficulty towards glory, but a rearrangement of scattered pieces, having the appearance of logic and pattern. In September 1973, John and Roberta visited Turkey, but this was a trip for pensioners, not the ideologically tinted venturers to East Germany, Yugoslavia, or Hungary. One might begin anywhere, almost at any date, to begin the summing up, but 1974 was an auspicious year, once newspapers and their death columns were discounted.

One of Hewitt's most substantial publications in retirement was *Rhyming Weavers and Other Country Poets of Antrim and Down*, issued by Blackstaff Press late in 1974. Its origins reached back to pre-exile days when, in 1951, Queen's University awarded him a Master's Degree for a thesis, 'Ulster Poets 1800–1870'. Even earlier, he had contributed three articles on the topic to an obscure journal *Fibres, Fabrics and Cordage*. A number of the poems themselves had been reprinted in the magazine *Rann* between 1948 and 1951. In a foreword to the book he recalled his first exploration of this popular culture, his appreciation of how 'the forgotten and often clumsy old poets' had given him in one turn of phrase or another verbal felicity 'some feeling that, for better or worse, they were my own people'.[1]

What people? If we look into the anthology itself, the work of fifteen writers is represented, of whom the oldest was Francis Boyle (of County Down), who was born about 1730. At least two of the others had not died when Hewitt arrived in 1907—Henry Fletcher being still alive in 1909 and Thomas Given staying as late as 1917. Hewitt had his own family connections back into rural east Ulster (Armagh rather than Down or Antrim) and he was not ashamed to indicate their lowly status. In a sense, the anthology and the introduction he wrote for it constituted an indirect and impersonal form of autobiography. His concentration on the two most eastern maritime counties of the province was largely determined by the sources then available to him in libraries where fragile chapbooks and broadsheets were preserved, notably the Linen Hall collection in Belfast. But among Hewitt's cited authorities and sources, we do not find Colm Ó Lochlainn's *Irish Street*

[1] John Hewitt, ed., *Rhyming Weavers and Other Country Poets of Antrim and Down* (Belfast: Blackstaff, 1974), p. vii; see also Hewitt's MA thesis, p. iv.

Ballads (1939) or *More Irish Streets Ballads* (1965), though these contained some appropriate material and many splendid woodcut illustrations from the original broadsheets. The compilation of the book was a demonstration of Hewitt's continuing interest in regionalism as a 'way out' of more rigid divisions and incorporations.

Another consideration was at work. The thesis and the published book differ more extensively than Hewitt publicly admitted. The writers treated in 1951 were drawn from more Ulster Counties than just Antrim and Down, and weavers constituted only a fraction (yes, a large-ish fraction) of their number. Less important, the thesis (while quoting generously in each chapter) made no attempt to be an anthology. *The Rhyming Weavers* was a far more original publication that it posed as. By bringing weavers to the fore, Hewitt gave the book a solider foundation in the economic and semi-industrial reality of nineteenth-century Ulster. By printing the poems, he substantiated that reality for the modern reader, who was not asked to take on trust the word of a critic. But he also finessed expectations of a political commentary.

Just as the thesis had avoided the United Irishmen, and even discounted James Hope's compositions, so *The Rhyming Weavers* adopted a Brechtian cunning.[2] It would have been easy and, in some quarters, popular to write up a 'continuity' between Jacobin-inspired rebellion and the resurgent turmoil of Northern Ireland in the early 1970s. Nationalist tradition performed the operation on a weekly basis with no more than a local anaesthetic, invoking Wolfe Tone and his determination to break the link between 'us' and Britain. Hewitt was, in an exact sense, a republican, but he was never a nationalist. His links with Irish republicans had been intermittent—yes, to Peadar O'Donnell in the late 1930s and 1940s; no to Sean MacBride in the late 1940s and early 1950s.

By the mid-1970s, *The Irish Democrat* had reached complacent middle-aged Cominternity, propounding the doctrines of a socialist nationalism to come, nodding to the republican dissenters of the past, and lambasting Dublin governments of whatever hue. It no longer styled itself a New Series, having sunk its namesake of 1937 below recollection: it was now 'founded 1939', an impossible date given the Stalin–Hitler pact. Every issue carried a full page of singalongs, 'Kelly the Boy from Killane', 'The Old Rustic Bridge by the Mill', and others. Meanwhile a banner line denounced 'Conor Cruise O'Brien, Enemy of Irish Culture', anonymously. In this context, Hewitt's *Rhyming Weavers* was favourably reviewed (August 1975) by Eavann Conor. Among contributors, the only recognizable survivor of Hewitt's Belfast circle was John Boyd, an occasional reviewer.

Despite the fossilized brain-pan of the Stalinist Left, and the sub-Trotskyite ecstatics of People's Democracy, some comparison of the situation in 1971 with that of 1937 is advisable as a measure of Hewitt's long political interest. The Northern Irish constitutional arrangement was more exposed and vulnerable in the 1970s than it ever was in the 1930s. Nationalism and republicanism had acquired

[2] Hope did not write very much verse, and it achieved late publication through the historian R. R. Madden. Hewitt was well aware of Hope and Madden's cooperation, for the two appear together in the final scene of his play known as 'The McCrackens'.

a more sophisticated leadership, even if the republican movement was split (since 1970) between two factions. More important, Unionism too was split: in party terms, the landed and middle-class establishment enshrined in *the* Unionist Party would face an implacable rival in Ian Paisley's Democratic Unionist Party (founded 1971), especially among working-class and *petit bourgeois* Protestants. Underlying the latter development lay the demoralization of many among Belfast's young men, as recruitment into the British armed forces was progressively curtailed with the shrinkage of empire. Wild boys from the Shankill, who had previously been packed off to learn a trade in the Navy or RAF, were now (to borrow a phrase, inappropriately, from Marx) murderous dreamers on street corners. Hewitt knew this part of Belfast well—he had been born there, his wife's brother-in-law sold boots and shoes there. In harmonious contrast, discontent with the Marxist line of the (official) IRA led, after 1970, to outright sectarian terrorism. Finally, in the 1930s it had been legitimate to cite European fascism as the looming spectre haunting everywhere else; in the 1970s, the idiom of a civil rights movement echoed battles already if painfully won in the United States.

*

Publication of verse resumed in the modest fashion which had served before *Collected Poems*. MacGibbon and Kee had been absorbed by a colossal organization principally active in television—'the Granada monster', Hewitt called it.[3] The first casualty was not quite truth but poetry. In 1974, he privately issued two small items—*The Chinese Fluteplayer* and *Scissors for a One-Armed Tailor*, the latter subtitled *Marginal Poems 1929–1954*. Both were released in editions of just 200 copies. Belfast's slow development of modern publishing had borne fruit in 1971 with Jim and Diane Gracey's Blackstaff Press, a venture supported by an Arts Council grant. Hewitt would publish a great deal with Blackstaff, poetry, some art criticism, and literary history, in the decade and more still left to him. *Out of My Time; Poems 1967–1974*, the first collection under the imprint, appeared in the same year as the two very limited, private issue pamphlets.[4] In all three volumes, material from the past—even the remote past in *Scissors*—was mobilized. 'S. S. K.', written in 1939, discloses Roberta's stepfather as a man who attended séances. 'Second Front: Double Summertime, July 1943' links manipulation of clock time to expectations of an ultimate, humanly expensive victory: 'and all the guns in Europe wait / for all the men who are to die'. It is work like this which Derek Mahon had in mind when he detects occasional 'worthiness and dullness', though, far more incisively, he associates Hewitt's regionalism with Edmund Burke's idea of 'the little platoon' as the essence of social well-being.[5]

[3] Private collection, JH to Alan Warner, 15 September 1973.

[4] *Out of My Time* had been a title used by Hewitt in 1952 when submitting, unsuccessfully, to Faber. It may be reasonable to assume that some of the material first gathered in 1952 survived into the publication of October 1974, though the author stresses his English Midlands years in the preface. Nevertheless, the commence-date given in the subtitle, 'poems 1967 to 1974', disguises the title's earlier origins.

[5] Derek Mahon, *Journalism* (Loughcrew: Gallery, 1996), p. 94.

In the same year, Jim Stewart died suddenly (sitting on the toilet), and the New University of Ulster conferred the degree of Doctor of Letters, on Hewitt. In 'Flight of the Earls Now Leaving' James Simmons, then on the NUU staff, proclaimed him 'the daddy of us all'.[6] Honours were interwoven with griefs and losses. The following year his only sister, Eileen died (24 February 1975); later he was elected vice president of the Dublin-based Irish Academy of Letters, founded by Yeats and Shaw in 1932 to combat censorship. During September 1975 he and Roberta took their last foreign holiday together, visiting the USSR with some political interest, and getting as far east as Samarkand.

Hewitt maintained active links with southern Ireland, despite Clarke's death in March 1974. He participated in an early Kilkenny Arts Week, noting its equal attention to literature and painting. His study of John Luke was jointly published by the two Arts Councils in 1978. But, for the southern state's most ambitious cultural project, he was overlooked and underestimated. Aosdana was formally launched on 5 March 1981 and, by the end of the year, thirty-seven writers were nominated by the Arts Council as foundation members (together with musicians and visual artists). Hewitt's name appears nowhere in the surviving papers for consideration, nor was he later proposed for election. Perhaps he rebuffed approaches. Certainly, he would feature as the darling neither of Whitehall nor of Merrion Street.[7]

In June 1974, Roberta Hewitt had authorized ultimate release of her dead body to Queen's Medical School. More than a year later, she died on 19 October 1975 in the Royal Victoria Hospital, Belfast. The stated cause of death was bronchopneumonia, with a brain tumour detected earlier.[8] There is even some evidence of symptoms occurring in 1971.[9] The poet naturally received a large number of letters offering condolences and sympathy. Many proceeded to record memories, or pay tribute to her character, her achievements, and her role in Hewitt's creative and personal life. Their final three years together had been marked by unceasing violence and communal conflict across the province.

Ulster writers were notable among those offering their condolences—among them Sam Hanna Bell, Gerald Dawe, Seamus Heaney, Paul Muldoon, and Jimmy Simmons. Also Harden Rodgers, daughter of the Hewitts' late friends, the poet Bertie Rodgers and his first wife Marie, whose funeral Roberta had attended on her own. John Boyd appreciated the profound loss of a wife who had loved Hewitt dearly, and protected him 'like a mother her child'. Less acutely, Boyd judged that the death caused the widower to write some of his most deeply felt poems.[10] What one notices among these communications is the high proportion of addresses outside Ulster from which they write to the tiny home on Stockman's Lane. If Hewitt had returned to Ulster, others had left. Heaney was living on the edge of what had been the Synge Estate at Glanmore in Wicklow; Dawe was teaching in Galway

[6] James Simmons, 'Flight of the Earls Now Leaving' [poem], *Irish Times*, 4 June 1974, p. 10.
[7] See Arts Council of Ireland, archives, file 2616/1981/1.
[8] See PRONI, D/3838/1/1/4 and D/3838/1/1/23.
[9] *Journal*, PRONI, D/3838/4/7, note headed 1971.
[10] John Boyd, *The Middle of My Journey* (Belfast: Blackstaff, 1990), p. 199.

and editing a literary page for the local newspaper; Harden Rodgers was doing something of the same at Trinity College Dublin.

Heaney had found it advisable to move out of Belfast, taking his family southwards and finding a post in Carysfort Teacher Training College outside Dublin. From Glanmore Cottage he wrote,

> I heard last night of Roberta's death, bleak and brutal news that I have no style for except to tell you of my own sadness and sympathy. Your own solitude and sorrow are probably enough for you to have to endure at the moment, but I just want to gesture as well as I can across the distance and the absence. Her smiling, lively face stays in my mind, her good concern and concerns, and the memory in particular of my first visit with you both in Coventry.

Roberta was not forgotten in Britain. From Scotland, a distant relative recalled with affection 'the wild organised chaos of her kitchens'. The Hewitts' GP and friend Joe Spears, together with Peggy his wife, wrote in sympathy. A Coventry neighbour assured John that 'you will take pleasure in the knowledge you have bequeathed your beloved wife a measure of immortality in your beautiful poems' and then signed off, 'Courage, Lilac'. Closer to home, there were exceedingly few tributes from the Establishment, though Rae Stirling (sometime Principal of Edenderry Nursery School), and James Ford Smith of the Ulster Museum, communicated. The redoubtable Arthur Agnew still ministered to dwindling Unitarians at All Souls, Elmwood Avenue, but associated the Roberta of old with diminishing numbers in York Street Non-Subscribing Church. His own intellectual or theological position, by implication close to hers, indicates the breakdown of Ulster radicalism into benign and ineffectual coteries: 'I have pondered much over death and my own comfort comes from Socrates.' He opined that either death would lead to a wonderful experience or be a dreamless sleep. 'Of course I have no use for the orthodox belief in Heaven and Hell and certainly not the latter.' Roberta's mother, Agnew noted even-handedly, had become a spiritualist.

The Hewitts had no family, in the colloquial sense that they had no children—or, naturally, grandchildren. The Millars rallied in John's support, with Keith writing to record how Aunt Ruby had taken him to his first hill-country youth hostel, and recalling with love 'her talks on music, plants & birds'.[11] Family was a relative matter: among the sympathizers was Morag McKinlay, sister of Jean Craig, both daughters of Hewitt's technique-bound painter friend, Billy McClughin.

The years after Roberta were conducted with Hewitt's customary attention to duty and public obligation. He had no time for sentimental rhetoric about sacrifice, mocking it by preferring a semi-articulate, 'I seen my duty and I done it.' The public, or the more enlightened corners of it, responded. In 1976, he was appointed the first Writer-in-Residence at Queens, holding the position for three years. The Department of English at Queen's developed a particular affection for Hewitt, and contributed to the father figure he (rather ironically) became. Much credit in this regard goes to Edna Longley, a Dubliner by birth and one who knew the actuality

[11] All quotations from material in tribute to Roberta are taken from PRONI, D/3838/3/19.

of Protestant–Catholic accord in her own family. Belfast could field an impressive team of poets. In 1979, he was elected first president of the Northern Ireland Fabian Society (Jim Stewart had been an active chairman in the 1960s), but turned down the proposed OBE. The year 1983 saw him doubly honoured—with a second doctorate (from Queen's) and with the Freedom of Belfast City. According to Kenneth Jamison, director of the Arts Council, Hewitt in the latter connection had considered quoting Samuel Johnson's famous reply to Lord Chesterfield, 'The notice you have been pleased to take of my labours, had it been early, had been kind, but it has been delayed till I am indifferent and cannot enjoy it; till I am solitary and cannot impart it; till I am known and do not want it.' This, frankly, was a false comparison, and Hewitt forbore. Yet the admission of 'indifference' would have been honest.[12] In 1984, he was presented with the Gregory Medal by Peadar O'Donnell at a ceremony in Cushendall, O'Donnell acting in his role as president of the Dublin-based Irish Academy of Letters.

*

The poet's life cannot be siphoned off from the life of art, and while it is helpful to know the public events and the domestic emotions, only Hewitt's poems ultimately justify the enquiry. His best editors, Longley and Ormsby, rightly speak of 'this profoundly egalitarian poet [who] is concerned to interact with his readers' while approving a mode of address that sounds confidential'.[13] A taut resonance between those apparently at-odds adjectives—'egalitarian' and 'confidential'—should be given its hearing. As a young man Hewitt wrote prolifically and, if there were dry periods during his years in Coventry, the ease of publication with Blackstaff Press led to a second, late prolific phase. Consequently, a proportion of the writing falls below his high standard. Judgement in this area is complicated by Hewitt's often elliptic syntax; a poem which seems too straightforward to be interesting can turn out to contain challenging technical accomplishments which send the reader back to reconsider a too casual dismissal. Here, he may have learned a trick or two from Robert Frost.

For the purposes of summary in a biographical context, let us gruffly propose three classes of poem by John Hewitt—the good, the bad, and the ugly, the first and last of which are positively charged. The bad may be disposed of fairly quickly. In the late 1920s and early 1930s, much of Hewitt's literary energy went into avowed propaganda: 'A Labour Victory', 'The Song of the Shipyard Men', 'The Simple Minded Christian', and many more. Among later poems, I think too many of the personal tribute pieces fall under the same heading: they lack variety as a group, and individually they display little vivacity or distinction of language. None of these went into either of the substantial volumes (*No Rebel Word* 1948 and *Collected Poems* 1968) which Hewitt controlled. When the type appears or reappears in the last fifteen years of his life, the period evoked is childhood. *Kites in Spring; a Belfast Boyhood* (1980)

[12] Kenneth Jamison, 'John Hewitt, a Personal Reminiscence', in *John Hewitt, a Poet's Pictures* (Hillsborough: Shambles Art Gallery, 1987), p. 11.

[13] Longley/Ormsby, p. xxiii.

consists of more than one hundred pieces, sonnets all: in a note to Alan Warner, Hewitt recorded that 'the sequence was written from October '78 to August '79, with frequent revisions during that period'. One discernible feature of the volume is its occasional use of the earlier Troubles to describe incidents occurring or recurring in the 1970s—'A Case of Mistaken Identity', for example. To Warner, in the note just quoted, Hewitt made the telling admission, 'I don't know if I shall continue it into the less nostalgic decades.'[14] The book was reviewed by Paul Durcan in *The Cork Examiner*, and generally appealed to a new readership.

In a draft introduction to *Kites*, the seventy-year-old widower reflected, 'it was perhaps natural that I should brood on the idea of death, at the dismal outset of winter, in a deeply riven and violent society, tortured by a cruelly remembered past'.[15] The personal situation is neatly inscribed, but impersonal or general or structural implications leach everywhere. Is it the violent society which is tortured by the past or is it the individual? Is the remembering cruel (malicious, deliberate, or whatever); or is the past cruel? And if the latter, does it imply an active influence of the past upon the present, as in some ancient Greek scenario? Hewitt addressed the latter question in 'Parallels Never Meet', written in September 1969 and included in *An Ulster Reckoning*.

The following year, still in Coventry, he seized gratefully on phrases used by John Boyd in a centenary issue of the *Belfast Telegraph*. The exile wrote home congratulating his friend for 'sounding the honest note, facing not dodging the "communal menace" in "our fractured society"'.[16] He added, perhaps self-laceratingly, fond recollections of the American radical Horace Traubel and his 'Chants Communal' of 1915. But the questions and implications persist. If Ulster society is deeply riven—that is, split into two—then violence is the form in which it denies and possibly overcomes that split condition. In tougher terms, does a language inevitably generate indeterminates in leaving open the issue of how subject and predicate 'translate' in social relations? What exactly had Boyd meant by 'communal menace'?

The early 1980s were years of high-speed writing and publication. *Kites in Spring* (February 1980) was followed by *The Selected John Hewitt* (September 1981), *Mosaic* (November 1981), *Loose Ends* (April 1983). (There was more to come.) *Loose Ends* opens with 'For Jean':

> Dear girl, dream daughter of the childless years—
> known all your days—of such a surrogate,
> of her too, hearthstone of my prime's estate,
> staff, anchor, buttress, when beset by cares—
> those forty vivid years none living shares—
> till riven from me by a witless fate
>
> when I most needed, older grown; so great
> a sheaf of masks your single visage wears.
> When, that bright day, chance brought beneath my roof

[14] Private collection, JH to Alan Warner, 22 March 1980.
[15] Quoted in Ormsby, p. 617.
[16] Linen, JH to John Boyd, 14 November 1970.

you and your sons, I snatched at the relief,
a sounding house to stem my lonely grief.
Now, six years later, with the daily proof
of this assuagement, to your bracing care
may these brief lines my lucky debt declare.

More information than aesthetic pleasure may be gleaned from these lines prefacing a collection of less than compelling substance. The reader is to know that in 1976 Jean Craig, with her two sons (Colin and Ian), moved into the Stockman's Lane cottage, a year after Roberta died. But the language is reaching backwards to formulas which, even in the 1980s, were decidedly old-fashioned—'my prime's estate', 'riven from me', 'these brief lines my lucky debt declare'. Formally, the dedicatory poem is a sonnet, for what that's still worth, and we do not recognize a successor to Shakespeare or Milton, nor a rival to John Berryman among contemporary sonneteers. The 'dream daughter' may be the child of childless years, but also 'of such a surrogate / of her too, hearthstone'. Agency, in this family romance, is identified as 'witless fate' or 'chance'.

A poem such as 'At the Newsagents'' (written 7 February 1981, but evidently revised or extended later) can be taken to exemplify the ugly classification. It unquestionably responds to day-to-day violence, dealing with the shooting dead of a reserve policeman outside a shop, close to Stockman's Lane, on 6 February. Hewitt regularly bought pipe tobacco in the same shop. The text consists of two numbered sections, the first made up of six four-line 'clusters', the second of three clusters unequal in length. The poem has been considered as free verse by some; certainly the second portion pays no regard to regular line length or stanza formation. The diction is plain, offering no aesthetic consolation in the face of a man's summary execution in broad daylight on the public street:

One of the bullets cut a hole
in the upper panel
of the glass and metal door
which had closed behind him.

This is meticulous, unostentatious and unyielding, sticking to the ugly facts without emotive elaboration. Two further clusters ('stanza' is not quite right) modify the perspective without altering the tone:

And every time
I pushed open that door,
though the shattered glass
has since been replaced,

I think fleetingly
of the bullet hole;
this, I suppose, might be considered
'an objective correlative'.

And so the first section ends, leaving the stranded reader uncertain about the implications of the poet's thinking of the bullet hole, not the dead fellow shopper.

Dropping T. S. Eliot's theoretical pearl into quote marks achieves a closing line which questions the value of poetry amid casual slaughter.

The second section moves rapidly to shift the weight of this uncertainty. It reads in its entirety:

> Colleagues of the murderer
> or murderers—I do not know
> how many guns were then fired—
> captured, sentenced, imprisoned, insisted
> that they were 'political prisoners';
> and to assert the status they claimed
> neither washed, shaved, nor cut their hair;
> they wore no clothes except a blanket,
> and smeared their cell walls with their shit.
> This exercise was known as 'On the Blanket'
> Or 'The Dirty Protest'.
>
> Some months later
> ten of the younger prisoners
> starved themselves to death
> to sustain the protest.
>
> None of these happenings,
> widely communicated through
> the popular media,
> even flickers, however faintly,
> among the reflecting grimaces
> in that glass door.[17]

An attempt at close reading may lead to other observations. Significant yet ordinary words are repeated. The following occur twice—*newsagents'*... *hole*... *murderer/s*... *prisoners*... *blanket*; the words *bullet/s*... *glass*... *door* three times. These are the nodal points from which the poem is suspended in its uncanny stillness. The node in geometry is a double or multiple point, and one can trace a series of doublings or merging in the poem. For example, *newsagents'* relates first to the policeman, then to the poet; the repetition *murderer/s* in the singular and then plural may emotively heighten the phrase, but the immediately preceding *Colleagues* has anticipated and negated the effect. (*Colleagues*, indeed, is worthy of Swift.) In the last line *glass* and *door* come together, re-establishing the crime scene which had been displaced by the cool journalese of section two. In its eschewal of ornament whether of diction or form (no wreaths, no rhyme), its acceptance of the prosaic, this is an ugly piece of work.

It is also a devious piece of work. If we look outside the poem and inside the prison, the dirty protest had begun in 1976 and had no originating link to the events of February 1981. It is true, however, that the first of the hunger strikers to die (Bobby Sands) died in May 1981, to be followed slowly by the next and the next, a programme carefully orchestrated by the republican leadership. Hewitt's

[17] Ormsby, pp. 357–9.

reference to ten prisoners starving themselves to death dates the poem's completion to no earlier than late August, that is, over a period of seven months. Balance, it might be argued, would require a twin poem dealing with violent mistreatment of prisoners or internees by the authorities, or with Bloody Sunday (thirteen shot dead by the Paratroop Regiment), or with the covert policy of shoot to kill.

Perhaps the poem which follows in *Loose Ends*—'The Bombed Public House'—may provide balance of a kind, in that it recalls Hewitt's taking Brendan Behan for a pint which the republican future playwright could not afford. (That was back in 1951.) More cogently, however, both poems conclude with images involving mirrors or other reflecting surfaces. These are moments of irresolution, admissions of not knowing. In 'At the Newsagents", the final cluster of lines suggests that the dirty protest and the hunger-strike deaths are elided, not by the poet or not only by him, but by the grim bustle of morning trade—'None of these happenings... / even flickers, however faintly, / among the reflecting grimaces/in that glass door.' As for the Crown Bar (damaged by a kickback from bombs across the street), conversations with Behan and, much later, the Russian poet Yevgeny Yevtushenko:

> When this interior is restored, re-covered
> with fashionable surfaces and textures,
> will any mirror echo such reflections
> or cushioned corner's covers bounce them back?[18]

The cosy alliteration hints that only a too-easy reconstruction of the past may be possible, a simulacrum of locations and incidents beyond recovery, this in keeping with the fleeting effect of any revisiting of the newsagents' glass door.

The good poems are not always easier to fathom, and some of them have their ugly side, for example 'The Splendid Dawn'. Perhaps Jack Lynch's quotation in 1971 gave 'The Colony' an extra-literary boost, yet it should be recalled how the few acute reviewers of the *Collected Poems* (1968) had singled it out for close attention. Here, let us examine a short poem of the same period, 'The Ram's Horn', written in the summer of 1949, published by *The New Statesman* the following May, and much anthologized:

> I have turned to the landscape because men disappoint me:
> the trunk of a tree is proud; when the woodmen fell it,
> it still has a contained ionic solemnity:
> it is a rounded event without the need to tell it.
>
> I have never been compelled to turn away from the dawn
> because it carries treason behind its wakened face;
> even the horned ram, glowering over the bog hole,
> though symbol of evil, will step through the blown grass
> with grace.
>
> Animal, plant, or insect, stone or water,
> are, every minute, themselves; they behave by law.
> I am not required to discover motives for them,
> or strip my heart to forgive the rat in the straw.

[18] Ormsby, p. 359.

I live my best in the landscape, being at ease there;
the only trouble I find I have brought in my hand.
See, I let it fall with a rustle of stems in the nettles,
and never for a moment suppose that they understand.

If this is nature poetry in some English Romantic tradition, then it has pushed Wordsworth out of sight, though not entirely out of mind. The poem is often cited because its opening line is read as a manifesto, albeit in the present perfect tense. Yet the first and last stanzas refer to the landscape, rather than to nature. Landscape is not wholly distinct from the human realm, for landscape has been shaped or (at least) conceived and perceived by a human presence. (Here the influence not only of Scottish Geddes and an English 'back to the land' movement can be noted but, more locally, that of the Welshman Estyn Evans.) The intervening stanzas employ negative constructions—'never been compelled... not required'—to establish what relations there are between these realms. Hewitt's terms are his own. The dawn carries no treasonable/treacherous intent as (by implication) some men do or did. Under its light, the horned ram *will* move with grace, a solitary instance in the poem of a future tense. The animal is recognized as a symbol of evil, yet it is capable of grace or graceful movement. It is not evil.

Nevertheless, 'the horned ram, glowering over the bog hole' remains a powerful image, announced in the poem's title. How can it be a symbol of evil capable of grace? We need recourse to a standard appropriated by Ulster Protestant thought and feeling, though one infrequently associated with Hewitt—the Bible. Extremes of that constituency, including Dr Ian Paisley, whom Hewitt identified in 1968 as a destructive foe, were fond of the prophetic books, not just for their supposed Messianic trailblazing but for models of catastrophe. Take the eighth chapter of Daniel, verses three and four:

> Then I lifted up mine eyes, and saw, and, behold, there stood before the river a ram which had two horns: and the two were high; but one was higher than the other, and the higher came up last. I saw the ram pushing westward, and northward, and southward; so that no beasts might stand before him, neither was there any that could deliver out of his hand; but he did according to his will, and became great.

The bestiary is extended by the arrival of a he-goat, and complicated by arcane discussion of sacrifice and sanctuary. But in verses 19–20, the archangel Gabriel provides a reading or interpretation for Daniel's enlightenment—'The ram which thou saw having two horns are the kings of Media and Persia. And the rough goat is the king of Grecia'.

Hewitt is not engaging in apocalyptic speculation; on the contrary, he works against it. If the ram at the bog hole was observed one damp Saturday Antrim afternoon as a (relatively) natural phenomenon, it was yet possible to recall the biblical image, and to do so conscious of the unparalleled evil disclosed in a few preceding years—the bombing of Dresden, the extermination camps, Hiroshima. Intelligent people, who had pooh-poohed the objective existence of Evil, including the philosopher Stuart Hampshire, thought again when confronted by Kaltenbrunner or Mengele. In one realm, that of an inherited religion, the ram is a symbol of evil and rampant aggression; in another, that of casual mountain farming, he will move with grace or at least natural ease. The trouble in the poem, the unease which shifts from the ionic tree to the rat in the straw, but also from evil to nettles, relates to the double realm of the human, involving both thought and sensation, mind and body. From these materials, it is difficult to imagine—let alone create—a Utopia, and even more difficult to make a socialist one.

In 1948, Hewitt had naturally given a copy of *No Rebel Word* to Roberta (co-dedicatee, with his mother), adding a 14-line poem (not a sonnet) which remained unpublished until 1991.[19] I count it among the good, not for technical excellence or intellectual depth, but for its dedication to the problem of reticence, or reserved expression. The—'For Busha'—makes use of a family pet name, more intimate than Ruby. The first six lines read:

> This is your own who patiently
> stood by my side as time limped by,
> and when I swithered in and out
> through streams of hope and bogs of doubt,
> watching the long tedious vigil wear
> from month to month to month and year to year
> till faith became a token of
> the perfect craftsmanship of love.

Bearing in mind the prolonged gestation of *No Rebel Word*, the reader of these lines will take lines 5–6 as a reference to the 'tedious vigil' from early 1946 (if not even earlier) to late 1948 (see Chapter 1). The concluding lines instance the ordinary and mainly natural phenomena through which he and she had passed, less bogs of doubt than 'the song, the leaf, the lake, the stone' etc. Then line 12 ends with an ellipsis (…), signalling non-verbally a species of non-ending. Then the poem itself ends:

> Of vanished moments this endures,
> I cannot give what's also yours.

Here, I suggest, is a brave if utterly private attempt to divulge the burden of reticence which plays reservoir for the very utterance the poem is—or *No Rebel Word* is. Inevitably, perhaps, the book's title is recalled for the adjective (rebel) so potent in twentieth-century Irish vocabularies. Hewitt's reticence (or, as I prefer, *reserve*) is paradoxically central to the alienation, loneliness, critique of identity, sturdy independence his readers have noted. Perhaps the author of the 1948 collection was a reserved rebel, awaiting historical circumstances which, like earlier moments, disappointed in their time.

'An Irishman in Coventry' (written mid-1957, published in *The New Statesman* in 1958) was much anthologized, starting with *The Guinness Book of Poetry 1958–59* (London, 1960). In theme it is closer to the received characterization of Hewitt, as a figure inevitably displaced yet preoccupied with the minutiae of his surroundings (past and present). Speaking of this characterization, we might note in passing

[19] See Ormsby, p. 435.

how difficult it has proved to associate his work with any movement in Anglophone literature. He was little if at all affected by the Imagism of the Great War years: the tough nuts of that phenomenon (Doolittle, Flint, Hulme, Pound etc.) were never part of his diet, despite their camaraderie with minor Irish writers such as Desmond FitzGerald and (less minor) the Ulsterman Joseph Campbell. The Georgians, a looser federation pre-dating and outliving Imagists, included Gordon Bottomley (1874–1948) who shared with Hewitt a respect for William Morris as writer and thinker, and shared with Hewitt a passion for collecting pictures. Austin Clarke also respected Bottomley—but none of this helps to assign 'An Irishman in Coventry'. Yet it remains in the good category for many readers who do not insist on measuring every writer against the sticking-post of Auden, Eliot, Carlos Williams, or Yeats.

Two further poems deserve consideration under the same heading, 'A Little People' (June 1986), and 'The Mortal Place (August 1986)', written just a year before he died.[20] The first belongs to the group headed by 'The Colony' and including 'An Irishman in Coventry', and constitutes the poet's final thoughts on the mesh of themes—history, identity, place—which gather very individual poems under a common heading. Its title is an obvious nod (hardly respectful) towards Yeats and his celebration of the Anglo-Irish in 1925—

> We against whom you have done this thing, are no petty people. We are one of the great stocks of Europe. We are the people of Burke; we are the people of Grattan; we are the people of Swift, the people of Emmet, the people of Parnell. We have created the most of the modern literature of this country. We have created the best of its political intelligence.[21]

The political and ideological context in which Yeats uttered these words was far from transparent. The great national poet whose work had sent forth 'certain men the English shot' in 1916 had more recently been in cahoots with the southern Unionists and, in June 1925, was involved in plans (never finalized) to establish a National Unionist Party, along somewhat fascist (reactionary, without question) lines. Among Yeats's boasts about the 'great stock' he came from was a confident prediction aimed at the Catholic majority:

> I shall be able to find out, if not I, my children will be able to find out whether we have lost our stamina or not. You have defined our position and have given us a popular following. If we have not lost our stamina then your victory will be brief, and your defeat final.

Stamina here is a eugenic term, part of Yeats's cult of selective breeding as it will develop in the 1930s. 'A Little People' is Hewitt's response sixty years later:

> we've hugged our sod for nigh four hundred years
> since the last ripples of migration placed
> our grip upon this soil that once was theirs.

[20] Fair copies of the two poems, in Hewitt's handwriting, are preserved in the Linen Hall Library, differing from the published texts only in small matters of punctuation.

[21] *Seanad Eireann Debates*, 5, 11 June 1925, col 443.

As with Yeats, the history evoked in these lines is not unchallengeable: migration cannot adequately cover invasive armies, though it may properly name the process by which camp-followers and tradesmen arrived, some of them after the battles were decided. But migration does not of itself place the *grip* of these humble newcomers on the land. In 'A Little People' Hewitt advances a more open, vulnerable argument, concedes attachment to and decline of the 'empire-Commonwealth'. As with Yeats at the opening of 'Nineteen Hundred and Nineteen', Hewitt looks back to an earlier, deceptively secure phase and cites a notion (mastery) dear to the older man:

> Those happier decades we were dominant,
> but now that mastery has flaked away,
> those trades and crafts which fed us have grown scant.[22]

The resolution of 'A Little People' is remote from Yeats and his delight in conflict; it commends and longs for friendship between once violent neighbours, but does not indulge the longing under the banner of hope.

'The Mortal Place' was printed immediately before 'A Little People' in the winter 1986/87 issue of *Threshold*. In pervasive loyalty to its title, the poem attends to place, and particular street names in Belfast, whereas 'A Little People' dealt with history and affiliations. The poet's infancy is recalled, his first recorded words—'ship, boat, water'. For the infant in (say) 1909, these are emblems of the city's industrial wealth and strength, its association with naval power. For the octogenarian, they doubly signify the agencies of departure and return, rejection and dissent. More than the poet's life is reviewed; two nostalgic poems about his childhood, 'My First Recorded Words' and 'The River Streets'—both already published in *Kites in Spring: a Belfast Boyhood* (1980)—are condensed into grimmer images of the modern city. Murders or executions are summarized in a line or two—'a Catholic shot by gunmen never named'. 'The Mortal Place' consists of four clusters of lines, apparently unrhymed. The fourth, however, diverges from the loco-descriptive pace and pattern of the earlier three, to offer something like an analysis which then turns quizzical:

> Now just last week a taximan who lived
> in Manor Street was gunned remorselessly,
> and in between the streets,
> Roe Street and Avonbeg, a wall's being raised
> to hold the tribes apart. For in recent years
> there's been a drift of folk from distant places
> for kinships, friendships, comfort, security;
> to paraphrase those words of Baudelaire,
> a town's more mortal than a people's fears.

The rhyme of years/fears lends a tone of resolution which seems remote from an invocation of Baudelaire after a list of violent casualties. The taxi man may be identified with Paddy McAllister, who was shot in his home by the Ulster Freedom

[22] For the entire poem, see Ormsby, pp. 539–41.

Fighters on 26 August 1986 while watching television. An obstacle to this identification arises with Mr McAllister's address—not Manor Street, but Rodney Drive off the Donegall Road in West Belfast.[23] Has Hewitt transferred an actual sectarian killing into the terrain familiar to him since childhood? Or had the taxi man previously lived in Manor Street, a fact known to the poet but unreported in any newspaper? We might equally ask how Hewitt introduces a nineteenth-century French poet into a distinctly local and immediate scenario.

Baudelaire (1821–67), however, saw the contemporary metropolis as a flimsy and distracting veil drawn over an underlying archaic reality. The modern city is a labyrinth of arcades within which the correlative of the ancient Minotaur remains voracious. The island of Cythera is, for Baudelaire, 'a banal El Dorado'. These images, savage and resonant, could in the right hands become amenable to Irish appropriation. Hewitt's rather jaunty penultimate line in 'The Mortal Place' does not encourage the view that his are the right ones—Thomas Kinsella might be the better bet. Nevertheless, the French poem behind the allusion is certainly apt to the condition of Belfast in 1986 and the situation the ageing poet found himself.

'Le Cynge' (The Swan) was published in the *Tableaux Parisiens* (1861) and dedicated to Victor Hugo, then exiled in Brussels finishing *Les Miserables.* During his months in Belgium, he visited the battlefield at Waterloo, which uniformed French soldiers were forbidden to visit. The poem is address to Andromache, widow of the Trojan warrior, Hector. These details alone indicate a motorway pile-up of defeats and incidental betrayals—the Trojan and Napoleonic wars, the lesser French upheavals of 1848 and 1851, the physical reconfiguration of Paris and its streets by Haussmann from 1853 onwards partly at least to facilitate military operations against rioters and protesters. Baudelaire's poem takes its title from a swan which he imagines escaped from its cage near the Louvre art gallery, an image of the primary Greek god (cf. Leda and the Swan), the emblem of fidelity and death-inspired song, lost in the wreckage of a city. Baudelaire's *correspondances* of the contemporary and the archaic city, the ruined city and the planner's blueprint have an a priori applicability to Hewitt's native place as he found it in retirement, within a year of the medical laboratory's grateful dissection of his body. It would overload speculation about 'The Mortal Place' to consider the second victim mentioned—'her only crime to marry outside her faith'[24]—as somehow echoing or corresponding with Homer's Helen, who eloped with Paris and was possibly the daughter of Leda and Zeus. Overloading, but not abusing, for if the Belfast woman's 'crime' was as described, it was by no means hers alone, in the Belfast 1986, or in South Africa

[23] McKittrick et al., *Lost Lives: the Stories of the Men, Women and Children Who Died as a Result of the Northern Ireland Troubles* (Edinburgh: Mainsteam, 2004), p. 1047.

[24] This was probably Margaret Caulfield, killed 7 May 1986 in her bedroom in Ballysillan by the UDA because she (a Protestant) had married a Catholic (who was seriously injured in the incident.) See McKittrick et al., *Lost Lives: the Stories of the Men, Women and Children Who Died as a Result of the Northern Ireland Troubles*, pp. 1036–7. It seems very probable that the individuals noted by Hewitt were all killed by loyalists, though it seems equally likely that none of them lived in the area so clearly delineated as the poet's childhood beat. There is, then, an undeclared Aesopian politics in commemorating victims of Protestant sectarianism, drawing them into a mortal place, in part fiction and in part bitter recollection of a happier past.

under apartheid, among fundamentalist Muslims, or in the older homes of racial and fideist intolerance.

The problem with Hewitt's reference to Baudelaire is not one of relevance but of political aesthetics. For a start, the two lines inscribed at the head of this chapter are not easily rendered into a convincing English verse idiom. Robert Lowell, always willing to risk a deliberate error in the name of a higher cause, has:

> Old Paris is done for. (Our cities find
> new faces sooner than the heart.)[25]

This downplays the strong implication that an old Paris is replaced by a new megapolis faster than mortal (a key term omitted in the translation) change of heart which, by a subdued implication, is lethally slow. Rather than find this evidence of man's fallen condition, and so endorse claims that Hewitt was, somehow, a Calvinist, we should remember the balanced discussion of evil in 'The Ram's Horn'.

'The Mortal Place' comes too late in his career to solve the problem, though it certainly casts an interrogatory shadow over the calm yet uncomfortable final lines of 'A Little People'—the dialectic can be at times dyspeptic. The colossal interest in Baudelaire among twentieth-century writers and thinkers—most strikingly those associated with the School of Social Research in pre-war Frankfurt—evoked little response in Ireland. For balance, one might note Michael McLaverty's life-long dedication to the fiction of Thomas Mann and, in later generations of Ulster writers than that of Hewitt and McLaverty, John Montague's and Derek Mahon's translations of French drama and poetry from Molière to Claude Esteban.

In retirement Hewitt the gallery-man tended to be eclipsed by Hewitt the poet. His publications in art history had been numerous but small-scale, beginning with notes in the Belfast Museum and Gallery's *Quarterly Notes*, but expanding with time into the reviewing of exhibitions and writing forewords to catalogues. The forewords were often short monographs. By its nature and mode of production, this work served an educational purpose, informing the public of what was significant in (usually) contemporary painting, and directing them into appreciation and criticism.

Art in Ulster (2 vols, 1977) made considerable advances in the treatment of Irish painting and sculpture. Hewitt wrote the first volume, covering 400 years from 1557 to 1957 or, crudely measured, from the coming of the Reformation to his own departure for Coventry. His interest in the very early period is not great. He reaches his preferred material in the late eighteenth century, deals with the British Association of the 1830s, the art schools which spring up in the mid-Victorian period, and the development of commercial patronage in Belfast, notably by the firm of Marcus Ward after which a street is named. Echoing Conor Cruise O'Brien on the Irish dilemma generally, Hewitt defines an Ulster artist, not by birth or blood or accent but through 'the condition of being involved in Ulster life and

[25] Robert Lowell, *Imitations* (London: Faber, 1962), p. 57. JH's library at UU includes copies of two collections by Lowell, both signed by the author for JH: *For the Union Dead* (London: Faber, 1965) and *Poems 1938–1949* (London: Faber, 1960).

Irish landscape, and finding therein the material for his art'.[26] In this way, seventeenth-century planters and twentieth-century refugees such as Paul Nietsche and Zoltan Frankl are accommodated side by side with Daniel O'Neill and other bearers of Gaelic names. Illustrations include numerous paintings on which Hewitt had pronounced informally—Lavery's portrait of Cardinal Logue, for example; and, predictably, the work of John Luke. There was an inevitable valedictory undertone—writer and artist friends were dying off, most notably Bertie Rodgers in 1969, Austin Clarke in 1974, and Luke the following year.[27]

Though the second volume was written by Mike Catto, the material covered owes much to Hewitt's activities before 1957, and indeed after. For example, the summary list of T. P. Flanagan's exhibitions (and his collaborations with Seamus Heaney) is indirectly a tribute to Hewitt's nurture of the young, orphaned painter and to his desire for a practical engagement between the verbal and the visual arts. Catto's fourth chapter 'Notes from a Small War: Art and the Troubles' takes the narrative into a realm where Hewitt had no wish to function. *Art in Ulster 1* was to be his final substantive publication, joining *No Rebel Word* and *Collected Poems 1932–67*. There would be further discrete forays into the world of poetry, fiction, and criticism.

[26] John Hewitt, *Art in Ulster I* (Belfast: Blackstaff, 1977), p. 146.
[27] Seamus Treacy reviewed *Art in Ulster* in *The Irish Democrat* for October 1979.

Break for Text IV

Daybreak; or, I Solve the Irish Problem

Answer: A collideoscape!
James Joyce, 1939

Among Hewitt's late papers is an undated typescript (with some alterations) oddly titled, 'I Solve the Irish Problem'. Any hint of pride is immediately dispelled—'I had a dream. I solved the Irish problem. But I must not claim any credit personally since the solution was borne in on me by a succession of Irish patriots who appeared before me.' Use of the term 'patriot' in the 1970s was, in many eyes, monopolized by those least qualified to distribute it as a reward; or, it was an old-fashioned term, reserved for the long dead. Care, therefore, should be taken when interpreting Hewitt's meaning. As if to emphasize the point, the narrator admits that he did not recognize the first apparition until he 'solemnly uttered these words: ESSE EST PERCEPI'. Finally identifying the eighteenth-century philosopher George Berkeley (1685–1753), he proceeds to account for the succession of advisers, employing a species of golf-club idiom—'it dawned on me... none other than... all very interesting... that's really bad...' It would be rash to conclude that the narrator is Hewitt in any simple sense.

He and Berkeley click when the bishop wittily observes, 'indubitably you see me, therefore I exist' and announces that all the succeeding figures in the dream are Irish Protestants, 'though sadly I must qualify this statement: while they all come of good Protestant stock two of them switched to Rome... as a consequence they hav'nt joined us in Heaven: they are in Purgatory'. The full list of apparitions is:

George Berkeley (1685–1753)
Jonathan Swift (1667–1745)
Henry Grattan (1746–1820)
Theobald Wolfe Tone (1763–98) and Edward FitzGerald (1763–98)—appearing together
Robert Emmet (1778–1803)
Isaac Butt (1813–79)
Thomas Davis (1814–45)
John Mitchell [*sic*] (1815–75)
James Stephens (1825–1901)
C. S. Parnell (1846–91)
Edward Carson (1854–1935)

Horace Plunkett (1854–1932)
Douglas Hyde (1860–1949)
Roger Casement (1864–1916)
W. B. Yeats (1865–1939)
Robert Erskine Childers (1870–1922)
Countess Markievicz (1868–1927) and Maude [*sic*] Gonne (1865–1953)—appearing together

Towards the close of 'I Solve the Irish Problem', the narrator remarks 'Sixteen Irish patriots appeared before me, all Protestants... four of them met an untimely end.' These numbers would need adjustment if historical veracity were the objective: the list contained eighteen names, and five of those named died violent deaths.[1] The verbal exchanges between the dreamer and the apparition are, in most of these cases, unremarkable, leaving aside words of advice to be noted in due course.

Some inclusions and exclusions deserve comment. Carson, whom Hewitt heartily disliked (though he attended the funeral), earns his place by virtue of having a strikingly distinctive notion of Irish patriotism, based on attachment to Britain. Plunkett represents the other side of the paradox, a practical leader of the Irish Cooperative Movement whose other leader was G. W. Russell, publisher of Hewitt's first printed poem. Plunkett, though born in England and educated at Eton and Oxford, was a member of the Norman-Irish aristocratic Dunsany line. The inclusion of Stephens, if it was grounded in supposed Protestantism in childhood, was mistaken: the Kilkenny-born founder of Fenianism may have been confused in Hewitt's mind with the poet James Stephens (1880–1950), raised a pauper Protestant. Only two Ulster-born individuals feature—Butt (Donegal) and Mitchel (Londonderry), whereas Henry Joy McCracken and Jemmy Hope among United Irishmen had earned Hewitt's extended celebration. Among other northern likely names one might mention Russell and Bulmer Hobson (1883–1969). No visual artists feature.

The advice given by the apparitions, intended to advance the possibility of a United Ireland, varied considerably. Swift observed 'I was right to blame the English Government for much of Ireland's ills in my time but it would be very wrong of me to do so now. Please pass on that message on to the foolish Brits-out-agitators.' Grattan said 'My message to you is that if you must have two separate governments let there be more thought for the religious minority in each [state,] and the first step forward in solving the Northern Ireland problem will be reasonable power sharing.' Pressed to explain how the United Irishmen's ideals might be renewed, Fitzgerald and Tone chorused 'Join the Alliance Party'. Stephens made a lengthy speech, citing the Diet of Speyer (1529) and denouncing Provos and Stickies as unworthy of the Fenian legacy.[2] Casement regretted that he could find no helpful advice to offer. Markievicz and Gonne recited their activities,

[1] The five are Tone (self-inflicted), Fitzgerald, Emmet, Casement, and Childers.

[2] 'Stickies' was a nickname given to the left-wing Official IRA, when the Provisional IRA was set up in January 1970.

nothing more. Childers spoke against harbouring bitterness. The apparitions fade away, and the narrator recovers consciousness. 'When is it ever going to end?... The only way we will ever break the Republican and Loyalist shells of ignorance and terrorism is for all history in the Catholic schools to be taught by Orangemen and all history in the Protestant schools to be taught by Republicans for at least a generation.'

None of this advice could be classified under a socialist heading. The Alliance Party (founded in April 1970), governmental power-sharing, and a modest degree of integrated education amounted to a liberal agenda of no great ambition.[3] Furthermore, the document omits all reference to nationalism and regionalism, one a bugbear and the other a panacea in Hewitt's thinking for much of the mid-century. As an implicit critique of Northern Ireland's politics in the very early 1980s, the implied programme stands well off from *An Ulster Reckoning* (1970) with its sharp delineation of living individuals, not historical icons. Certainly, no rebel word could be detected in the distant utopian solution hinted at.

Another of Hewitt's most intriguing late publications is a short story appearing in the Autumn/Winter 1980 issue of *Threshold* of which he was guest editor; that is almost six years before publication of the two poems just examined in Chapter 10. Editorial modesty may have prompted him to revive the pseudonym, Richard Telford, last used in *The Irish Democrat* of 1937. This, though his last published fiction, was by no means his last word. His reputation and his new audience ensured that Blackstaff Press was happy to publish further collections of poems—*Mosaic* (1981), *Loose Ends* (1983), *Freehold and Other Poems* (1986), together with the revised version of *The Day of the Corncrake* (1984; 1st ed. 1969).

Hewitt was unused to this ready access to public print, and his substantial output included a few poems which, in the astringent past, he might have left among the insatiable notebooks. As several subtitles among the rapidly published volumes indicate, a high degree of retrospection was at work, either in the form of reminiscence ('a Belfast Boyhood') or in the (re-)publication of earlier material. The most significant instance of the latter comes with *Freehold and Other Poems*, where the title piece (originally published in *Lagan*, 1946) frames some newer material, with 'The Bloody Brae' (written 1936) closing the frame. In relation to the story 'Daybreak', now to be examined, one should note how Richard/Robert Telford Hewitt is once again celebrated in the second section of 'Freehold'. The poet's last collection gathers in and reissues the longest of his filial tributes. Against what outsiders might think the unchallengeable evidence—the devotion of his

[3] There is no evidence that JH joined, or more loosely affiliated with, the Alliance Party, apart from a few of its leaflets preserved (with others issued by the Northern Ireland Labour Party) in UU, Hewitt, Box 20. In 1984, the *Irish Times* published an angry letter from Ms D. A. Freer (of Belfast) castigating the editor for his 'green miasma (very slightly tinged with the palest of pale pinks)'. Her few positive comments were reserved for the Alliance Party, and she concluded 'I have written with great passion... I make no apology for I am writing of what our Ulster poet, John Hewitt, once defined as the task of true democracy, the keeping of the people "in good heart".' *Irish Times*, 11 August 1984, p. 17. Ms Freer misquotes JH who, in 'Neither an Elegy nor a Manifesto' had written 'Patriotism has to do with keeping / the country in good heart...' The poem first appeared in the June 1972 issue of *Alliance; the Newspaper of the Alliance Party of Northern Ireland.*

son, popularity as a teacher, long commitment to colleagues through the Irish National Teachers' Organisation, and some public impact as a broadcaster and writer—Hewitt Senior is fondly commemorated both as 'the lonely heart', and 'the greatest man of all the men I love', in a reprise of lines published forty years earlier, a year after the old man's death. Loneliness and love are scarifying namesakes, even with the passage of decades.

In mitigation, Hewitt's long-practised awareness of slow time offers pointers towards understanding. The poles we find slow time slung between are several—eternity and human life, history and the present, various histories ranging from the tundra to the rantings of Paisley and the booming Provisionals or, more compactly, from the Celtic saints to the 'planters'. Landscape is its name and its pseudonym, identity, and cunning alibi. Every 'now' requires more than one 'here', otherwise we have nothing but the unrelated self. Edwin Muir's *Variations on a Time Theme* (1934) suggests affinities; perhaps even constitutes an influence.[4] Muir's Orkney, isolated physically and all-but monolithic in its religious culture, stood in extreme contrast to Hewitt's birthplace, industrialized and divided along sectarian fault lines. Hewitt's socialism was always a heroic-desperate mediation between a community (Catholic, Protestant, English, Irish) he could never quite join and an individualism he despised (or feared). He remained concerned about European politics and, shortly before his death, discussed Antonio Gramsci and the prospects for socialism in Italy.[5]

What if the determinants (e.g. 'witless fate' or 'lucky debt') had not applied, or could be suspended, or were never more than fantasies? 'Daybreak', the last short story which Hewitt published, toys with this possibility to deliver a happy, if humdrum ending for the narrator. Though duly listed in Tom Clyde's bibliography of the prose, it is only one of Hewitt's fictions to have evaded critical notice. *Threshold* No. 31 allowed him to play several roles between (or under) one set of covers. He was the guest editor, supplying a prose editorial; with 'Variations on a Theme' he was also a contributing poet; and, in some oblique or inverted manner, he was Richard Telford, author of 'Daybreak', courtesy of the self-same guest editor who modestly acknowledged the assistance of John Boyd and Diane Hyde.

The first-person narrator remains nameless, almost to the end of the story. He is however just once or twice addressed as 'Andy' by the central figure whose own name is first given as G. V. King. The narrator is a shop-keeper, who prospers to the point where he runs a network of Transprovincial Stores. At the time of the action, Andy had a small business in a West of Ireland town, holding on to it 'until the setting up of the two Governments in Ireland, after which he concentrated on the branches established in the North'. In the lives of John Hewitt and Robert Telford Hewitt, a shopkeeper called Andy [Millar] married Peggy Black.[6]

4 Republished in Edwin Muir, *Collected Poems* (London: Faber, 1963), pp. 37–53.

5 John Boyd, *The Middle of My Journey* (Belfast: Blackstaff, 1990), p. 199.

6 The sliding of personal names from one 'referent' to another—in this case from Andy Millar to a Hewitt-narrator—is not entirely without parallel in the Belfast circle. The sculptor George McCann published several short stories; in 'Journey to China', the first-person narrator refers to his wife as Sophie, adding that this is 'not her right name'. McCann's wife was Mercy, not a name easily used in

The association of biographical datum and fictional detail may seem strained, and worse is to come. The central character is gradually named as George Valentine King, a painter successful in youth, born near Ballymena in County Antrim, and 'about my own age' (the narrator discloses.) The two become friends in the little western town, to which G. V. (as Andy prefers to call him) has retired early with his Hungarian wife. In the kaleidoscope, G.V. might look like a king's name (George the Fifth), and indeed G. V.'s surname is King. On the other side of the kaleidoscope, Andy's (not G.V.'s) wife is named Mary. On the assumption, reasonable but as yet unproven, that the widower Hewitt read his late wife's journal and noted the anguish of 1953 at the time of Old Queen Mary's death, the story 'Daybreak' can be read as fictional or fantastic autobiography, thriving without determinants. Read in this light, its conclusion is that life as one's own father might have been preferable to an enforced self-hood, painting might have given a greater degree of companionship than writing. The realization of unavoidable necessity is a kind of freedom. Is this the only utopia available to the disillusioned man of the left?[7]

*

Freehold and Other Poems was Hewitt's last collection, published in 1986. Though it shares the now established practice of recycling material from the past, it displays a greater sense of organization than preceding volumes. The title poem may partner *Conacre* (1943) in that both terms relate to modes of holding land, but 'Freehold' (first published complete in *Lagan*, 1946) relies on a notion of freedom which is challenged in the even older piece which closes the volume. 'The Bloody Brae', with its prolonged emergence into print, deserved some prefatory lines which conclude with the essential relationship between John Hill and Bridget Magee 'for she was papist, he a protestant. / Four decades on, the heartbreak's relevant.' Whether in the Lyric Theatre or *Threshold* (both 1957), or in the Blackstaff collection (1986), relevance must seem a euphemism. Hewitt had little opportunity to reflect on intimate relations between the two versions (broadly defined) of Christianity practised (not to perfection) in Northern Ireland. In the Glens, he and Roberta mixed affably with their Catholic neighbours, exchanging hospitality and gifts, over two decades. When, in 1980, John Turnly was murdered (the tombstone reads 'assassinated') a few miles down the Antrim coast, the killers were his 'fellow Protestants'. In May 1986, Margaret Caulfield was murdered by her 'fellow Protestants'. (One thinks of Swift's bitter—indeed sectarian—jibe that any talk of

fiction, and in any case facticity was not the writer's primary objective; Sophie, however, was the name of Jim Stewart's wife. To complicate things Mercy Hunter had travelled to China in her youth. In a small way, these details suggest a peculiar difficulty in establishing a thoroughly fictive world from amidst the limited resources of a coterie where the Protestant suspicion of literary invention (creativity) exercised a continuing if mellowed influence. For a description of the McCann story, see R and B Rowan's *Catalogue 81* (2011), item 233.

[7] The conviction that 'the only person who never disappointed [John Hewitt] was his father and this relationship is beautifully explored in many poems', raises rather than dissolves the issue. Geraldine Watts adopts a more revealing perspective when she declares R. T. Hewitt as someone whom the poet could eventually 'see in himself'. G. Watts, 'Utility Clashes with Emotion', *Fortnight* (1989), Hewitt Supplement, p. v.

'Brother Protestants' reminds him the rat is 'our fellow creature'.) This latter killing in part prompted Hewitt to write 'The Mortal Place', though it came too late for inclusion in *Freehold and Other Poems*. It is a striking feature of 'The Mortal Place' that it contrives to ground the killings it notes in streets known to the poet from early childhood.

The book also contains 'Hesitant Memorial', the poet's gesture of commemoration towards Dorothy Roberts. In the title poem he goes back even further, to call up once again the spirit of his father. The second section 'The Lonely Heart' pays tribute to him—through him, 'I have understood / just how the meek, the merciful, the good / possess the kingdom...'. If this is the kingdom of God, it is an internal one, not of this world nor of any church. Between 'Freehold' and its parental tribute and 'The Bloody Brae' with its relentless interrogation of personal guilt, Margaret Caulfield and Dorothy Roberts are not the only human figures. Two poems, 'Tryst' and 'Age and Youth', venture beyond the exclusive zone of a mono-faith population. In the first, the speaker and a companion walking in an unfrequented lane come unexpectedly upon a couple 'standing face-to-face'. The scene might be 'minor Preraphaelite', except that the two are 'a handsome tall young priest and a young nun'. The incident, if actual incident there had been, belonged to the Hewitts' years at Cushendall, spent in a cottage owned by the local convent.

'Age and Youth' is less sweet. It might be classified among Hewitt's ugly pieces. The scene is a railway carriage which the speaker shares with two nuns. He inclines to think of them as 'circumscribed by edict of the Vatican', but then proceeds to note:

> Age drifting towards a death long overdue,
> Youth ebbing as all urge to live withdrew,
> while, paradoxically, the ancient one
> had slithered back to childhood's innocence
> with slack-held beads, there sagged, with no defence
> from time's brusque thrust, her faint companion.[8]

While the poem is only one of many which deal with the rough indignity of old age and hurrying death, it is remarkable in Hewitt's canon as a study of Catholic women—somewhat picturesque the merchants of unpleasant facts might imply, but complexly 'ugly' in the knotted syntax allowing a sighting of youth in the old, but not indulging it.

*

Hewitt maintained his judicious public interventions even in old age. In 1982, he supported the case brought by Jeff Dudgeon to the European Court of Human Rights seeking decriminalization of male homosexuality in Northern Ireland, when none of the established political parties would 'open their bakes'.[9] On May Day 1985, he formally inaugurated the Belfast Unemployed Resource Centre.

[8] Ormsby, p. 392.
[9] See Jeff Dudgeon in the *Belfast Telegraph*, 29 July 2011.

After the eclipse of the Northern Ireland Labour Party, as far back as 1971, and the split in Unionism which partly resulted from that collapse, Hewitt's politics had abjured party identification. When Paul Bew showed him one of the several jointly authored books which emerged from the non-nationalist Belfast Left, he observed, 'I always knew there was something wrong about James Connolly', whom he had celebrated in early poems.[10] Quite what Hewitt 'always knew' remains—as with many busy thoughtful and long-lived people—a challenge. A more painful admission had come in 1980 when, in an interview with a Dublin-based journal, he conceded that he had no evidence whatsoever to suggest that poetry had made any difference at all to the situation in Northern Ireland.[11] Had Auden been right all along?

John Hewitt died on 27 June 1987 in what the *Irish Times* described as 'his family home'. Deirdre Todhunter, a favourite niece, spoke of sudden death without any long or prevailing illness. Michael Longley lamented the passing of 'a father figure'. Ciaran McKeown, once a leader of the Peace People and by 1987 active in the Lyric Theatre management, shrewdly recognized someone who 'was able to risk non-conformity to his own tradition, without falling helplessly into another'. To thwart a ritual of conformity popular among all Irish traditions, Hewitt had expressly forbidden the holding of any funeral ceremony. His body was left to Queen's University for medical research.[12] The news reached Coventry. The stalwart of Herbert Gallery committees, Ian Hollick wrote to Keith Millar several times in July 1987, mourning 'a gentle, kind, gifted and wonderful man' adding, in the second letter, 'in a strange way it is a comfort to know of the last few days of John Hewitt... I'm glad that he was still enjoying life to the end'.[13]

The Lyric Theatre mounted a tribute to their late director on 5 July 1987, with three hundred people in attendance. Others found other ways around the prohibition, using the approaching eightieth birthday (28 October) for a variety of events, including the reshowing on BBC 1 of 'I Found Myself Alone', a documentary premiered in 1978. In a folding commemorative card, Tom Paulin described Hewitt as 'an internationalist who loved his native province'. Jimmy Simmons picked up the implications of a body given to science: 'Your work is alive and kicking / in our heads and hearts. / After a life of service / your body is spare parts.'

The Arts Council, which had been planning birthday celebrations long before Hewitt's death, sponsored an exhibition of paintings which he and Roberta had collected. Not everyone was bowled over. The critic Brian McAvera acknowledged a much-loved poet though not perhaps a very interesting art historian, going on to complain—'not an abstract in sight' among the pictures on show; instead he thought of himself on a gentle trawl through rural Ireland. This was, of course, a

[10] Personal communication from Paul Bew to the author.

[11] See Timothy Kearney, 'Beyond the Planter and the Gael: Interview with John Hewitt and John Montague on Northern Poetry and the Troubles', *Crane Bag* 4, no. 2 (1980–81), pp. 85–92.

[12] *Irish Times*, 30 June 1987, p. 5. See also Ciaran McKeown, 'John Hewitt; Appreciation', *Belfast News-Letter*, 29 June 1987, and 'John Hewitt, Committee Man', *Threshold* 38 (Winter 1986/87), pp. 42–3.

[13] Private collection, Ian Hollick to Keith Millar, 3 July and 14 July 1987.

borderline dispute, the border lying between contemporary art practice (video, installation, and enduring abstraction) and the well-established genres of landscape, street-scene, and the human figure. Nevertheless, McAvera noted the presence of three important pictures—David Bomberg's 'Self Portrait', L. S. Lowry's 'Cherry Ripe', and Stanley Spencer's 'Portrait of Daphne'—none of these artists being Irish.[14]

One week short of what would have been his eightieth birthday, a gathering took place in the Lagan Social Club, Friendly Street, Belfast, to honour 'John Hewitt Poet Socialist Dissenter', augmented with 'an appreciation by Seamus Heaney, published by the Belfast Workers' Festival Committee'.[15] It was, however, the younger Dublin-born poet Eavan Boland who synthesized the apparent contradictions in Hewitt's aesthetic. Eschewing the usual tribal name calling, she defined him as the voice and conscience of 'a fragmented culture', fragmentation being (as I understand her argument) a more terrifying and disorientating modern condition than the binary oppositions of Catholic and Protestant, Planter and Gael. His subjects were linked (but hardly in any supportive way); they were historical isolation and private loneliness. As an exacting stylist, she could proceed further in characterizing him as 'by no means an exciting technician'. His craft often was conservative and old-fashioned.[16] Yet, he had accepted James Simmons's verdict on *Out of My Time*—'lack of consistent style is Hewitt's style'—declaring this 'an estimate I do not dispute'.[17]

Northern poets were warmer but perhaps less critical—Derek Mahon is a mild exception. Seamus Heaney, Michael Longley (Edna's husband), and Mahon were all in their thirties, with Montague and Simmons standing behind them as elders of a decidedly youthful kind. Each and all had welcomed Hewitt, conscious that their own breakthrough into widely circulating publication had been much easier than his. His father-figure-hood was important for them, partly because the only alternative, Louis MacNeice, had died in 1963 when Northern Ireland seemed beyond change. MacNeice had moved through the gradations of English public school, Oxford, a spell in America, and the BBC's London circle. Hewitt's very different course provided a closer parenting for young poets brought up through the A-Level system (as Heaney has recorded) and Irish universities north or south.[18] And he had returned at a crucial moment, when inchoate fragmentation was swept up in the brush-and-pan of sectarian conflict.

14 'Hewitt Memorial Show in Belfast', *Irish Times*, 9 November 1987, p. 14. See also *A Poet's Pictures; a Selection of the Works of Art Collected by John Hewitt (1907–1987)* (Hillsborough: Shambles Art Gallery, 1987). The Hillsborough exhibition did not include work by Bomberg, Lowry, or Spencer, but non-Irish artists included Thomas Sturge Moore (English), Leonid Pasternak (Russian), and Peter Peri (Hungarian). These are not great names, but they disrupt the impression of unrelieved Ulster landscape and portraiture.

15 An invitation card is preserved among the Roy McFadden Papers in QUB.

16 *Irish Times*, 30 June 1987, p. 8.

17 See Poetry Society Bulletin, Christmas 1976.

18 See the first chapter of Michael Parker, *Seamus Heaney; the Making of a Poet* (Iowa City: University of Iowa Press, 1993) for an extensive investigation of this dimension to Heaney's progress. The 1947 Northern Ireland Education Act brought pupils such as Seamus Deane and Heaney into Catholic grammar schools which had previously little concern with the lower classes.

Frank Ormsby summarized Hewitt's problem as 'the tensions and paradoxes of a particular fragmented culture'.[19] No one would deny this. It may be helpful to look beyond the particular case, to the world beyond Northern Ireland. This considerable expanse should not be assumed unfragmented, culturally, socially, or economically. Northern Ireland was in several profound ways shaped by the Great War to which it contributed dearly. The much commented-upon silence of returned veterans, the shell-shocked, the amputees, the blind and halt from mustard-gas attacks was an immeasurable fracture into which were poured the consolations of religious solidarity (for some) and the phoney wholeness of ethnic nationalism (for others.)[20]

How do we find John Hewitt at the end of these biographical enquiries? Roy McFadden recalled a non-literary, chilling, and yet deeply humane exchange. 'Towards the end... he said to me, perhaps sentimentally, perhaps with the wisdom of hindsight: "Having children is best." And a little later, 'I said that once round was enough. He nodded.'[21] Evidence could be cited to prove that Hewitt's manner in personal exchanges was often abrupt, as on his first encounter with that 'practical friend', John Montague. Roberta's journal presents a man willingly absorbed in his business, whether Muse or Museum. A man who wrote millions of words in notebooks, letters, reports, magazines, and books had little time for small talk. Yet in the competitive forum of Cushendall, its pubs and farm kitchens, he was warmly received. He was also generous, assisting younger writers such as Robert Greacen and Derrick Birley, and supporting a succession of little magazines, *Rann, Lagan, Threshold.* His advocacy of John Luke's art sometimes outstripped his private judgement. His bequest to the Ulster Museum included five works by Basil Blackshaw, three by T. P. Flanagan, four by Mercy Hunter (wife of George McCann), seven by John Luke, three by W. J. McClughin, four by Colin Middleton, one by Paul Mosse, and one by Daniel O'Neill—all exhibited at Hillsborough.

Edmund Gosse's *Father and Son* (1907) sets up one extreme in these enquiries, with the assumed relations of the Hewitts, *père et fils*, bidding fair to occupy decent space at the other extreme exemplifying mutual support, concurrence in thought, interests, and values. But what if one were to question John Hewitt's relationship with Richard Telford Hewitt? There is no reason to suspect concealed emotions of the hostile kind nurtured by Louis MacNeice. Yet the very number of poems invoking the beloved father suggests an unresolved concern and recurrent failure ever to comprehend its full complexity. If not hostility, what? Guilt? Envy? A sense of superiority, unearned but undeniable?

[19] Ormsby, p. lxiii.

[20] Walter Benjamin's reflections on the Great War offer a broader perspective; see in particular 'Experience and Poverty', in Benjamin, *Selected Writings vol 2 1927–1934*, trans. Rodney Livingstone et al. (Cambridge Mass.: Belnap Press, 1999), pp. 731–6; and 'The Storyteller; Reflections on the Work of Nikolai Leskov', in Benjamin, *Illuminations*, edited with an introduction by Hannah Arendt; trans. Harry Zohn (London: Cape, 1970), pp. 83–109.

[21] 'A Poet Wholly Independent of Fashionable Expectations' (anonymous obituary for Roy McFadden), *Irish Times*, 25 September 1999, p. 18. The remark about having children is best echoes Sophocles, 'not to have lived is best'.

Freud basically regarded belief in God as the longing for a father untouched by Oedipal rivalry. Hewitt never quite resolved his attitude towards religion, except to deny the Ulster churches any claim on his allegiance or on his body-in-death. The sustained commemoration of his earthly father was disturbed only by R. T. Hewitt's lapse into mental incoherence in the months before he died in 1945, a god that failed rather than a God that Died. These uneasy exchanges had their political register in the 1930s, when pacifism and opposition to fascism overlapped in mutually compromising ways. The Hewitts were stalwarts of the Belfast Peace League, and Bishop MacNeice was an advocate of internationalist politics, the League of Nations, etc. But the Hewitts also supported the Republican cause in Spain, and John worked with the veteran Frank Ryan on *The Irish Democrat*. Domestically, the paper's politics certainly required the Rebel Word; even if the IRA had split on the issues of socialist and nationalist priorities.

Pursued with forensic zeal, these details could be arranged to resemble a duplicitous persona, one who played up to the Rebel Word and then abjured it, rather like the ghostly Home Ruler MacNeice Senior, but moving in the opposite direction. Any such arraignment would, however, depend on a simplistic notion of the self, and a grossly simplistic notion of how poetry relates to and derogates from the authorial self. The sonnet from 1941, beginning 'Among the many selves that throng my flesh...' should not be discarded. Nor the undated 'Sentences that begin with "I" imply / an absence...' The rival zealotries of Louis-MacNeicians and the British and Irish Communist Organisation amount to a zero sum, allowing for a more nuanced and less frantic assessment of a poet whose thought and practice (after an apprenticeship under the Great Depression) advised recognition of politics as a sustained and ever changing relationship between the non-political and the political. This seeming paradox can be explored in a reading of 'The Colony'.

On the question of his regionalism, Heather Clark has assembled evidence to persuade us that Hewitt did not succeed in convincing his literary successors. Seamus Heaney, though deeply appreciative of all that Hewitt's poetry had contributed to his own development, felt that the doctrine had failed to reconcile the two traditions; that it had been 'slightly Nelson-eyed...more capable of seeing over the water than over the border'. Derek Mahon, a long-term resident of Dublin, London, and then Kinsale, asked somewhat petulantly, 'Why couldn't his region be Ireland?' Paul Muldoon called 'The Colony' a powerful political poem, yet complained that its dialogism allowed Hewitt 'to say what would otherwise be unsaid, or unsayable'—for example, 'they breed like flies'.[22] Some of these observations are vulnerable to rebuke—after all, Hewitt knew southern Ireland well, at first hand, and at a time when it was no bed of roses (though, arguably, of rosaries.) Muldoon does not pause to consider if the challenge of 'The Colony' was not to confront the murmurers of anti-Catholic prejudice with the same words in cold print. Clark is surely right to conclude that 'ultimately, regionalism could not accommodate the

[22] Heather Clark, *The Ulster Renaissance: Poetry in Belfast 1962–1972* (Oxford: Oxford University Press, 2006), pp. 126–7. The remark attributed to Mahon was never uttered by him in public, but recorded by an interviewer who chose (or agreed) to omit it.

increasingly grim realities of life in Northern Ireland, for how could the region open up a conciliatory space when that very space was contested?'[23] The best of Hewitt's late poems attempt to deal with this impasse, even to the point of (once) invoking Baudelaire. It was too late for the political situation to be ameliorated through culture, too late for a near-octogenarian to learn a new trade.

At the time of his death, John Hewitt's name appeared frequently in the newspapers. Various tributes to the poet have already been cited. There was also the Catholic martyr John Hewitt (d.1588), the football player (Aberdeen centre forward; later managed Dundalk), John Hewitt the Downing Street official, John Hewitt the rugby player (Ulster centre), John Hewitt father-in-law of the poet Adrian Mitchell, and John Hewitt the actor (Joe Keller in 'All My Sons' at the Belfast Civic).[24] We may have to deal with one more, in the Appends. From among these quick figures, the dead namesake moved on to the Elysian Fields, or into the gentle shades, beyond the determinants of loneliness, prolixity, reticence, disappointment, and the Troubles. I have heard his gruff laughter several times during the writing-up of his lifelong achievement.

[23] Clark, *The Ulster Renaissance*, p. 127.

[24] In September 1926, John Hewitt 'a young man residing in the Kilmore district of Lurgan' (County Armagh), together with a Portadown knacker (one who boils dead horses for their glue content) named McNeice, were charged with larceny. 'Hewitt was discharged, and McNeice was returned for trial.' *Irish Times*, 28 September 1926, p. 3.

APPENDS

The purpose of this final Part is multifold. Append A dwells on the significance of a strange textual presence and absence, the phrase 'no rebel word', together with Hewitt's spectral 1945 pamphlet (or less) of that name which has disappeared *in toto*. Append B investigates a minor textual possibility noted in Chapter 2, the authorship of a very short play. Technically, these are limited, distinct, and separate enquiries, yet together they will illuminate John Hewitt's mentality of publication. In turn, Append C involves scrutiny of one hero among his favourite public speakers in the 1930s, Alexander Irvine.

APPEND A

Missing the Rebel Word

The seven-page letter of spring 1964 to John Montague was constructed round a number of issues posed by the younger man the previous November. Among these was the origin of, or rationale for, the title of Hewitt's first full-sized collection, issued belatedly by Frederick Muller in the autumn of 1948. Having summarized his work from 1927 onwards, the poet turned to the point once again under consideration:

> Now about No Rebel Word: the title, a quotation from a sonnet of mine, was deliberately ambiguous, meaning no word leaping or tugging out of the consigned order, and at the same time no word by a rebel? [*sic*], asserting as it were that I was no rebel whatever folk might think. I corrected the page proofs in 1947 and it was published a year after. So by that time my interest had appreciably diminished. In addition, it contained nothing written after 1944, so that it was faraway [*sic*] from my active thought. It sold about 150 copies, got some good reviews (Irish Times, Tribune, T.L.S.). It has now only the relevance of a period piece, being in fact 18 years old.[1]

The full strangeness of this account deserves recognition. Though Hewitt specifies a poem from which the phrase was quoted, he does not admit its exclusion from the volume thereby named, nor does he indicate that the poem in question had not (evidently) been preserved in the collection of 'fair-copy' exercise books he had earlier described for Montague. Choice of a suppressed or discarded phrase for one's first major title page is more ambiguous than the phrase itself; in some internal or hermetic sense, it had not been discarded. His presentation of its 'deliberately ambiguous' meaning relates it to a consigned order of words, without elaborating on what 'consigned' means. Its usual context in ordinary language often involves a suggestion of dismissal or justified rejection—'consigned to prison... outer darkness' etc.—though there is a primary definition of the verb, 'to mark with the sign of the cross'. Perhaps Eliot's 'pneumatic' in the phrase 'pneumatic bliss' would serve as an example of the rebel word, or Yeats's 'slouching' in the last line of 'The Second Coming'. More extreme instances occur throughout Ezra Pound's *Cantos*.

In 'The Happy Man', written in 1942, Hewitt considers a variety of types—including the frightened man, the cynic, and the rebel—against a lightly suggested background of childhood instruction or schooling. The rebel, it seems, is formed by antagonist elders, yet the line following his cameo description curiously involves an identifying scribal act:

> The rebel always carries on his back
> the roaring master or the prim-lipped aunt.
> The sprawling signature curves back in time.[2]

I take this to mean that rebellion results from negative or oppressive causes, but the characteristic gesture of rebellion—self-proclamation in a name—does not mimic release but a

[1] UU, Hewitt, Box 9, undated and unsigned carbon copy, (f. 4). Hewitt's dating of the book—'18 years old'—would assign *No Rebel Word* to 1945/46, rather than 1948 when it was published.

[2] Ormsby, p. 41.

careless return of the gaze towards the oppressors. Much though it would amuse John Hewitt, these lines anticipate theories of 'the minor writer' first expounded by Gilles Deleuze and Félix Guattari in *Kafka: Towards a Minor Literature* (French, 1975; English, 1986). In the third chapter of this once renowned work, a number of propositions are advanced which may simply be noted *en passant*. In minor literatures 'language is effected with a high coefficient of deterritorialization'. But, simultaneously, 'everything in them is political'.[3] Between these frontier markers, Hewitt's rebel word resists the former and gives away the latter.

Some comments on synonyms or near-synonyms may clarify the structure of 'rebel' as a lexical item, with specific reference to its place in Irish discourse. Let us begin with a longer close-cognate—rebellion, the act committed by a rebel or rebels. In April 1916, a rebellion took place in Dublin. Or a rising, or an insurrection. Or, less plausibly, a revolt. In relation to these nouns, verbs can be found in some cases but not in all. The Irish Volunteers *rebelled*. Or, more idiomatically, the country *rose* (though not in 1916). But no comparable verb is available to describe what happened in the insurrection. And, as for the nouns, there are insurgents and rebels—but no risers or revolters (cf. the French *hommes revoltés*). All this is to say that the word 'rebel' is more richly varied than its seeming synonyms—a rebel rebels in a rebellion.

Yet, the rebel word (stylistically defined as it tentatively is by Hewitt) does not require any necessary connection with politics, with rebellion, or individual rebels. However, if the source-sonnet failed to gain admission to the Muller collection, so was the poem 'Ireland' (written 1932) removed from the final contents, explicitly because of its political associations or content. Hewitt's wartime politics, though unashamedly left-wing (e.g., in *The Northern Star* of 1941), was not characterized by links to rebellion in the sense generally understood in Belfast—that is, 'advanced' Irish nationalism. Such an association had been more obvious in 1937 and the Dublin-printed *Irish Democrat* of Frank Ryan and Peadar O'Donnell. By following the word with a question mark, mid-sentence, Hewitt goes some way towards undermining by over-egging his nicely balanced arguments for an ambiguous title phrase.

The second *Collected Poems* (edited by Frank Ormsby) provides one illuminating use of a term close to the anti-rebel verbal adjective *consigned*. 'The Scar', treating a sombre incident of family history in the Famine of 1845–47, includes the lines:

> and that chance meeting, that brief confrontation,
> conscribed me one of the Irishry forever.[4]

In *Out of My Time* (1974), Hewitt annotated the poem with a single sentence, 'My grandfather, John Hewitt, born in 1841 in Co Armagh, told me how his mother died in the Famine year, 1847.' The poem tells of fever transmitted when the woman gave bread to a suppliant at her window. The long consequence is stated plainly enough: 'in that woman's death I found my nation; / the old wound aches and shews its fellow-scar'. The wound and scar denote a traumatic event, perpetuated. So much is clear.

Can we accept the poem as a statement of origin? After all, the incident supposedly recounted had occurred when the old man was six. Rather, is it not exemplary of the theme announced in the 1974 collection's title, and the folkloric worldview accepted in pieces like 'The Fairy Thresher'? The incident is at once dated in history and yet out of time, just as

[3] Gilles Deleuze and Félix Guattari, *Kafka: Towards a Minor Literature*, trans. Dana Polan (Minneapolis: University of Minnesota Press, 1986), pp. 16–17.

[4] Ormsby, p. 177; see also notes, p. 603.

'Mary Hagan, Islandmagee 1919' is imaged or immobilized 'in that one gesture, knuckles on the gunwale...'.

The word 'conscribed' attracts attention here because it associates with 'consigned' in Hewitt's account for Montague of the rebel word and its absence. Yet, in 'The Scar', it is muddled by the late Yeatsian notion of the indomitable Irishry (see 'Under Ben Bulben'). More fustian than Hewitt officially allows swells the poem. Unadorned, the Irishry was an early modern term used to demark on maps either: (i) territory held by the native population (as against the Normans, then the English and Scots) or (ii) that population itself identified in pre-Reformation times by the language spoken. How do we construe the rest of the sentence? 'Conscribed me of'—are matters clarified by replacing *of* with (say) *to have been one of*? No, because the latter proposed phrase depends or insists upon a temporal order. Con*scribed* reports a change already effected, and effected (implicitly or subliminally) by writing. In relation to Hewitt's letter to Montague in 1964, and his effort to describe what it is the rebel word rebels against, we can take from 'The Scar' a context of traumatic contact (touch becoming contagion) in 1847 and the disappearing context of a century later. These are not personal slippages or political stratagems; they instantiate the mischief of language itself. *Consign* and *conscribe* are neither synonyms nor homonyms, but they nearly are both, a threatening abolition by agreement.

As for the elusive rebel word, Hewitt does positively assist in dating the source-sonnet. Describing *Conacre* (written April to June 1943) he wrote that his wife, 'then working in the Censorship' [branch of the post office] had the poem printed 'as a brochure for Christmas'.[5] She, in the belatedly inserted preliminaries to her journal, lists *Compass [Two Poems]* under the date January 1945, though the publication was dated 1944—Davy McLean took sixty-two copies at 1/6d each. Directly below this note, there follows her reference to 'No Rebel Word 1/6 each'. It seems reasonable to conclude that all these private printings were her doing, and that the source-sonnet was written between June 1943 and December 1944. All three titles may have been produced with an eye to Christmas sales through the Progressive Bookshop. Hewitt's brief but deliberate correspondence with Herbert Read in March 1944 and January 1945 referred to *Conacre*, and evidently included two newer poems: no reference to 'no rebel word'.[6]

In March 1945, Roberta records sending forty poems (including 'Conacre' and 'Compass') to Jonathan Cape, only to receive a rejection on 26 March. Then, in May, a collection she names as *No Rebel Word* was sent to Macmillan, with the rejection ('a nice letter') arriving on 1 June. The letter of 16 May, though signed by John, is a good deal less prosey than its predecessors and, under the signature, 'pp. RH.' is appended in miniscule.[7] As the submission cannot have consisted of just one sonnet, we may assume that the title poem was included in May 1945, but dropped before the submission to Muller later that year or early in 1946, or dropped in the early period between submission to Muller and the point at which now-traceable correspondence begins. Cape were offered forty poems, Muller finally published thirty-six. Though one cannot be certain that all these thirty-six had been present in the Macmillan typescript, the numerical difference might be explained as forty minus 'Conacre', 'Compass', 'No Rebel Word', 'Ireland', to leave thirty-six. Against this, one should note that the ten-page publication, *Compass*, included two poems ('The Return' and 'The Ruins Answer') or three if the dedicatory verse to R. T. Hewitt is counted. In refutation of the last objection, note that Roberta cites *Compass* as if it were a unitary item, thereby making plausible the calculation given above.

5 UU, Hewitt, Box 9, f.1. 6 Brotherton, Read C4362 and C4363.

7 University of Reading, Macmillan & Co Records, JH (or RH?), dated 16 May 1937.

If, despite Roberta Hewitt's pricing of it, no publication called *No Rebel Word* was actually issued in 1944–5, its next-door neighbour in the journal is exceedingly rare. The only examples of *Compass; Two Poems* I have traced in Irish libraries are an autographed copy in the Linen Hall, and a copy autograph dedicated 'to Lilian and Norman with best wishes from John Xmas 1944', the length [2] + 10 pages, in NLI.[8] Given the identity of prices provided by Roberta, we might conclude that the ghostly *No Rebel Word* was about the same length and format, if indeed it ever reached physical completion.

So much for negative forensics. The disappearance of a sonnet among 3500 unpublished poems is itself hardly surprising. The likely non-appearance of a second pamphlet at the end of 1944 or early in 1945 could be explained simply in terms of domestic economics: David McLean, with one such item on his shelves, may have advised against proceeding with the other, which would have involved doubled expenditure by the Hewitts. It is, however, the semantic and thematic implications which deserve consideration: dropping *No Rebel Word*, did Hewitt assert or imply some attitude of sustained rebelliousness, even silently?

In 1935, he and Roberta take a summer holiday on Rathlin Island, returning home to a Belfast caught up in riots. Later in the year, while attending a Museums Association course in Bristol, he took the opportunity to explore the neighbouring countryside. 'The Return', a poem of more than two hundred lines, deals with a number of returns—from the island to the city, from England to Ireland—with a good deal of attention to seabirds and life between the land masses. One verse paragraph (lines 44–64) alludes to the Ulster Unit and the Belfast Peace League in which he and Roberta were active. The urgent situation locally is not neglected, summarized memorably (but without detail):

> an electric day with that high-volted rebel,
> who has battered the walls of folly with his head
> for longer than I've cried upon this planet;[9]

Though Edward Carson, the satanic opponent of any democratically approved Rome/Home Rule, fits the description, it matters relatively little who the 'rebel' was, for the lines clearly indicate the poet's divergent attitude.[10] Populism, of whatever hue, never appealed. Hewitt's approach in 'The Return' is not reportive. Riots in mid-September 1934 led to the arrest of twenty-two men, who pleaded guilty and were released on probation.[11] In July the following year, by contrast, at least nine people were killed in rioting, leading Frederick MacNeice (the local Church of Ireland bishop, and Louis' father) to declare 'greater numbers had suffered grievous wrong, and not only men but women and children had been piteously driven from house and home, not for any crime proved against them by processes of law, but because they happened to be Protestants or Roman Catholics'.[12] The poem organizes itself round a thematic mosaic, and not a narrative.

In the dismal mid-Thirties, Hewitt's views shifted rapidly. If, in 1935, he deplored the high-volted rebel of 1912, two years later he was writing for Frank Ryan in *The Irish*

[8] Norman Kirkham married Lilian Black (older sister of Roberta Hewitt). The only copy listed in COPAC is in the Brotherton Collection, University of Leeds Library, where it forms part of the Herbert Read archive. In autumn 2013, the bookseller Paul Rassam had a further copy for sale, privately purchased.

[9] Ormsby, p. 14. Sir Edward Carson, the charismatic leader of Unionist opposition to Home Rule before the Great War, died on 22 October 1935, aged eighty-one. He was buried in St Anne's Cathedral, an electric day for Belfast.

[10] JH may additionally have been outraged by the participation of a former president of the Methodist Church in the funeral; see David Fitzpatrick, *'Solitary and Wild': Frederick MacNeice and the Salvation of Ireland* (Dublin: Lilliput, 2012), p. 233.

[11] *Irish Times*, 3 October 1934, p. 4.

[12] *Irish Times*, 27 July 1935, p. 1.

Democratic. Certainly his politics in the final year of the war remained unambiguously left-wing, though without the brief republican/nationalist entanglement of 1937. Yet it was only one year into peacetime when he began the negotiations with Muller which resulted in *No Rebel Word* (1948), by which point the title phrase had no formal context in either sonnet or pamphlet. Muller, of course, was London-based, where Irish politics might count negatively.

Hewitt specifically raised the matter of the title's suggesting that the author was not a rebel 'whatever folk might think'. Even he sought to qualify the issue by claiming ambiguity on its behalf. The folk, we may conclude, were based closer to home than London. An inky trail of apostasy passes close to many a writer's desk. St John Ervine was a celebrated Ulster instance, but not perhaps of great literary significance. In 1938 the *soi-disant* Anglo-Irish Cecil Day-Lewis moved his family to an idyllic Cornish cottage, 'noiselessly slipping the painter' of his eloquent Communist Party affiliations.[13] Auden had preferred New York. Earlier, Swinburne had earned the scorn of Oscar Wilde for abandoning liberal views of Ireland, and earlier still Wordsworth was mocked by Browning—'Just for a handful of silver he left us, / Just for a riband to stick in his coat...' Cries of apostasy for the most part relied on the assumption that the cause abandoned had been the one true faith, with which the apostate had earnestly and fully identified. What if more than one cause had been initially taken up, equally, but at odds with each other, or deemed by many to be at odds? Such was John Hewitt's case.

One extensive work deals with the issue of the double cause, using rebellion as a mobile point of encircling reference. 'The Angry Dove', however, never saw the light of day until 1999, twelve years after Hewitt's death. Originally intended as a radio play in 1945, it proved too long for successful broadcast. Almost two months after despatching a first draft, Roberta typed a revised script, sending it to the BBC on 6 August. During Hewitt's reworking the script, his father died on 17 July. On the previous day, the enfeebled old man had said to his son, 'No nation can live alone—I have been too much alone.'[14] Something of both the playwright and Robert Telford Hewitt might be traced in the central figure of 'The Angry Dove'.

The title character, the early Irish St Columcille bears a name combining Latin and Gaelic elements, which can translate as Dove of the Church.[15] The action commences when the future saint transcribes a valuable manuscript without permission, and refuses to be disciplined, with war resulting. The term 'rebellion' features in the opening speech with reference to Satan's offence, as told in *Paradise Lost*—Milton's influence re-emerges on several occasions, also Yeats's. It then occurs in the tempting demon's account of Columcille's superior, 'a haughty priest / swift to discern rebellion in the least, / quick flicker...'. Then finally, the chastened saint uses it in describing nettles 'for chastisement of the rebellious flesh'.[16] The flesh in question is not his own; throughout 'The Angry Dove' no rebel word is attached to Columcille, despite his pride, fiery anger, and refusal of church discipline.

[13] Peter Stanford, *C. Day-Lewis, a Life* (London: Continuum, 2007), pp. 163–7.

[14] Roberta Hewitt records JH sending an early treatment of the Columcille script to Louis MacNeice on 6 June 1945. In the middle of the month, she 'typed for days' at the script, which MacNeice quickly approved. Other mid-June activities involved Roberta in a street-corner flirtation, herself and JH addressing electioneering envelopes, and a trip to Dublin. See *Journal TS*, prelims, pp. v–vi.

[15] For a succinct and scholarly account see Aidan Breen's article in the *Dictionary of Irish Biography*, edited by Maguire and Quinn (Dublin: Royal Irish Academy; Cambridge: Cambridge University Press, 2009), vol. 2, pp. 706–8.

[16] John Hewitt, *Two Plays: the McCrackens and The Angry Dove*, edited by Damian Smyth (Belfast: Blackstaff, 1999), pp. 75, 80, 106.

The one marginal case arises where Demal characterizes Finnian in hostile terms, indirectly suggesting rebellion in his pupil.

In mitigation, Columcille is a poet and a writer who, in contrite exile, pities the poor and converts the powerful to Christian truth. Even his original offence (based on traditional lore) focuses on literature and access to it. In old age Columcille is invited to advise on a dispute about the role of poets, and advances a clever response—'the stuff that poets play with is a fire, / and, like a fire, has uses manifold'.[17] A little later, his argument turns on a more general notion of freedom ('the blessed thing'). These explicitly political considerations are studded with further latter-day concepts—'your nation', 'the Irish Kingdom', 'the nation's judgment', 'the wide enfranchised world'. The historical Columcille had inspired the affection of Irish Catholics and Protestant alike; there was even a proud claim that he had been a Presbyterian, virtually.[18] In more conventional style, the play concludes with the saint dying a pious death, surrounded by devoted followers, but not before Columcille has ventured a rebellious gesture. His last (but ultimately abandoned) offence is to support a younger son against a rightfully expectant older one.[19] The consigned order prevails.

In the years after publication of *No Rebel Word*, Anglophone literary circles felt an influx of new ideas from France. Though Albert Camus' *L'Etranger* (1942) had appeared in English in 1946, the cumulative significance of his work emerged in the early 1950s, notably with *L'Homme Révolté* (1951; English as *The Rebel*, 1953). Only one factor encourages the thought that Hewitt might have paid attention—*The Rebel* carried a foreword by Herbert Read. Camus' theme is at once metaphysical and political. In a late chapter he considers 'rebellion and style', in which the true artist (writer, painter, whatever) is observed always to work between limits, as both total realism and total formalism are impossible and inconceivable. Thus in writing, the artist imposes a 'correction' by his language and by a selectivity or redistribution of elements derived from reality. At the other end of the problem, creative forces or the fecundity of rebellion are contained in a 'distortion which represents the style and tone of the work'.[20] These are then the limits of all possible art—correction and distortion. None of this was available to Hewitt when he chose to use the phrase 'no rebel word' as a title, but it was available when he strove to explain himself to John Montague in 1964. None of the colossal horrors to which Camus was responding—fascism, colonial torture in Algeria, Stalinist terror—affected the Ulster writer. Yet in miniature (the B-Specials) or at a distance (suppression of Mau Mau), they were present too.

[17] Hewitt, *Two Plays: the McCrackens and The Angry Dove*, p. 114.

[18] See Thomas Hamilton, *History of the Presbyterian Church in Ireland* (1886), cited in the *Dictionary of Irish Biography* (2009), vol. 2, p. 707, col 2.

[19] Hewitt, *Two Plays: the McCrackens and The Angry Dove*, pp. 103–5. Primogeniture (the right of the firstborn) had no place in early Irish law of Columcille's period and, strictly, is anachronistic in the play. The poets' harshest critic cites another anachronistic phrase—'the slogan's "Root and Branch", destroy or expel' (p. 113). The original 'root and branch petition' of 1641 and after sought totally to abolish the English episcopacy. The political term 'radical' is constructed on this commitment to treat issues at the root (Latin *radex*) rather than to trim them. The phrase became proverbial and is echoed in James Connolly's pamphlet of 1906, *The Axe to the Root*.

[20] Albert Camus, *The Rebel*, trans. Anthony Bower (Harmondsworth: Penguin Classics, 1971), pp. 233–7.

APPEND B

Africa Calling (1926), Unwanted Words

Damian Smyth's edition of 'The McCrackens' and 'The Angry Dove' in 1999 drew attention to Hewitt's more than occasional commitment to playwriting in the 1930s and Forties. Indeed, premonitions of both can be traced in 'The Red Hand' notebook. Nevertheless, 'The Bloody Brae' continued to be taken as his significant contribution to the genre, a preference endorsed by the merging of its subject matter with notable poems—'An Irishman in Coventry' and 'The Colony'. If the latter is taken as representative of John Hewitt's most complex, thoughtful, and finished work, few of the approvers will regard *Africa Calling* as an addition to the canon worth claiming. Its faults are adequately noted (Chapter 2)—wooden dialogue, pious plot, negligible dramatic action, frozen climax. Its manifest concern with Christian missionary vocations does not gel with the poet's long familiar themes of nature and politics, time and solitude, a secularist blast of trumpets against Ian Paisley and the raised hand, or the gallery-man's commitment to visual art in Europe, including the islands. Superficially at least, 'The McCrackens' chimes with Hewitt's man-of-the-left self-image, though by the same token it raises the issue of rebellion and rebels—or what is often called the tragedy of pre-mature revolution.

Yet, with other religious or a-religious plays in mind ('The Bloody Brae', 'The Angry Dove', and, perhaps, the never completed 'Salute to the Red Army' [February 1943]), we cannot simply abandon *Africa Calling* as the impossible recruit to an awkward squad of guerrilla activities. In a narrow compass, both the Columcille radio drama and the piece published under the Hewitt name in 1926 are plays about Christian missionaries. In a larger view, the investigation may illuminate wider European contexts, personal silences, and apparent conflicts in Hewitt's emergence from late childhood.

He was only nineteen when the little play was published, further evidence surely for a not-guilty-of-authorship verdict.[1] Against this, at least to emphasize that he was already writing, he had begun to compose poems in 1924 and, in the year that *Africa Calling* appeared, began to maintain the fair-copy notebooks of finished verse, breaking into print by 1928, aged twenty or twenty-one. From 1924 to 1930, he struggled between two educational institutions; in Queen's he contributed energetically to the poetry scene, but

[1] It is only proper to note some rival suspects: John Alexander Hewitt (1907–42; died in a Japanese prison camp) was an Irish missionary sponsored by the Plymouth Brethren; after the war, his ashes were interred in the Kilmore churchyard celebrated by the poet John Hewitt in 'Planters' Gothic'. See 'Echoes of Service' archive in John Rylands Library, University of Manchester, GB 133 EOS. See also J. G. Hutchinson, *Missionaries from Ireland Now with the Lord* (Glasgow: Gospel Tract Publications, 1988), pp. 61–4 (with portrait photo). Hutchinson was a long-serving leader of the Plymouth (or Christian) Brethren. A Presbyterian, John Hewitt evidently missioned in India; a brief biography published in Belfast during the 1950s is known only through copies preserved in Yale University Library. There is no reason to think that he would have written a play specifically about Methodists and published by HPH. From the year that *Africa Calling* appeared in London, two local publications deserve notice: Edith Buxton, *Chocolate and Cream; Tales of African Missions* (Belfast: Graham and Heslip, 1926); and R. M. Sibbett, *For Christ and Crown, the Story of a Mission* (Belfast: The Witness, 1926).

loitered academically; in Stranmillis he underwent training as a teacher, like his father before him, yet never taught. The period surrounding the play's appearance involved shifts of direction, with some evidence of other difficulties.

Rather than squeeze the lemon of personal data, it may prove more illuminating to begin with the London firm issuing the play in question. The Holborn Publishing House (hereinafter HPH) or a related imprint (Holborn Hall) began to publish material on Africa and the missions in 1907 or earlier. This was a high imperial Victorian mission already turning sour. The war over, HPH produced less didactic books between 1919 and 1932, and was associated with the widely respected *Holborn Review*.[2] Its point of institutional attachment, the Primitive Methodists, differed from the original association of Methodist societies which had seceded from the Church of England *c.*1818. The Primitives were less centralized, less clergy-led, and more democratic in their procedures. Some had been politically radical along millenarian and even republican lines. Anti-Catholicism also had its extended moments.[3] This history of the movement is little evident in the Holborn publications, though Primitive Methodism is faithfully acknowledged.[4] More emphatically, HPH after 1918 specialized in lengthy works of thoughtful reflection, scholarship, or (sometimes) applied scholarship. J. G. Bowran's *Christianity and Culture* (1923) was followed by detailed studies of African societies, E. W. Smith's *The Golden Stool, Some Aspects of the Conflict of Cultures in Modern Africa* (1926) for example.[5] Later, H. G. Meecham's *The Oldest Version of the Bible: 'Aristeas' on its Traditional Origin: a Study in Early Apologetic, with Translation and Appendices* (1932) was among the last heavyweight volumes appearing under the HPH imprint. A post-war generational *Angst*, far from exclusive to small religious movements, is unmistakable.

The thumbnail sketch above should indicate that *Africa Calling* issued from no mere distributer of pious tracts, nor a pure voice of unrelieved evangelicalism—though the latter aspect of Methodism got good measure. Distant from the bitter sectarianism of twentieth-century Belfast, HPH offered an intellectualist platform to British (with Irish) Protestant non-conformity in the aftermath of the Great War. On the latter question it contributed *The Life of James Flanagan* (1920), whose background was Catholic and Irish but whose career as evangelist and author had been pursued in England. On the intellectualist side, the publication closest to the poet Hewitt's concerns was *Sociality, the Art of Living Together* (1927), a fervent post-war attempt to assemble philosophical arguments in favour of a new (but not too new) humane social order. Its authorities ranged from Plato to Harold Laski; it endorsed the aesthetic and the utopian with specific reference to William Morris (a Hewitt hero), quoted Thomson and Geddes on Evolution (also approved by Hewitt), and advanced 'Art the Sociologizer' (Plato, Ruskin, Tolstoy, Morris etc.) as a revolutionary

[2] It began life in 1879 as the *Primitive Methodist Quarterly Review and Christian Ambassador*, grew weary of the *Christian Ambassador* in 1888, and, with other modifications, became the *Holborn Review* in 1910.

[3] For an account of the Primitive movement in Ireland, see D. L. Cooney, *The Methodists in Ireland: A Short History* (Dublin: Columba Press, 2001), pp. 65–80. Organizationally, the Primitives abandoned Ireland in 1905, and various mergers between their congregations and those of the central church took place in the years following. By an arrangement of 1910 the Primitive Methodist congregation on the Shankill Road was transferred to the Agnes Street circuit where the Hewitt family attended. The Hewitt parents' refusal to have their son baptized in 1907, based on a disagreement between RTH and the local minster, may reflect transitional circumstances and tensions of those years.

[4] *Handbook of Primitive Methodist Church Principles, History* (1928), and a printed church service deriving from the 'last session of the last Primitive Methodist Conference' (1932).

[5] Also an anthology of Tonga folk tales, conundrums, etc. 'primarily for school use'.

panacea.[6] W. Lansdell Wardle's *Israel and Babylon* (1925), while remaining within the fold of orthodox belief, raised questions about similarities between the two kingdoms and Abraham's Babylonian origins.[7]

Scholarly and critical HPH publications might have encouraged or, on the other hand, dismayed a youthful reader swaddled in the faith—if, indeed, Johnny had been swaddled. The post-war shift, anxious or confident, of a missionary focus from India to the African colonies, raised issues noted even by W. B. Yeats; India being home to ancient, learned, and literate cultures known to Western scholars, Africa a seeming patchwork of diverse, unlettered, and historyless tribalisms.[8] Lee's book—more reflective than scholarly, but well informed—works from the assumption that, where politics and diplomacy and war have failed, culture may lead human beings to find or build 'sociality'. (Freud and Adler do not feature in these aspirations.)

In the Northern Irish context, what our encounter with Lee recalls is less Hewitt's own early writings in the 1920s than the grand strategy of the Arts Council in Belfast from 1968 onwards to solve, dissolve, or at least dilute the Troubles by means of cultural (usually literary) partnership—Longley and Heaney (1968), Montague and Hewitt (1970). There was never another tour involving (say) Thomas Kinsella (author of *Butcher's Dozen*, 1972) and Roy McFadden. While Sarah Ferris's complaints about the official patronage afforded Hewitt after 1972 have a point—namely, that he suited a Higher Agenda—the point is lost in the bile. There is a less frantically urgent logic. Historically, the wartime CEMA formula (extended to Northern Ireland in 1943) was applied to the emergent internal Troubles. Furthermore, and further back, an intellectual post-Great-War programme of similar kind had been explicitly advanced by Lee in *Sociality* (HPH, 1927), with profounder philosophical abstractions in support. Doubtless Lee had comrade-rivals, but the names he invokes prominently include some Hewitt favourites. HPH anticipated the means—culture as politics by other means—through which his late writings reached the Irish public.

Africa Calling deserves some attention in its own right. It was not typical of the HPH list, being literary rather than discursive. It was not unique, either: *The Island Heritage; Episodes from the Missionary History of Fernando Poo, West Africa, a Play for Young People* appeared in the same year.[9] In the Anglican compound, something similar had appeared the previous year—*Africa Calling; a Set of Missionary Scenes for Boys and Girls* (London: Church Missionary Society, 1925).[10] Though the evidence is slight, one might conclude that, *c.*1926, these publishers experimented with short dramatic texts illustrating the missionary in West Africa. The year had been celebrated as a metropolitan anniversary for missions,

[6] Atkinson Lee (1880–1955), *Sociality, the Art of Living Together* (London: Holborn Publishing House, [June or earlier] 1927). Lee's book was positively reviewed by John Macmurray in *The Journal of Philosophical Studies* 4, no. 13 (January 1929), p. 147. Lee also published *Groundwork of the Philosophy of Religion*. From 1922 to 1928, Macmurray was a philosophy Fellow at Balliol College, Oxford. His socialist sympathies at this time, and his practical concern for the Workers' Educational Association, are well described in a broader context of left-liberal intellectual activity; see John E. Costello, *John Macmurray: A Biography* (Edinburgh: Floris Books, 2002), pp. 171–8.

[7] Reviewed favourably by Jacob Hoschander in *The Jewish Quarterly Review* New Series 21, no. 3 (January 1931), p. 299–303.

[8] See J. B. Hardy, 'The Education of an African Native', *Holborn Review* (July 1926), pp. 333–41.

[9] The author was Philip J. Fisher, author of *The Opening Door* etc. Holborn also issued several volumes of suitably Methodist fiction during the 1920s.

[10] *A Call from Africa; Being a Comprehensive Statement of the Facts which Constitute the Call from Africa to the Church of England*, preface by the Right Reverend St Clair Donaldson (London: Board of the Church Assembly for the Missionary Council, 1926).

with a young people's rally in Holborn Hall on 8 May, that is, smack in the middle of the General Strike (4–13 May).[11]

Despite its literary shortcomings, the play discloses material worthy of consideration in the poet Hewitt's context. Some linguistic points. The dialogue of *Africa Calling* possesses little flexibility or individuality. Crude content apart, the utterance of one character could be transferred with little or no alteration to another. Virtually every word, and the rhythm of every sentence, proceeds from UKSE (United Kingdom Standard English), a product and a prerequisite of state radio broadcasting, which was chartered in December 1926, drawing on principles laid down in John Reith's *Broadcast over Britain* (1924). One little phrase and one noun deviates from this mono-idiom. The play centrally concerns three male students about to enter the Methodist ministry—Oliver, Roland, and Tom. Each of these uses the expression 'Why man' as a form of emphasis (actually 'oh man' in Tom's case). This could be heard as an Ulster or Scottish expression (cf. 'hoots man' in the extreme usage). So far, so very little good. One of the female characters, Mrs Jennie Forester, refers to her daughters as 'the bairns': this is unmistakably Scots or Scots-influenced East Ulster dialect. Otherwise the locations are England and Africa, the latter explicitly, but without any place names.

An ideological point. Although virtually all the characters are active as ordained ministers (or married to same), there is virtually no religious feeling or invocation in their dialogue. To a great extent, this dimension is corralled within the words of a hymn ('Break, day of God', by Henry Burton, 1840–1930) repeatedly sung throughout the action. Instead of piety or faith, teaching is emphasized as the task of the missionary—'teaching, interpreting, translating'. Additionally, social issues are positively considered—dire living conditions in the slums at home, the temperance movement, and 'the colour problem'.

The absent character. Jimmy Johnson is variously treated by the others as a figure of fun. He is 'our solitary misogynist' or 'our only woman-hater'. Much merriment arises from the prospect of Jimmy preaching on the text parodied as, 'Now abideth muddle, fuddle, and cuddle, these three, but the greatest of these is cuddle' (cf. I Corinthians, 13:13). Ironically, it is Jimmy who exemplifies a notion of Christian self-sacrifice; he drowns in England (off-stage of course) in attempting to save a young girl's life.

A motivator. Although Oliver, Roland, and Tom are dedicated to their vocation, Roland, alone of the three, actually reaches Africa. He has been additionally stirred by the enthusiasm of his supervisor or superintendent, Joseph Forester, 'the big popular city preacher, the howling pulpit success'. The business of examining this play-text as potentially the poet Hewitt's work will involve a reconsideration of the one 'howling pulpit success' (cf. Chapter 2) he admired (with reservations) and the notion of poemosaic investigated in Chapter 3.

However, the root question of authorship cannot be postponed forever. *Africa Calling* is, on its title page, attributed to a John Hewitt, and the possibility of this being a pseudonym is slight, given the publisher involved. Consequently, the objective can be narrowed to establishing *which* John Hewitt was the author. The British Museum library cataloguer in 1926 uses the identifier 'John Hewitt, religious writer', which does no more than report the work itself: the Museum never assigned a second work under the name John Hewitt, thus tagged.[12] In 1926, the poet John Hewitt was involved in some kind of crisis which had led

[11] *The Island Heritage* was performed on this occasion; a list of characters and a synopsis were included in the programme. The missionary play phenomenon lasted many decades but flourished between the Wars; see Anon., *What is a Missionary Play?* (London: London Missionary Society, [1920?]).

[12] Likewise, the Oxford (Bodleian Library) copy is assigned to 'John Hewitt, writer of plays', which does no more than identify the author as himself, no other plays being attributed to a John Hewitt.

to his taking six years to complete a degree at QUB and which involved two years devoted to training for a career as a teacher. The evidence takes the form of vacancy, the non-discussion of Methody or Queens in the preliminaries to *A North Light*. The prose sketches he wrote (cf. 'The Parcel of Thorns') at this time involved religious themes, and indeed a pelagic maintenance of the concern can be observed feeding just under the surface of some manifestly non-religious work. Robin Roddie, however, can report that no copy of the play is to be found in the various collections overseen by the Methodist Historical Society of Ireland. If this is seen as evidence against Irish authorship, one must bear in mind Hewitt's rapid distancing of himself from conventional religion to the point, perhaps, of suppressing the play (as he later suppressed the 'No Rebel Word' sonnet). In a different perspective, Primitive Methodist ministers contributed extensively to HPH; one might expect to find the author of *Africa Calling* among their number. Dr Roddie, however, reports that no minister named Hewitt of that period bore the initial J.[13] Finally, in this area of enquiry, one can also report that collections at, or catalogued by, the Oxford Centre for Methodism and Church History (Oxford Brookes University) contain no copy of *Africa Calling*. It is truly an elusive text. In terms of positive evidence, we have a late sonnet, 'The Open Eye' written in February 1979, specifically the first eight lines:

> Those yawning mornings moored among the pews,
> our creek of vantage once a month would yield
> adventure in the current *Foreign Field*
> which offered fancy freedom in a cruise
> along the Congo; other voyages
> promised pagodas, pigtailed Chinamen,
> but with old Leopold's atrocities
> I swore to be a missionary then.[14]

This provides little guidance in dating Hewitt's youthful commitment, for the Belgian monarch's sadistic regime had been exposed in 1904, three years before his birth. That the exposé was the work of a fellow-Ulsterman certainly bore in on Hewitt, who alluded to Casement favourably in 'The Laying on of Hands' and 'I Solve the Irish Problem'. The sonnet of 1979 provides a textual basis for Hewitt's passing interest in missionary work, but does not attach it or limit it to any decade.

Rival candidates for assignment of the authorship are equally rare. The two clergymen mentioned in fn1 above are not known to have published; the Plymouth Brother certainly would not have written a play for the stage, even a pious one. And neither he nor the diligent Presbyterian could have rendered faith, hope, and charity as 'muddle, fuddle and cuddle'. This joke, in dubious taste, is perhaps as strong an argument as any for assigning the piece to the poet John Hewitt. Align it with the character names Roland and Oliver (from the *Chanson de Roland*) with the admission of 'The Open Eye', and an errant literary undergraduate becomes a suspect-type.

[13] Robin Roddie to the present writer, 5 September 2013.

[14] Ormsby, p. 292. *The Foreign Field* was published irregularly between 1904 and 1932 by the London-based Wesleyan Methodist Society.

APPEND C

Alex Irvine, Luther, and Rebellion

The issue of John Harold Hewitt's likely authorship of *Africa Calling* should be held open partly because, on a positivist vetting, no conclusive evidence has been cited, but partly also in a less narrowly defined argument, discussion of his attitude to the intertwined issues of politics and religion has never escaped from the local sectarian framework. These problems have not been exclusively Hewitt's. In 'The Man Who Invented Sin', Sean O'Faolain had explored the cruel intensity of the Catholic Church's fear of sex, but conducted his enquiry against the background of an Ireland gripped no less fiercely by the passions of nationalist rebellion and imperial repression. *The Man Who Invented Sin and Other Stories* was published in 1948.

In the same year, John Hewitt published 'The Laying on of Hands' in *The Bell*, of which O'Faolain had been the founding editor. He was on good terms with O'Faolain, whose 1937 story 'A Broken World' (like Hewitt's also of 1948) is set in a railway carriage. Both stories deal with frustrated spiritual undertakings linked to social reform or better. In the southern story, it emerges that a Catholic priest has been silenced as punishment by the official church for his involvement in agrarian politics, while he has been simultaneously demoralized by the apathy of peasants he had hoped to revolutionize. Hewitt's story is less polished, but also less dependent on a lineage including James Joyce's 'Ivy Day in the Committee Room' and George Moore's 'The Wild Goose'. One could trace the theme of these stories—the tortured interaction of political radicalism and religious adherence—to the campaign for Catholic Emancipation in the 1820s, or further back to the 1790s and the United Irishmen's efforts to substitute the common name of Irishman, in place of the denominations of Protestant, Catholic, and Dissenter.

Hewitt was apt to invoke the earlier movement, usually through Ulster participants, Jemmy Hope and others. A play, now known as 'The McCrackens' (also written *c.*1948), features Hope, Thomas Russell, and the McCracken family in a drama closing in the winter of 1845.[1] This is classic Irish rebellion in its most resonant but tragic instance, the event which gave priority to the term 'rebel' in Irish contexts and which, consequently, provided the ideological framework (ironically or otherwise) for Hewitt's twice proposed 'no rebel word' banner phrase. Bearing this in mind, we might return to Alexander Irvine's *The Carpenter and His Kingdom*, while also bearing in mind a need to remain in earshot of *Africa Calling.*

A few pages after Irvine's anti-Calvinist account of sin, pinpointed by Hewitt, we find a passage rich in sympathy for the poor, ancient and modern, learned in the Protestant tradition, and keen to perpetuate an imperial view of the Great War:

> The early church tried communism. Mammon pointed out the foolishness of the venture, and introduced the competitive system—which is war in industry. There the battle is to the strong and the race to the swift, and the weak and slow are gathered together and cast into the Gehenna of modern industrial methods.... In the peasants' revolt [Germany, 1524],

[1] See John Hewitt, *Two Plays: The McCrackens; The Angry Dove*, edited by Damian Smyth (Belfast: Lagan Press, 1999).

> when the overlords slaughtered a hundred thousand labourers, Luther was Mammon's chief defender. He said that a prince could get to heaven as easily by slaughtering peasants as by prayer. His chief literary contribution to this bacchanalia of the god Success was a pamphlet entitled, *Against the murderous thieving hordes of Peasants*. 'A rebel', said the great theologian and son of a miner, 'is outlawed of God and Kaiser. Therefore who can and will first slaughter such a man, does right well, since upon such a common rebel every man is alike judge and executioner. Therefore who can, shall here openly or secretly smite, slaughter, and stab; and hold that there is nothing more poisonous, more harmful, more devilish, than a rebellious man!' His advice was taken and religiously followed even to peasants of Belgium in 1914.[2]

As Hewitt was familiar with the Irvine of page 206, in a book presented to him by the author, it is reasonable to assume that he read pages 220 to 221. Irvine does not misrepresent Luther, though perhaps he over-lards the 1914 German invasion of Belgium. A former miner who served very effectively (if briefly) as a British super-*padre* during the Great War, he was entitled to have a last swipe at the Boche in the January 1922 publication.[3] What *The Carpenter* does not report is the author's ministry in Ireland to the brutal Auxiliaries of 1921, and his (possible) meeting with Michael Collins, details he only published in 1930.[4] In this context, he might be described as a compassionate imperialist, hardly meat for Hewitt's pantheon.

A wider context is available. Luther's view of the Peasants' Revolt had not been the only Protestant response. The Anabaptist Thomas Müntzer (1489–1525) adopted quite the opposite position, supporting the peasants in their claims, and suffering condemnation by Luther, torture, and execution for his pains. Irvine makes no reference to Müntzer, though the German Social Democratic opposition in exile at the end of the Great War found solace in his courage and, to that extent, his example. Particularly attentive were a group of Marxists and others, including the Dadaist poet Hugo Ball (1886–1927) and the philosopher Ernst Bloch (1885–1977). Bloch's *Thomas Müntzer als Theologe der Revolution* appeared in 1921, but remains untranslated into English.[5] The mix of messianic thinking, utopianism, revolutionary Marxism, and Dadaism which swirled round these figures in the immediate post-war years had no equivalent on the British (or Irish) Left. But if Hewitt had never heard of Müntzer, he did in time come to revere the fourteenth-century English rebel John Ball (1338–81), principally by reading William Morris's 'A Dream of John Ball' (1888). For his part in Wat Tyler's Rebellion, the Lollard priest was hanged, drawn, and quartered in the presence of the king. Rebellion, the action of individual rebels, was a crime infinitely fouler than treason (as we have come to formulate it; it was an offence against God and the cosmological order established at the Creation). Both Ball and Müntzer were priests who judged that the social order of their day travestied the original Christian message.

[2] Alexander Irvine, *The Carpenter and His Kingdom* (New York: Scribner's, 1922), p. 221. Irvine appears to have taken this translated passage from Karl Pearson, *The Ethic of Free Thought* (London: A and C Clark, 1901) directly or indirectly. Dublin-born J. B. Bury referred to Luther's reformation as rebellion, not as an outraged Catholic but as an atheist of Irish Protestant background; see his *History of Freedom of Thought* (London: Williams and Norgate, 1913).

[3] According to Linda Linney, author of Irvine's entry in the *Dictionary of Irish Biography*, the book was written (perhaps drafted) during the Somme retreat of 1918.

[4] Alexander Irvine, *A Fighting Parson* (London: Williams and Norgate, 1930), pp. 197–8.

[5] The most relevant of Bloch's works in English is *The Spirit of Utopia*, trans. Anthony A. Nassar (Stanford: Stanford University Press, 2000), pp. 235–6. On Müntzer, see Hans-Jurgen Goertz, *Thomas Müntzer: Apocalyptic Mystic and Revolutionary*, trans. Jocelyn Jacquiery (Edinburgh: T. & T. Clarke, 1992).

In safer times and places Alexander Irvine said much the same thing. Hewitt could record with pride that his hero 'had exposed the outrages of the chain gangs in the southern states' of the US.[6] Nevertheless he regarded the juncture between Irvine's socialism and his religious teaching as a geological fault or—far more concessively—as an ambiguity. His account of *The Carpenter and His Kingdom* disingenuously presents it as not dealing with politics. With Luther's condemnation of the Peasants' Revolt echoing across all its pages, one could rapidly twist the argument tighter to suggest that Irvine, while condemning Luther's harshness towards the poor and the iniquities of industrial capitalism, used *no rebel word*. Though Britain experienced nothing like Germany's Spartacus Rising of January 1919, nor produced anything to match the *Freikorps* veterans who suppressed it, in the other part of the United Kingdom the Irish war of independence was triggered by the Solaheadbeg incident, also of January 1919. The threat of rebellion had been heard loud in Ulster in 1912 (with Robert Shepherd Black's wobbly approval) and in Dublin in April 1916 with massive amplification.

Irvine was a self-educated man, with a broad range of interests and sympathies. Touring the Irish midlands in an armoured car, he visited localities and buildings associated with Oliver Goldsmith. He met Yeats, whom he found inattentive. He admired Mark Twain and could quote Nietzsche on the loneliness of those who quit the conventional paths of thought. When Twain, under populist pressure, resigned from a welcoming party due to meet Maxim Gorki, for Irvine 'it was as if a fine piece of statuary had fallen to fragments'.[7] Irvine was John Hewitt's Twain, and Hewitt's writings on the great orator are attempts to reassemble the fragments, one or two in sonnet form dropping totally out of sight. In 'The Return', he had listed significant components of which he could say, 'these are Man'. Together with the chiselled face and the temple, he named the sonnet.

A couple of unpublished sonnets is no adequate salute to Irvine. In 'Alex of the Chimney Corner' Hewitt provided an account of the York's Street's Labour Hall occasion:

> After an embarrassingly adulatory though mercifully short introduction from [Harry] Midgley, Irvine rose. He spoke of social justice and the historical role of the Christian church in relation to it, of the message of the agitator Christ and the communism of the early disciples... And the crowd took to it with clenched attention: the catholic shoemaker, the arid atheist, the militant freethinker, the saintly old Quaker, the fat union official, the rest of us.[8]

The passage is not without its challenges. 'Clenched attention' is too close to the clenched fist of 1930s' European communist display to be more than an overworked metaphor. The communism of Mathew, Mark, Luke, and John etc. offered only a sentimental pedigree for the beliefs and practices of Lenin or even Harry Pollitt. Yet Hewitt's own desire for social justice rings through, with his qualified admiration of Alex Irvine.

[6] *Ancestral*, p. 41. [7] Irvine, *Fighting Parson*, p. 288. [8] *Ancestral*, p. 41.

Selected Bibliography

John Hewitt arranged for a division of his archive between the Public Record Office of Northern Ireland in Belfast (PRONI) and the library of the University of Ulster at Coleraine (UU), the former receiving personal correspondence (but also Roberta Hewitt's journal), and the latter receiving his large collection of compositional notebooks, literary manuscripts, proofs and typescripts of certain texts (including *A North Light* in various forms), and his own library of printed books. Holdings in these and other institutions (e.g. the National Library of Ireland, the Linen Hall Library, University of Reading, etc.) are specified in the appropriate footnotes—see List of Abbreviations, p. xiii.)

What follows indicates printed sources used for the present work.

1. ESSENTIAL TEXTS BY JOHN HEWITT

'Aesthetics in the Museum and Art Gallery', *The Museums Journal* 36, no. 6 (1936), pp. 229–35.

Alicia Boyle; a Retrospective Exhibition of Paintings Completed Since 1938 (Belfast: Arts Council of Northern Ireland, 1983).

Ancestral Voices: the Selected Prose, ed. Tom Clyde (Belfast: Blackstaff, 1987).

Art in Ulster I: 1557–1957 (Belfast: Blackstaff, 1977).

'Belfast Art Gallery', *The Studio* (January 1947), pp. 14–24.

Catalogue of the Collection of Warwickshire Watercolours ([Coventry], 1972); Introduction by John Hewitt.

The Chinese Fluteplayer (Lisburn: [privately printed], 1974).

Colin Middleton (Belfast: Arts Council of Northern Ireland, 1976).

Collected Poems, ed. Frank Ormsby (Belfast: Blackstaff, 1991).

Collected Poems, 1932–1967 (London: MacGibbon & Kee, 1968).

Compass: Two Poems (Belfast: [privately printed], 1944).

Conacre (Belfast: [privately printed], 1943); two printings, of 100 copies each; the second incorporating a small number of corrections.

The Day of the Corncrake; Poems of the Nine Glens ([n.p.]: Glens of Antrim Historical Society, 1969; revised edition, 1984).

'Daybreak' [short story], *Threshold* 31 (Autumn/Winter 1980), pp. 69–79.

'Foreword' to Cathal O'Byrne, *As I Roved Out* (Belfast: Blackstaff, 1982).

Freehold and Other Poems (Belfast: Blackstaff, 1986).

John Luke, 1906–1975 (Belfast and Dublin: Arts Councils of Ireland, 1978).

Kites in Spring: a Belfast Boyhood [poems] (Belfast: Blackstaff, 1980).

Loose Ends (Belfast: Blackstaff, 1983).

Mosaic (Belfast: Blackstaff, 1981).

A North Light: Twenty-Five Years in a Municipal Art Gallery, ed. Frank Ferguson and Kathryn White (Dublin: Four Courts, 2013).

No Rebel Word (London: Muller, 1948).

Out of My Time; Poems 1967–1974 (Belfast: Blackstaff, 1974).

The Planter and the Gael: Poems by John Hewitt and John Montague (Belfast: Arts Council of Northern Ireland, 1970).

The Poems of William Allingham, ed. with an introduction by John Hewitt (Dublin: Dolmen Press, 1967).
The Rain Dance: Poems New and Revised (Belfast: Blackstaff, 1976).
Rhyming Weavers and Other Country Poets of Antrim and Down (Belfast: Blackstaff, 1974).
Scissors for a One-Armed Taylor: Marginal Verses 1929–1954 (Belfast: [privately printed], 1974).
The Selected John Hewitt, ed. Alan Warner (Belfast: Blackstaff, 1981).
Tesserae (Belfast: Festival Publications, 1967).
Those Swans Remember: A Poem (Belfast: [privately printed], 1956).
Time Enough: Poems New and Revised (Belfast: Blackstaff, 1976).
Two Plays: The McCrackens; The Angry Dove, ed. Damian Smyth (Belfast: Blackstaff, 1999).
Ulster Poets 1800–1850 (a paper read to the Belfast Literary Society 2 January 1950). No imprint. 28pp.
'Ulster Poets 1800–1870', MA thesis, QUB, 1952.
An Ulster Reckoning (Belfast: [privately printed], 1971).

2. RELATED TEXTS

[proposed attribution] *Africa Calling, a Missionary Play* (London: Holborn Publishing House, 1926).
'I Found Myself Alone'. Landseer Films for Northern Ireland Arts Council, 1978.
A Poet's Pictures: a Selection of the Works of Art Collected by John Hewitt (1907–1987) (Hillsborough: Shambles Art Gallery, 1987). (Contains material by Shelagh Flanagan, T. P. Flanagan, Seamus Heaney, Kenneth Jamison, Michael Longley, and James Simmons.)

Roberta Hewitt, from 'Diary 1948–1972', in *The Field Day Anthology of Irish Writing, 4: Irish Women's Writing and Traditions* (Cork: Cork University Press, 2002), pp. 1012–26.
Ian McIlhinny (ed.), *The Green Shoot; a One-Man Show Based on the Life and Writings of John Hewitt, and the Diaries of His Wife Roberta* (Belfast: Lagan, 1999).

3. SECONDARY READING

Adams, J. R. R., *The Printed Word and the Common Man: Popular Culture in Ulster 1700–1900* (Belfast: Institute of Irish Studies, 1987).
Adams, Mark, 'A Northern Maecenas [i.e. Zoltan Levinter Frankl]', *Irish Arts Review* 20, no. 3 (2003), pp. 98–103.
Akenson, D. H., *Between Two Revolutions: Islandmagee, County Antrim 1798–1920* (Port Credit, Ontario: Meany, 1979).
Akenson, D. H. and W. H. Crawford, *Local Poets and Social History: James Orr, Bard of Ballycarry* (Belfast: Public Record Office of Northern Ireland, 1977).
Annesley, Mabel, *As the Sight is Bent: an Unfinished Autobiography* (London: Museum Press, 1964).
Bardon, Jonathan, *The Ulster Plantation: British Colonisation in the North of Ireland in the Seventeenth Century* (Dublin: Gill & Macmillan, 2011).
Baudelaire, Charles, *Selected Poems*, trans. Carol Clark (London: Penguin, 1995).
Black, Eileen, *Art in Belfast 1760–1888: Art Lovers or Philistines?* (Dublin: Irish Academic Press, 2006).
Black, Eileen (ed.), *Drawings, Paintings, & Sculptures* ([Belfast]: Museums & Galleries of Northern Ireland in association with Nicholson & Bass, 2000).

Blackburn, Robin, *The Unfinished Revolution; Karl Marx and Abraham Lincoln* (London: Verso, 2011).
Boyd, John, *The Middle of My Journey* (Belfast: Blackstaff, 1990).
Boyd, John, *Out of My Class* (Belfast: Blackstaff, 1985).
Bradley, Anthony, *Contemporary Irish Poetry* (Berkeley: University of California Press, 1980).
Breatnach, Caoimhin, 'The Religious Significance of Oidhreadh Chloinne Lir', *Eriu* 50 (1999), pp. 1–40.
Brooke, Peter, *Ulster Presbyterianism, the Historical Perspective, 1610–1970* (Dublin: Gill & Macmillan, 1987).
Brown, Terence, *Ireland's Literature: Selected Essays* (Dublin: Lilliput, 1988).
Brown, Terence, 'John Hewitt: an Ulster of the Mind', in Dawe and Foster (1991), pp. 299–311.
Brown, Terence, *Northern Voices: Poets from Ulster* (Dublin: Gill & Macmillan, 1975).
Brown, Terence, *The Whole Protestant Community, the Making of a Historical Myth* (Derry: Field Day, 1985).
Buckland, Patrick, *Ulster Unionism and the Origins of Northern Ireland 1886 to 1922* (Dublin: Gill & Macmillan, 1973).
Bury, J. B., *The History of Freedom of Thought* (London: Williams & Norgate, 1913).
Carr, E. H., *The Romantic Exiles: A Nineteenth-Century Portrait Gallery* (Harmondsworth: Penguin, 1949; first published 1933).
Carr, Frank, 'Municipal Socialism: Labour's Rise to Power', in Bill Lancaster and Tony Mason eds., *Life and Labour in a Twentieth Century City: The Experience of Coventry.* (Coventry: Cryfield Press, [n.d.]), pp. 172–203.
Clark, Heather, *The Ulster Renaissance: Poetry in Belfast 1962–1972* (Oxford: Oxford University Press, 2006).
Clarke, Austin, *Selected Poems*, ed. W. J. Mc Cormack (London: Penguin, 1992).
Clayton, Pamela, *Enemies and Passing Friends; Setter Ideologies in Twentieth Century Ulster* (London: Pluto Press, 1996).
Clyde, Tom, *Irish Literary Magazines: An Outline History and Descriptive Bibliography* (Dublin: Irish Academic Press, 2003).
Clyde, Tom, 'The Prose Writings of John Hewitt; a Bibliography', MA thesis, QUB, 1985.
Cooney, Dudley Levistone, *The Methodists in Ireland: A Short History* (Dublin: Columba Press, 2001).
Coulter, Riann, 'John Hewitt: Creating a Canon of Ulster Art', *Journal of Art Historiography* 8 (December 2013), https://arthistoriography.files.wordpress.com/2013/12/coulter.pdf.
Crick, Bernard, *George Orwell: A Life* (London: Secker, 1980).
Cunningham, Valentine, *British Writers of the Thirties* (Oxford: Oxford University Press, 1989).
Dallat, Cathal, 'The Nine Glens of Antrim', in Dawe and Foster (1991), pp. 17–29.
Davies, J. McG., 'A Twentieth-Century Paternalist: Alfred Herbert and the Skilled Coventry Workman', in Bill Lancaster and Tony Mason eds., *Life and Labour in a Twentieth Century City: the Experience of Coventry* (Coventry: Cryfield Press, [n.d.]), pp. 98–132.
Dawe, Gerald (ed.), *Earth Voices Whispering; an Anthology of Irish War Poetry 1914–1945* (Belfast: Blackstaff, 2011).
Dawe, Gerald and J. W. Foster, *The Poet's Place: Ulster Literature and Society; Essays in Honour of John Hewitt 1907–87* (Belfast: Institute of Irish Studies, 1991).
Dawe, Gerald and Edna Longley, *Across a Roaring Hill: the Protestant Imagination in Modern Ireland* (Belfast: Blackstaff, 1985).

De Paor, Liam, *Divided Ulster* (Harmondsworth: Penguin, 1970).
Deleuze, Gilles and Félix Guattari, *Kafka: Towards a Minor Literature* (Minneapolis: University of Minnesota Press, 1986).
Devlin, Paddy, *Yes We Have no Bananas; Outdoor Relief in Belfast 1920–1939* (Belfast: Blackstaff, 1981).
Dunn, Douglas (ed.), *Two Decades of Irish Writing* (Manchester: Carcanet Press, 1975).
Edwards, Aaron, *A History of the Northern Ireland Labour Party: Democratic Socialism and Sectarianism* (Manchester: Manchester University Press, 2009).
Elliott, Marianne, *Watchmen in Sion, the Protestant Idea of Liberty* (Derry: Field Day, 1985).
English, Richard, 'Cultural Traditions and Political Ambiguity', *Irish Review* 15 (1994), pp. 97–106.
Evans, E. Estyn, *Irish Folk Ways* (London: Routledge, 1957).
Evans, E. Estyn, *Irish Heritage: the Landscape, the People, and their Work* (Dundalk: Dundalgan Press, 1942).
Evans, E. Estyn, *Mourne Country: Landscape and Life in South Down* (Dundalk: Dundalgan Press, 1951).
Fulton, Terence, 'Through the Artist's Eyes: Presidential Address to the Ulster Medical Society in the Session 1981–82', *The Ulster Medical Journal* 51, no. 1 (1982), pp. 1–22.
Fenwick, Gillian, *George Orwell, a Bibliography* (Winchester: St Paul's Bibliographies & New Castle, DE: Oak Knoll Press, 1998).
Ferris, Sarah, 'An Exemplary Protestant: A Study of the Myth of John Hewitt and its Place within Contemporary Literary Debate in Northern Ireland', PhD thesis, Newcastle University, 1998.
Ferris, Sarah, *Poet John Hewitt 1907–1987 and Criticism of Northern Irish Protestant Writing* (Lampeter: Edwin Mellen Press, 2002).
Fitzpatrick, David, 'Methodism and the Orange Order in Ireland', *Bulletin of the Methodist Historical Society of Ireland* 17 (2012), pp. 5–38.
Fitzpatrick, David, *'Solitary and Wild': Frederick MacNeice and the Salvation of Ireland* (Dublin: Lilliput, 2012).
Fleming, W. E. C., *The Diamond, a North Armagh Parish* ([privately published], 2009).
Fortnight (1989) 'John Hewitt Supplement', with contributions by Terence Brown, Sam Burnside, Patricia Craig, Damian Smyth, and Geraldine Watts.
Foster, John Wilson, *Colonial Consequences; Essays in Irish Literature and Culture* (Dublin: Lilliput, 1991).
Foster, John Wilson, 'The Landscape of Planter and Gael in the Poetry of John Hewitt and John Montague', *The Canadian Journal of Irish Studies* 1, no. 2 (November 1975), pp. 17–33.
Gilmore, George, *The 1934 Republican Congress*, 2nd edn. (Inistioge: George Brown Memorial Committee, 2011).
Greacen, Robert, *Even without Irene: An Autobiography*, 2nd edn., expanded (Belfast: Lagan, 1995).
Greacen, Robert (ed.), *Northern Harvest: a Collection of Stories, Essays and Poems* (Dublin: New Frontiers Press, 1946).
Green, E. R. R., 'The Cotton Hand-Loom Weavers in the North-East of Ireland', *Ulster Journal of Archaeology* 7 (1944), pp. 30–41.
Green, E. R. R., *The Lagan Valley, 1800–1850: A Local History of the Industrial Revolution* (London: Faber, 1949).
Hanna, Dennis O'Dea, *The Face of Ulster: Antrim, Londonderry, Fermanagh, Tyrone, Armagh, Monaghan, Cavan, Donegal and Down* (London: Batsford, 1952).

Hannigan, Ken, 'Wicklow Garden City: an Unrealised Vision', *Wicklow Historical Society* 4, no. 5 (2013), pp. 44–51.

Heaney, Seamus, *The Government of the Tongue: the 1986 T. S. Eliot Lectures* (London: Faber, 1988).

Heaney, Seamus, *Preoccupations; Selected Prose 1968–1978* (London: Faber, 1980); includes 'The Poetry of John Hewitt', pp. 207–10.

Heaney, Seamus, *The Redress of Poetry: Oxford Lectures* (London: Faber, 1995); on Hewitt, see 'Frontiers of Writing', pp. 186–203, esp. pp. 195–8.

Heller, Erich, *In the Age of Prose: Literary and Philosophical Essays* (Cambridge: Cambridge University Press, 1984).

Hempton, David and Myrtle Hill, *Evangelical Protestantism in Ulster Society 1740–1890* (London: Routledge, 1992).

Hewitt, Robert Telford, *Drawing for Schools: Teachers' Notes of Lessons Based on Official Recommendations* (Dublin: Browne & Nolan, 1928).

Holt, R. V., *The Unitarian Contribution to Social Progress in England*, 2nd edn. (London: Lindsey Press, 1952).

Irvine, Alexander, *The Carpenter and His Kingdom* (New York: Scribners, 1922).

Irvine, Alexander, *A Fighting Parson* (London: Williams & Norgate, 1930).

Irvine, Alexander, *My Lady of the Chimney Corner* (London: Eveleigh Nash, 1913; new edn.: Belfast: Appletree Press, 1980).

James, Kevin J., *Handloom Weavers in Ulster's Linen Industry 1815–1914* (Dublin: Four Courts, 2007).

Jamieson, Ken, 'Edward Norman Carrothers (1898–1977)', *Irish Book Lore* 4, no. 1 (1978), pp. 5–6.

Kennedy, Dennis, *The Widening Gulf; Northern Attitudes to the Independent Irish State 1919–49* (Belfast: Blackstaff, 1988).

Kennedy, Liam and Philip Ollerenshaw (eds.), *An Economic History of Ulster 1820–1939* (Manchester: Manchester University Press, 1985).

Kennedy, S. B., *Irish Art & Modernism 1880–1950* (Belfast: Institute of Irish Studies, 1991).

Kennedy, S. B., *The White Stag Group* ([Dublin]: Irish Museum of Modern Art, [n.d.]).

Kilfeather, John, 'Remembering John Hewitt', *Threshold* 38 (Winter 1986/87), pp. 31–6.

Kirkland, Richard, *Cathal O'Byrne and the Northern Revival in Ireland 1890–1960* (Liverpool: Liverpool University Press, 2006).

Levine, K., 'A Tree of Identities, a Tradition of Dissent: John Hewitt at 78', *Fortnight* 213 (1985), pp. 16–17.

Loan Exhibition of the Lewinter-Frankl Collection of Contemporary Irish Drawings, 20 June–21 July 1956 (Belfast: Belfast Public Art Gallery and Museum, 1956).

Longley, Edna, *The Living Stream: Literature and Revisionism in Ireland* (Newcastle upon Tyne: Bloodaxe, 1992).

Longley, Edna, *Poetry in the Wars* (Newcastle upon Tyne: Bloodaxe Books, 1986).

Longley, Edna, 'Progressive Bookmen: Politics and Northern Protestant Writers in the 1930s', *The Irish Review* 1 (1986), pp. 50–7; reprinted in *The Living Stream*, with references.

Loraux, Nicole, *The Divided City; On Memory and Forgetting in Ancient Athens* (New York: Zone, 2002).

McCabe, Richard, *Spenser's Monstrous Regiment: Elizabethan Ireland and the Poetics of Difference* (Oxford: Oxford University Press, 2002).

McCormack, W. J. 'The Protestant Strain; a Short History of Anglo-Irish Literature from S. T. Coleridge to Thomas Mann', in Dawe and Longley, *Across a Roaring Hill*, pp. 48–78.

MacDiarmid, Hugh, *Complete Poems 1920–1976*, ed. Michael Grieve and W. R. Aiken (London: Martin, Brien, & O'Keefe, 1978).

McDowell, Florence Mary, *Other Days Around Me* (Belfast: Blackstaff, 1972).

McDowell, Florence Mary, *Roses and Rainbows* (Belfast: Blackstaff, 1974).

McFadden, Roy, *Collected Poems, 1943–1995* (Belfast: Lagan, 1996).

McIntosh, Gillian, *The Force of Culture; Unionist Identities in Twentieth-Century Ireland* (Cork: Cork University Press, 1999).

McKittrick, David (et al.), *Lost Lives: The Stories of the Men, Women and Children who Died as a Result of the Northern Ireland Troubles* (Edinburgh: Mainsteam, 2004).

MacMahon, Sean, 'Obituary, Sam Hanna Bell', *Linen Hall Review* 7, nos. 1–2 (1990), p. 7.

McNeice, Louis, *Collected Letters* (London: Faber, 2010).

Mahon, Derek, *Journalism* (Loughcrew: Gallery, 1996); includes 'An Honest Ulsterman', a review of *Ancestral Voices*, pp. 92–4.

Manvell, Roger (ed.), *Three British Screen Plays: Brief Encounter; Odd Man Out; Scott of the Antarctic* (London: Methuen, 1950).

Markey Robinson: Exhibition of Recent Paintings, foreword by Z. Lewinter-Frankl (Belfast: CEMA, 1952).

Marsh, Robert Gerald, 'John Hewitt and Theories of Irish Culture: Cultural Nationalism, Cultural Regionalism, and Identity in the North of Ireland', PhD thesis, QUB, 1996.

Matthews, Kelly, *The Bell Magazine and the Representation of Irish Identity* (Dublin: Four Courts, 2012).

Matthews, Steven, *Irish Poetry: Politics, History, Negotiation; the Evolving Debate 1969 to the Present* (Basingstoke: Macmillan, 1997).

Maxton, Hugh, *Waking: an Irish Protestant Upbringing* (Belfast: Lagan, 1997).

Montague, John, *The Pear is Ripe, a Memoir* (Dublin: Liberties Press, 2007).

Montague, John, 'Regionalism into Reconciliation: the Poetry of John Hewitt', *Poetry Ireland* 3 (Spring 1964), pp. 113–15; collected in Montague, *The Figure in the Cave and Other Essays* (Dublin: Lilliput, 1989), pp. 147–53.

Montague, John, 'Spiritual Maverick', *Threshold* 38 (Winter 1986/87), p. 17.

Morris, William, *A Dream of John Ball, and A King's Lesson* (London: Reeves & Turner, 1888).

Morrow, John Patrick, 'The Flourishin' Whin: a Critical Biography of John Hewitt', DPhil, UU, 1999.

Muir, Edwin, *Collected Poems* (London: Faber, 1963).

Mumford, Lewis, *The Culture of Cities* (London: Secker & Warburg, 1938).

Mumford, Lewis, *Technics and Civilization* (London: Routledge, 1934).

O'Connell, T. J., *History of the Irish National Teachers' Organisation, 1868–1968* (Dublin: Irish National Teachers' Organisation, [*c.*1970]).

Ó Drisceoil, Donal, *Peadar O'Donnell* (Cork: Cork University Press, 2001).

Ó Glaisne, Risteard, *Denis Ireland* ([Baile Atha Cliath]: Coiscéim, 2000).

O'Malley, Ernie, *Broken Landscapes: Selected Letters of Ernie O'Malley 1924–1957* (Dublin: Lilliput, 2011).

O'Malley, Mary, *Never Shake Hands with the Devil* (Dublin: Elo, 1990).

O Seaghdha, Barra, 'Ulster Regionalism: the Unpleasant Facts', *Irish Review* 8 (Spring 1999), pp. 51–64.

Orwell, George, *Orwell in Spain*, ed. Peter Davison (London: Penguin, 2001).

Patten, Eve (ed.), *Returning to Ourselves; Second Volume of Papers from the John Hewitt International Summer School* (Belfast: Lagan Press, 1995).

Prince, Simon, *Northern Ireland's '68; Civil Rights, Global Revolt and the Origins of the Troubles* (with a foreword by Paul Bew) (Dublin: Irish Academic Press, 2007).

Reilly, Patricia, *A Journey Through Time: a History of Kilmore Parish, Co. Armagh* (Armagh: Trimprint, 2009).

Richardson, Kenneth, assisted by Elizabeth Harris, *Twentieth-Century Coventry* (Coventry: City of Coventry, 1972).

Rodgers, W. R., *Collected Poems* (London: Oxford University Press, 1971).

Rosenfield, Judith and Ray, *Group Theatre, a Souvenir History* (Belfast: printed by Century Services, [n.d.]).

Scott, Maolcholaim, 'When the Planter was the Gael', *Fortnight*, no. 316 (April 1993), pp. 25–7.

Sheehy Sheffington, Andrée, *Skeff: A Life of Owen Sheehy Skefffington, 1909–1970* (Dublin: Lilliput, 1991).

Smith, Adrian, *The City of Coventry, a Twentieth-Century Icon* (London: Tauris, 2006).

Smyth, Damian, 'Joseph Tomelty' [Obituary], *The Independent*, 13 June 1995.

Snoddy, Theo, *Dictionary of Irish Artists: 20th Century*, 2nd edn. (Dublin: Merlin, 2002).

Spencer, Stanley, *Letters and Writings*, ed. Adrian Glew (London: Tate, 2001).

Stallworthy, Jon, *Louis MacNeice* (London: Faber, 1995).

Stewart, A. T. Q., *The Ulster Crisis* (London: Faber, 1967).

Talen, Emily, *The New Urbanism and American Planning; the Conflict of Cultures* (London: Routledge, 2005).

Taylor, Geoffrey, 'Time and Poetry', *The Bell* 6, nos. 2–4 (1943), pp. 210–12, 288–9, 488–9.

Thompson, E. P., 'John Hewitt 1907–1987', *Labour History News* [Dublin] 4 (Summer 1988), p. 4.

Thompson, E. P., *The Making of the English Working Class* (London: Penguin, 1991; first published 1963).

Thompson, E. P. (ed.), *Warwick University Ltd; Industry, Management and the Universities* (Harmondsworth: Penguin, 1970).

Thompson, E. P., *William Morris; Romantic to Revolutionary* (Stanford: Stanford University Press, 1988; first published 1955).

Tomelty, Joseph, *The End House* (Belfast: Duffy, 1962).

Walker, Brian (ed.), *Parliamentary Election Results in Ireland, 1918–92: Irish Elections to Parliaments and Parliamentary Assemblies at Westminster, Belfast, Dublin, Strasbourg* (Dublin: Royal Irish Academy; Belfast: Institute of Irish Studies, 1992).

Walker, Dorothy, *Modern Art in Ireland*, with a foreword by Seamus Heaney (Dublin: Lilliput, 1997).

Walker, Graham, *The Politics of Frustration; Harry Midgley and the Failure of Labour in Northern Ireland* (Manchester: Manchester University Press, 1985).

Walsh, Patrick, '"Too much alone": John Hewitt, Regionalism, Socialism, and Partition', *Irish University Review* 29, no. 2 (Autumn/Winter 1999), pp. 341–57.

Wang, Li-hsi, *Exile and Wars* [poems] (Chungking, 1939).

Watts, Geraldine, 'John Hewitt; the Non-Conformist Conscience of Northern Ireland', MLitt. thesis, TCD, 1987.

White, Lawrence William, 'Peadar O'Donnell, "Real Republicanism" and *The Bell*', *The Republic* 4 (June 2005), <http://theirelandinstitute.com/republic/04/html/white004.html>.

Wills, Clair, *That Neutral Island; a Cultural History of Ireland During the Second World War* (London: Faber, 2007).

Wilson, Judith C., *Conor 1881–1968, the Life and Work of an Ulster Artist* (Belfast: Blackstaff, 1981).
Woodward, Guy, '"We must know more than Ireland": John Hewitt and Eastern Europe', in Aidan O'Malley and Eve Patten (eds.), *Ireland West to East; Irish Cultural Connections with Central and Eastern Europe* (Frankfurt: Peter Lang, 2014), pp. 101–13.
Wordsworth, William, *Poetry and Prose*, ed. W. M. Merchant (London: Hart-Davis, 1969).
Yeates, Padraic, *A City in Wartime: Dublin 1914–1918* (Dublin: Gill & Macmillan, 2011).
Yeats, W. B., *The Poems*, ed. Daniel Albright (London: Dent, 1994).

General Index

Index of Hewitt's Writings